Copper, Cuneiform Inscriptions, and Other Finds

In memoriam Poul Kjærum

Danish Archaeological Investigations on Failaka, Kuwait

FAILAKA | DILMUN
THE SECOND MILLENNIUM SETTLEMENTS

volume 6
Copper, Cuneiform Inscriptions and Other Finds

by Flemming Højlund

with contributions by Ann Andersson, Eddy Faber, Anna Hilton, Gianni Marchesi, Sarah Morriss, David Mulder, Holly Pittman, Helle Strehle, Emma Watt, and Lloyd Weeks

Jutland Archaeological Society

Moesgaard Museum, Denmark
National Council for Culture, Arts and Letters, Kuwait

Failaka | Dilmun
The Second Millennium Settlements
volume 6
Copper, Cuneiform Inscriptions, and Other Finds

ISBN 978-87-93423-94-7
ISSN 0107-2854

Jutland Archaeological Society Publications vol. 17:6

Design: Jens Nygaard
Drawings: Jens Aarup-Jensen, Orla Svendsen, Flemming Højlund, Carsten Sønderby, Anna Hilton, Ann Andersson, Alessandra Lazzari
Digitization of drawings: Nicolaj Duus Linnet, Phine Wiborg, Ann Andersson, Anna Hilton, Jens Nygaard
Photos: Lennart Larsen, Svend Aage Lorentz, Hans Henrik Frost Larsen, Photo and media Moesgaard/ Rogvi N. Johansen, Gérard Franceschi, Hasan Ashkanani, Anna Hilton, Ann Andersson, Helle Strehle, Sarah Morriss, Henrik Brahe, Jozef Ďuriš/Kuwaiti-Slovak Archaeological Mission, Jacob Gonge Due
English revision: Sharon E. Rhodes
Printed by Stibo Complete, Horsens, Denmark

Published by Jutland Archaeological Society in cooperation with Moesgaard Museum and the National Council for Culture, Arts and Letters, Kuwait

Distributed by Aarhus University Press
Finlandsgade 29
DK-8200 Aarhus N
www.unipress.dk

The publication is funded by the Carlsberg Foundation (grant CF23-0295)

MIX
Papir fra ansvarlige kilder
FSC® C010651

Contents

Fig. 1. Aerial photo of the southwest corner of Failaka looking southwest with the four fenced-in archaeological excavations, Tell F5 (left), Tell F6 (foreground, middle), Tell F4 (background, close to the shore), and Tell F3 (right) (1961/62).

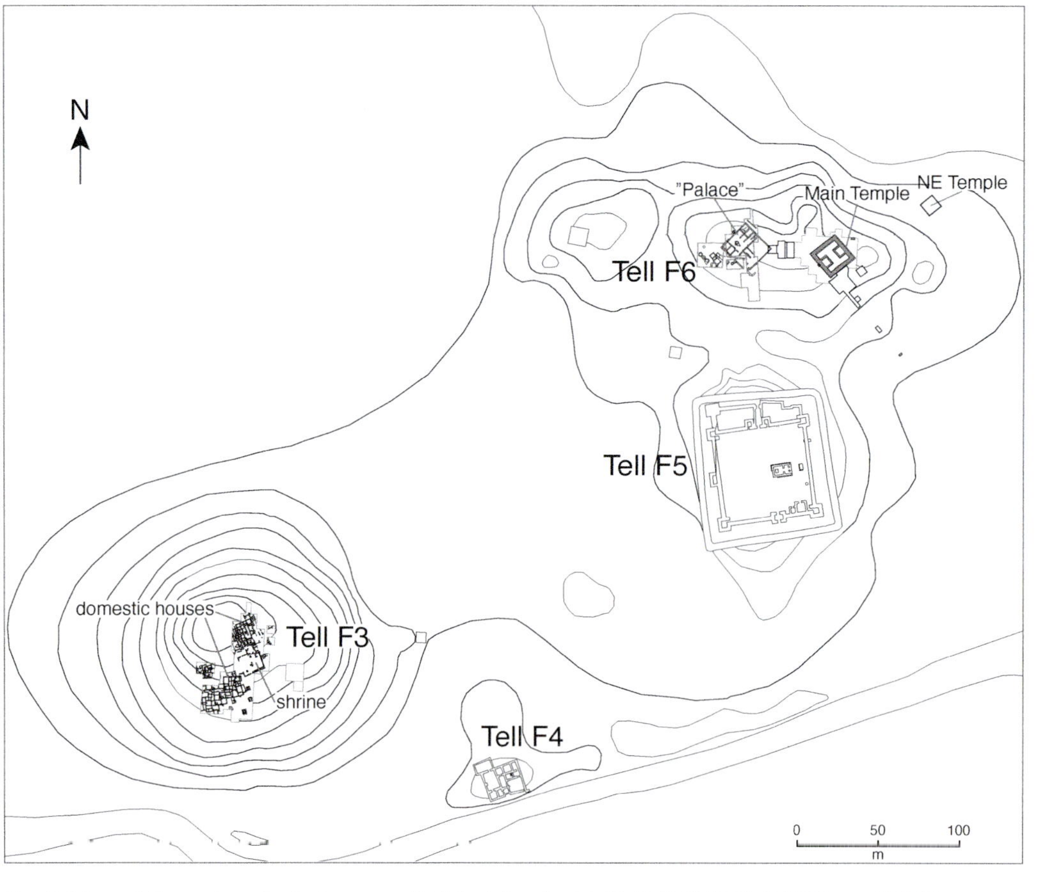

Fig. 2. Map of the archaeological area on Failaka Island with Tell F3, Tell F4, Tell F5 and Tell F6.

1. Preface

The first Danish excavations on the island of Failaka in Kuwait took place between 1958 and 1963. They were focused on four tells located on the southwest shore, Tell F3 and Tell F6 dating to the second millennium BC, and Tell F4 and Tell F5 dating to the Hellenistic period (figs. 1-2) (Glob 1959a-b. 1960. Bibby 1965. 1969).

The results of the early excavations in Tell F3 and Tell F6 have been presented in five monographs dealing with the stamp and cylinder seals (Kjærum 1983), the pottery (Højlund 1987), the architecture (Kjærum & Højlund 2013), the stone vessels (Hilton 2014), and the beads (Andersson 2022). The present monograph, the sixth and final, presents the remaining objects from these excavations, that is, copper weapons, tools and ornaments, crucibles, moulds and ingots, metal analyses, cuneiform inscriptions, miniature sculptures, and artefacts of stone, pottery, glass, bone, ivory, shell, gold, plaster, pearls, silver, iron, and bitumen.

In appendices 1-3 a number of stamp seals, stone vessel fragments and beads have been added to those previously published by Kjærum (1983), Hilton (2014) and Andersson (2022). Appendix 4 presents a few Bronze Age objects found in the Hellenistic Tell F5 and Appendix 5 discusses a new method for conserving bitumen.

The animal bones from the excavations were retrieved but have not been studied, apart from an analysis of the strontium isotope contents of fifteen cattle and sheep/goat teeth (Gregoricka 2013a-b).

The excavation of Tell F3 was carried out over five campaigns, 1958, 1959, 1960, 1961/62 and 1962/63, and revealed several complexes of domestic buildings and a small open-air shrine. The work in Tell F6 took place over the course of three campaigns, 1960, 1961/62 and 1962/63, and revealed a large building, named the "Palace". In 1973-74 a mission from Johns Hopkins University opened further trenches in Tell F3 and Tell F6 (Howard-Carter 1984), and subsequent work by a French team in 1983-88 revealed a temple to the east of the "Palace" (Calvet & Pic 1990).

In 2008-2012, new excavations were carried out in Tell F6 in the area between the "Palace" and the temple (Højlund & Abu-Laban 2016). The excavations were continued in Tell F3 in 2012-2017 (Højlund & Hilton 2021), and in 2017 a new temple platform, the NE temple, was uncovered at Tell F6 (Højlund & Hagelquist 2019).

All finds from the 1958-1963 excavations, apart from those of the last campaign, were shipped to the Prehistoric Museum in Aarhus (later Moesgaard Museum) to be registered, conserved, and studied. In the early 1970s they were returned to the Kuwait National Museum (Højlund 2008a and b). Here their studies were continued in 1975 by a group of researchers from Moesgaard Museum and Aarhus University (Poul Kjærum, Kristian Jeppesen, Lise Hannestad, and Hans Erik Mathiesen) assisted by draughtsmen and registrars (Jens Aarup Jensen, Lotte Jeppesen and Carsten Sønderby) as well as a photographer (Henrik Frost Larsen) (Højlund 2008a and b). The present volume was prepared in 2021-2024.

Since 1958, Danish archaeological research on Failaka has been generously supported by the Government of Kuwait, first through the Ministry of Education, headed by Sheikh Abdullah Al Jabir Al Sabah, then the Ministry of Information and, in recent years, the *National Council for Culture, Arts and Letters*, headed by Secretary General, Mr Ali Hussein Al Youha and his successors Mr Kamel Al-Abdul Jalil, Dr Eisa Al-Ansari and Dr. Mohammad Khaled Al-Jassar. We are also indebted to Assistant Secretary General, Mr Shehab A.H. Shehab, Directors of Museums and Antiquities, Dr. Sultan Dueish and Mr Mohammad Bin Redha, and NCCAL Consultant for Antiquities and Museum Affairs, Prof. Dr. Hasan Ashkanani.

For this volume we are grateful to Superintendent Mr Hasan Al-Failakawi and to Storeroom Manager Ms Hadeel Al-Shammari and her team, consisting of Mr Abdullah Al-Ansari, Ms Alymamah Rashed, Ms Badour Al-Senan, Ms Huwaida Ali, and Mr Abdulatif Sadeqi, for their kind and efficient assistance in the storerooms of the Kuwait National Museum. We would like to extend our warmest thanks to all our friends and colleagues in Kuwait for their great hospitality. The manuscript has benefitted from the constructive scrutiny of an anonymous reviewer.

Sincere thanks are owed to the *Carlsberg Foundation* for supporting Moesgaard Museum's archaeological investigations in the countries along the Arabian Gulf since 1955 as well as the publication of the present volume.

This book is dedicated to the memory of Poul Kjærum (1926-2010) who was in charge of the excavations on Failaka in 1960-1963 and who never ceased to care deeply for the ancient history of the island.

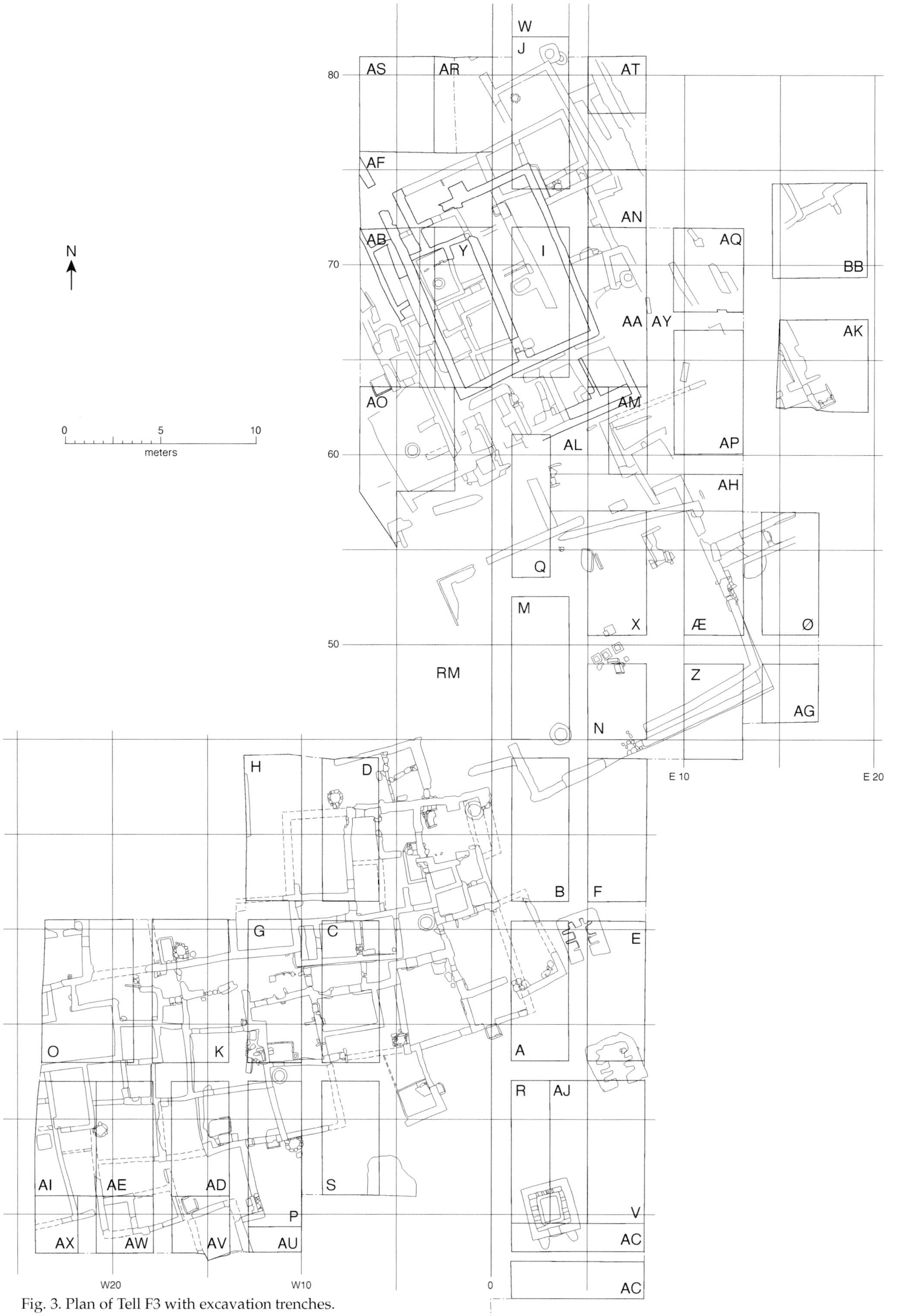

Fig. 3. Plan of Tell F3 with excavation trenches.

2. Introduction

The objects presented in this volume were collected from layers excavated in 75 trenches, mostly 3 x 8-9 m, covering Tell F3 and Tell F6 (figs. 3-4). The layers were horizontal and about 30 cm thick, rarely thinner, and often thicker, 40-60 cm. They were mostly arbitrarily defined, that is, they did not normally correspond to the discrete deposition of materials during the accumulation of the tell. A small part of the objects derives from a specified stratigraphical context, such as being found on or below the floor of a particular room or in a similarly well-defined relation to other structures. Objects, such as seals, copper artefacts, and stone vessel fragments, were, however, normally plotted in three dimensions. All excavated deposits were sieved.

The vertical measurements of layers and objects in Tell F3 were normally taken with the help of a theodolite in relation to a reference point on top of the tell that was assigned the arbitrary value of 10.00, in relation to a datum line approximately 2.90 m below sea level. Thus, levels are always positive above this datum, the lowest culture horizon recorded being level c. 5.30 (with the exception of a lot from level 5.50-4.84 and a lot from level 5.15), and the top of the tell in the excavated area reading level 9.76 (fig. 5). Sometimes the height was measured in relation to the surface of the tell in that particular trench, and this measurement has, if possible, been converted.

In the excavation of Tell F6, the threshold stone of the north gate in the fortress of the adjacent Tell F5 (Mathiesen 1982 p. 10: D/j) was employed as reference point, situated 4.20 m above sea level. Measurements taken above this line are positive, below it negative. The top of the tell in the excavated area read +1.30, the lowest cultural deposit -2.64 (fig. 6).

In the field, the finds were furnished with a field number and entered in the daybook. During registration at Moesgaard Museum, the field number was supplemented by an accession number. The field number always begins with the tell designation, F3, F5 or F6, followed, in the case of F3, by one to three digits (in 1958 with a prefixed asterisk) or by one to three small letters, and in the case of F6 by one to four digits. The accession number starts with the official site number in the Moesgaard Museum register, 881 (= Tell F3), 883 (= Tell F5) or 1129 (= Tell F6) followed by one to three capital letters. After their return to Kuwait, the objects were furnished with KM numbers.

The numbering system for **Tell F3/881** is as follows:

Season	Field number F3	Accession number 881
1958	*1-*68	A-BR
	Trench BB:	
	topsoil, layers 1-8	BS-CB
	Trench AK:	
	Layers 1-5	CC-CH
1959	1-329	CI-PM
	330-331	(-)
	(-)	PN-TO
		(not used: TH-TO)
1960	a-pg	TP-AKC
		(not used: AKD-AKG)
	aaa-auo	AKH-BEY
		(not used: BEZ-BGZ)
1961/62	ph-åå	BHA-BVS
	ava-awa	BVT-BXY
1962/63	awb-bjs	BXZ-CMA

The numbering system for **Tell F6/1129** is as follows:

Season	Field number F6	Accession number 1129
1960	1-607	A-XH
1961/62	608-949	XI-AML
1962/63	950-1245	AMM-BAI

The method of excavating in horizontal layers (spits) set certain limits on the chronological reliability of the excavated lots, as each spit may belong to more than one stratigraphic level. Additionally, the ubiquitous use of stone for construction made Dilmun architectural remains vulnerable to stone plundering. Indeed, evidence that old, abandoned and buried buildings were plundered for stone, presumably to be used in new constructions, has often been encountered during recent excavations in Tell F3 and Tell F6.

Especially during the 2008-2012 excavations in Tell F6, where solid clay or plaster floors covered

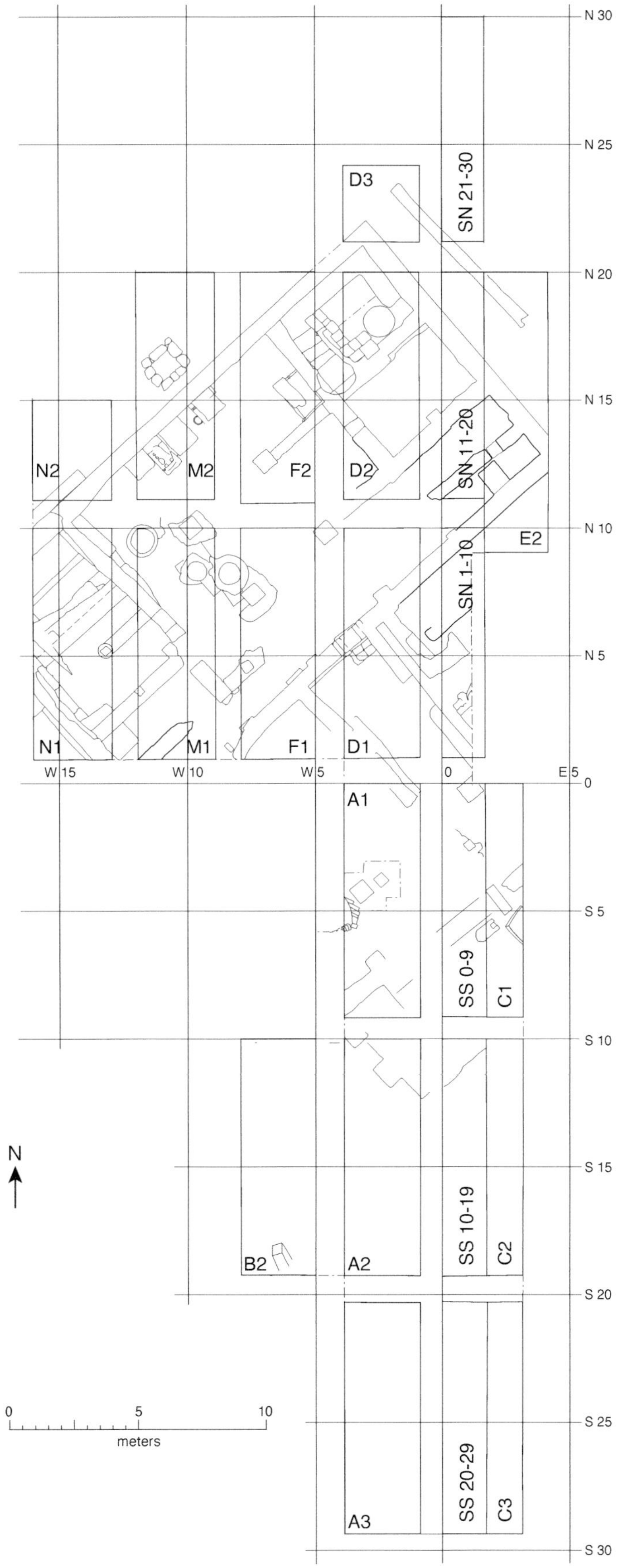

Fig. 4. Plan of Tell F6 with excavation trenches.

large stretches between the "Palace" and the temple, stone plundering holes were easily noted (Højlund & Abu-Laban 2016 p. 59-60, figs. 70 and 72), and the contents of such holes could be distinguished from that of the levels they broke through.

Stone plundering holes were also noted in the 2012-2017 excavations of Tell F3 (Højlund & Hilton 2021 figs. 104-105), but less often, perhaps because of less solid floors or less plundering activity in Tell F3 due to the use of smaller, less valuable stones in the walls. During the 1958-1963 excavations the stone plundering pits were rarely recognized in the field, and this has inevitably led to disturbances in the find contents of the excavated layers.

In terms of the pottery, the sheer number of sherds kept from the 1958-1963 excavations (c. 25.000 from Tell F3 and Tell F6) ensured that these disturbances were of minor significance. Comparing the pottery from each excavated layer, trench by trench, it was still possible to detect the typological changes through time and to delimit a periodic system for the two tells consisting of seven periods, 1, 2A, 2B, 3A, 3B, 4A, and 4B (Højlund 1987 fig. 707) (fig. 7).

The following scheme (fig. 8) summarises the pottery datings of the excavated layers in Tell F3, trench by trench, in relation to vertical levels. This gives a date for the pottery found at a certain level, but there is no certainty that the context is undisturbed. Accordingly, these datings should be treated with caution and can only indicate trends in the material. Based on these dating indications the architectural phases of Tell F3, identified by Kjærum (1986a), were dated to Periods 2, 3A, 3B, 4A, and 4B (Højlund 1987). The subsequent excavations in 2012-2017 revealed three additional occupation phases dating to Period 3B (figs. 5 and 7).

The stone plundering disturbances of Tell F6 were more severe than those of Tell F3, perhaps due to the larger sizes and greater amounts of building stone that could be quarried from the "Palace" (Kjærum & Højlund 2013 p. 99-101). A similar scheme showing the typological changes in pottery, trench by trench, could therefore not be made. Instead, the dating of the architecture took advantage of several assemblages of complete, datable pots that had survived the stone plunder (Højlund 1987 p. 138-149).

Based on the 1960-1963 excavations, the occupation of Tell F6 was separated into a Pre-"Palace" phase dating to Period 1, the construction of the "Palace" in Period 2 or 3A, followed by two further occupation phases in the "Palace" dating to Period 3B and 4A, and a phase post-dating the "Palace" and Period 4A (figs. 6-7) (Højlund 1987). The excavations in 2008-2012

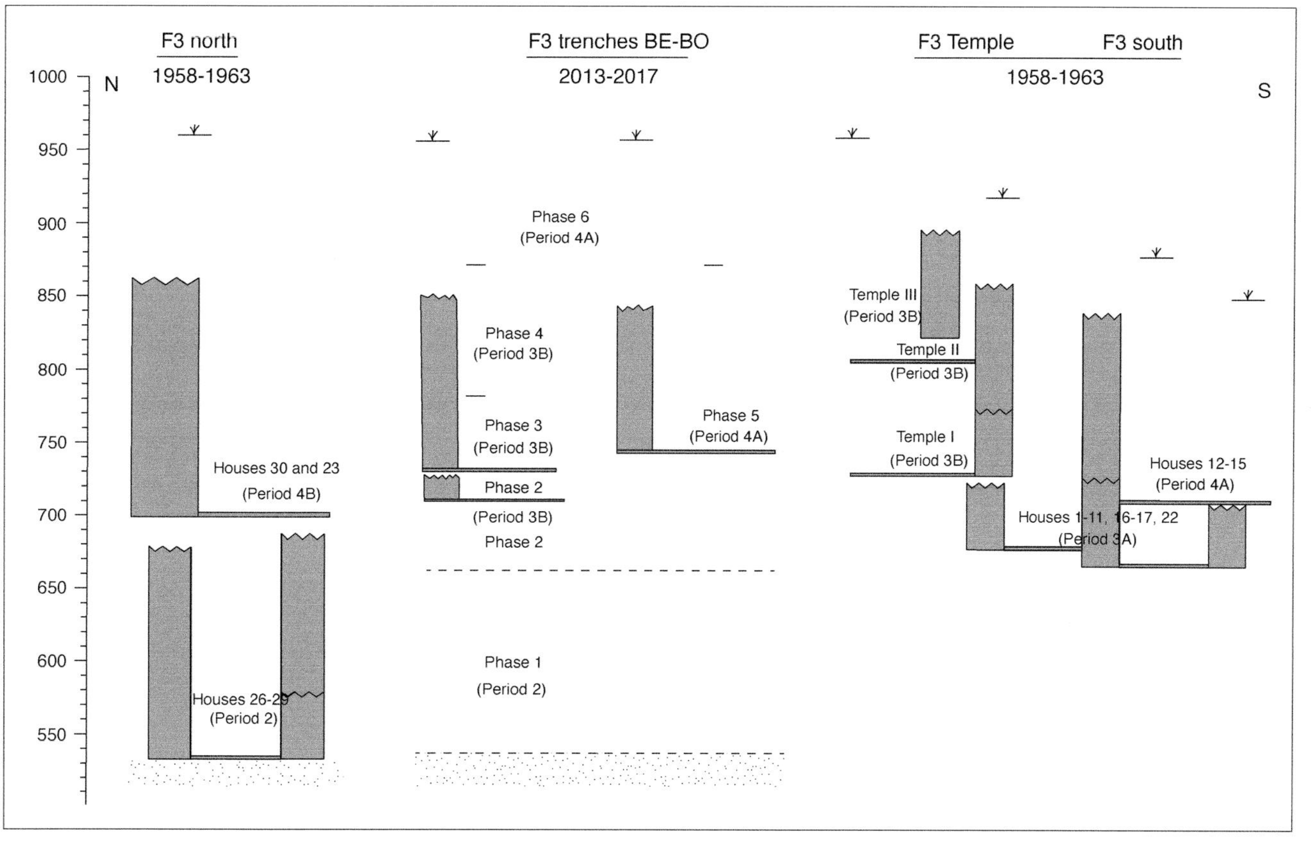

Fig. 5. Main stratigraphy of Tell F3 (Højlund & Hilton 2021 fig. 49).

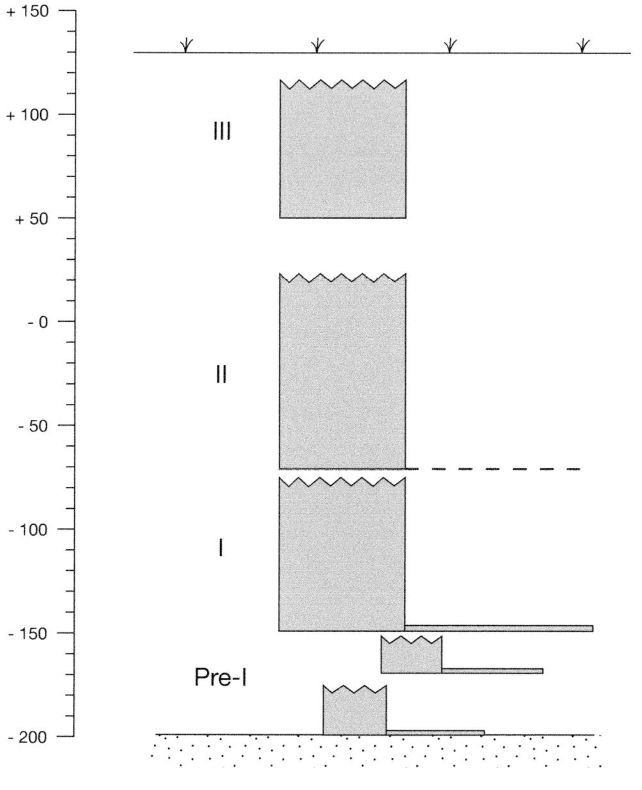

Fig. 6. Main stratigraphy of Tell F6 (Kjærum & Højlund 2013 fig. 132).

supported this chronology and narrowed down the dating of the construction of the "Palace" to Period 2 (Højlund & Abu-Laban 2016 p. 43, fig. 6).

With regards to the non-ceramic finds from the 1958-1963 excavations, the problems of dating are great. Because of the excavation method and the plundered and therefore disturbed nature of the site, it is not possible to date single finds based on their find contexts alone, because of the risk that they may have intruded into their find positions from later contexts or be residual from earlier contexts.

The following chapters will present the remaining finds from the 1958-1963 excavations in Tell F3 and F6, divided according to type of objects. Not all objects were available at the writing of this manuscript; some have been described on the basis of drawings, photos or day-book entries. The dating of the associated pottery, if available, is given after each find, however, for the reasons given above, these datings should only be viewed as indicative.

The following abbreviations are used: L length, W width, Th thickness, D diameter, PD perforation diameter.

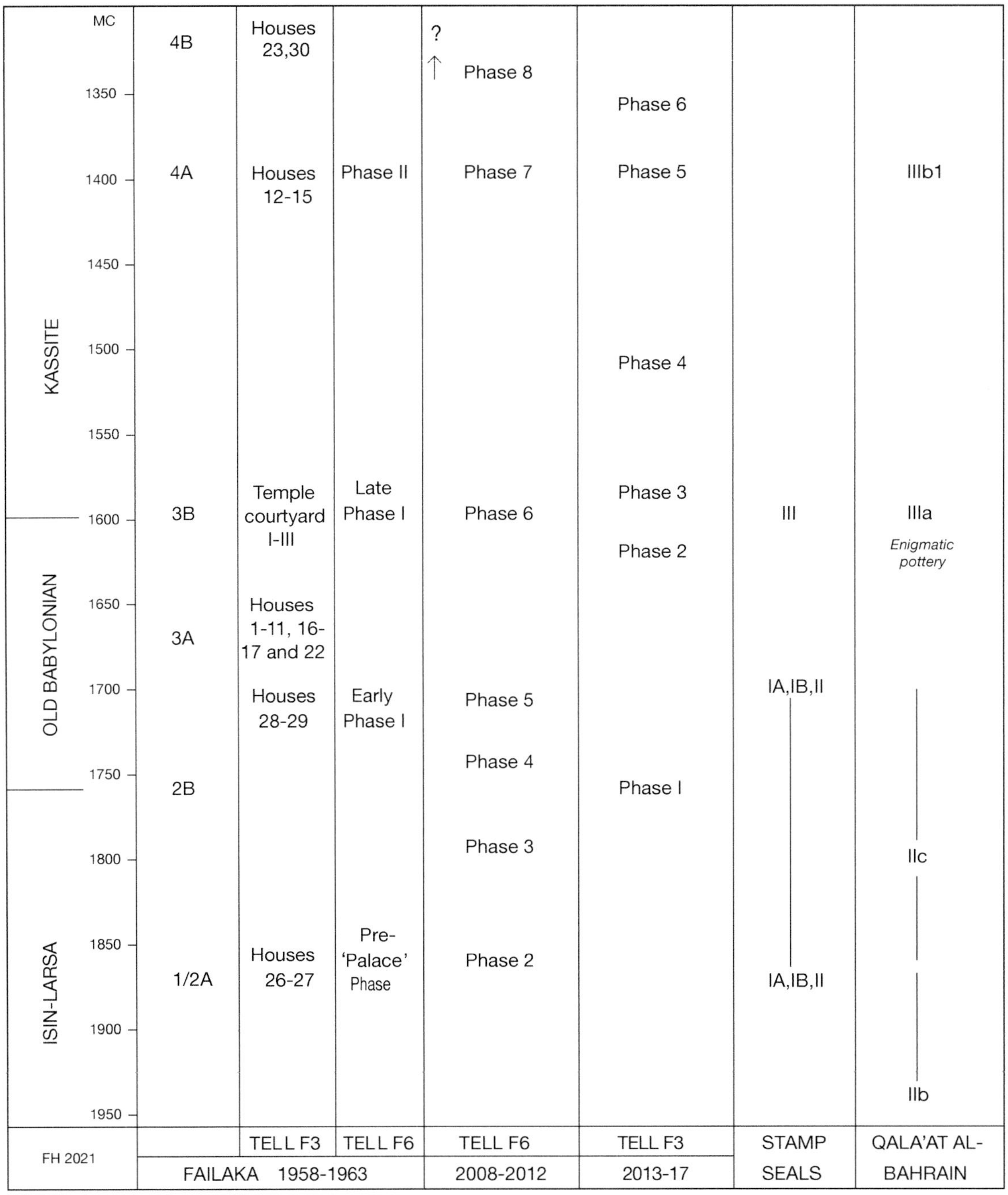

Fig. 7. Chronological chart for the 2nd millennium BC in the upper Arabian Gulf. Mesopotamian periods follow the Middle Chronology (Højlund & Hilton 2021 fig. 50).

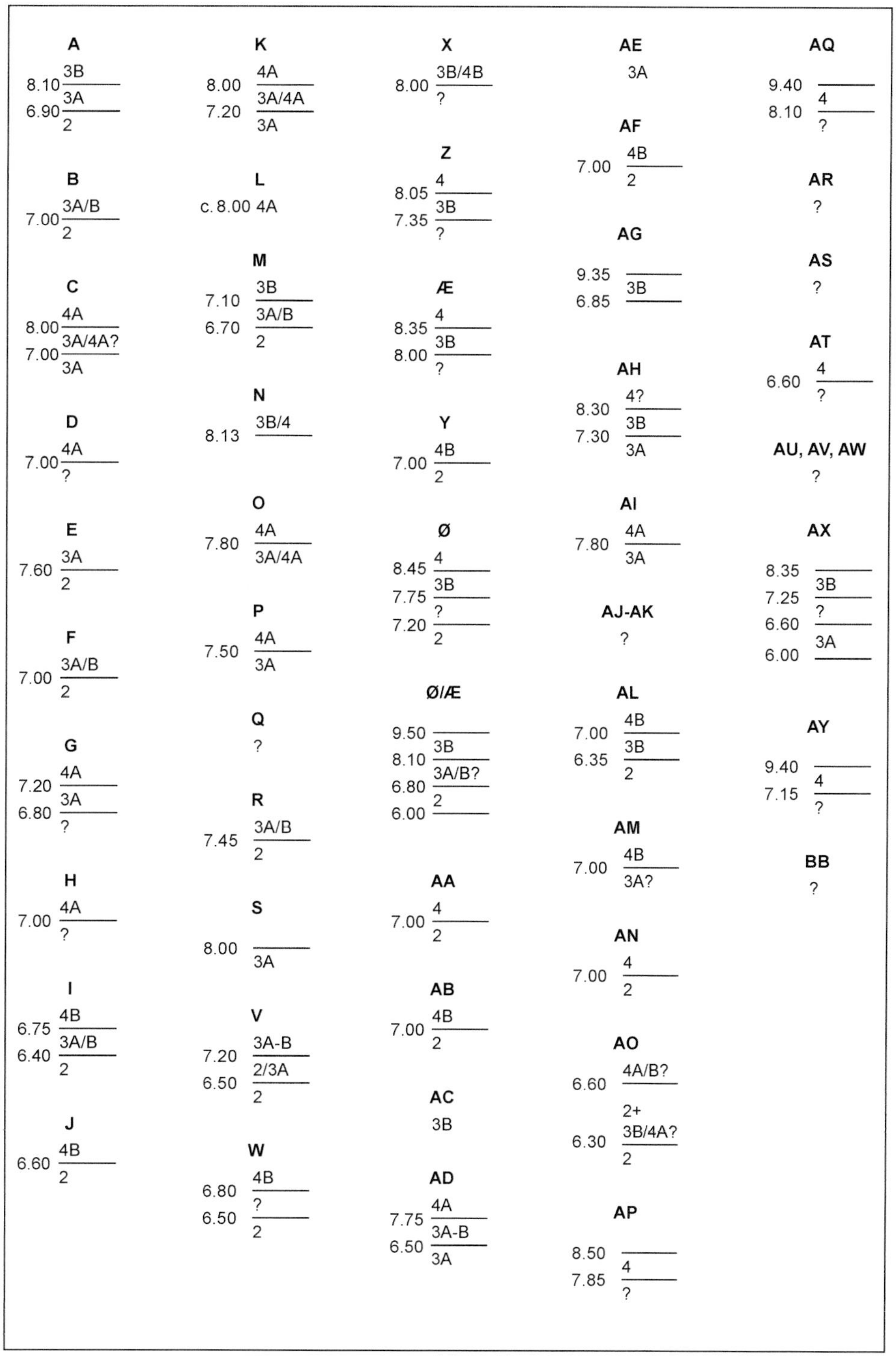

Fig. 8. Tentative ceramic dating of excavated layers in Tell F3 trenches with vertical levels indicated.

3. Copper objects

Copious quantities of copper base objects were found during the excavation of Tell F3 and Tell F6. All copper finds, apart from those found during the last campaign in 1962/63, were shipped to the museum in Aarhus where the majority were cleaned and conserved in the early 1970s by conservator Elmer Fabech and subsequently returned to Kuwait. The finds from the 1962/63 campaign remained in Kuwait and have not been conserved. Their original shape is thus obscured by a thick layer of corrosion, and they are therefore rarely included in this publication. Numerous fragments of copper sheet and simple rods with round or square cross section have also not been included in the following register.

Approximately 400 copper objects have been registered, and it is the largest collection of copper objects known from the land of Dilmun. They have been divided into around thirty object types: daggers with grip tang, daggers with riveted grip plate, daggers with riveted grip plate and bent edges, daggers with riveted grip plate and S-shaped bent edges, dagger blade fragments, spears, arrows, socketed hoes, axes, ridged cylinders, knives, chisels/drills, chisels with raised edges, drills, awls, needles, tweezers, barbed and unbarbed fishhooks, nails and rivets, staples, rods with round and square sections, vessels, handles, fittings, scrap metal, pins, rings, cymbals, boxes and other objects.

The inventory of copper objects from Tell F3 and Tell F6 comprises a simple, utilitarian repertoire. Around 300 of the registered objects are tools, while 66 are weapons, and 24 ornaments. It has not been possible to discern any typological developments in the metal object types through the 2nd millennium occupation on Failaka. An examination of the tentative pottery contexts of the thirty object types suggests that they occur in all periods of Tell F3 and Tell F6; none seem to be concentrated in certain periods or entirely absent from other periods.

Reference is made to the metallurgical analyses carried out on the copper material presented in Chapters 3-4, see Weeks et al. in Chapter 5, fig. 378.

Daggers

Daggers are plentiful and seem to appear in all periods. They occur with four different hafting methods, grip tang, riveted grip plate, riveted grip plate with bent edges, and riveted grip plate with S-shaped bent edges.

The type with grip tang is never equipped with rivets. The hafting of the non-grip tanged daggers all make use of one to four rivets. Sometimes the edges of the grip plate have been hammered around a single shaft plate, likely made of wood or bone. In a special type, which does not seem to occur outside of Dilmun, the grip plate has S-shaped bent edges and, in this case, the shaft consisted of two plates of bone or wood (cf. Højlund & Hilton 2021 fig. 478. Trier & Højlund 1986).

Daggers have often been extensively sharpened, so that only a small part of the original blade is preserved, but complete, apparently unworn specimens also occur.

The blade may be completely flat and only a few millimetres thick, but more often it is slightly thickened in the middle - sometimes the centre is demarcated with a line, though a true midrib is rare.

The same inventory of daggers is found in the burial mounds, temples and settlements of Bahrain (Trier & Højlund 1986. Killick & Moon 2005 fig. 5.1: d-e. Ibrahim 1982 fig. 47: 4-6, pl. 55:5-7. Mughal 1983 fig. 27: 1-2, pl. LII: 4-5. Srivastava 1991 fig. 59B, pl. XLIIIA. Vine 1993 p. 61. Andersen & Højlund 2003, vol. 1, figs. 670-671, 722-725, 734).

Grip tang

Dagger with broad blade and grip tang (fig. 9) (F3.172). Trench RM, 50-60 N, level c. 7.30-8.60, sieve.

Dagger with grip tang (fig. 10) (F3.id). Trench Q, 60 N, 1.6 E, level 9.31.

Dagger with broken grip tang and broken blade (fig. 11) (F3.is). Trenches A, B, E, or F, sieve.

Dagger with grip tang (fig. 12) (F3.ke). Trench B, 40 N, 0.5 E, level 7.99. Associated pottery: Period 3A/3B.

Dagger with grip tang (fig. 13) (F3.mc). Trench J, northern part, level c. 8.51. Associated pottery: Period 4B.

Dagger with grip tang, blade 2.5 mm thick (fig. 14) (F3.pb). Sieve.

Dagger with grip tang and broken flat blade (fig. 15) (F3.xk). Baulk between Trenches X and Æ, level 9.60-8.15. Associated pottery: Period 3B/4B.

Dagger with grip tang (fig. 16) (F3.yp). Trench AB, sieve.

Dagger with grip tang and flat blade (fig. 17) (F3.adh). Trench C, 30.05 N, 7.03 W, level 7.00. Associated pottery: Period 3A/4A?

Dagger with grip tang and broken blade, all three edges of blade are battered (fig. 18) (F3.ain). Trench H, 38.15 N, 12.2 W, level 7.39. Associated pottery: Period 4A.

Dagger with grip tang and broken blade (fig. 19) (F3.bej.A). Trench AA, level 6.52-6.43. Associated pottery: Period 2.

Dagger with oval grip tang (fig. 20) (F3.no number). Tell F3.

Dagger with grip tang (fig. 21) (F6.759). Trench F2, 12 N, 6 W, level 1.98. Associated pottery: Period 1.

Dagger with broken grip tang, 4 mm thick blade, corroded (fig. 22) (F6.1194). Trench F1, 4-5 N, 6-7 W, level -1.94. Associated pottery: Period 1.

Riveted grip plate

Dagger with grip plate and rivet hole, thickness 2.5 mm (fig. 23) (F3.hg). Trench A, 32.35 N, 0.80 E, level 6.85. Associated pottery: Period 2.

Dagger with grip plate and three rivet holes, heavily worn on both edges, with a slight midrib (fig. 24) (F3.lb). Trench A, 36 N, 2.90 E, level 6.96. Associated pottery: Period 3A.

Fragment of dagger with grip plate and one rivet in situ (fig. 25) (F3.ahå). Trench G.

Dagger with grip plate and three rivet holes (fig. 26) (F3.ajc). Trench K, level c. 8.90-8.40, sieve. Associated pottery: Period 4A.

Dagger with grip plate and three rivet holes (fig. 27) (F3.alc). Trench K, level c. 7.20-7.40. Associated pottery: Period 3A/4A.

Dagger grip plate with four rivet holes (fig. 28) (F3.apv). Trench O, level c. 7.20-6.80. Associated pottery: Period 3A/4A.

Dagger with concave grip plate. On the photo (fig. 29) the dagger exhibits different stages of cleaning and conservation (F3.avo). Trench AL, 63 N, 4.50 E, level 6.82. Associated pottery: Period 3B.

Dagger with flat, 2 mm thick blade and one rivet hole in grip plate (fig. 30) (F6.698). Trench F2, 17 N, 7 W, level -1.15.

Dagger with two 1-1.3 cm long rivets in situ in the grip plate, blade 3 mm thick (fig. 31) (F6.1015.B). Trench N2, 13-14 N, 14-16 W, level -1.65. Associated pottery: Period 1.

Grip plate with bent edges

Dagger with grip plate with bent edges (fig. 32) (F3.225). Trench RM, 40.20 N, 4.05 W, level 7.40.

Dagger with grip plate with both edges bent to the same side and flat, 3 mm thick, blade (fig. 33) (F3.rv). Trench Y, 66.80 N, 2.5 W, level 7.40. Associated pottery: Period 4B.

Dagger with grip plate with bent edges, blade flat, 2.5 mm thick (fig. 34) (F3.aqt). Trench K, c. level 7.00-6.50. Associated pottery: Period 3A.

Riveted grip plate with S-shaped bent edges

Dagger with flat grip plate with S-shaped bent edges and one rivet hole (fig. 35) (F3.ary). Trench O, 33.20 N, 18.85 W, level 7.14. Associated pottery: Period 3A/4A.

Dagger with a slight midrib and flat grip plate with S-shaped bent edges and three rivets in situ (fig. 36) (F3.avu). Trench AL, 64.20 N, 4.95 E, level 6.72. Associated pottery: Period 3B.

Dagger with grip plate with S-shaped bent edges and one rivet hole (fig. 37) (F3.azp). Trench AO, level 6.87-6.63. Associated pottery: Period 4A/4B?

Dagger with grip plate with remains of S-shaped bent edges and two rivet holes (fig. 38) (F3.bhq). Trench AO, 58-61 N, 6-7 W, level 5.62-6.19. Associated pottery: Period 2.

Fragment of grip plate with S-shaped bent edges and two rivets in situ and two more rivet holes. Rivet length 3.3 cm, diameter 0.7 cm (fig. 39) (F3.bjl). Sieve.

Dagger with midrib and grip plate with S-shaped bent edges and two rivet holes (fig. 40) (F6.296). Trench SN1-10, 5.3-7 N, 0-1.5 E, level -1.49.

Dagger with grip plate with S-shaped bent edges and two rivets in situ. Around the rivets are handle remains with a longitudinal structure, probably wood or bone (fig. 41) (F6.696). Trench F2, 16.10 N, 7.5 W, level -1.11.

Blade fragments

Dagger blade, 3.5 mm thick, slightly thickened in the middle (fig. 42) (F3.278). Trench RM, sieve.

Dagger blade point, 3.5 mm thick (fig. 43) (881.TE). Trench RM.

Dagger blade point, 3 mm thick, flat (fig. 44) (F3.jø). Trench Q, 59 N, 3 E, level 7.34.

Dagger blade point (fig. 378: sample 325) (F3.te). Trenches Æ and Ø, sieve.

Dagger blade point, 2 mm thick, flat (fig. 45) (F3.øm.A). Trench AE, sieve.

Dagger blade, 3 mm thick (figs. 46 and 378: sample 410) (F3.øm.B). Trench AE, sieve.

Dagger blade point, 3 mm thick (figs. 47 and 378: sample 413) (F3.øm.C). Trench AE, sieve.

Dagger blade, 2.5 mm thick (fig. 48) (F3.ajp). Trenches C-D, G-H, K-L.

Dagger blade, lower part flat, upper part with faint midrib (fig. 49) (F3.ajx). Trench H, 42.90 N, 10.57 W, level 7.06. Associated pottery: Period 4A.

Dagger blade point with midrib (fig. 50) (F3.avw). Trench AI.

Dagger blade (fig. 51) (F3.bcn). Trench I, level 6.55-6.35. Associated pottery: Period 2 or 3A/3B.

Dagger blade (figs. 52 and 378: sample 338) (F3.bej.B). Trench AA, level 6.52-6.43. Associated pottery: Period 2.

Dagger blade, hafting part broken off, middle part of blade is slightly thickened up to 3 mm (fig. 53) (F6.830). Trench M2, 14 N, 9.5 W, level -1.58. Associated pottery: Period 1.

Dagger blade, covered in corrosion, length 7.6 cm, width 2.3 cm, thickness 0.45 cm (F6.1005.A). Trench F1, 1-2 N, 7-8 W, level -1.48.

Spears

Spears are relatively rare in Tell F3 and Tell F6 but occur often in burials in Bahrain (cf. Ibrahim 1982 fig. 47:1-3 and pl. 55:1-4. Mughal 1983 fig. 26 and pl. 53a. Højlund 2007 fig. 35. Trier & Højlund 1986. Killick & Moon 2005 fig. 5.1:c). Socketed spearheads are also widespread in the U.A.E. and Oman (Yule & Weisgerber 2015 fig. 8). The socket can often be seen to have been made by rolling a sheet so that it either overlaps itself or has been smithed together.

Spear with marked midrib and long socket, which is folded (fig. 54) (F3.242). Trench RM, 39.50 N, 4.50 W, level 7.10.

Spear with marked midrib and socket; socket has a slit, probably folded together (fig. 55) (Ashkanani 2021 p. 114) (F3.aib). Trench G, level 6.87. Associated pottery: Period 3A.

Spear with marked midrib and socket (fig. 56) (F6.1015.A). Trench N2, 13-14 N, 14-16 W, level -1.65. Associated pottery: Period 1.

Socket, 8.1 cm long, 2.1-2.6 cm in diameter, probably for spear (F6.1054.B). Trench N2, 14 N, 12-14 W, level -1.64. Associated pottery: Period 1.

Socket, 12.1 cm long, 2.1-3.5 cm in diameter, probably for spear (F6.1124). Trench F1.

Arrows

The arrows presented here are extremely varied and probably encompass a range of dates and purposes. The blade may be slightly thickened in the middle but more often there is a marked midrib.

Arrow (fig. 57) (F3.æ). Trench A, sieve from level 7.85-8.15. Associated pottery: Period 3A.

Arrow (fig. 58) (F3.lq). Sieve.

Arrow (fig. 59) (F3.rq). Trench Æ, 54.20 N, 10.30 E, level 8.56. Associated pottery: Period 4.

Arrow (fig. 60) (F3.sf). Trench Æ, sieve.

Arrow (fig. 61) (F3.tf). Trench Ø, sieve.

Arrow (fig. 62) (F3.zk). Trench AF, sieve.

Arrow (fig. 63) (F3.æg). Trenches AB-AF, sieve.

Arrow (fig. 64) (F3.anv). Trench O, 30.10 N, 19.75 W, level 7.06. Associated pottery: Period 3A/4A.

Arrow (fig. 65) (F3.aol). Trench D, 43.95 N, 8.45 W, level 7.60. Associated pottery: Period 4A.

Arrow, corroded (fig. 66) (F3.bgm). Sieve.

Arrow. The point is missing in the photo but preserved, giving the arrow a total length of 11.7 cm (fig. 67) (F6.1114). Trench F1, level -1.17. There are good parallels to this type of arrow from Period 4A context in Tell F3 (Højlund & Hilton 2021 figs. 480-481) and from Tell Khaiber (Moon 2023 figs. 6.82-6.83).

Arrow (fig. 68) (F6.1182). Trench F2, 11 N, 6 W, level -1.90. Associated pottery: Period 1.

Arrow, corroded (figs. 69 and 378: sample 373) (F6.1205). Trench M1, 1-2 N, 8-10 W, level -1.28.

Arrow, 3 mm thick (fig. 70) (KM1626). Tell F3.

Socketed hoes

Hoes with a socket at right angles to the blade are common throughout Eastern Arabia in the 2nd-1st millennia BC (Potts, D.T. 1994 p. 158. Højlund & Andersen 1997 fig. 310. Killick & Moon 2005 fig. 5.3: b). Up to the present day the same shape, produced in iron, continue to be used as a basic farming tool in the countries along the Gulf. Possibly the modern word for this tool (*ṡaxxin*) was also used in the second millennium BC (Holes 2005 p. 52-54).

Normally the blade has an even thickness, but two examples have a reinforcing ridge leading up to the socket. The few pottery contexts of the hoes suggest that they belong to the whole chronological sequence on Failaka.

Fragment of a socketed hoe (fig. 71) (F3.4). Trench RM, 12.80 N, 1 W, 0.77 m below surface.

Possibly fragment of hoe (fig. 72) (F3.xh). Trench AF, level 9.50-8.05. Associated pottery: Period 4B.

Possibly point of hoe, 4.5 mm thick (fig. 73) (F3.xm). Trench AD, 7.30-7.05. Associated pottery: Period 3A-3B.

Hoe blade, 0.9 cm thick, with socket broken off (figs. 74 and 378: sample 316) (F3.bfc). Trench J, 76 N, 3 E, level 6.42. Associated pottery: Period 2.

Front part of a hoe blade (fig. 75) (F6.655). Trench F2, 17-18 N, 5-6 W, level -0.57.

Socketed hoe with heavily battered blade (fig. 76) (F6.1086). Trench N1, 2 N, 13 W, level -0.34.

Complete hoe with short socket and reenforcing ridge (fig. 77) (KM5892). Found during Kjærum's sounding in room 10 in the "Palace" in Tell F6 in 1988 (Kjærum & Højlund 2013 p. 145). It lay at level -1.53, corresponding to the earliest floor of the building, at the base of the northern pillar, covered by a paved floor with surface in level -1.35. Associated pottery: Period 2.

Hoe blade possibly (fig. 78) (F6.nonumber).

Fragment of hoe blade, 9 mm thick near shaft, 7 mm at tip, corroded (fig. 79) (F6.u.nr).

Complete hoe with socket and reinforcing ridge (fig. 80) (KM2259). The provenience of this object is uncertain. It was not registered during the Danish excavations, but only drawn and photographed by the Danish team in 1975. It was likely found during maintenance and cleaning of the sites by the Kuwait museum staff between 1963 and 1975.

Axes

Some of the axes from Tell F3 and Tell F6 are simple axe blades (cf. Killick & Moon 2005 fig. 5.2: a), and some have been furnished with a socket. One such socket was adorned with two bands of ridges, and it is likely that the ridged cylinders described below derive from such broken artefacts. The socketed axe with ridges has a parallel from a burial in Hamad Town in Bahrain which shows two groups of five to seven ridges (Trier & Højlund 1986: Hamad Town 1982-83, BS 2135 F213. Vine 1993 p. 61). Adzes with similar ridged sockets are known in Mesopotamia from mid 2nd mill. Tell Khaiber (Moon 2023 fig. 6.79) and late 2nd millennium Ur (Woolley & Mallowan 1965 p. 104-105, pl. 36: U.6927).

An adze was used to prepare the oolitic limestone ashlars for the temple in Tell F6. This is revealed by the cutting marks on the ashlars found there, identical to those found on ashlars in the Barbar Temple (Højlund & Abu-Laban 2016 p. 83-87 and 259, figs. 119-120. Andersen & Højlund 2003, vol. 1, p. 327-328, figs. 190-191).

Axe with rectangular cross section, thickness at neck 1.4 cm, in the middle 1.8 cm and by the battered edge 1.9 cm (fig. 81) (F3.ayr). Trench AO, level 7.00. Associated pottery: Period 4A/4B?

Axe with battered edge, thickness at neck and edge 0.8 cm, in the middle 0.9 cm (figs. 82 and 378: sample 358) (F3.bbc). Trench AO, 63.25 N, 5 W, level 6.65, on plaster floor. Associated pottery: Period 4A/4B?

Axe with battered edge and part of a socket preserved. The transition between blade and socket is decorated with two groups of each three ridges on both sides. The broken edges of the socket are also battered (fig. 83) (F6.562.A). Trench D2, 12.25 N, 2.65 W, level -1.40.

Axe with socket, diameter 2.2 x 2.6 cm, wall thickness 0.9 cm, decorated with four ridges. The blade is narrow, 3 cm thick, and almost completely worn down and battered, thick at the edge, decorated on two sides with about three ridges. Covered with corrosion (fig. 84) (F6.1028). Trench N1, 2 N, 14-15 W, level +0.24.

Axe/hammer with both ends flat and expanded, deformed by hammering, thickness between 1.5 and 2 cm (fig. 85) (F6.1147). Trench N1, level -1.06.

Ridged cylinders

A number of broken cylinders with a diameter of c. 4 cm exhibit up to two bands of two to five ridges. A vertical ridge is always present, perhaps indicating where the cylinder was forged together and may suggest that the cylinder was not cast. They probably belonged to socketed axes like those described above.

Three ridged cylinders are preserved all around and were thus not attached to a blade and may have ended a staff as a ferrule. One of these has two groups of ridges, like the broken cylinders described above, in addition to an engraved face, consisting of two eyes, a mouth and a moustache. One cylinder dates to Period 2 and four have pottery contexts of Period 4A and 4B.

Ridged cylinder (fig. 86) (F3.nf). Trench Q, level 6.15. Associated pottery: Period 2.

Ridged cylinder (fig. 87) (F3.pb). Sieve.

Ridged cylinder (fig. 88) (F3.vh). Trench AB, 68 N, 3.1 W, level 7.89. Associated pottery: Period 4B.

Ridged cylinder (fig. 89) (F3.ån). Trench AF, sieve.

Ridged cylinder (fig. 90) (F3.abg). Trench C, level c. 8.25-7.95. Associated pottery: Period 4A.

Ridged cylinder (fig. 91) (F3.ajp). Trenches C-D, G-H, and K-L.

Ridged cylinder, 3.9 cm long, 2.7 cm wide, 0.7 cm thick, with 5-6 ridges, corroded (F3.avb). Trench AF, 72.5 N, 3 W, level 7.33. Associated pottery: Period 4B.

Ridged cylinder (fig. 92) (F3.avw). Trench AI.

Ridged cylinder (fig. 93) (F3.azr). Trench AO, 62 N, 3.10 W, level 6.75. Associated pottery: Period 4A/4B?

Ridged cylinder (fig. 94) (F6.295). Trench SN1-10, 1-4 N, 0-1.5 E, -1.27.

Ridged cylinder with male face engraved (fig. 95) (KM52). The exact provenience of this object is uncertain. It was not registered during the Danish excavations, but only drawn and photographed by the Danish team in 1975. It was likely found during maintenance and cleaning of the sites by the Kuwait museum staff between 1963 and 1975.

Knives

Knife (fig. 96) (F3.æ). Trench A, sieve from level 8.15-7.85. Associated pottery: Period 3A-3B.

Knife? (figs. 97 and 378: sample 406) (F3.qt). Trenches X-Z, sieve.

Knife (figs. 98 and 378: sample 348) (F3.baf). Trench AO, level 7.63-6.63. Associated pottery: Period 4A/4B?

Knife (fig. 99) (F3.baj). Trench AO, level 6.54. Associated pottery: Period 2, 3B/4A?

Knife with grip tang (fig. 100) (F6.417). Trench D2.

Knife with grip tang with broad midrib (fig. 101) (F6.562.B). Trench D2, 12.25 N, 2.65 W, level -1.40.

Knife, upper blade 4 mm thick (fig. 102) (F6.1178). Trench F1, 7 N, 6 W, -1.89. Associated pottery: Period 1.

Chisels/drills

These objects have a length of up to 15 cm. Their cross section is square or rectangular, measuring 3 to 11 mm (*M* 5 mm), and their edges have a similarly narrow width of 3-11 mm. They have never been found fitted with a bone handle like the awls described below, but they may have been inserted as chisels in a wooden handle and worked with a mallet. If used as chisels their narrow edge indicates that they may have been used to produce very small holes, probably in wood. The possible traces of hammering, as a slight expansion of the butt, have been noted in only one case.

Another more likely possibility is that they were in fact not chisels but drill heads to be inserted in a drill shaft and worked with a bow in order to make holes, again rather small holes, not much larger than the width of the edge, that is, 3-11 mm.

The obvious use of such a tool, whether worked as a chisel or as a drill, would have been in building or repairing *lashed* or *sewn boats*. Along the shores of the Arabian Gulf and the Indian Ocean, boats were traditionally built by drilling or chiselling holes along the edge of wooden planks and sewing or lashing them together. Impressions in bitumen found in archaeological excavation show that such techniques were already in use in the 3rd-2nd millennium (Vosmer 1996 p. 229, figs. 13-15. Cleuziou & Tosi 2020 fig. 183. Højlund & Abu-Laban 2016 p. 210, figs. 1071-1072).

The large number of chisels/drills found at Tell F3 (at least 19) may be seen as evidence for the importance of building or repairing boats on the island, especially with regard to Tell F3, as only a few of these tools have been found at Tell F6 (c. 3). They were found scattered all over Tell F3, and they apparently occur in all periods.

The long production length of the chisels/drills underscores their practical purpose as the need to constantly sharpen the edge would cause them to gradually loose length. It was therefore economical to produce them with a long length.

A few similarly long, narrow chisels/drills have been found at Al-Khidr (Benediková 2010 figs. 48-49).

Chisel/drill (fig. 103) (F3.89). Trench RM.

Chisel/drill (fig. 104) (F3.124). Trench RM, 3-15 N, 1.00-2.45 m below surface, sieve.

Chisel/drill, square cross section (fig. 105) (F3.179). Trench RM, 24.3 N, 2.2 W, level 6.86.

Chisel/drill (fig. 106) (F3.kt). Trench J, 74.90 N, 3.70 E, level 6.06. Associated pottery: Period 2.

Chisel/drill (figs. 107 and 378: sample 432) (F3.ro). Trench Y, 64 N, 1.5 W, level 7.06, on stone floor. Associated pottery: Period 4B.

Chisel/drill (fig. 108) (F3.xk.1). Baulk between Trenches Æ-X, level 9.60-8.15. Associated pottery: Period 3B/4B.

Chisel/drill, cross section at butt 4 x 4.5 mm (fig. 109) (F3.xk.2). Baulk between Trenches Æ-X, level 9.60-8.15. Associated pottery: Period 3B/4B.

Chisel/drill (fig. 110) (F3.yu). Trench AB, sieve.

Chisel/drill (fig. 111) (F3.æh). Trench AI, level 8.94-6.49.

Chisel/drill (fig. 112) (F3.øm.1). Trench AE, sieve.

Chisel/drill (fig. 113) (F3.øm.3). Trench AE, sieve.

Chisel/drill (fig. 114) (F3.aam). Trench C, 28.47 N, 8.12 W, level 8.52. Associated pottery: Period 4A.

Chisel/drill, pointed edge (fig. 115) (F3.acq). Trench C, level c. 7.65-7.35. Associated pottery: Period 3A/4A?

Chisel/drill (fig. 116) (F3.aeg). Trench C, 30.47 N, 7.84 W, level 7.15. Associated pottery: Period 3A/4A?

Chisel/drill (fig. 117) (F3.aep). Trench C, 30.95 N, 8.22 W, level 7.10. Associated pottery: Period 3A/4A?

Chisel/drill (fig. 118) (F3.ajp). Trenches C-D, G-H, or K-L.

Chisel/drill (fig. 119) (F3.ast). Trench E, level c. 7.80-8.80. Associated pottery: Period 3A.

Chisel/drill (fig. 120) (F3.avø). Trench AF, sieve, c. level 7.22. Associated pottery: Period 4B.

Chisel, covered in corrosion (F3.azp). Trench AO, level 6.87-6.63. Associated pottery: Period 4A/4B?

Chisel/drill (fig. 121) (F6.732). Trench F2, 20 N, 5-9 W, level -1.73. Associated pottery: Period 1.

Chisel/drill, sharp edge, broken butt, cross section 6 x 8 mm (fig. 122) (F6.880). Trench M2, sieve above level -2.04.

Chisel/drill (fig. 123) (F6.926). Trench E2, sieve.

Chisels with raised edges

The edges of some chisels are raised, thereby creating a longitudinal furrow on both sides and an H-shaped cross section. This method strengthened the chisel, perhaps making it possible to apply a mallet to the butt without causing the blade to bend.

Chisel (fig. 124) (F3.297). Trench RM, 40 N, c. 1 W, level c. 7.34.

Chisel, broken at both ends, blade thickness 3 mm, raised edges on both sides, 5 mm thick (fig. 125) (F3.abø). Trench C, level c. 7.70-8.00. Associated pottery: Period 3A/4A?

Chisel (fig. 126) (F3.amæ). Trench O, c. level 8.00. Associated pottery: Period 4A.

Chisel, edge broken off (figs. 127 and 378: sample 390) (F6.58). Trench SS 21.6 S, 1.4 E, level -1.80.

Chisel, blunt edge, butt slightly battered (fig. 128) (F6.519). Trench D3, 21-24 N, 1-4 W, level 0.01.

Chisel, flat-hammered head (fig. 129) (F6.622). Trench D2, level -2.03. Associated pottery: Period 1.

Chisel (fig. 130) (F3.no number).

Drills

Two fragments of a rod, both with a starshaped cross-section with the same number of points. The two pieces cannot be fitted together exactly, perhaps because they were both covered with a layer of corrosion when found and the removal of this corrosion may have modified the breakages. Nevertheless, the shape and size of the individual indentures are so similar that there is no doubt in the present author's mind that they originally fitted together.

Encapsulated in a wooden shaft this object may have been worked with a bow for drilling holes in wood, such as for fitting beams together with dowels. One end of the drill was heavily worn before it finally broke. The small worn piece was found in Tell F6, and one may speculate that this was where it was operated when it finally broke. Perhaps the worn piece was left embedded in a wooden beam at Tell F6 and the craftsman took the rest of the tool back to his house in Tell F3 where it was found.

Smooth, round end of a rod with starshaped cross-section (fig. 131) (F3.sk). Trench Ø, 56 N, 14.7 E, level 8.78. Associated pottery: Period 4.

Rod with starshaped cross-section (fig. 132) (F6.262). Trench B2, level -0.11.

Awls

Awls have a pointed working end with round cross section and a hafting end with square or rectangular cross section. The awls of the extant collection have lengths varying between 4.7 and 11.5 cm, the handle parts have a maximum thickness of between 2.5 and 7 mm (*M* 4 mm) and the maximum diameter of the round ends varies from 2 to 5 mm (*M* 3 mm). In addition to the specimens registered below, there were also many fragments of rods with a square or rectangular cross section all the way to the pointed end.

Thirteen of the thirty-six awls listed below were found inserted into bone handles and this must be assumed to have been the general rule when operational. The handles were made of the distal ends of the metapodia of sheep/goat. The copper rod was rammed into the spongious tissue of the tubular bone, and the square section of the awl must have been essential in situating the awl securely inside the handle, especially when used in a rotary movement. The copper rod was likely hammered into the handle before the pointed end was shaped.

Remains from the production of these bone handles were found in abundance during the 2012-2017 excavations at Tell F3 (Højlund & Hilton 2021 p. 141, figs. 551-563). Bitumen has been noted in the hafting part of awls from Al-Khidr (Benediková 2010 p. 54), but so far not in awls from Tell F3 and Tell F6. Perhaps it was used only for repairs.

The thirty-two awls from Tell F3 were found throughout the site and date to almost all periods. Of the four awls found in Tell F6, three were found in Pre-"Palace" layers.

Similar awls, often hafted in bone handles, have been found at Al-Khidr (Benediková 2010 fig. 50), at Saar settlement in Bahrain (cf. Killick & Moon 2005 fig.

5.2c) and in contemporary burials in Bahrain (Ibrahim 1982 fig. 46: 6-9 and pl. 54: 11-14. Mughal 1983 fig. 27: 7. Srivastava 1991 fig. 59B: 2. Trier & Højlund 1986).

The presence of awls in burials suggests that they were considered to be personal equipment, perhaps a multipurpose tool worn in the belt, in contrast, for instance, to the chisels/drills treated above which have never been found in graves.

Awl (fig. 133) (F3.9), round cross section in the pointed end and square section, 5 x 5 mm, in the handle part. Trench RM.

Awl (fig. 134) (F3.21), point broken off. Trench RM, 19.45 N, 4.20 W, 60-65 cm below surface.

Awl, round cross section in the pointed end and square cross section in the hafting end (fig. 135) (F3.98). Trench RM, 7.10 N, 2.60 W, 2.10 m below surface.

Awl, square section 3 x 3.5 mm, at butt end 2 x 2 mm, one end pointed (fig. 136) (F3.217). Trench RM, 51 N, 2.25 W, level 6.90.

Awl, point broken off, square cross section at butt, 0.35 x 0. 3.5 mm, round cross section at pointed end (fig. 137) (F3.æ). Trench A, level 8.15-7.85, sieve. Associated pottery: Period 3A-3B.

Awl, square section at butt, 2 x 2.5 mm, and middle, 3 x 3 mm; round cross section at pointed end and up to 2.7 mm from the point, sitting loose in bone handle with parallel stripes from shaping the bone (fig. 138) (F3. hg.1). Trench A, 32.35 N, 0.80 E, level 6.85. Associated pottery: Period 2.

Awl sitting firm in bone handle (fig. 139) (F3.hg.2). Trench A, 32.35 N, 0.80 E, level 6.85. Associated pottery: Period 2.

Awl, full length preserved, 6.9 cm, square section in upper part, 4 x 5 mm, and square section in lower part, 4 x 4 mm (F3.ta). Trench Ø, level 8.97-8.46. Associated pottery: Period 4.

Awl, point broken off, pointed end round in cross section until 1 cm from end where it becomes square (fig. 140) (F3.wå.1). Trench AE, level 7.75. Associated pottery: Period 3A.

Awl with bent point (fig. 141) (F3.wå.2). Trench AE, level 7.75. Associated pottery: Period 3A.

Awl (fig. 142) (F3.xb). Trench AB, sieve.

Awl (fig. 143) (F3.yv). Trench AH, 58 N, 12 E, level 8.10. Associated pottery: Period 3B.

Awl, square cross section, 3 x 3.5 mm (fig. 144) (F3.zn). Trench Ø, level 6.80-6.00. Associated pottery: Period 2.

Fragment of awl sitting in opening of handle. The surface of the handle is covered with parallel striations (fig. 145) (F3.ød.1). Trench AK, level 6.28.

Awl, diameter 3.5 mm (fig. 146) (F3.ød.2). Trench AK, level 6.28.

Awl, diameter 3.5 mm (fig. 147) (F3.ød.3). Trench AK, level 6.28.

Awl (fig. 148) (F3.øm.2). Trench AE, sieve.

Awl (fig. 149) (F3.ada). Trench C, level c. 7.65-7.35. Associated pottery: Period 3A/4A?

Awl with handle (fig. 150) (F3.aeq). Trench D, 37.80 N, 7.10 W, level 7.82. Associated pottery: Period 4A.

Awl (fig. 151) (F3.aia). Trench G, fireplace.

Awl with handle, the part of the awl sitting in the handle has a square section, 5 x 5 mm, the part outside the handle has a round section, 3 mm in diameter (fig. 152) (F3.ajo.A). Trenches C-D, G-H, K-L.

Awl (fig. 153) (F3.ajo.B). Trenches C-D, G-H, K-L.

Awl (fig. 154) (F3.ajo.C). Trenches C-D, G-H, K-L.

Awl, upper end with oval section, 3 x 5 mm, square section in the middle, 4 x 4 mm (fig. 155) (F3.akz). Trench H, level c. 7.65-7.15. Associated pottery: Period 4A.

Awl with handle, the awl is 5.9 cm in length and 4 mm in diameter, square cross section inside the handle and round outside. The surface of the handle is covered with parallel striations from shaping (fig. 156) (F3.amw). Trench D, level c. 7.00-6.50.

Awl, length 3.5 cm, diameter 3 mm (fig. 157) (F3.aoh). Trench S, level c. 8.30.

Awl with bone handle, point broken off, awl diameter outside handle 4 mm, inside 6 mm (fig. 158) (F3.

aon). Trench D, 37.45 N, level 7.76. Associated pottery: Period 4A.

Awl with bone handle (fig. 159) (F3.aræ). C. 1 cm of the awl extends outside the handle, but the bone is broken. The section of the awl is rectangular, 0.2 x 0.25 cm, in the shaft. The handle is made of the distal part of the left tarsometatarsus of an extinct giant heron, *Ardea bennuides* (Hoch 1979 p. 626). Trench G, in the east baulk.

Double awl in handle. Distance between points 2 mm (fig. 160) (F3.arø). Trench G. Possibly used to carve the dotted circles on soft stone stamp seals (pers. comm. Kjærum 1979. David-Cuny & Azpeitia 2012 p. 25).

Awl with bone handle (fig. 161) (F3.atq). Trench K, level c. 7.00-6.50. Associated pottery: Period 3A.

Awl (fig. 378: sample 357) (F3.bdr). Trench Y, level 5.36. Associated pottery: Period 2.

Awl (fig. 162) (F3.bjl). Sieve.

Awl (fig. 163) (F6.585). Trench D1, 6.7 N, 3.2 W, level -1.47.

Awl with bone handle (fig. 164) (F6.617.A). Trench D2, 15-16 N, 1-2 W, level -1.84. Associated pottery: Period 1.

Awl, 8.8 cm long, in damaged bone handle. Outside of handle the awl has a round cross section, diameter 4 mm (fig. 165) (F6.617.B). Trench D2, 15-16 N, 1-2 W, level -1.84. Associated pottery: Period 1.

Awl, 8.7 cm long, with broken bone handle (fig. 166) (F6.820). Trench F2, 14.50 N, 4.5 W, level -1.84. Associated pottery: Period 1.

Needles

Needles have a length of 10-17 cm and a round cross section of 3 to 6 mm in diameter (*M* 4). The eye was shaped by hammering the end of the pin into an elongated point, which was bent back and joined onto the shaft.

Twenty-seven needles derive from Tell F3 and only five from Tell F6, a ratio that is reflected in the numbers from the recent excavations, namely seven from Tell F3 (Højlund & Hilton 2021 figs. 469, 475-476, 483-484, and 494-495) and none from Tell F6 (Højlund & Abu-Laban 2016). The needles from Tell F3 were found spread throughout the site and dating to all periods. Similar needles were found at Al-Khidr (Benediková 2010 fig. 51), and at Qala'at al-Bahrain (Højlund & Andersen 1994 fig. 1868). From Bahraini burials, one example is known (Mughal 1983 fig. 27: 3).

These needles are remarkably uniform in length and thickness and intended for heavy duty. A relatively large number were found in complete condition, so they appear to have been lost where they were used, rather than being collected for remelting.

They resemble the needles *(makher)* used by Bedouins to sew together long strips of cloth for tents (Højlund & Hilton 2021 p. 131). They may have been used for sewing textiles for sails for boats, sewing palm leaf mats (Frifelt 1995 p. 190, fig. 278), constructing boats of reed bundles or *barasti/areesh* buildings, or for passing cordage through holes drilled along the edge of wooden planks for boat building.

Needle, broken in two parts, an eye part with round cross section, 4 mm in diameter, and a pointed end, 4 mm in diameter (fig. 167) (F3.*60). Trench BB, level 5.99.

Needle (F3.60). Trench RM, 31.35 N, 2.80 W, level c. 8.21-8.06.

Needle head, shaft diameter 4 mm (fig. 168) (F3.264.A). Trench RM, sieve.

Needle head, shaft diameter 5 mm (fig. 169) (F3.264B). Trench RM, sieve.

Needle head, shaft diameter 6 mm (fig. 170) (F3.278). Trench RM, sieve.

Needle, shaft diameter 4.5 mm (fig. 171) (F3.312). Trench RM, sieve from 0-20 N, until 1.50 m below surface.

Needle head, round cross section, 3 mm in diameter (fig. 172) (881.SY.A). Trench RM, sieve.

Needle head, round cross section, 4 mm in diameter (fig. 173) (881.SY.B). Trench RM, sieve.

Needle head, round cross section, 6 mm in diameter (fig. 174) (881.TE.A). Trench RM.

Needle head, round cross section, 6 mm in diameter (fig. 175) (881.TE.B). Trench RM.

Needle, shaft diameter 3.5 mm (figs. 176 and 378: sample 434) (F3.dt). Trench F, 40.80 N, 5.10 E.

Needle, point broken off, shaft diameter 3-4 mm (fig. 177) (F3.jn). Trench I, level 6.55. Associated pottery: Period 3A/3B.

Needle, shaft diameter 4 mm (fig. 178) (F3.kl). Trench B, 39.60 N, 0.65 E.

Needle, shaft diameter 3 mm (fig. 179) (F3.nh). Trench B, level 6.75. Associated pottery: Period 2.

Bent needle with pointed end but without head, round cross section, diameter 5 mm (fig. 180) (F3.py). Trench X, level 8.24. Associated pottery: Period 3B/4B.

Needle head (fig. 181) (F3.vf). Trench Ø, level 6.83-6.37. Associated pottery: Period 2.

Needle head (fig. 182) (F3.xk.A). Baulk between Trenches Æ and X, level 9.60-8.15. Associated pottery: Period 3B/4B.

Needle head (fig. 183) (F3.xk.B). Baulk between Trenches Æ and X, level 9.60-8.15. Associated pottery: Period 3B/4B.

Needle eye, diameter of shank 4 mm (fig. 184) (F3.xu). Trench AB, sieve.

Needle, shaft diameter 4 mm (figs. 185 and 378: sample 435) (F3.yt). Trench AI, level 8.69-8.30. Associated pottery: Period 4A.

Needle, diameter 3 mm (fig. 186) (F3.zc). Trench AI, level 7.85. Associated pottery: Period 4A.

Needle, shaft diameter 4 mm (figs. 187 and 378: sample 473) (F3.abø). Trench C, level c. 7.95-7.65. Associated pottery: Period 3A/4A?

Needle with only the lower part of the eye preserved, 5 mm diameter shaft (fig. 188) (F3.asr). Trench K, level c. 7.20-7.00. Associated pottery: Period 3A.

Needle, round cross section, 4 mm diameter, eye broken off (fig. 189) (F3.atq). Trench K, level c. 7.00-6.50. Associated pottery: Period 3A.

Needle, diameter 4 mm (fig. 190) (F3.avs). Trench AL, 64.50 N, 6 E, level 6.80. Associated pottery: Period 3B.

Needle, point broken off, preserved length 12.5 cm, diameter 6 mm (fig. 191) (F3.avw). Trench AI, sieve.

Needle, 13.5 cm long, diameter 6 mm (F3.bhh). Trench AO, level 5.63-6.63. Associated pottery: Period 2, 3B/4A?

Needle, oval cross section, 3.5 x 5 mm, eye broken off (fig. 192) (F6.491). Trench E2, 19 N, 2.5 E, level -0.48.

Needle, diameter 4 mm (fig. 193) (F6.743). Trench F2, 13-14 N, 6.5-8 W, level -1.32.

Needle, upper shaft cross section 3 mm, lower shaft cross section 2.5 mm (fig. 194) (F6.937). Trench A3, level -1.16.

Needle, 5 mm in diameter, eye broken off, bent together (fig. 195) (F6.1194). Trench F1, 4-5 N, 6-7 W, level -1.94. Associated pottery: Period 1.

Fragment of needle without eye, round cross section up to 6 mm in diameter (fig. 196) (F6."A3").

Tweezers

Tweezers (fig. 197) (F3.102). Trench RM, 0-10 N, sieve.

Tweezers (fig. 198) (F3.136). Trench RM, 16.30 N, 2.50 W, level 5.15.

Tweezers (fig. 199) (F3.146). Trench RM, sieve.

Tweezers (fig. 200) (F3.258). Trench RM, 22 N, 0.20 W, 1.45 m below surface.

Fragment of tweezers (F3.pb). Sieve.

Fragment of tweezers, 4.9 cm long (F3.sk). Trench Ø, 56 N, 14.7 E, level 8.78. Associated pottery: Period 4.

Tweezers, 5.8 cm long (F3.bct). Trench I, level 6.35-6.25. Associated pottery: Period 2.

Fishhooks

A total of forty-nine copper objects were identified as fishhooks. Many more were undoubtedly broken during excavation and ended up as small bits of wire. Fourteen were equipped with a barb, whereas twenty-seven seem to have been unbarbed (Cf. Højlund & Andersen 1994 figs. 1856, 1865-1866. Benediková 2010 figs. 53: c-d, 54-56. Killick & Moon 2005 fig. 5.3: g-m). A fishhook found during the 2012-2017 excavations in Tell F3 shows how the string was attached by knots to the shank (Strehle 2021 p. 165-166, figs. 1-3). In fourteen cases the end of the shank was hammered flat and wide to prevent the string from slipping off. In two cases the shank ends in an eye, a feature well-known from the Indus region (Mackay 1937-1938 Pl. 114: 6, 125: 48, 132: 23 and 25. Mackay 1943 p. 184, Pl. 73: 5-8, 17-18, 76: 15).

Judging by the find circumstances fishhooks occurred in all periods of the two tells' occupation, more from Tell F3 (40) than from Tell F6 (8). Additionally, five complete fishhooks were found in Tell F3 during the 2012-2017 excavations (Højlund & Hilton 2021 figs. 465-468 and 496) and two fragments of fishhooks were found in Tell F6 in the 2008-2012 excavations (Højlund & Abu-Laban 2016 figs. 1060 and 1070).

Parallels have been found at other Dilmun sites: Al Khidr on Failaka (Benediková 2010 figs. 53a-d, 54a-f, 55a-f, and 56a-f), and in Bahrain at Qala'at al-Bahrain (Højlund & Andersen 1994 fig. 1865), Saar burial mounds (Ibrahim 1982 fig. 46.5) and Saar Settlement, where a small number of the fishhooks were also barbed (Killick & Moon 2005 fig. 5.3:g-m).

Barbed fishhooks

Barbed fishhook, shank diameter 4 mm, with flat attachment area, 1 x 7 mm (fig. 201) (F3.10). Trench RM, 17.5 N, 4 W, above 1 m depth.

Barbed fishhook (881.RO). Trench RM, 40-60 N, above level c. 6.50, sieve.

Fragment of barbed fishhook, shaft diameter 4 mm (figs. 202 and 378: sample 500) (F3.j). Trench A, 28.72 N, 3.82 E, level 8.23. Associated pottery: Period 3B.

Barbed fishhook, the shank has a 4 mm thick, round cross section with flat-hammered end, 1 x 6 mm (fig. 203) (F3.ab). Trench B, 36.85 N, 2.68 E, level 8.10. Associated pottery: Period 3A/B.

Barbed fishhook (F3.pb). Tell F3, sieve.

Barbed fishhook, shank diameter 4 mm, and flat-hammered head, 6.5 mm wide (fig. 204) (F3.qæ). Trench Z, sieve.

Barbed point of fishhook, shank 5 mm in diameter (fig. 205) (F3.xk). Baulk between Trenches Æ and X, level 9.60-8.15. Associated pottery: Period 3B/4B.

Two barbed fishhooks corroded together, shank diameters 3.5 and 4 mm, one with flat, 6 mm wide, attachment area (fig. 206) (F3.æz). Trench AD, sieve.

Barbed fishhook, shaft diameter 4 mm (fig. 207) (F3.øx). Trench AE, sieve.

Barbed fishhook with an eye for fastening the line (fig. 208) (F3.afd). Trench G, level c. 8.93-8.43. Associated pottery: Period 4A.

Barbed fishhook with square, 2 x 3.5 mm, shank and 6 mm wide, flat attachment area (fig. 209) (F3.aqj.1). Trench O, level c. 7.20-6.60. Associated pottery: Period 3A/4A.

Barbed fishhook with flat attachment area (fig. 210) (F6.444). Trench D2, level -1.31.

Barbed fishhook with flat attachment area (fig. 211) (F6.802). Trench M2, sieve from above level -1.07.

Unbarbed fishhooks

Fishhook, 0.4 cm diameter cross section of shank (fig. 212) (F3.36). Trench RM, 19.65 N, 4.33 W, 0.95 m below surface.

Fishhook (fig. 213) (F3.47). Trench RM, 16.6 N, 3 W, 1.08 m below surface.

Fishhook, shaft 0.45 cm in diameter (fig. 214) (F3.74). Trench RM, 16.30 N, 1.5 W, 1.7 m below surface.

Fishhook, shaft diameter 2-4 mm (fig. 215) (F3.103). Trench RM, 0-10 N, sieve.

Fishhook, shaft diameter 3.5 mm (fig. 216) (F3.104). Trench RM, 0-10 N, sieve.

Fishhook, 5 mm diameter (figs. 217 and 378: sample 491) (F3.115). Trench RM, 3-15 N, 1-2.45 m depth.

Fishhook, shaft diameter 4 mm (fig. 218) (F3.155). Trench RM, 35.70 N, 3.5 W, level 7.61.

Fishhook, shaft diameter 4.5 mm (fig. 219) (F3.187). Trench RM, sieve.

Fishhook, shaft diameter 3.5 mm (fig. 220) (F3.313). Trench RM, level 7.41.

Fishhook, diameter 5 mm (fig. 221) (F3.315). Trench RM, 49.60 N, 0.60 W, level 6.24.

Fishhook (fig. 222) (F3.323). Trench RM, 0-20 N, above 1.50 m depth.

Fishhook, shank diameter 4 mm (fig. 223) (881.TE). Trench RM.

Fishhook, shaft diameter 4 mm (fig. 224) (F3.m). Trench A, level 8.02-8.22, sieve. Associated pottery: Period 3A-3B.

Fishhook, shaft diameter 4 mm (fig. 225) (F3.fv). Trench F, 39.30 N, 5.10 E, level 6.30. Associated pottery: Period 2.

Fishhook, shaft square 3 x 4.5 mm (fig. 226) (F3.gu). Trench F, sieve.

Fishhook, shaft diameter 4 mm (fig. 227) (F3.jh). Trenches E-F, sieve.

Fishhook, 3 mm thick rod (fig. 228) (F3.ty). Found while cleaning up after the 1960 excavation in 1961.

Fragment of fishhook, shank diameter 3.5 mm (fig. 229) (F3.vå). Trench AA, sieve.

Fishhook, shank diameter 3 mm (fig. 230) (F3.øm). Trench AE, sieve.

Fishhook, round shaft 3.5 cm diameter (fig. 231) (F3. ada). Trench C, level c. 7.65-7.35. Associated pottery: Period 3A/4A?

Fishhook, point missing, shaft diameter 3.5 mm, the upper part of the shaft is hammered flat, 1.5 x 4 mm (fig. 232) (F3.ajo). Trenches C-D, G-H, or K-L.

Fishhook, square section, 2 x 2 mm (fig. 233) (F6.71). Trench SS 28, 1.90 E, level -0.47.

Fishhook, shank diameter 2.5 mm (fig. 234) (F6.185.A). Trench A3, level -1.20.

Fishhook (fig. 235) (F6.185.B). Trench A3, level -1.20.

Possible fishhook, shank diameter 6.5 mm (figs. 236 and 378: 494) (F6.803). Trench M2, sieve from above level -1.07.

Fishhook, 4 mm round cross section (fig. 237) (F6.855). Trench M2, sieve.

Fishhook with the beginning of an eye for fastening the line (fig. 238) (F6.913). Trench D1, 8-10 N, 1-3 W, level -2.00. Associated pottery: Period 1.

Fishhook (fig. 239) (no number).

Shank of fishhook, 3 mm diameter, with flat attachment area, 1 x 5 mm (fig. 240) (881.SY). Trench RM, sieve.

Shank from fishhook, diameter 2 mm, with bent over, flat, 5 mm wide attachment area (fig. 241) (F3.is). Trenches A, B, E, or F.

Three fragments of fishhooks, two flat-hammered attachment areas, one bent shank (fig. 242) (F3.xk). Baulk between Trenches Æ and X, level 9.60-8.15. Associated pottery: Period 3B/4B.

Shank of fishhook with 3 mm diameter and 1 x 9 mm, flat attachment area (fig. 243) (F3.aqj.2). Trench O, level c. 7.20-6.60. Associated pottery: Period 3A/4A.

Fishhook shank with square, 3 x 5 mm, cross section and flat, 2 x 7 mm, attachment area (fig. 244) (F3.avw). Trench AI.

Nails and rivets

The nails exhibit significant variation in size and shape in contrast to the remarkable uniformity seen among the nails excavated in the Barbar Temple (Andersen & Højlund 2003, vol. 1, figs. 666-743 passim), perhaps an example of decentralized, multicentred production versus centralized production. The point is missing from many of the nails described below.

Nail, diameter of head 1.1 cm, diameter of shank 5 mm (fig. 245) (F3.*57). Trench RM, 9 N, 1.55 W, 1.70 m below surface.

Nail (fig. 246) (F3.22), round cross section. Trench RM, 19 N, 0.60 W, 0.45 m below surface.

Nail (fig. 247) (F3.253). Trench RM, 4.10 N, 0.50 W, 1.10 m below surface.

Nail (fig. 248) (F3.nk), square section, 5 x 5 mm. Trench B, above level 6.60. Associated pottery: Period 2, 3A/3B.

Nail, square section, 8 x 8 mm (fig. 249) (F3.rn). Trench Y, 64.70 N, 0.10 E, level 7.06 on stone floor. Associated pottery: Period 4B.

Nail (fig. 250) (F3.rå). Trench Æ, sieve.

Nail, square section, 6 x 6 mm (fig. 251) (F3.te). Trenches Æ and Ø, sieve.

Nail (fig. 252) (F3.xk.A). From baulk between Trenches Æ and X, level 9.60-8.15. Associated pottery: Period 3B/4B.

Nail (figs. 253 and 378: sample 402) (F3.xk.B). From baulk between Trenches Æ and X, level 9.60-8.15. Associated pottery: Period 3B/4B.

Nail (figs. 254 and 378: sample 401) (F3.xk). From baulk between Trenches Æ and X, level 9.60-8.15. Associated pottery: Period 3B/4B.

Nail (figs. 255 and 378: sample 398) (F3.xw). Trench AG, level 9.35-8.03. Associated pottery: Period 3B?

Rivet (fig. 256) (F3.zc). Trench AI, level 8.16-7.85. Associated pottery: Period 4A.

Rivet, shaft diameter 4 mm (fig. 257) (F3.ajo). Trenches C-D, G-H, K-L.

Nail (fig. 258) (F3.avw.A). Trench AI.

Nail, square cross section, 4 x 5 mm (fig. 259) (F3.avw.B). Trench AI.

Nail (fig. 260) (F6.251). Trench C1, level -0.07.

Nail, just below the head square cross section, 5.5 x 5.5 mm, above the point square cross section, 3.5 x 3.5 mm (fig. 261) (F6.505). Trench E2, 15-18 N, 1.5-3 E, level -1.21.

Nail (figs. 262 and 378: sample 400) (F6.655.1). Trench F2, 17-18 N, 5-6 W, level -0.57.

Nail (fig. 263) (F6.655.2). Trench F2, 17-18 N, 5-6 W, level -0.57.

Nail, square head 12.5 x 13.5 mm, square shank 8.5 x 9 mm (fig. 264) (F6.830). Trench M2, 14 N, 9.5 W, level -1.58. Associated pottery: Period 1.

Nail with circular head, 3 cm in diameter (fig. 265) (F6.985.A). Trench F1, level -0.71, sieve.

Nail, 2.7 cm long, with square 6.5 x 7.5 mm cross section and square head, 8 x 10 mm (F6.985.B). Trench F1, level -0.71, sieve.

Nail, 2.8 cm long with square, 7 x 7 mm cross section and square, 9 x 9 mm head (F6.985.C). Trench F1, level -0.71, sieve.

Staples

Bands of sheet metal with a built-in nail in each end. Some of them have been found loose, and some have been noted in situ along the edges of copper plates with the nails hammered through the plates and into some, now disappeared, (wooden?) substructure.

Staple, 6.6 cm long, 1 cm wide and 0.3 cm thick band, both ends terminated with nails (fig. 266) (F3.131). Trench RM, 35.65 N, 3.1 W, level 7.75.

Staple, 4.3 cm long, 0.8 cm wide band, 0.25 cm thick, ending in nail-like parts, 0.2–0.35 cm in cross section, one nail 1.4 cm long, the other broken (fig. 267) (F3.øy). Trench AL, level 5.81. Associated pottery: Period 2.

Staple, 8.8 cm long, 1 cm wide, 2 mm thick, one end ending with a nail, 3.5 mm in diameter, the other end broken (fig. 268) (F3.aac). Trench C, level c. 9.15-8.85. Associated pottery: Period 4A.

Staple, 5.9 cm long, 1.4 cm wide band, 0.2 cm thick, ending in nail-like parts (fig. 269) (F3.aad). Trench C, level c. 9.15-8.85. Associated pottery: Period 4A.

Staple, 5.5 cm long, 1.9 cm wide, 0.2 cm thick, broken in both ends (fig. 270) (F3.avw). Trench AI.

Fragment of staple, preserved length 3.2 cm, 1.3 cm wide and 0.2 cm thick, ending in a round nail-like part with a diameter of 0.5 cm (F6.264). Trench SN 11-13 N, 0-1 E, level -0.69.

Fragment of sheet, 5.6 x 7.8 cm, 0.2 cm thick, with a staple in situ, 5 cm long and 1.9 cm wide, parallel to what may have been the original edge of the piece. On the other side, the two nails stick out obliquely 1.4 cm (fig. 271) (F6.819). Trench M2, sieve.

Circular, rather even plate, 40 x 47 cm, 0.2 cm thick. Along the rim, about 0.9 cm from the edge, a row of staples, 4-5 cm long and 0.6-0.8 cm wide with an internal distance of 1 cm (fig. 272) (F6.831). Trench M2, 11

N, 11-12 W, level -1.21, in baulk. The plate was likely attached by the staples to a wooden structure, perhaps as a symbol of the sun. Sun symbols are prolific on stamp seals (Kjærum 1983) and stone vessels in Failaka Figurative Style (Hilton 2014). Reference is made to a deep posthole in front of the temple in Tell F6 (Højlund & Abu-Laban 2016 fig. 16).

Staple, 6.7 cm long, 1.5 cm wide and 0.4 cm thick, possibly decorated, band ending in a narrow, 1.7 cm long nail-like part with a 0.4 x 0.4 cm cross section, the other end broken (fig. 273) (F6.1005.B). Trench F1, 1-2 N, 7-8 W, level -1.48.

Copper plate, 14 x 24 cm, with bent over, 3.6 cm wide, edge along one side and staples along the other three sides on the other face. Dimensions of staples: 1.3 x 5.2 cm, 1.4 x 4.4 cm and 1.8 x 5.1 cm (fig. 274) (F6.1143). Trench N1, 6-8 N, 13-15 W, level -0.90.

Rods with round section

Fragments of rods with round section were numerous in the excavation and only a small selection is described below.

Rod with rounded section (fig. 378: sample 404) (F3.49). Trench RM, 20.8 N, 3.45 W, 1.2 m below surface.

Rod with roundish section, length 9 cm, diameter 0.5 cm (fig. 378: sample 436) (F3.xk). Baulk between Trenches Æ and X, level 9.60-8.15. Associated pottery: Period 3B/4B.

Rod with round section, length 7.2 cm, diameter 0.5 cm (fig. 378: sample 460) (F3.xk). Baulk between Trenches Æ and X, level 9.60-8.15. Associated pottery: Period 3B/4B.

Rod with round section, length 6.7 cm, diameter 0.4 cm (fig. 378: sample 464) (F3.zc). Trench AI, level 8.16-7.85. Associated pottery: Period 3B, 4.

Rod with round section (fig. 275) (F3.øm).

Rod with round section, length 4 cm, diameter 0.4 cm (fig. 378: sample 462) (F3.ajo). Trenches C-D, G-H, K-L.

Rod with round section, length 4.2 cm, diameter 0.5 cm (fig. 378: sample 442) (F3.ajp). Trenches C-D, G-H, or K-L.

Rod with round section, length 7.8 cm, diameter 0.8 cm (F3.avw). Trench AI.

Rod with round section, length 5.1 cm, diameter 0.5 cm (fig. 378: sample 465) (F6.855). Trench M2, sieve.

Rod with round section (fig. 378: sample 361) (F6.1194). Trench F1, level -1.94. Associated pottery: Period 1.

Rods with square section

Fragments of rods with square section were numerous in the excavation and only a small selection is described below.

Rod with square, c. 0.5 x 0.5 cm, section, length 3.4 cm (fig. 378: sample 319) (F3.72). Trench RM, level c. 8.20.

Rod with square, 0.7 x 0.7 cm, section, pointed, length 5.5 cm (fig. 378: sample 405) (881.RS). Trench RM, 45-50 N, level c. 6.85-6.35.

Rod with square, 0.6 x 0.6 cm, section, length 4.8 cm (fig. 378: sample 322) (F3.bo). Trench B, sieve.

Rod with square, 0.6 x 0.6 cm, section, length 3 cm (fig. 378: sample 332) (F3.rt). Trench Æ, sieve.

Rod with square, 0.3 x 0.3 cm, section, length 3.8 cm (fig. 378: sample 479) (F3.xk). Baulk between Trenches Æ and X, level 9.60-8.15. Associated pottery: Period 3B/4B.

Rod with square, 0.4 x 0.4 cm, section, length 2.7 cm (fig. 378: sample 386) (F3.xk). Baulk between Trenches Æ and X, level 9.60-8.15. Associated pottery: Period 3B/4B.

Rod with square, 0.4 x 0.4 cm, section, length 8.4 cm (fig. 378: sample 388) (F3.xk). Baulk between Trenches Æ and X, level 9.60-8.15. Associated pottery: Period 3B/4B.

Rod with square, 0.4 x 0.4 cm, section, length 5.5 cm (fig. 378: sample 461) (F3.xk). Baulk between Trenches Æ and X, level 9.60-8.15. Associated pottery: Period 3B/4B.

Rod with square, 0.5 x 0.5 cm, section, c. 4 cm long (fig. 378: sample 385) (F3.ajo). Trenches C-D, G-H, K-L.

Rod with square, 0.5 x 0.5 cm, section, c. 6.5 cm long (fig. 378: sample 387) (F3.ajo). Trenches C-D, G-H, K-L.

Rod with square, 0.5 x 0.5 cm, section, c. 4.8 cm long (fig. 378: sample 389) (F3.ajo). Trenches C-D, G-H, K-L.

Rod with square, 0.7 x 0.7 cm, section, c. 5 cm long (fig. 378: sample 391) (F3.ajo). Trenches C-D, G-H, K-L.

Rod with square, 0.6 x 0.6 cm, section, c. 3.5 cm long (fig. 378: sample 443) (F3.ajo). Trenches C-D, G-H, K-L.

Rod with square section, 1.2 x 1.3 cm, length 6 cm (fig. 378: sample 360) (F3.bab). F3, sieve.

Vessels

A good deal of the sheet metal found during the excavation and described below as scrap metal probably derives from vessels, but little can be said about their shapes as only a few are well preserved. Copper vessels are known from elsewhere in Dilmun (Lombard 1999 nos. 47-49. Andersen & Højlund 2003, vol. 1, figs. 657. Højlund 2007 p. 167: figs. 1-2. Højlund & Abu-Laban 2016 fig. 1066. Højlund & Andersen 1994 figs. 1863-1864). Some fragments show that the rims were reinforced by an extra double layer. Copper vessels were sometimes equipped with handles (see below), like the basket-shaped containers known from the U.A.E. (Velde 2003 fig. 7: 7-8). The shape probably derives from baskets made of braded palm leaf bands (Ferdinand 1993 figs. 9:67-68) and is also known in pottery (Højlund & Andersen 1994 p. 91, figs. 187, 864-865).

Vessel rim, strengthened with piece of sheet bent over rim (F3.35). Trench RM, 5.35 N, 1.75 W, 1.05 m below surface.

Vessel rim with rivet hole, sheet thickness 2.5 mm (fig. 276) (F3.lw). Trench V, level 8.35-7.65. Associated pottery: Period 3A-3B.

Vessel rim (figs. 277 and 378: sample 418) (F3.qn). Trench Z, level 8.35-7.36. Associated pottery: Period 3B, 4.

Vessel rim (fig. 278) (F3.qo). Trench Z, level 7.19.

Vessel rim, strengthened with piece of sheet bent over the rim (F3.vw). Trench Ø, sieve.

Fragment of curved sheet, 2 mm thick, both upper and lower edge appear to be original though slightly irregular, possibly from a bracelet, diameter c. 8 cm (fig. 279) (F3.wc). Trench AB, 64 N, 6 W, level 7.44, in rubble. Associated pottery: Period 4B.

Almost complete rim of vessel with a diameter of 21 cm, sheet thickness 0.2 cm. The rim is strengthened by a plate which is folded/bent over both sides, c. 6 cm wide, and fastened by about seven rivets. May have fitted with the next item (fig. 280) (F3.ahø). Trench H, 39.5 N, 11.15 W, level 7.42. Associated pottery: Period 4A.

Bottom part of vessel with maximum diameter 24.5 cm. May have fitted with the preceding item (fig. 281) (F3.ajj). Trench H, 41.55 N, 10.85 W, level 7.01. Associated pottery: Period 4A.

Possibly rim of vessel carrying a cuneiform inscription, the rim is straight, however, not curved (figs. 282 and 422) (F3.avw) (Glassner 1984 no. 46. Marchesi below p. 100). Trench AI, sieve. Associated pottery: Periods 3A or 4A.

Rim of vessel (fig. 283) (F6.203). Trench B2, level +0.15.

Bottom part of round-bellied vessel, 20 cm diameter, with small foot, diameter 6.5 cm, sheet thickness 0.1 cm (fig. 284, Ashkanani 2021 p. 112-113) (F6.483). Trench D2, 14.75 N, 3.3 W, level -1.85. Associated pottery: Period 1.

Vessel rim, rim thickness 0.3 cm, lower down 0.1 cm (fig. 285) (F6.544). Trenches D3-E2.

Handles

One handle derives from Tell F3, while the other five derive from Tell F6. These handles probably belong to basket-shaped copper vessels (cf. Højlund & Hilton 2021 figs. 485 and 497. Andersen & Højlund 2003, vol. 1, fig. 741). They are also found in the Wadi Suq period in the U.A.E. and Oman (Yule & Weisgerber 2015 fig. 9).

Possible handle with split attachment with rivet holes, corroded together (fig. 286) (F3.yt). Trench AI, level 8.69-8.30. Associated pottery: Period 4A.

Handle (fig. 287) (F6.542). Trench D1, 7 N, 3 W, level -1.20.

Handle with double attachments and triangular decoration (fig. 288) (F6.615). Trench SN11-20, 13.5 N, 0.50 E, level -1.61. Associated pottery: Period 1.

Fragment of handle with rivet in situ (fig. 289) (F6.830). Trench M2, 14 N, 9.5 W, level -1.58. Associated pottery: Period 1.

Handle (fig. 290) (F6.1005.C). Trench F1, -1.48.

Fragment of handle with hole for rivet (fig. 291) (F6.1038). Trench N2, 12-14 N, 13-15 W, level -1.46.

Fittings

Cylinder in 0.25 cm thick copper sheet, along upper edge nine punched holes, punched inside out, one 0.45 cm in diameter, the rest between 0.7-0.9 cm, of which four with nails with head diameter of 1-1.2 cm. The lower edge ended in three points and three curves (fig. 292) (F3.apf). Trench C, 36 N, 8.25 W, level 8.07.

Pivot fitting (fig. 293) (F3.bbe). Trench AO, 61.55 N, 4 W, level 6.52. Associated pottery: Period 2, 3B/4A?

Pivot sheath with bottom edge worn sharp; sheet 0.2-0.5 cm thick, two holes, one with nail in situ (fig. 294, Ashkanani 2021 p. 96) (F6.584). Trench D2 east baulk, 15.5 N, 0-1 W, level -1.11.

Scrap metal

Sheet (fig. 295) (F3.*15). Trench AK.

Sheet metal (figs. 296 and 378: sample 303) (881.SD). Trench RM, 42-52 N, level 6.79-6.35.

Sheet with rivet hole (figs. 297 and 378: sample 417) (F3.xk). Baulk between Trenches Æ and X, level 9.60-8.15. Associated pottery: Period 3B/4B.

Scrap sheet, 2 mm thick, rolled into a cylinder, a hole at one end, broken at the other (fig. 298) (F3.tp). Trench Ø, level 8.46-7.74. Associated pottery: Period 3B/4.

Two pieces of sheet bent together, one with nail holes, sheet 0.2 cm thick (fig. 299) (F3.yt). Trench AI, level 8.69-8.30. Associated pottery: Period 4A.

Square fragment of sheet, 0.3 cm thick, with rivet in situ (fig. 300) (F3.æg). Trench AB-AF, sieve.

Fragment of sheet bent as if to form a socket (fig. 301) (F3.øm). Trench AE, sieve.

Sheet metal, length 10.4 cm, rolled around rod with square cross section, 0.7 x 0.8 cm (fig. 302) (F3.ajx). Trench H, 42.9 N, 10.57 W, level 7.06. Associated pottery: Period 4A.

Two pieces of sheet held together by rivet (fig. 303) (F3.aqæ). Trench K.

Scrap sheet folded (fig. 304) (F3.avw). Trench AI.

Scrap sheet, curved, with two nail holes (fig. 305) (F3.awa). Trench Y, level 7.05. Associated pottery: Period 4B.

Scrap sheet, 14.5 x 23 cm, 0.3 cm thick (fig. 306) (F6.212). Trench SN1-10 N, 0-1.5 E, level -0.75.

Scrap sheet, thickness 0.25 cm (fig. 307) (F6.314). Trench SN, 2-3 N, 0-1.5 E, level -1.44,

Scrap sheet (fig. 308) (F6.527). Trench E2, 17-18 N, 2-3 E, -1.85. Associated pottery: Period 1.

Scrap metal (fig. 309) (F6.648.1). Trench F2, 19-20 N, 6-8 W, level -0.25.

Two pieces of sheet, held together by 1.2 cm long rivet (fig. 310) (F6.648.2). Trench F2, 19-20 N, 6-8 W, level -0.25.

Band of sheet, 0.2 cm thick (fig. 311) (F6.759). Trench F2, 12 N, 6 W, level -1.98. Associated pottery: Period 1.

Piece of copper sheet with rivet in situ (fig. 312) (F6.880). Trench M2, sieve above level -2.04.

Scrap metal folded together (fig. 313) (F6.930). Trench D1, 7.2 N, 2.8 W, level -1.32.

Pins

Circular head

Pin with circular, bent around head (fig. 314) (F3.*45), shank round cross section, 2.5 mm in diameter, head rectangular cross section. Trench BB, level 5.31.

Head of pin, shaft diameter c. 0.3 cm (fig. 315) (F3.pb). Sieve.

Pin with circular, bent around head, point broken off, shank diameter 3.5 mm, cross section of head part 0.2 x 0.3 cm (fig. 316) (F3.tæ). Trench Ø, level 7.74-7.20.

Head of pin with circular, bent around head, shaft diameter 0.35 cm (fig. 317) (F3.vw). Trench Ø, sieve.

Head of pin with circular, bent around head, shaft diameter 0.3 cm (fig. 318) (F3.avw). Trench AI, sieve.

Moulded head

Pin with moulded head, shaft diameter 0.55 cm (fig. 319) (881.SR). Trench RM, sieve (cf. Højlund & Hilton 2021 fig. 472).

Moulded pin head, maximum diameter 0.95 cm (fig. 320) (F3.qæ). Trench Z, sieve.

Pin with moulded head, shank diameter 0.5 cm, head diameter 0.7 cm (fig. 321) (F3.xk). Baulk between Trenches Æ and X, level 9.60-8.15.

Pin with moulded head (fig. 322) (F6.655). Trench F2, 17-18 N, 5-6 W, level -0.57.

Conical head

Pin with conical head and ridged upper part (fig. 323) (F3.gu). Trench F, sieve.

Rings

Open rings

Open ring, rod diameter 3 mm (fig. 324) (F3.ej). Trench F, sieve.

Open ring, rod diameter 2.5 mm (fig. 325) (F3.le). Trench B, 43 N, 0.50 E, level 6.79, in rubble. Associated pottery: Period 2.

Open ring, rod diameter 3.5 mm (fig. 326) (F3.yu). Trench AB, sieve.

Open ring with overlapping ends, rod diameter 3 mm (fig. 327) (F3.zc). Trench AI, level 8.16-7.85. Associated pottery: Period 4A.

Open ring with the end wrapped around (fig. 328) (F3.ån). Trench AF, sieve.

Ring, open, pointed on both ends, diameter of rod 3 mm (fig. 329) (F3.akz). Trench H, level c. 7.65-7.15. Associated pottery: Period 4A.

Ring, open with overlapping, pointed ends, 4 x 6 mm (fig. 330) (F3.amg). Trenches K, G and C, sieve.

Ring, open, corroded (fig. 331) (F3.azi). Trench AO, c. 60 N, c. 3 W, level 6.82. Associated pottery: Period 4A/4B?

Ring, open (F3.bek). Trenches I, AN, and AO, sieve.

Ring or folded band (fig. 332) (F6.486). Trench D1, level -0.30.

Ring (fig. 333) (F6.628). Trench D2, 13-16 N, 1-3 W, level -2.10. Associated pottery: Period 1.

Ring, open, round cross section 4-5 mm in diameter (fig. 334) (F6.826). Trench M2, level -1.92. Associated pottery: Period 1.

Ring, covered in corrosion, cross section of rod 3.5-5 mm in diameter (fig. 335) (F6.1164). Sieve.

Closed ring

Ring with notches on opposed sides (fig. 336) (F6.482). Trench D2, level -1.60. Associated pottery: Period 1.

Cymbals

Two, possibly three, circular plates with a bulge and a hole in the middle. They resemble a musical instrument, occurring in pairs (*tus*), common in recent Arabian Gulf folk music (Rovsing Olsen 2002 p. 35, fig. 20).

Circular plate, 2 mm thick, diameter 6.1 cm, with 2.5 cm diameter bulge and 3.5 mm diameter hole in the centre (fig. 337) (F3.lr). Trench B, 39.80 N, 3.20 E, level 6.60. Associated pottery: Period 2.

Circular plate with a bulge in the middle but no hole noted (fig. 338) (F3.qo). Trench Z, level 7.19.

Circular plate with a bulge and a hole in the centre (fig. 339) (F3.afo). Trench G, level c. 7.93-8.43. Associated pottery: Period 4A.

Boxes

Fragment of box (figs. 340 and 378: sample 307) (F6.264). Trench SN11-13 N, 0-1.5 E, level -0.69 (cf. Højlund & Abu-Laban 2016 fig. 1067).

Box, remains of a hard, black, fine-grained, bituminous material inside, visible in the section and in the photo (fig. 341) (F6.314). Trench SN2-3 N, 0-1.5 E, -1.44.

Other objects

Stopper? (fig. 342) (F3.30). Trench RM, 20 N, 1.8 W, 20-60 cm below surface.

Miniature axe with blunt edge (fig. 343) (F3.lm). Trench Q, 58.40 N, 0.50 E, level 7.23.

Miniature axe (fig. 344) (F6.no number). Found 1960 in the spoils from Tell F6.

Unidentified object (fig. 345, Ashkanani 2021 p. 98) (F3. sg). Trench Ø, 55.80 N, 15.10 E, level 8.69. Associated pottery: Period 4.

Chisel with broad, sharp edge and bent grip, 2.5 mm thick (fig. 346) (F3.wd). Trench AD, 24 N, 16 W, level 8.25. Associated pottery: Period 4A.

Rod with hole in centre (fig. 347) (F3.wi). Trench AE, level 8.05. Associated pottery: Period 3A.

Rod, round, diameter 8 mm, cleaved in one end (fig. 348) (F3.xk). Baulk between Trenches Æ and X, level 9.60-8.15. Associated pottery: Period 3B/4B.

Triangular piece with two nail holes (fig. 349) (F3.zo). Trench AI, below level 7.85.

Bent band, 7.8 cm length, 1.2 cm wide, 0.2 cm thick (F3.aia). Trench G.

Unknown object, covered in corrosion, damaged at one end (fig. 350) (F3.azp). Trench AO, level 6.87-6.63. Associated pottery: Period 4A/4B?

Triangular copper plate, 7 mm thick in the narrow end and 2.5 mm thick in the broad end (fig. 351) (F3. no number).

Circular piece of copper, both faces even, thickness 5 mm in the centre and 3-4 mm near the edge (fig. 352) (F6.323). Trench C1, 1.80 S, 2.20 E, level -1.30.

Conical cylinder closed in one end, folded and smithed together (fig. 353) (F6.840). Trench M2, 17 N, 10 W, level -1.69. Associated pottery: Period 1.

Unidentified object with heads of two rivets preserved on its left side and holes for two others on its right side (fig. 354) (F6.848.F). Trench M2, 17-20 N, 9-11.50 W, level -1.70, north of the "Palace". Associated pottery: Period 1.

Cleaver with broken off handle (figs. 355 and 378: sample 317) (F6.1020.A). Trench F1, 1-3 N, 4-8 W, level -1.41.

Fig. 9. 1:2.

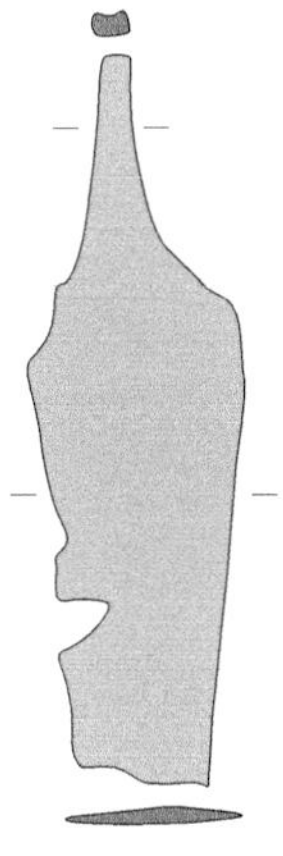

Fig. 10. 1:2.

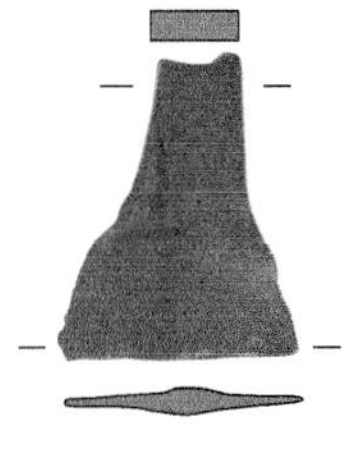

Fig. 11. 1:2.

Fig. 12. 1:2.

Fig. 17. 1:2.

Fig. 13. 1:2.

Fig. 14. 1:2.

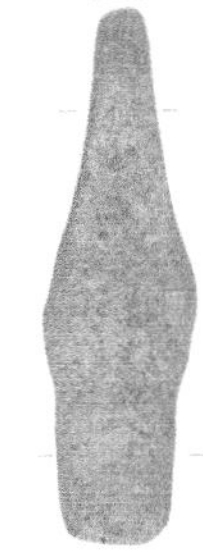

Fig. 15. 1:2.

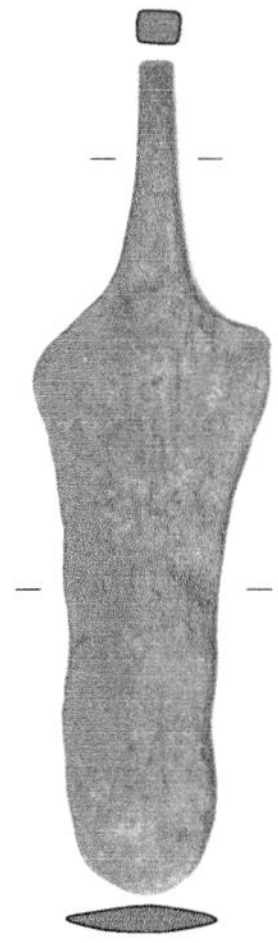

Fig. 16. 1:2.

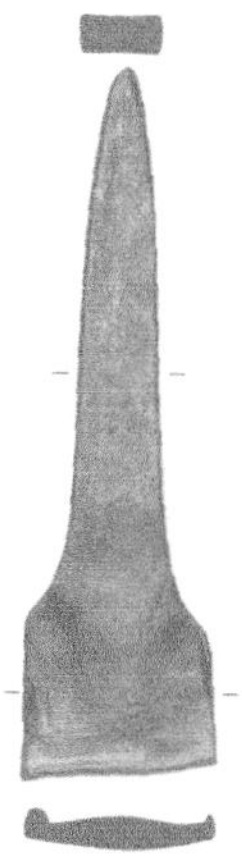

Fig. 18. 1:2.

Fig. 19. 1:2.

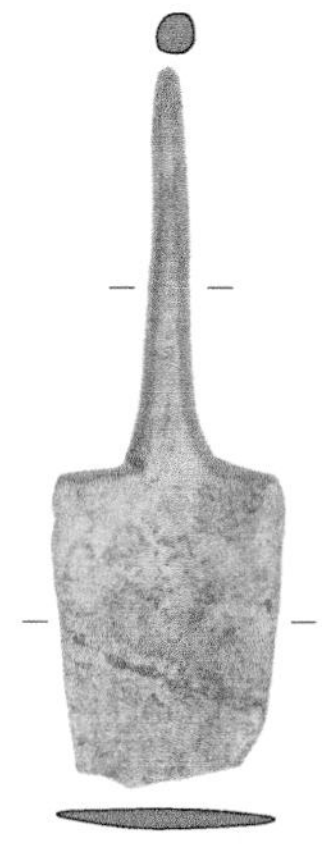

Fig. 20. 1:2.

Fig. 21. 1:2.

Fig. 22. 1:2.

Fig. 23. 1:2.

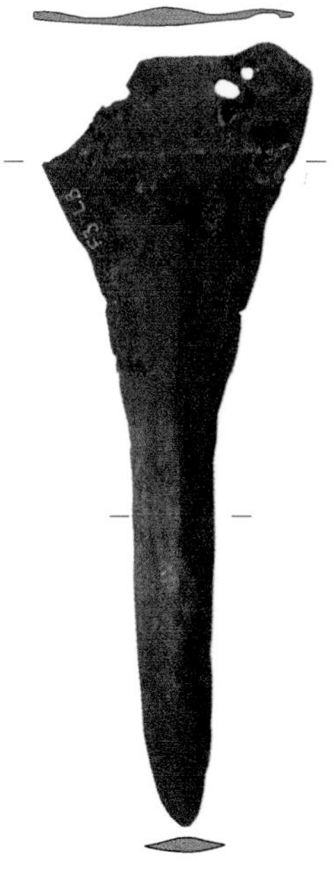

Fig. 24. 1:2.

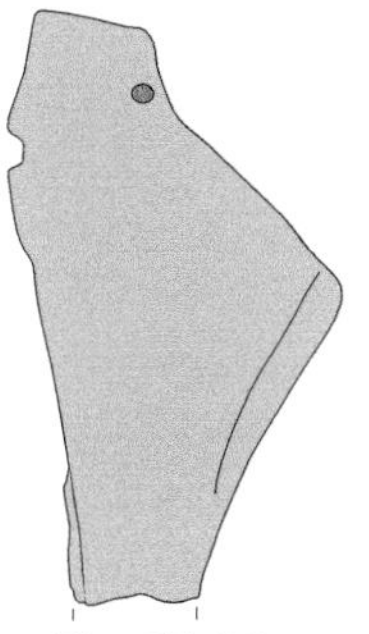

Fig. 25. 1:2.

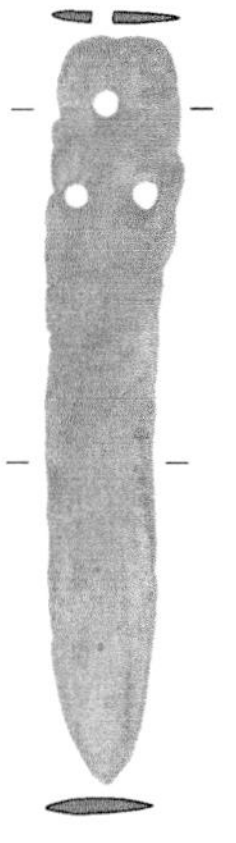

Fig. 26. 1:2.

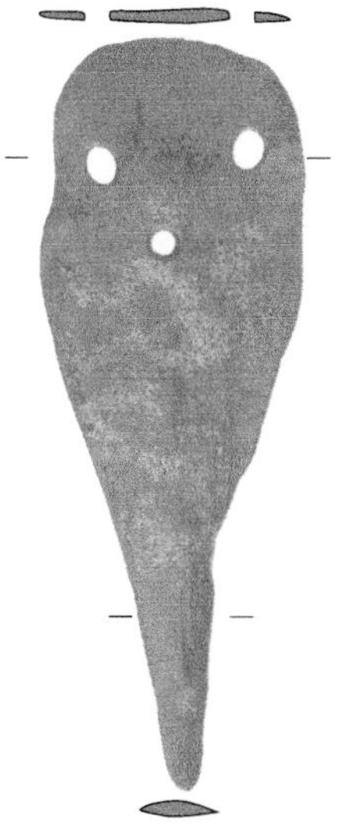

Fig. 27. 1:2.

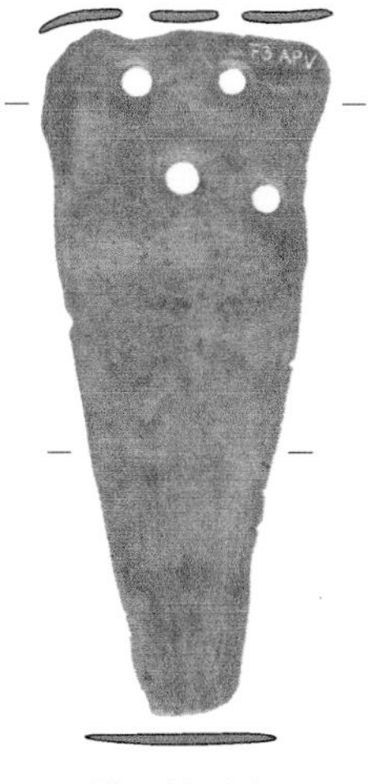

Fig. 28. 1:2.

Fig. 29. 1:2.

Fig. 30. 1:2.

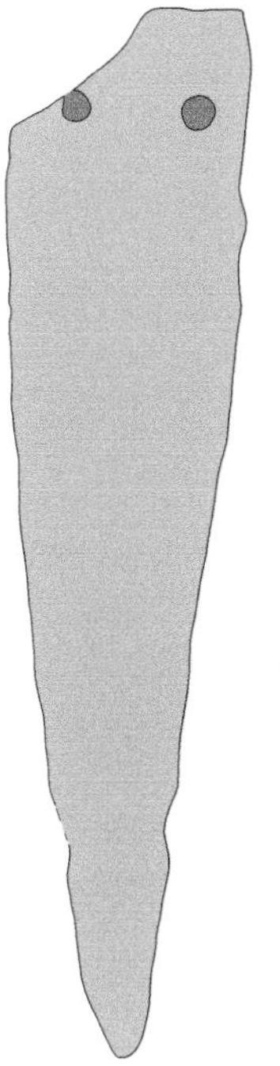

Fig. 31. 1:2.

Fig. 32. 1:2.

Fig. 33. 1:2.

Fig. 34. 1:2.

Fig. 35. 1:2.

Fig. 36. 1:2.

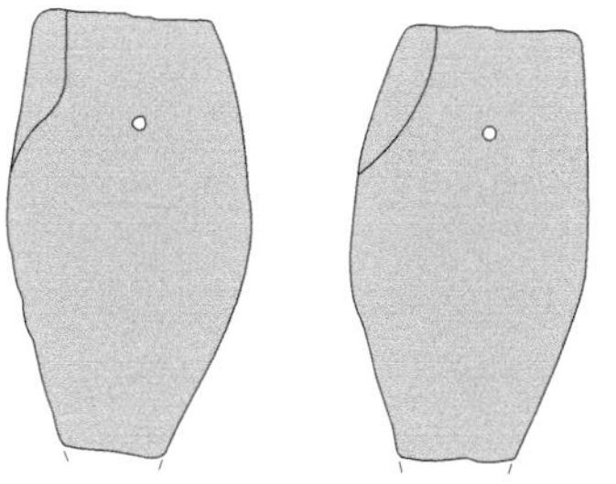

Fig. 37. 1:2.

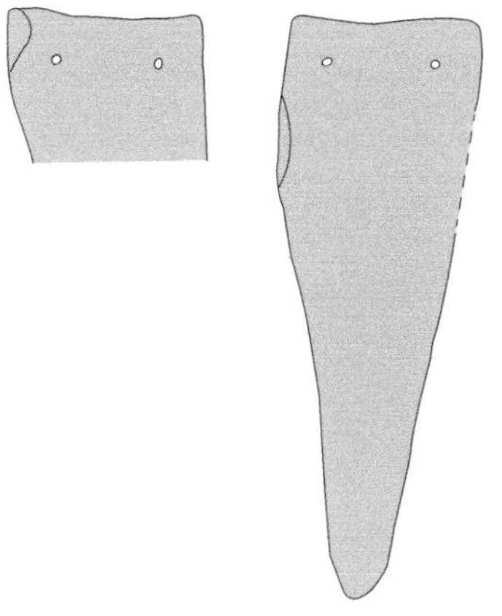

Fig. 38. 1:2.

Fig. 39. 1:2.

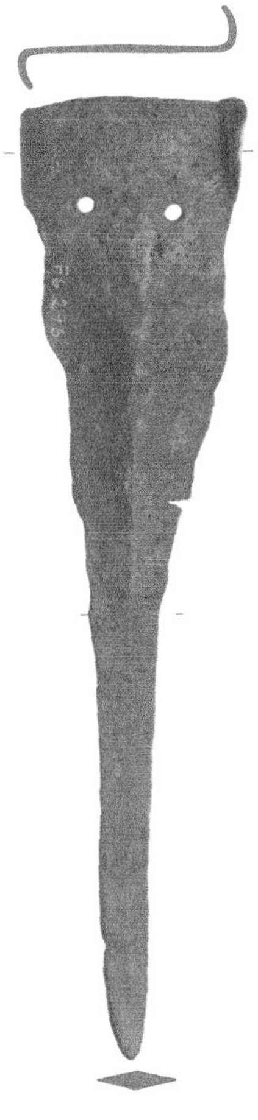

Fig. 40. 1:2.

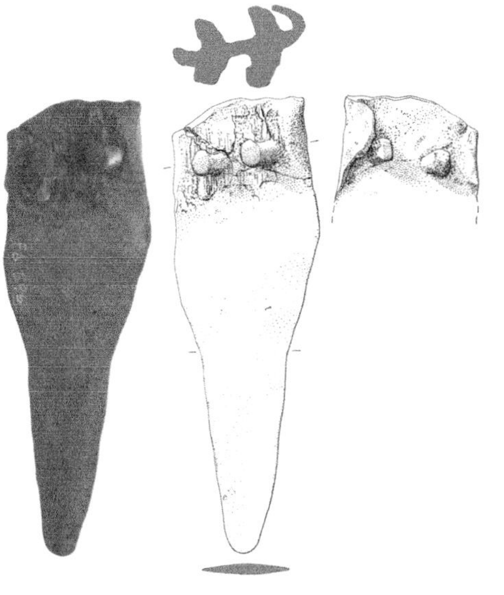

Fig. 41. 1:2.

Fig. 42. 1:2.

Fig. 43. 1:2.

Fig. 44. 1:2.

Fig. 45. 1:2.

Fig. 46. 1:2.

Fig. 47. 1:2.

Fig. 48. 1:2.

Fig. 49. 1:2.

Fig. 50. 1:2.

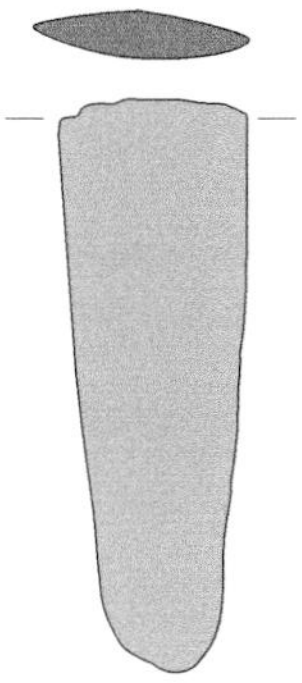
Fig. 51. 1:2.

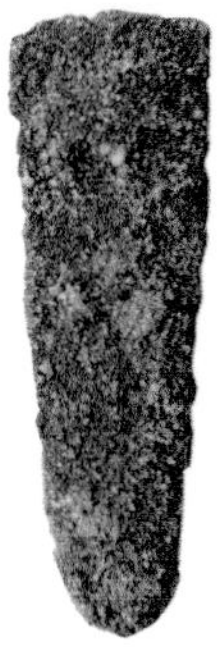
Fig. 52. 1:2.

Fig. 53. 1:2.

Fig. 54. 1:2.

Fig. 55. 1:2.

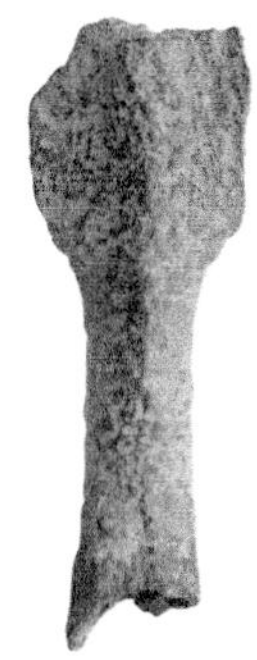
Fig. 56. 1:2.

Fig. 57. 1:2.

Fig. 58. 1:2.

Fig. 59. 1:2.

Fig. 60. 1:2.

Fig. 61. 1:2.

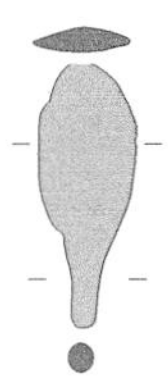
Fig. 62. 1:2.

Fig. 63. 1:2.

Fig. 64. 1:2.

Fig. 65. 1:2.

Fig. 66. 1:2.

Fig. 67. 1:2.

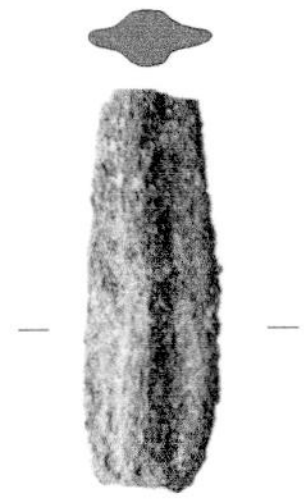
Fig. 68. 1:2.

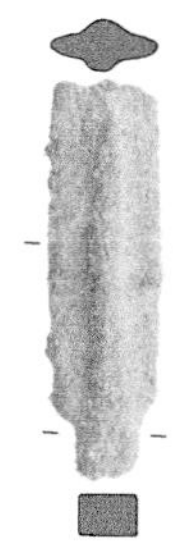
Fig. 69. 1:2.

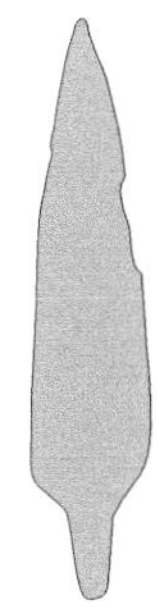
Fig. 70. 1:2.

Fig. 71. 1:2.

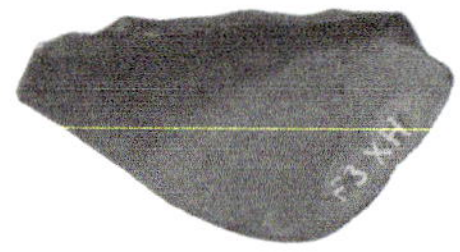

Fig. 72. 1:2.

Fig. 73. 1:2.

Fig. 74. 1:2.

Fig. 75. 1:2.

Fig. 76. 1:2.

Fig. 77. 1:2.

Fig. 78. 1:2.

Fig. 79. 1:2.

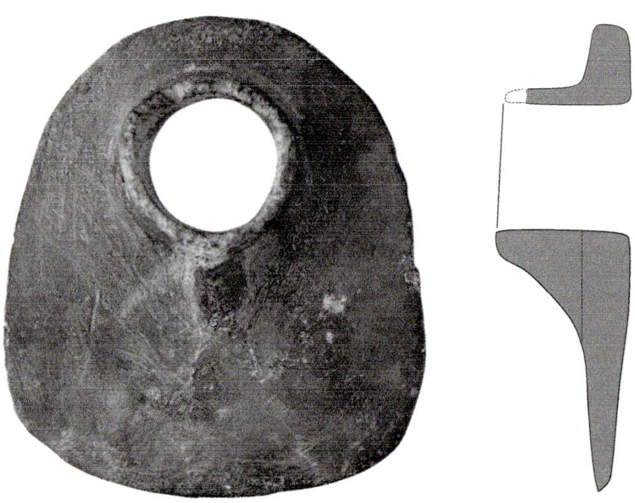

Fig. 80. 1:2.

Fig. 81. 1:2.

Fig. 82. 1:2.

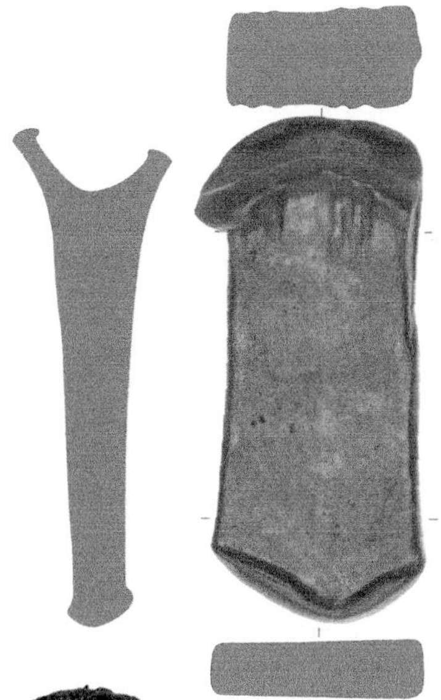

Fig. 83. 1:2.

Fig. 84. 1:2.

Fig. 85. 1:2.

Fig. 86. 1:2.

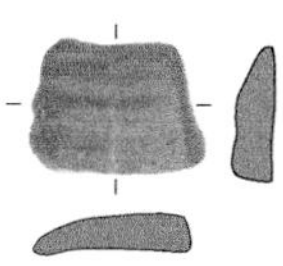

Fig. 87. 1:2.

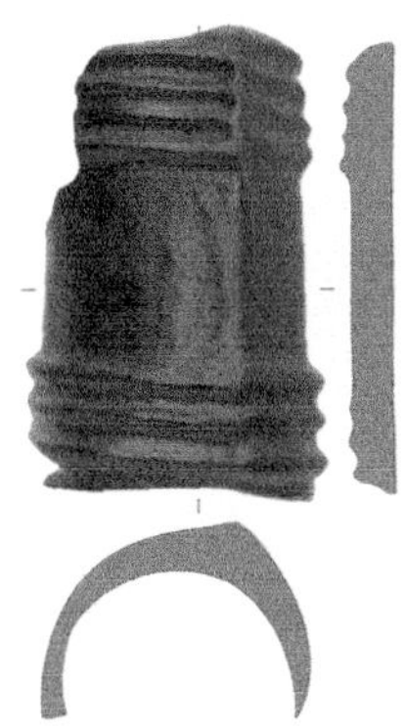

Fig. 88. 1:2.

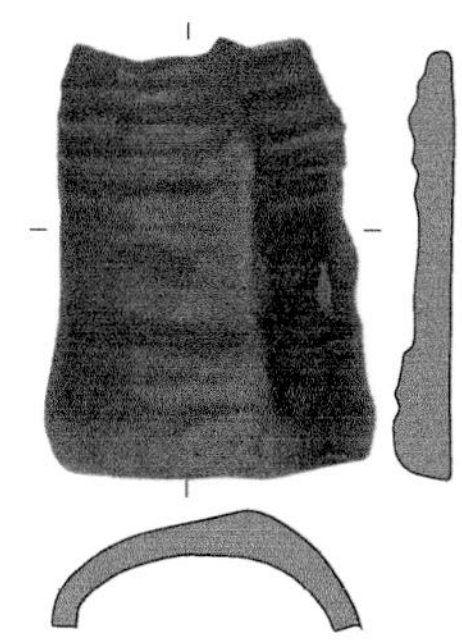

Fig. 89. 1:2.

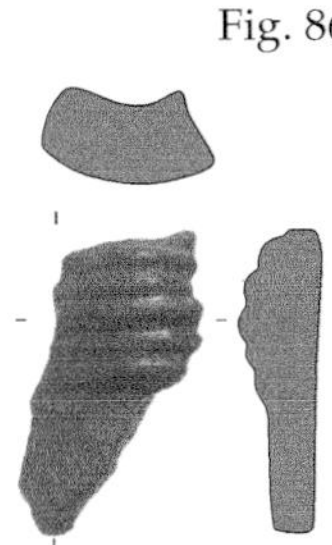

Fig. 90. 1:2.

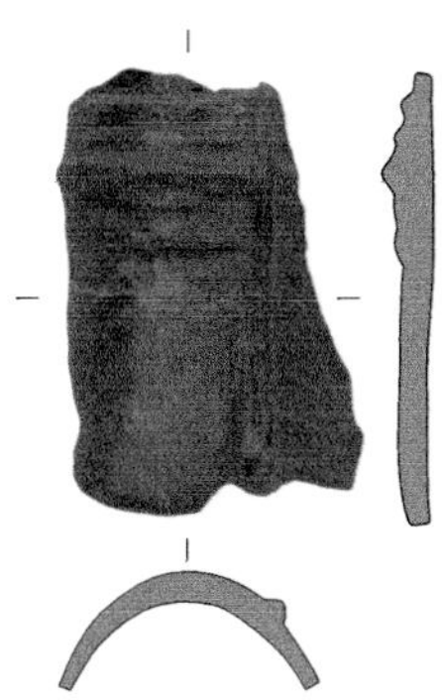

Fig. 91. 1:2.

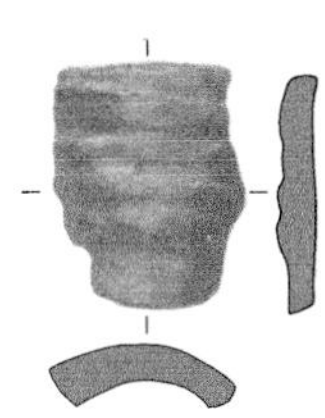

Fig. 92. 1:2.

Fig. 93. 1:3.

Fig. 94. 1:2.

Fig. 95. 1:2.

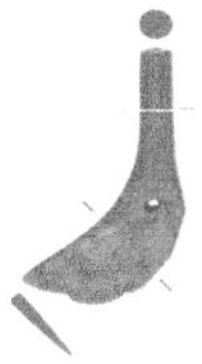

Fig. 96. 1:2.

Fig. 97. 1:2.

Fig. 98. 1:2.

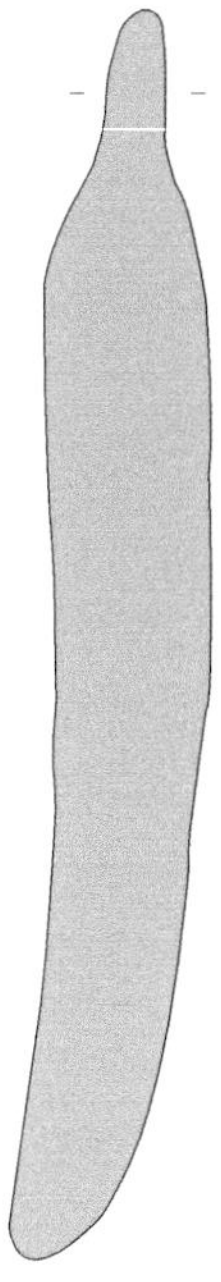

Fig. 99. 1:2.

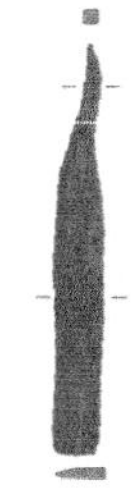

Fig. 100. 1:2.

Fig. 101. 1:2.

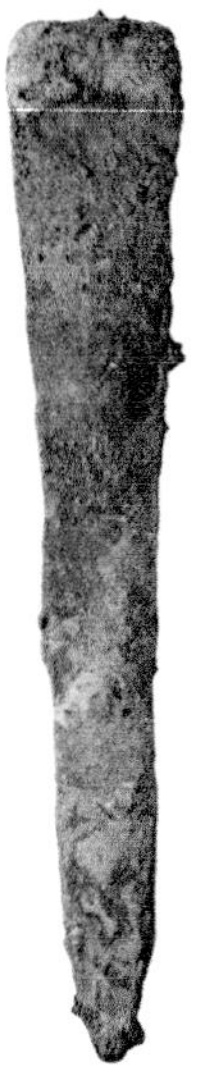

Fig. 102. 1:2.

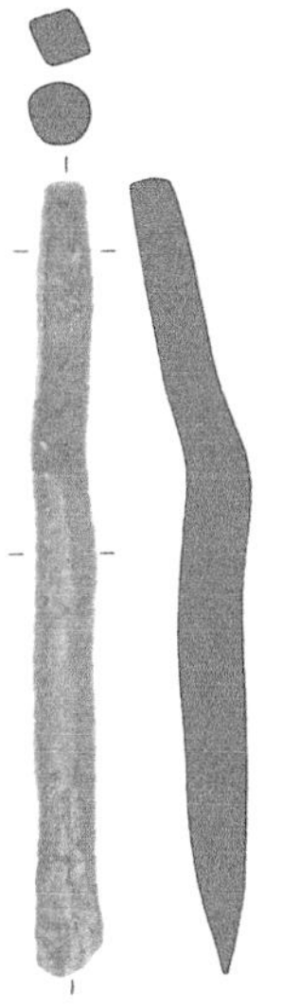

Fig. 107. 1:2.

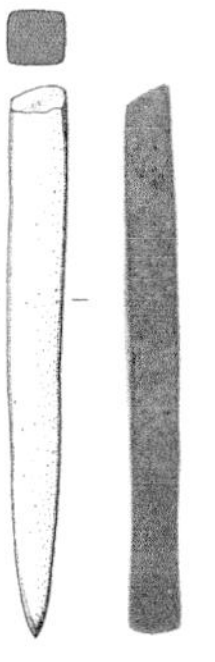

Fig. 108. 1:2.

Fig. 109. 1:2.

Fig. 103. 1:2.

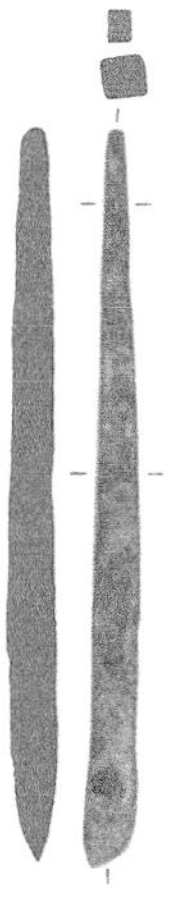

Fig. 104. 1:2.

Fig. 105. 1:2.

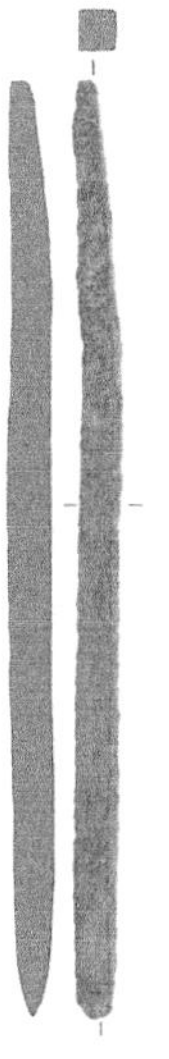

Fig. 106. 1:2.

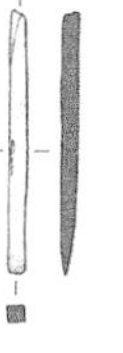

Fig. 110. 1:2.

Fig. 111. 1:2.

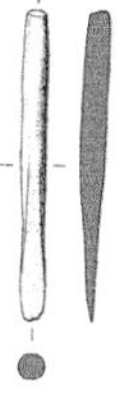

Fig. 112. 1:2.

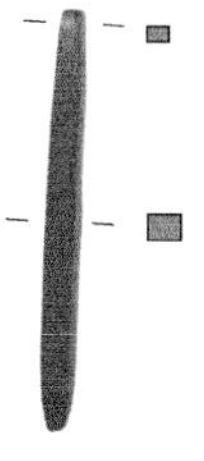

Fig. 113. 1:2.

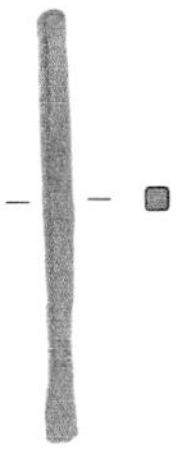

Fig. 114. 1:2.

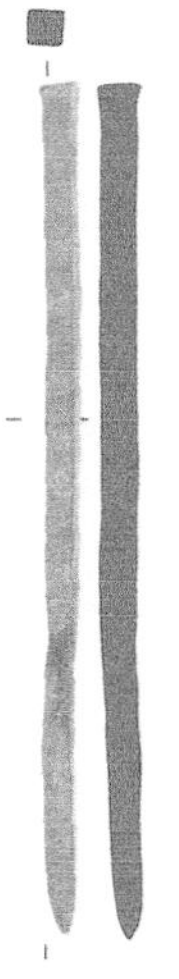

Fig. 115. 1:2.

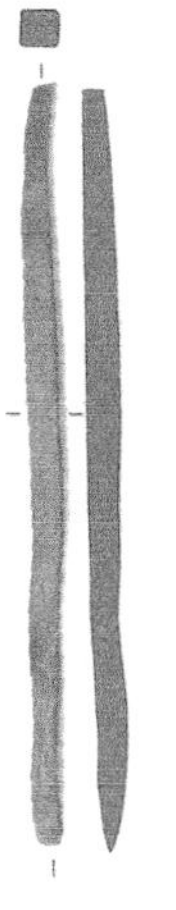

Fig. 116. 1:2.

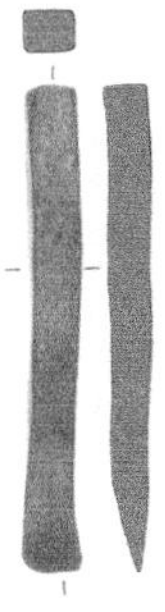

Fig. 117. 1:2.

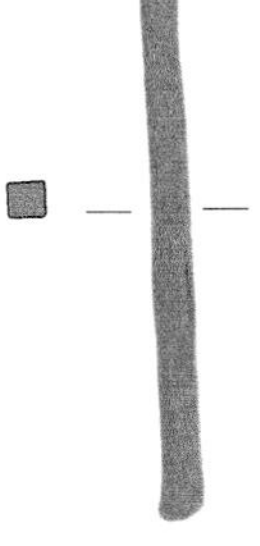

Fig. 118. 1:2.

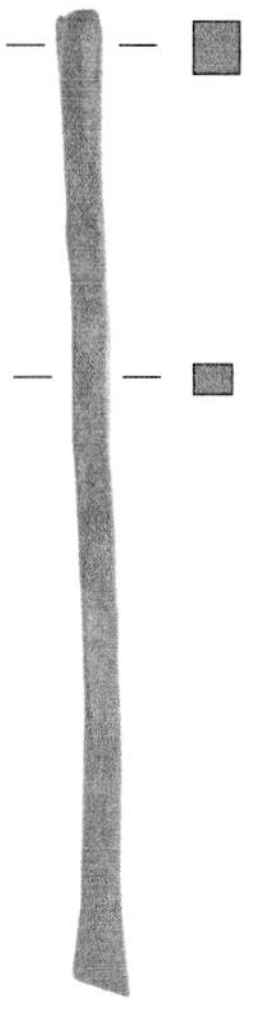

Fig. 119. 1:2.

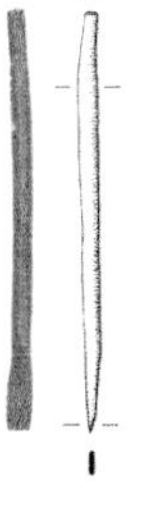

Fig. 120. 1:2.

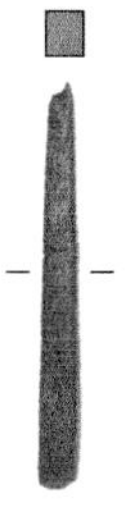

Fig. 121. 1:2.

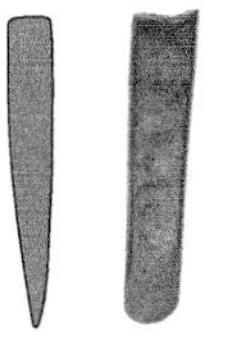

Fig. 122. 1:2.

Fig. 123. 1:2.

Fig. 124. 1:2.

Fig. 125. 1:2.

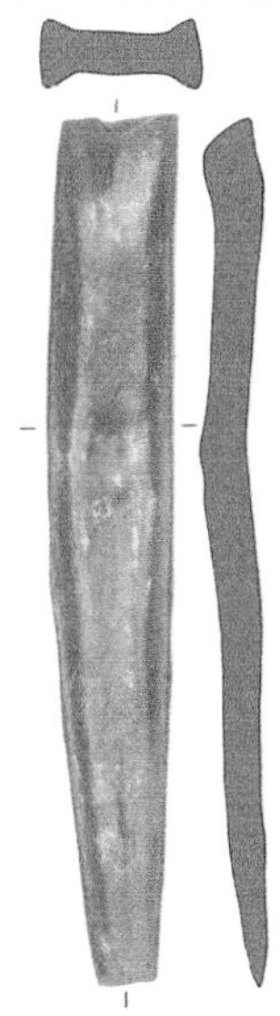
Fig. 126. 1:2.

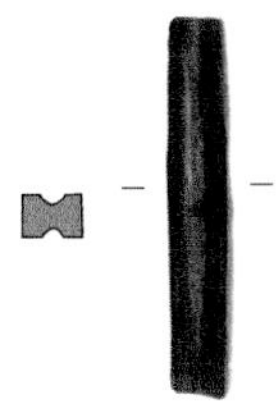
Fig. 127. 1:2.

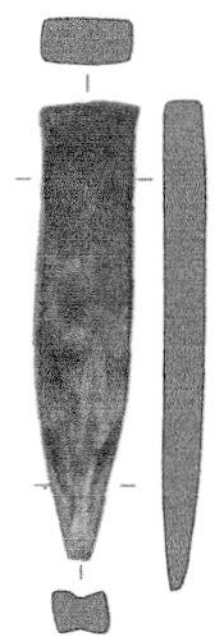
Fig. 128. 1:2.

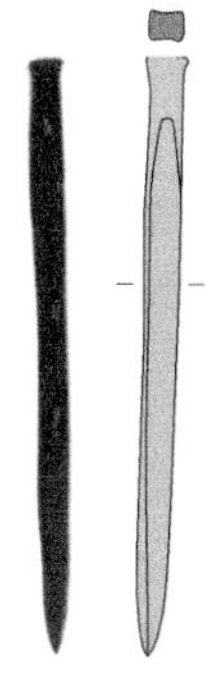
Fig. 129. 1:2.

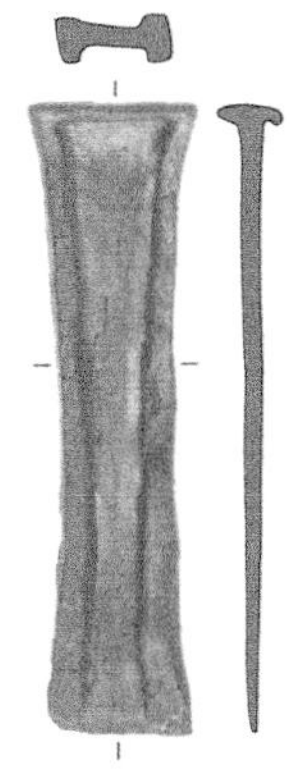
Fig. 130. 1:2.

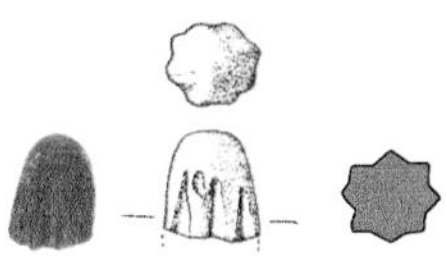
Fig. 131. 1:2.

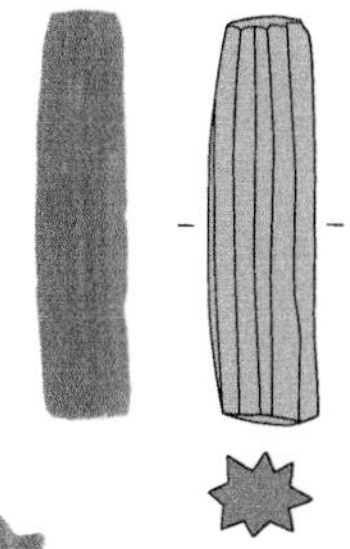
Fig. 132. 1:2.

Fig. 133. 1:2.

Fig. 134. 1:2.

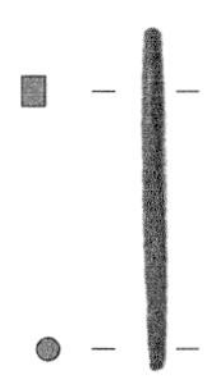
Fig. 135. 1:2.

Fig. 136. 1:2.

Fig. 137. 1:2.

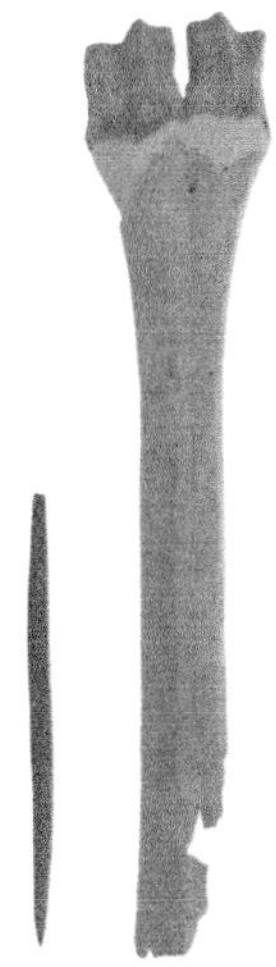
Fig. 138. 1:2.

Fig. 139. 1:2.

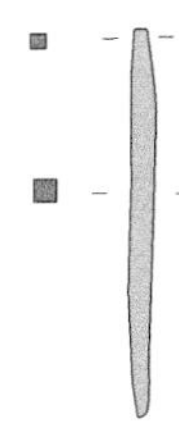
Fig. 140. 1:2.

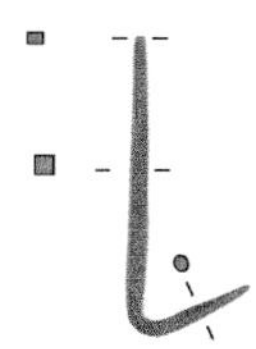
Fig. 141. 1:2.

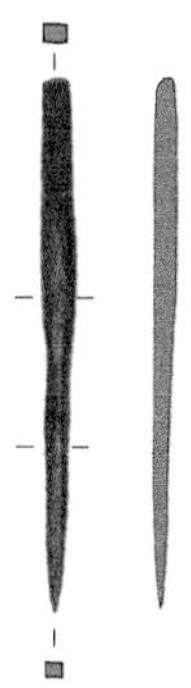
Fig. 142. 1:2.

Fig. 143. 1:2.

Fig. 144. 1:2.

Fig. 145. 1:2.

Fig. 146. 1:2.

Fig. 147. 1:2.

Fig. 148. 1:2.

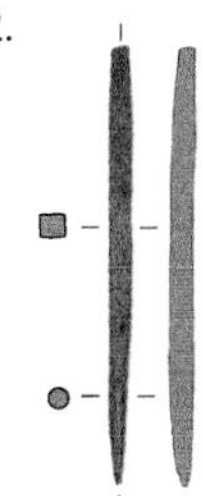
Fig. 149. 1:2.

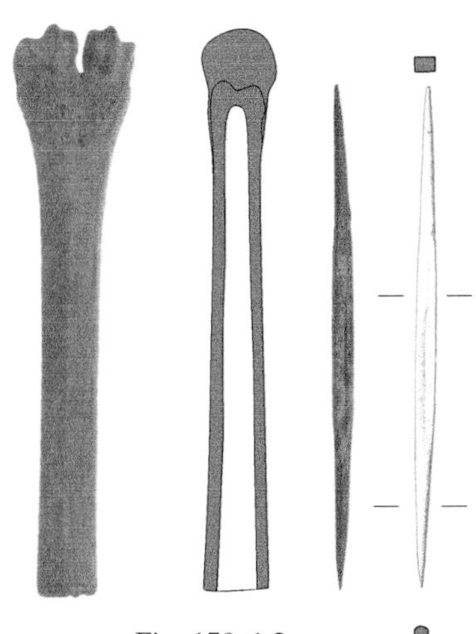
Fig. 150. 1:2.

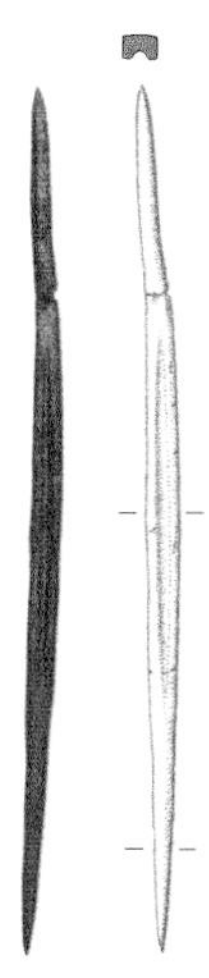
Fig. 151. 1:2.

Fig. 152. 1:2.

Fig. 153. 1:2.

Fig. 154. 1:2.

Fig. 155. 1:2.

Fig. 156. 1:2.

Fig. 157. 1:2.

Fig. 158. 1:2.

Fig. 159. 1:2.

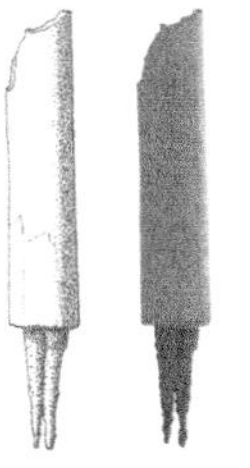
Fig. 160. 1:2.

Fig. 161. 1:2.

Fig. 162. 1:2.

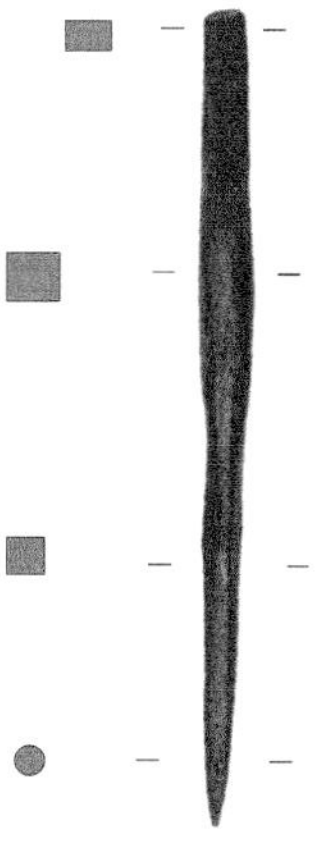
Fig. 163. 1:2.

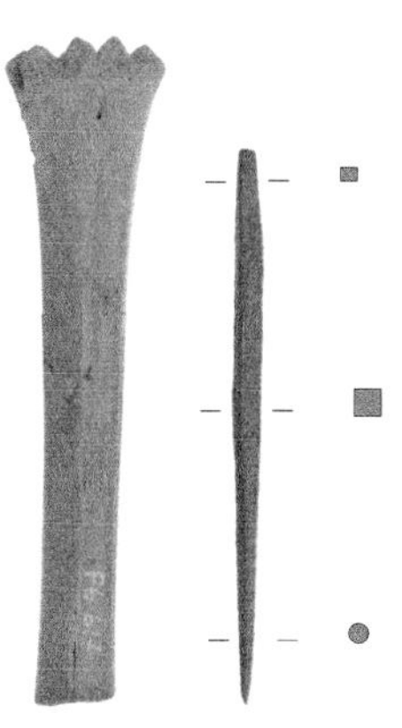
Fig. 164. 1:2.

Fig. 165. 1:2.

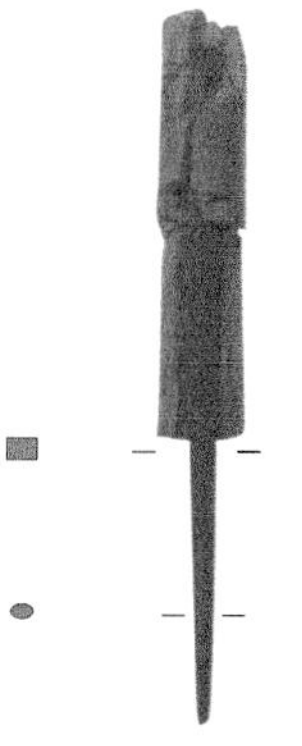
Fig. 166. 1:2.

Fig. 167. 1:2.

Fig. 168. 1:2.

Fig. 169. 1:2.

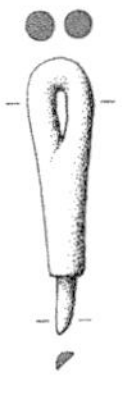
Fig. 170. 1:2.

Fig. 171. 1:2.

Fig. 172. 1:2.

Fig. 173. 1:2.

Fig. 174. 1:2.

Fig. 175. 1:2.

Fig. 176. 1:2.

Fig. 177. 1:2.

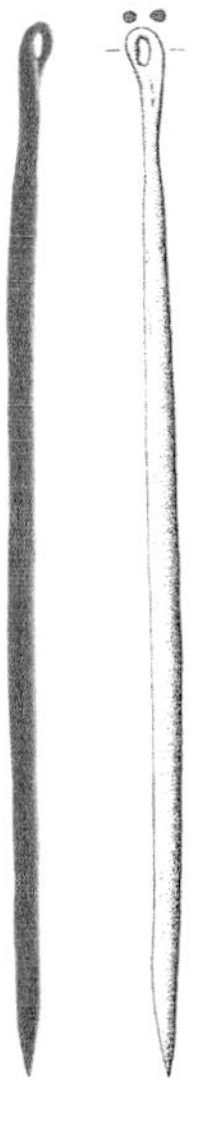
Fig. 178. 1:2.

Fig. 179. 1:2.

Fig. 180. 1:2.

Fig. 181. 1:2.

Fig. 182. 1:2.

Fig. 183. 1:2.

Fig. 184. 1:2.

Fig. 185. 1:2.

Fig. 186. 1:2.

Fig. 187. 1:2.

Fig. 188. 1:2.

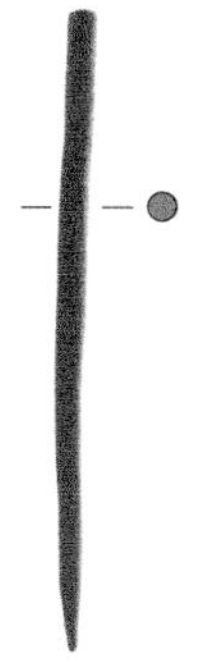
Fig. 189. 1:2.

Fig. 190. 1:2.

Fig. 191. 1:2.

Fig. 192. 1:2.

Fig. 193. 1:2.

Fig. 194. 1:2.

Fig. 195. 1:2.

Fig. 196. 1:2.

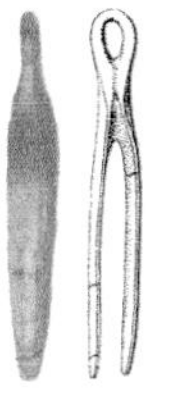
Fig. 197. 1:2.

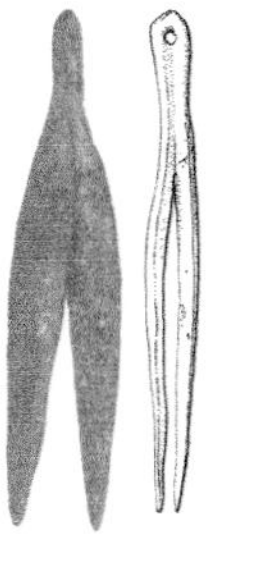
Fig. 198. 1:2.

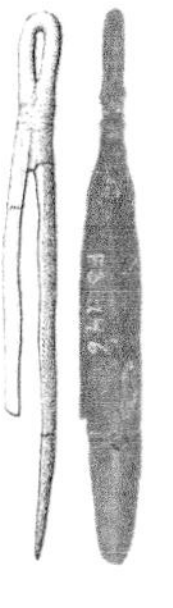
Fig. 199. 1:2.

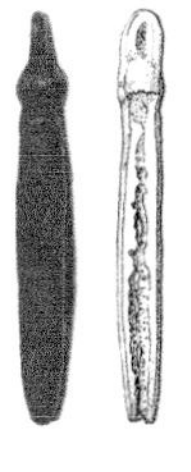
Fig. 200. 1:2.

Fig. 201. 1:2.

Fig. 202. 1:2.

Fig. 203. 1:2.

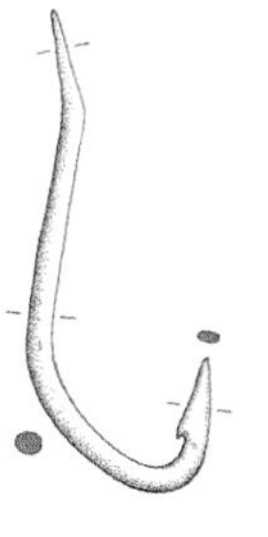
Fig. 204. 1:2.

Fig. 205. 1:2.

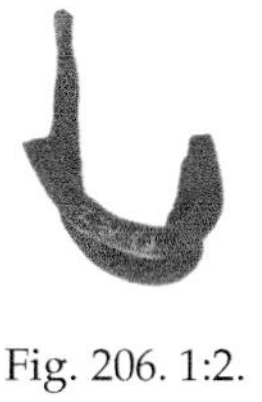
Fig. 206. 1:2.

Fig. 207. 1:2.

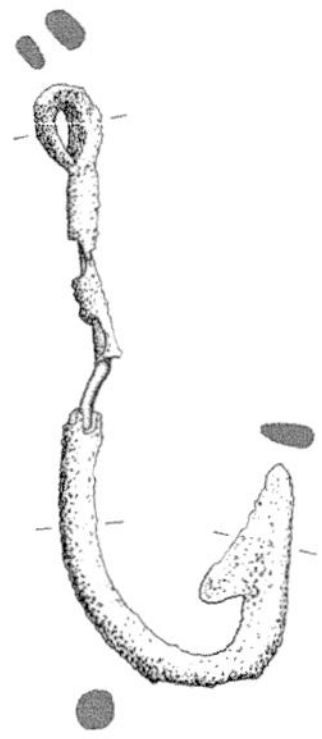
Fig. 208. 1:2.

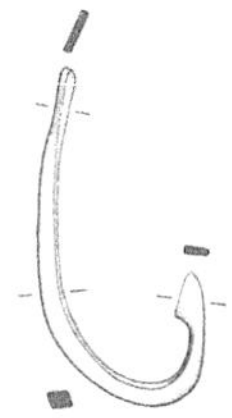
Fig. 209. 1:2.

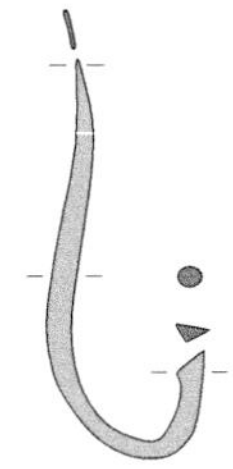
Fig. 210. 1:2.

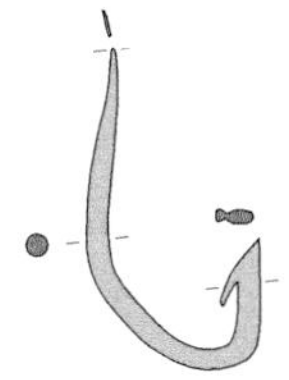
Fig. 211. 1:2.

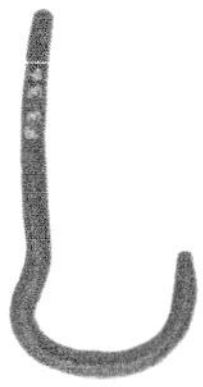
Fig. 212. 1:2.

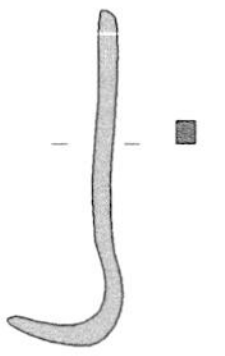
Fig. 213. 1:2.

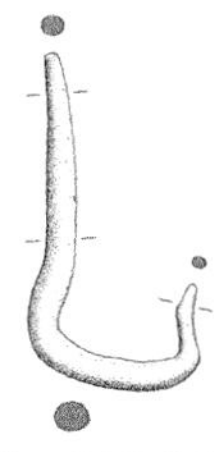
Fig. 214. 1:2.

Fig. 215. 1:2.

Fig. 216. 1:2.

Fig. 217. 1:2.

Fig. 218. 1:2.

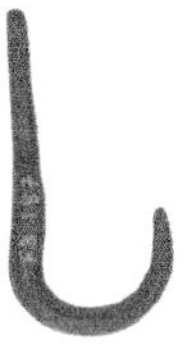
Fig. 219. 1:2.

Fig. 220. 1:2.

Fig. 221. 1:2.

Fig. 222. 1:2.

Fig. 223. 1:2.

Fig. 224. 1:2.

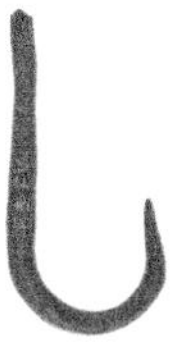
Fig. 225. 1:2.

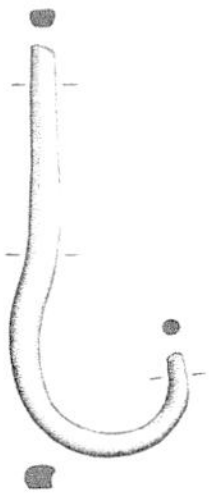
Fig. 226. 1:2.

Fig. 227. 1:2.

Fig. 228. 1:2.

Fig. 229. 1:2.

Fig. 230. 1:2.

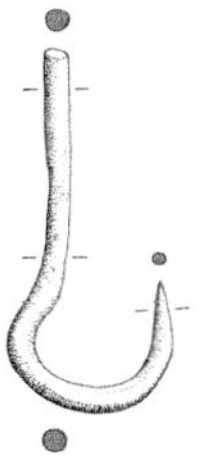
Fig. 231. 1:2.

Fig. 232. 1:2.

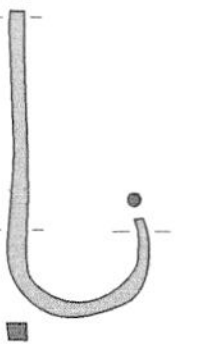
Fig. 233. 1:2.

Fig. 234. 1:2.

Fig. 235. 1:2.

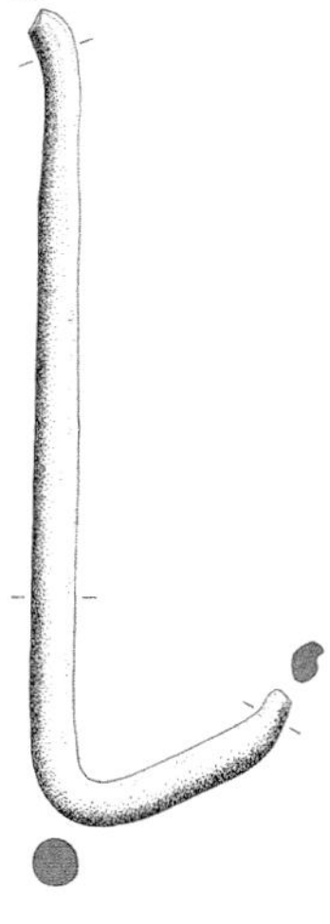
Fig. 236. 1:2.

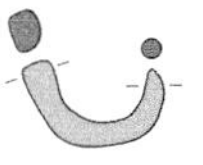
Fig. 237. 1:2.

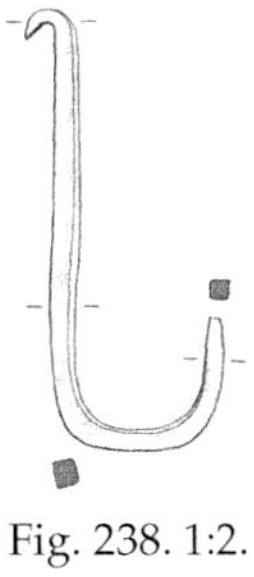
Fig. 238. 1:2.

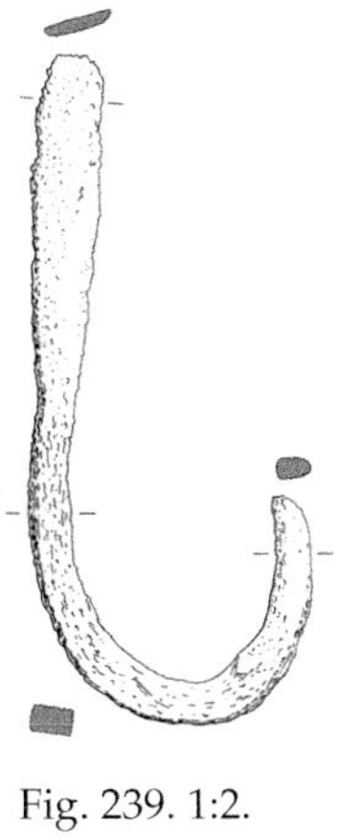
Fig. 239. 1:2.

Fig. 240. 1:2.

Fig. 241. 1:2.

Fig. 242. 1:2.

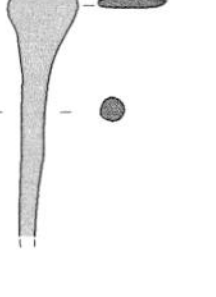
Fig. 243. 1:2.

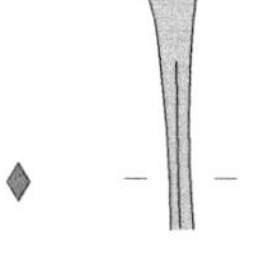
Fig. 244. 1:2.

Fig. 245. 1:2.

Fig. 246. 1:2.

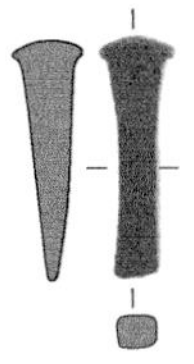
Fig. 247. 1:2.

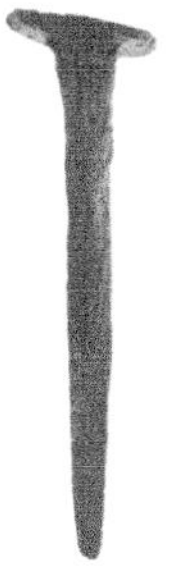
Fig. 248. 1:2.

Fig. 249. 1:2.

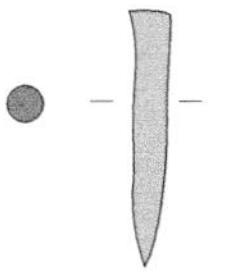
Fig. 250. 1:2.

Fig. 251. 1:2.

Fig. 252. 1:2.

Fig. 253. 1:2.

Fig. 254. 1:2.

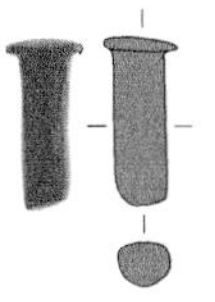
Fig. 255. 1:2.

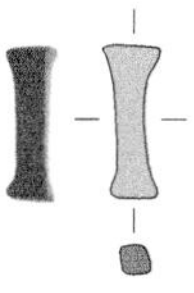
Fig. 256. 1:2.

Fig. 257. 1:2.

Fig. 258. 1:2.

Fig. 259. 1:2.

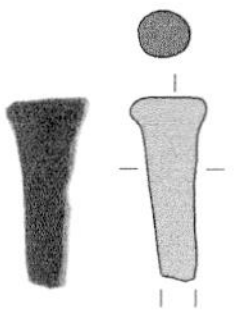
Fig. 260. 1:2.

Fig. 261. 1:2.

Fig. 262. 1:2.

Fig. 263. 1:2.

Fig. 264. 1:2.

Fig. 265. 1:2.

Fig. 266. 1:2.

Fig. 267. 1:2.

Fig. 268. 1:2.

Fig. 269. 1:2.

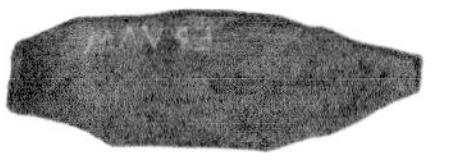
Fig. 270. 1:2.

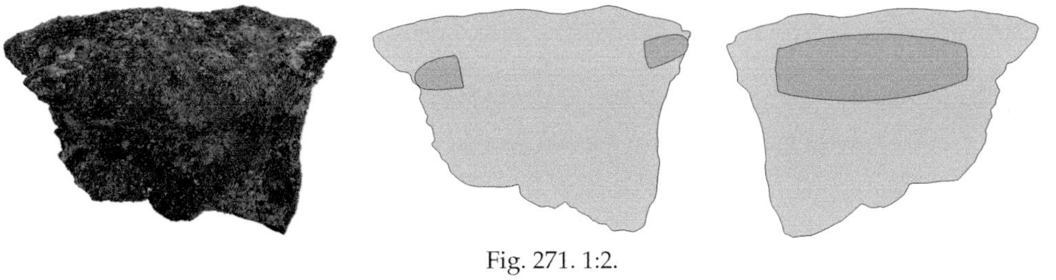
Fig. 271. 1:2.

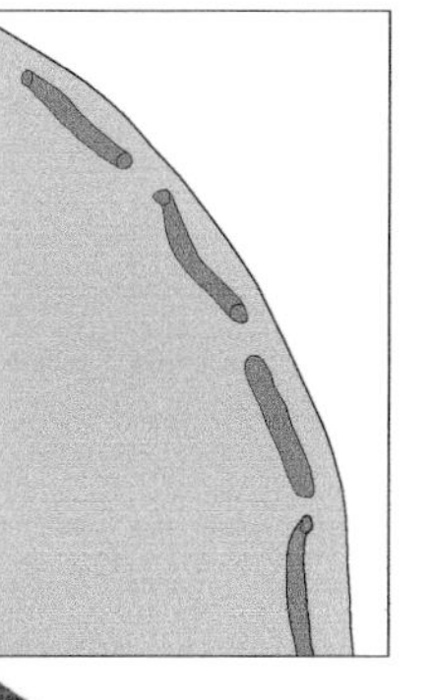

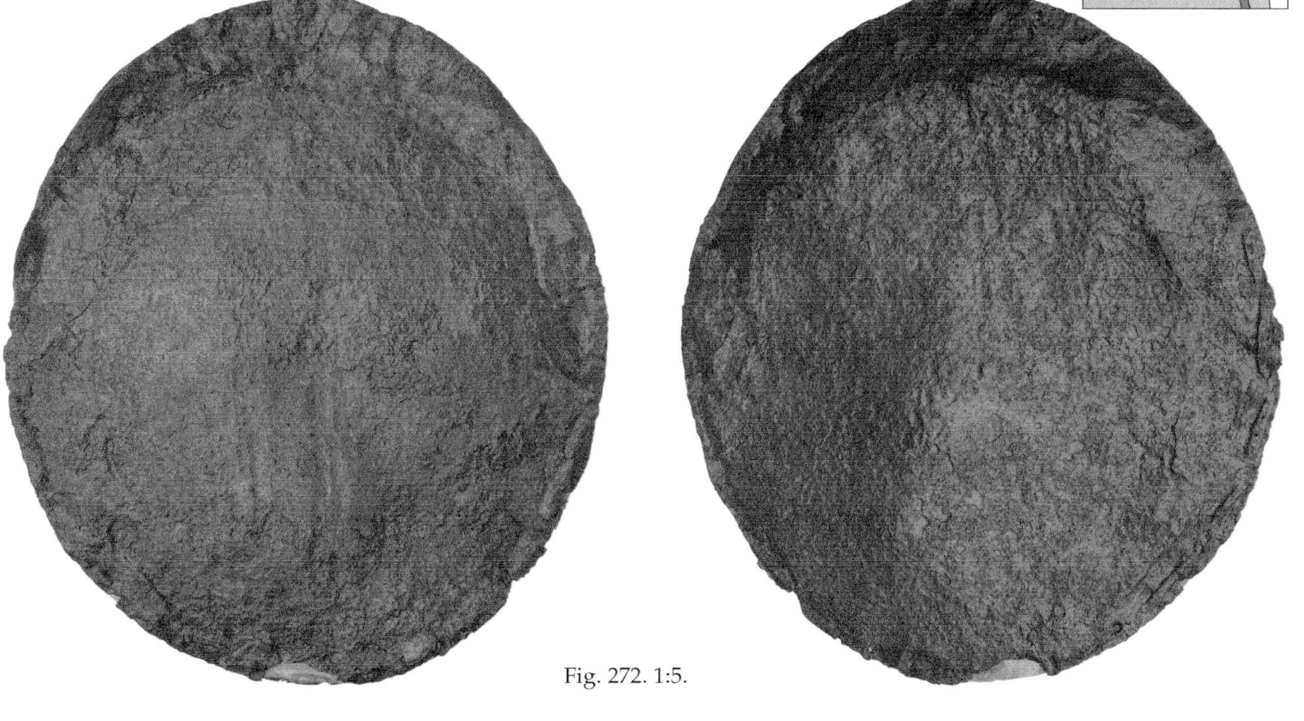
Fig. 272. 1:5.

Fig. 273. 1:2.

Fig. 274. 1:2.

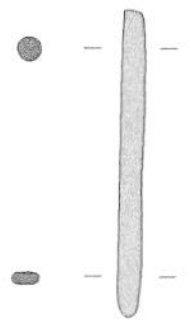

Fig. 275. 1:2.

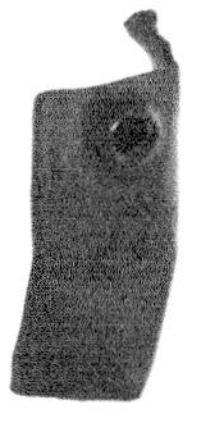

Fig. 276. 1:2.

Fig. 277. 1:2.

Fig. 278. 1:2.

Fig. 279. 1:2.

Fig. 280. 1:2.

Fig. 281. 1:2.

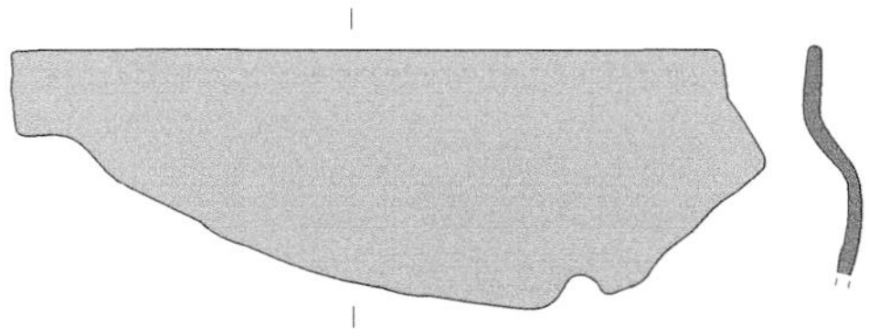

Fig. 282. 1:2.

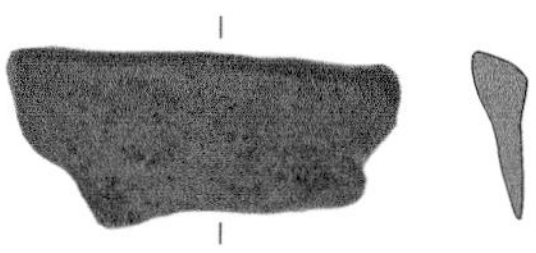

Fig. 283. 1:2.

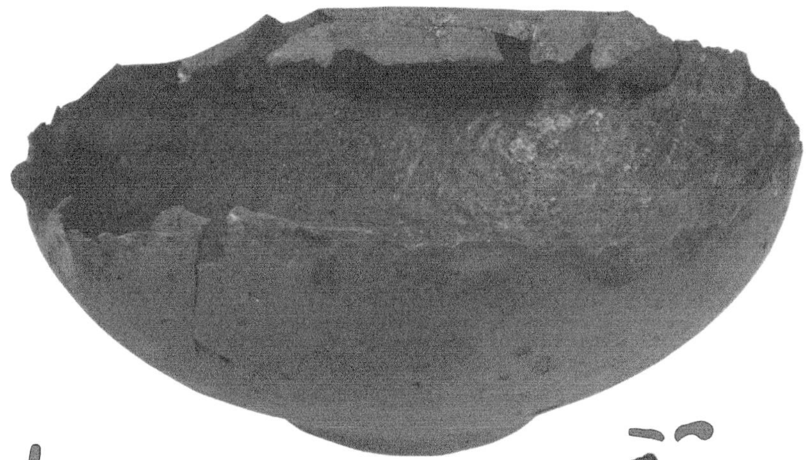

Fig. 284. 1:2.

Fig. 285. 1:2.

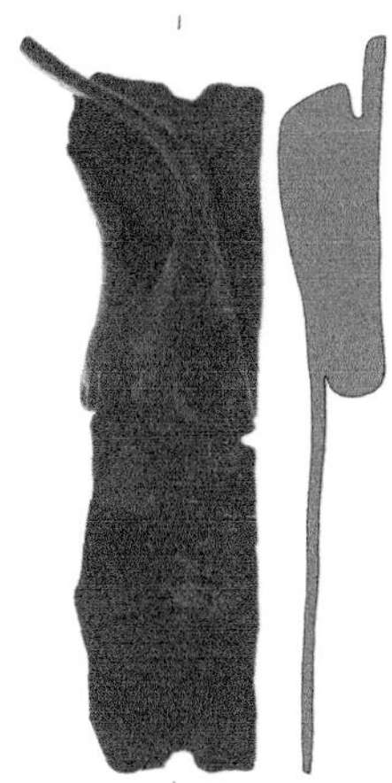

Fig. 286. 1:2.

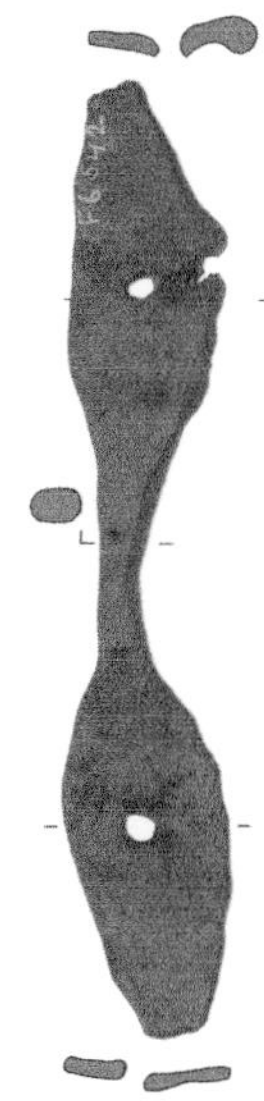

Fig. 287. 1:2.

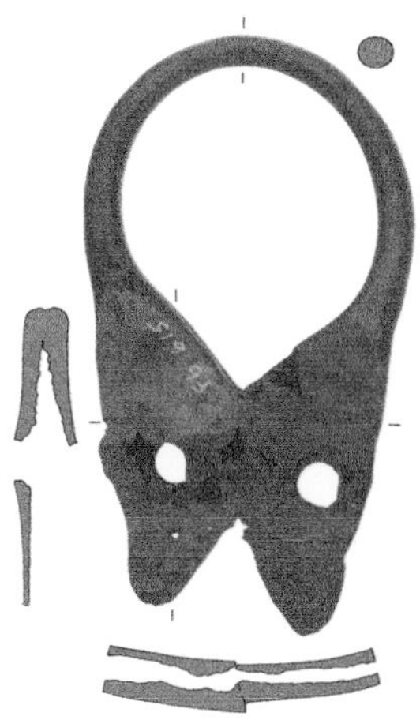

Fig. 288. 1:2.

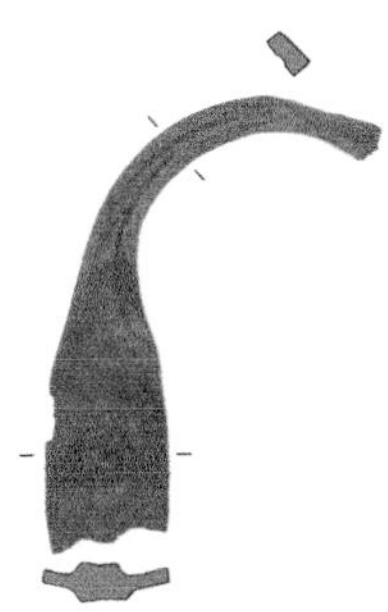

Fig. 289. 1:2.

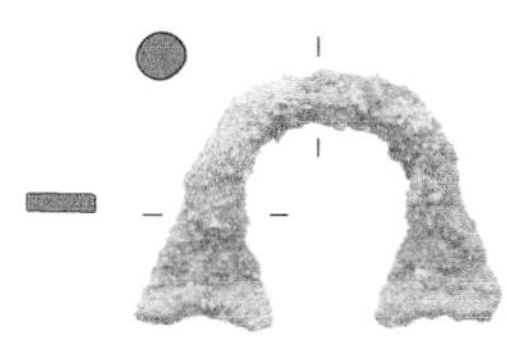

Fig. 290. 1:2.

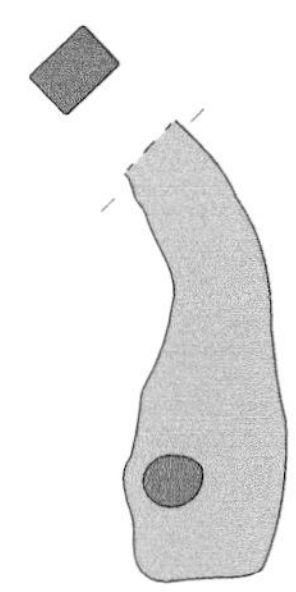

Fig. 291. 1:2.

Fig. 292. 1:3.

Fig. 293. 1:3.

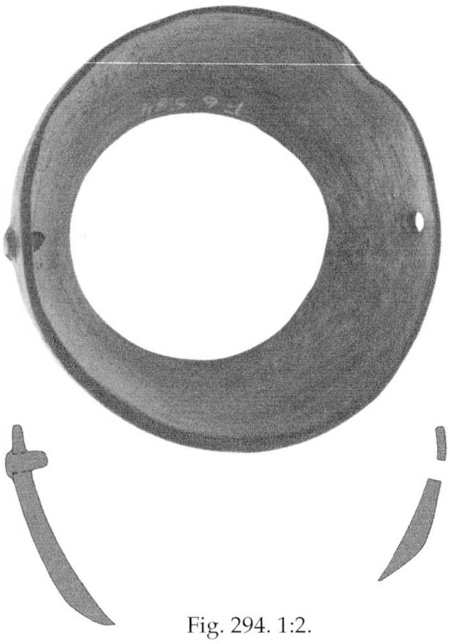

Fig. 294. 1:2.

Fig. 295. 1:2.

Fig. 296. 1:2.

Fig. 297. 1:2.

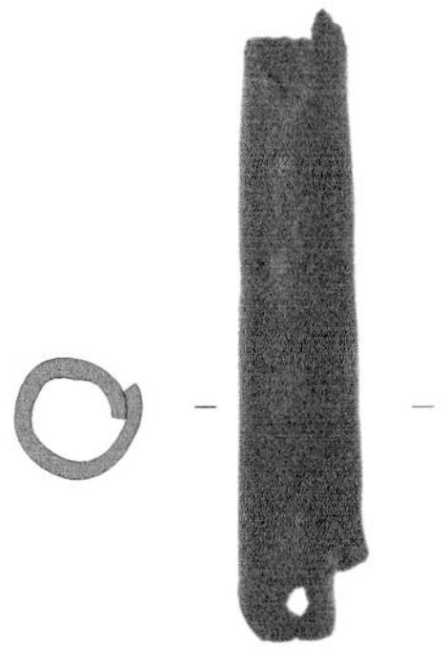

Fig. 298. 1:2.

Fig. 299. 1:2.

Fig. 300. 1:2.

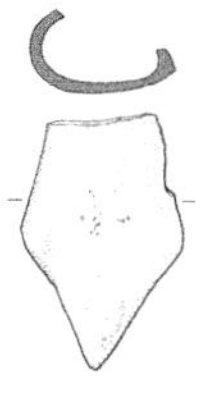

Fig. 301. 1:2.

Fig. 302. 1:2.

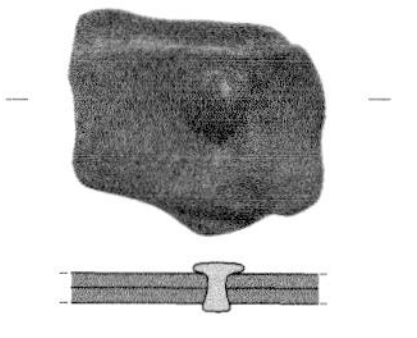

Fig. 303. 1:2.

Fig. 304. 1:2.

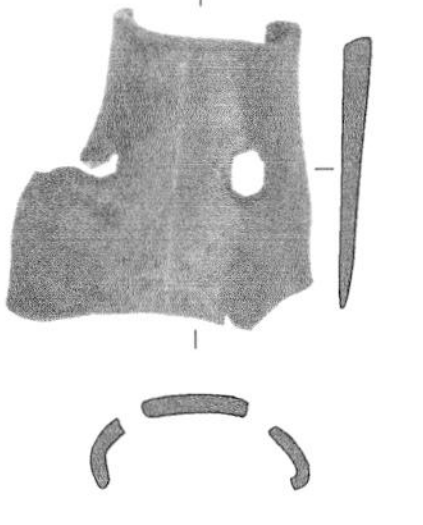

Fig. 305. 1:2.

Fig. 306. 1:3.

Fig. 307. 1:2.

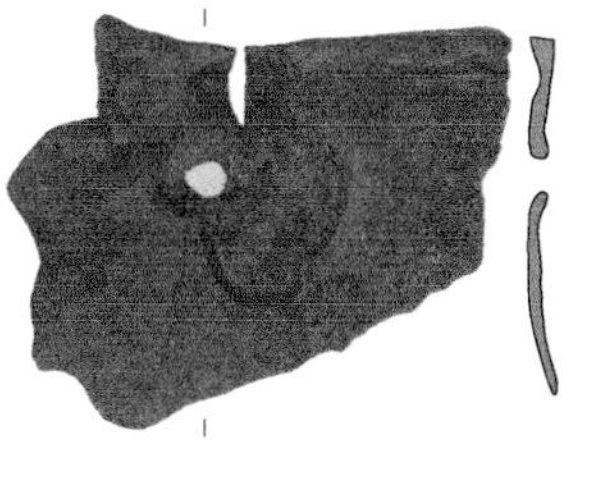

Fig. 308. 1:2.

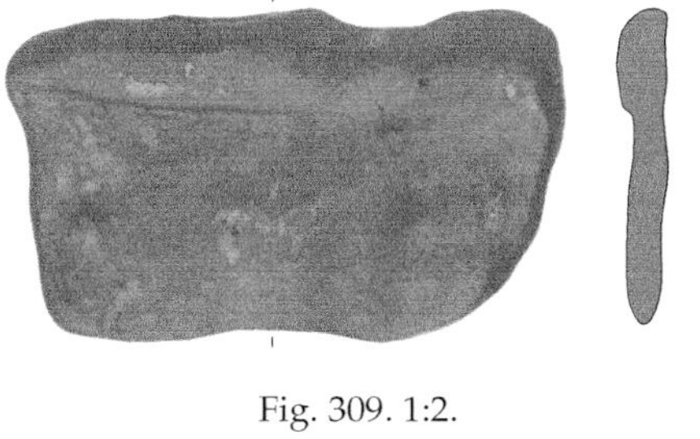

Fig. 309. 1:2.

Fig. 310. 1:2.

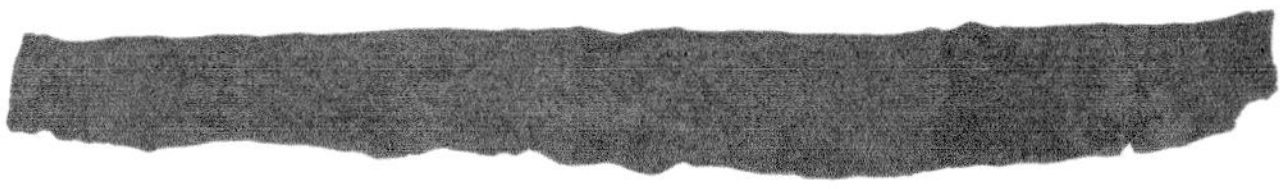

Fig. 311. 1:2.

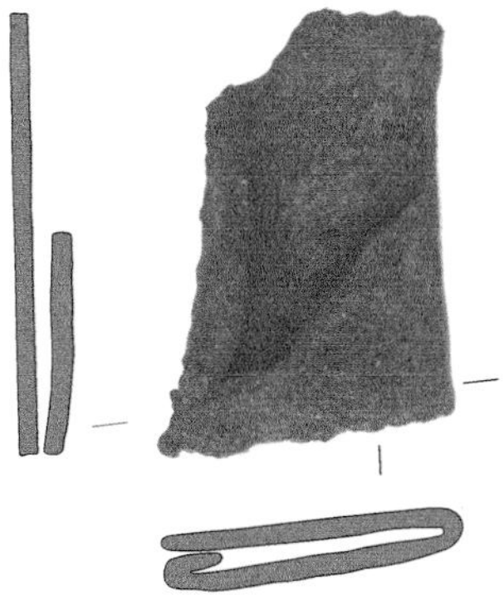

Fig. 313. 1:2.

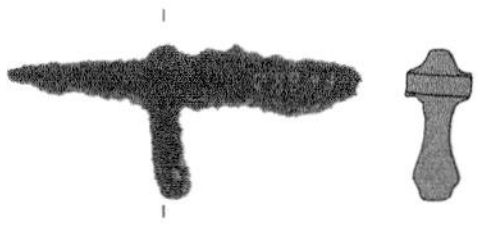

Fig. 312. 1:2.

Fig. 314. 1:2.

Fig. 315. 1:2.

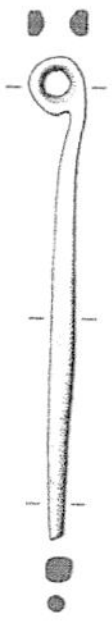

Fig. 316. 1:2.

Fig. 317. 1:2.

Fig. 318. 1:2.

Fig. 319. 1:2.

Fig. 320. 1:2.

Fig. 321. 1:2.

Fig. 322. 1:2.

Fig. 323. 1:2.

Fig. 324. 1:2.

Fig. 325. 1:2.

Fig. 326. 1:2.

Fig. 327. 1:2.

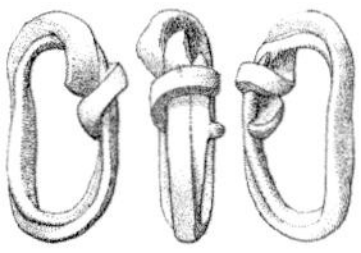

Fig. 328. 1:2.

Fig. 329. 1:2.

Fig. 330. 1:2.

Fig. 331. 1:2.

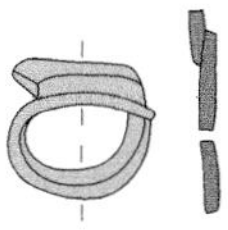

Fig. 332. 1:2.

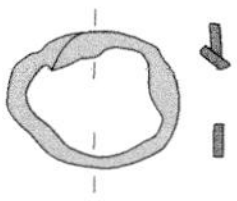

Fig. 333. 1:2.

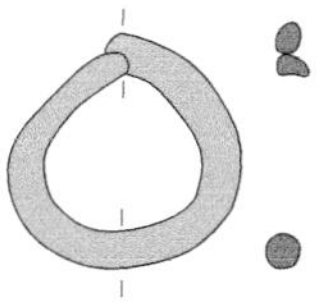

Fig. 334. 1:2.

Fig. 335. 1:2.

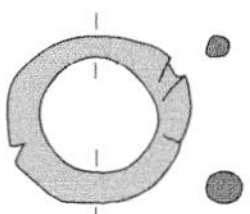

Fig. 336. 1:2.

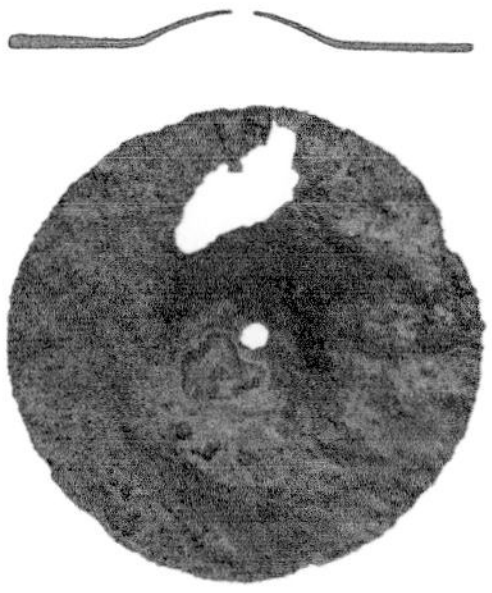

Fig. 337. 1:2.

Fig. 338. 1:2.

Fig. 339. 1:2.

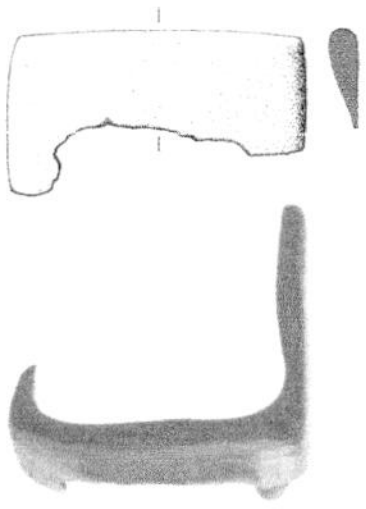

Fig. 340. 1:2.

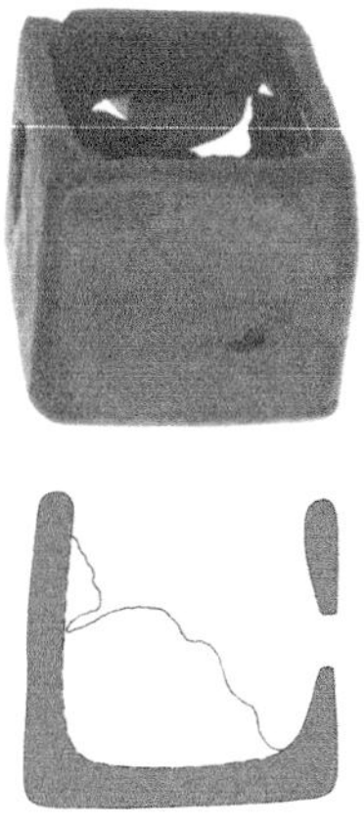

Fig. 341. 1:2.

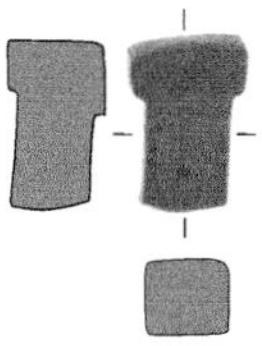

Fig. 342. 1:2.

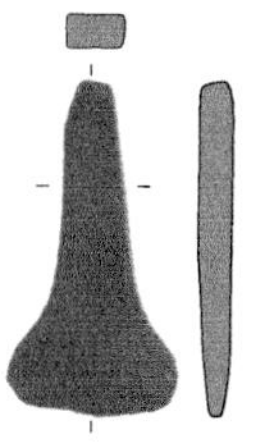

Fig. 343. 1:2.

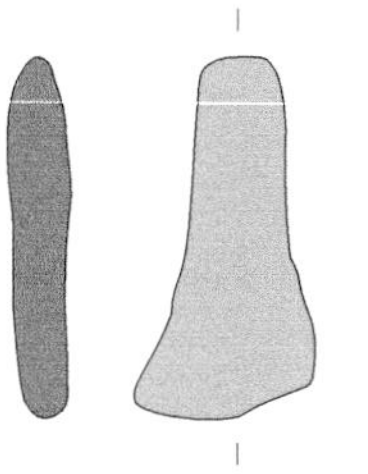

Fig. 344. 1:2.

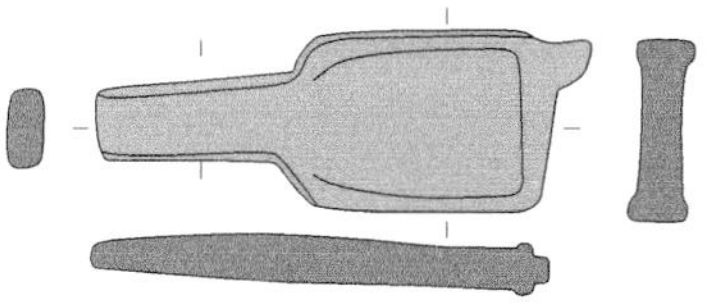

Fig. 345. 1:2.

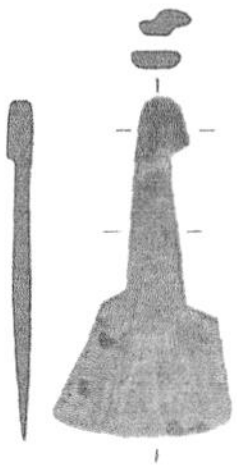

Fig. 346. 1:2.

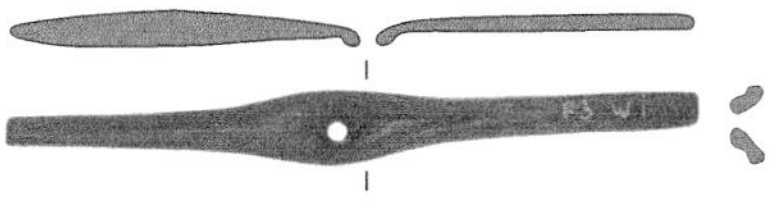

Fig. 347. 1:2.

Fig. 348. 1:2.

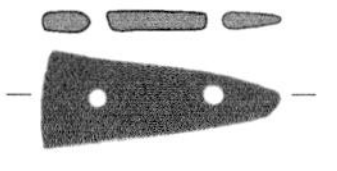

Fig. 349. 1:2.

Fig. 350. 1:2.

Fig. 351. 1:2.

Fig. 352. 1:2.

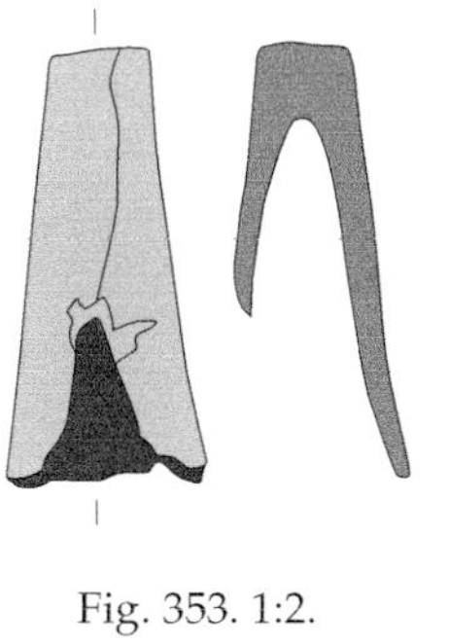

Fig. 353. 1:2.

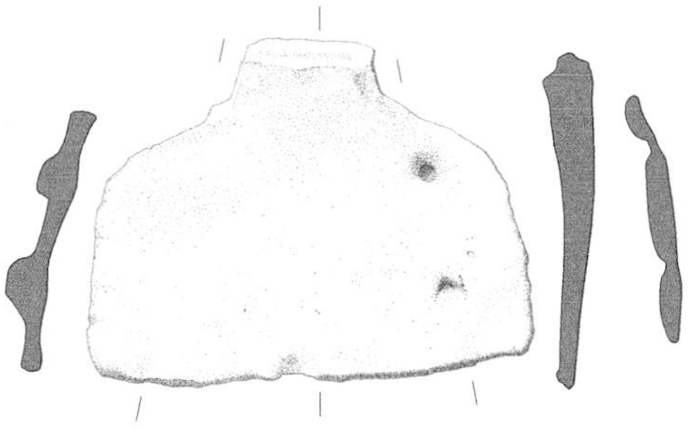

Fig. 354. 1:2.

Fig. 355. 1:2.

4. Crucibles, moulds, and ingots

Around twenty-three fragments of *crucibles* were found scattered across Tell F3 and Tell F6 during the 1958-1963 excavations. The crucibles were made of clay tempered with straw, but the clay has disappeared from most of the fragments leaving only the vitrified inside of the crucibles, that is, a layer of pottery fused with metal. The fragments were mostly small, down to a few centimetres, the largest being 12 x 12.5 cm and the only one where the diameter could be measured with any degree of confidence, to c. 20 cm.

M. Tosi described some of these fragments as "copper furnace lining", when he visited Kuwait in 1985, and this information has been added to the registration cards in the Kuwait National Museum. These fragments are, however, in all respects, similar to the crucible fragments found in other Dilmun excavations in Failaka and Bahrain, for example, the 2008-2017 excavations in Tell F3 and Tell F6 (Højlund & Abu-Laban 2016 p. 207, fig. 1050. Højlund & Hilton 2021 p. 130, figs. 463-464), Excavations 520 and 518 in Qala'at al-Bahrain (Højlund & Andersen 1994 p. 370-378, figs. 1818-1835. Højlund 2019 figs. 660-661), and the Barbar Temples (Andersen & Højlund 2003, vol. 1, figs. 745-751).

Fragments of two *moulds* were found in the 1958-1963 excavations. One of them is of the small variety with close parallels in Excavations 520 and 518 at Qala'at al-Bahrain dating to periods I and II (Højlund & Andersen 1994 figs. 1837-1853. Højlund 2019 fig. 662), and the other is of the large variety, dating to period II, found in the 2008-2012 excavations of Tell F6 (Højlund & Abu-Laban 2016 figs. 1051-1052), at the Barbar Temple (Andersen & Højlund 2003, vol. 1, figs. 752-756), and in Excavations 519 and 518 at Qala'at al-Bahrain (Højlund & Andersen 1997 figs. 87-89. Højlund 2019 p. 140, fig. 663).

Numerous small "metallic lumps" were found throughout the excavations and designated *slag* in the daybook, but their exact nature is often uncertain. Some may be fragments of crucibles, others look more like bits of corroded metal, and yet others look like production waste, such as casting spillage or impurities removed from the surface of molten metals in a crucible, comparable to the waste/spill from Saar Settlement in Bahrain (Weeks & Collerson 2005 p. 315-317).

In sum, there is no evidence for smelting of ore and no remains of furnaces from the 1958-1963 excavations, nor from any other excavations on Failaka or Bahrain. Copper probably reached Dilmun primarily in the shape of plano-convex ingots. Several ingots were actually found in the deepest, Pre-"Palace" levels of Tell F6 (cf. figs. 371 and 374. See also Hurtel and Tallon 1990 p. 52).

The two mould fragments suggest that the casting of copper objects in moulds took place somewhere in the neighbourhood of Tell F3 and Tell F6, like in the copper workshop found at the northern city wall at Qala'at al-Bahrain, where dozens of crucible and mould fragments occurred over a 15 x 35 m wide area (Højlund & Andersen 1994 p. 370-378, 467-468, figs. 1818-1853). Numerous fragments of crucibles and moulds were also found in Excavation 518 at Qala'at al-Bahrain (Højlund 2019 p. 140, figs. 660-663). The exact location of such a workshop on Failaka has, however, yet to be found. It is assumed that many of the copper objects described in the preceding section were produced in this workshop.

However, the many crucible fragments and production waste found throughout Tell F3 and Tell F6 and the few moulds raise the question of whether some kind of copper melting/working in which moulds were not utilized took place within the excavated area, such as the remelting of scrap metal into ingots in "sand moulds", working copper into shape, or repairing copper objects. There is certainly a good deal of worn-out objects, compressed artefacts and scrap metal in the metal assemblage from Tell F3 and Tell F6.

Evidence of such copper working may have been encountered in Trench Q in the middle of Tell F3. At level c. 6.10, a hard, clayey floor that covered most of the trench was found. It was quite greenish because of the inclusion of many small pieces of copper "slag". There was a round depression in the clay layer, full of ashes and slag/production waste. On the floor lay a fragment of a ridged cylinder in copper (fig. 86). The clay layer can be dated to Failaka Period 2, since it was deposited up against a wall belonging to the row of houses (26-29) in the north of Tell F3 dating to Failaka Period 2 (Kjærum & Højlund 2013 figs. 104-105). No remains of crucibles or moulds were found in this specific location, however, there is a scattering of crucible fragments from different levels in the area immediately south of Trench Q, in Trenches RM, B, M, and Ø.

In Excavation G3, a small tell lying 200 m north of Tell F6 similar evidence for metal working was found in the shape of slag and crucible fragments of which two were illustrated (Calvet 1984 p. 51-58, figs. 27: 59, 30: 94, 31: 108).

Crucibles

Fragment of crucible, 2 cm thick, vitrified layer with impression of pottery on the outer side (fig. 356) (F3.10). Trench RM, 17.05 N, 4 W.

Fragment of crucible, 5.2 x 6.9 cm, 0.7 cm thick, vitrified layer with 0.6 cm thick layer of pottery on the outside (fig. 357) (F3.24). Trench RM.

Fragment of crucible or perhaps of a special, enigmatic type known from Tell F6 and Qala'at al-Bahrain (cf. Højlund & Abu-Laban 2016 p. 207, fig. 1053. Højlund 2019 p. 140, fig. 664) (F3.202). Trench RM, c. 40 N, level 7.52.

Fragment of crucible. A 1-2 mm thick, green, vitrified layer attached to a 2 cm thick layer of light reddish-brown coarse pottery without the exterior face preserved (fig. 358) (F3.264). Trench RM, sieve.

Two fragments of crucible, 2.5 x 4 cm and 3.5 x 3.5 cm, both of them 1.2 -1.3 cm thick, vitrified layer with impression of pottery on one side (fig. 359) (881.RN). Trench RM, 40-60 N, above level c. 8.25.

Fragment of crucible (881.SR). Trench RM, sieve.

Fragment of crucible, consisting of 1.6 cm thick layer of green metal on a 1.4 cm layer of pottery (fig. 360) (F3.ad). Trench B.

Fragment of crucible (F3.bz). Trench B, north part, level 7.90-7.27.

Fragment of crucible, 5 x 7 cm, 0.8 cm thick, grey-green, vitrified layer and 0.8 cm thick layer of pottery (F3.ey). Trench B, level 6.75-6.54. Associated pottery: Period 2.

Fragment of crucible, 6.5 x 6.7 cm, 1.5-1.8 cm thick, vitrified layer with impression of pottery on the outside (fig. 361) (F3.fs). Trench B.

Fragment of crucible (F3.ib). Trench M, level 6.73-6.41.

Fragment of crucible, a grey-green, vitrified layer with brown slag and remains of pottery (F3.is). Trenches A, B, E, and F.

Fragment of 2 cm thick crucible wall of light brown coarse pottery with the exterior face partly preserved (fig. 362). On the inside layers of green metal and grey-black slag (F3.lu). Trench B, level 6.50. Associated pottery: Period 2.

Fragment of crucible wall, c. 3 cm thick, in light reddish-brown straw-tempered ware with 0.5 cm thick layer of green metal attached to the inner side (fig. 363) (F3.mu). Trench B/M baulk, between surface and level 8.00. Associated pottery: Period 3B.

Fragment of crucible, 2.1 x 3.4 cm (F3.sd). Trench Ø, 56 N, 16.40 E, level 9.07.

Five fragments of crucible, 0.7 cm thick vitrified layer with an up to 1.5 cm thick layer of light brown, straw-tempered pottery attached to the outside (F3.te). Trench Æ/Ø, sieve.

Crucible fragment, 3.8 x 7 cm (fig. 364) (F6.45). Trench SS, 5-9 S, 0-1.5 E, -0.71.

Crucible fragment (fig. 365) (F6.617). Trench D2, 15-16 N, 1-2 W, level -1.84. Associated pottery: Period 1.

Moulds

Mould rim fragment, reddish, heavily tempered with straw and a little sand, apparently round with a diameter of 30 cm (fig. 366) (F3.ey). The internal base of the bottom is grey-black. Trench B, level 6.75-6.54. Associated pottery: Period 2.

Mould rim fragment, straight side, heavily tempered with straw, buff surface, grey-black in section (fig. 367) (1129.916). Trench D1/D2, 8-11 N, 3 W-1 E, level -2.20. Associated pottery: Period 1.

Ingots

Irregular lump of solid copper, 0.9 x 3 x 7 cm (881.RN). Trench RM, 40-60 N, above level c. 8.25.

Lump of pure copper, 4.2 x 5 cm (figs. 368 and 378: sample 333) (F3.rt). Trench Æ, sieve.

Lump of pure copper, 3.7 x 7 cm, 1.5 cm thick (fig. 369) (F3.yt)

Two lumps of solid, pure copper, 1 x 3 x 5 cm (fig. 370) and 2.8 x 3 x 3.5 cm (F3.avæ).

Fragment of ingot, 4 x 6.1 x 8 cm, weight 695 g (F6.198). SS1N, 1-10 N, 0-1.5 E, level -0.58.

Lump of solid copper, 2.5 x 4 x 7 cm (no number)

Copper ingot, plano-convex, 4 cm thick, weight 4 kg (fig. 371) (F6.615). Trench SN11-20, 13.50 N, 0.50 E, level -1.61. Associated pottery: Period 1.

Copper ingot, 3.3 cm thick, oval cross section, pure copper, rust patches on both sides, weight 475 g (fig. 372) (F6.917). Trench M2, 16.2 N, 8 W, level -1.81. Associated pottery: Period 1.

Lump (figs. 373 and 378: sample 315) (F6.1035). Trench N2, level +0.78.

Copper ingot, plano-convex, 4.3 cm thick (fig. 374) (F6.1200). Trench M1, 4-5 N, 11-12 W, level -1.80. Associated pottery: Period 1.

Lump of copper, irregular, 1.9-3 cm thick (fig. 375) (F6. no number).

Fig. 356. 1:2.

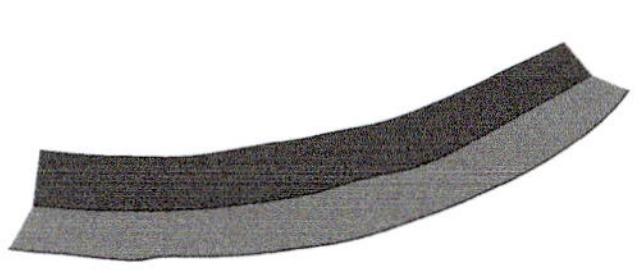

Fig. 357. 1:2.

Fig. 358. 1:2.

Fig. 359. 1:1.

Fig. 360. 1:2.

Fig. 361. 1:2.

Fig. 362. 1:2.

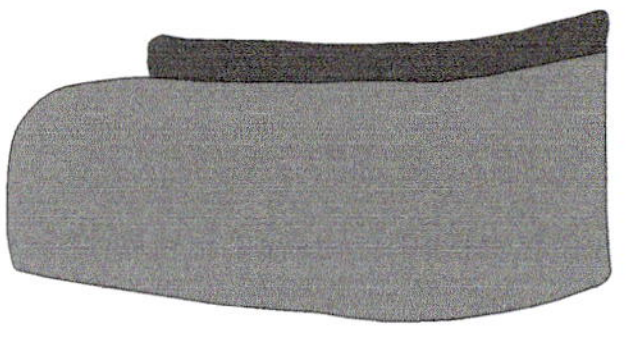

Fig. 363. 1:2.

Fig. 364. 1:2.

Fig. 365. 1:2.

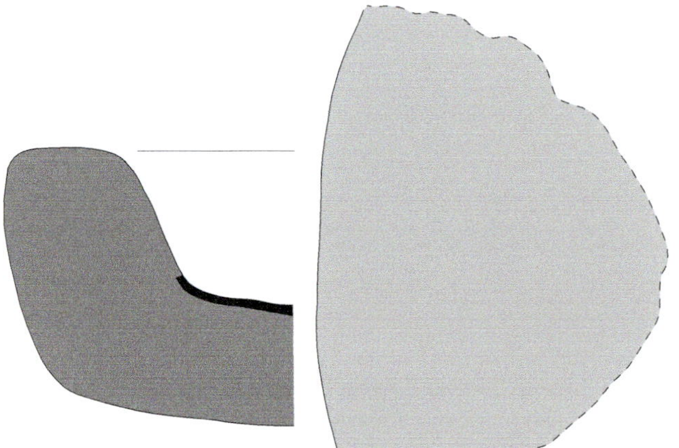

Fig. 366. 1:2.

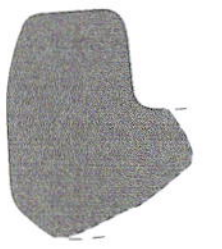

Fig. 367. 1:2.

Fig. 368. 1:2.

Fig. 369. 1:1.

Fig. 370. 1:1.

Fig. 371. 1:2.

Fig. 372. 1:2.

Fig. 373. 1:1.

Fig. 374. 1:2.

Fig. 375. 1:2.

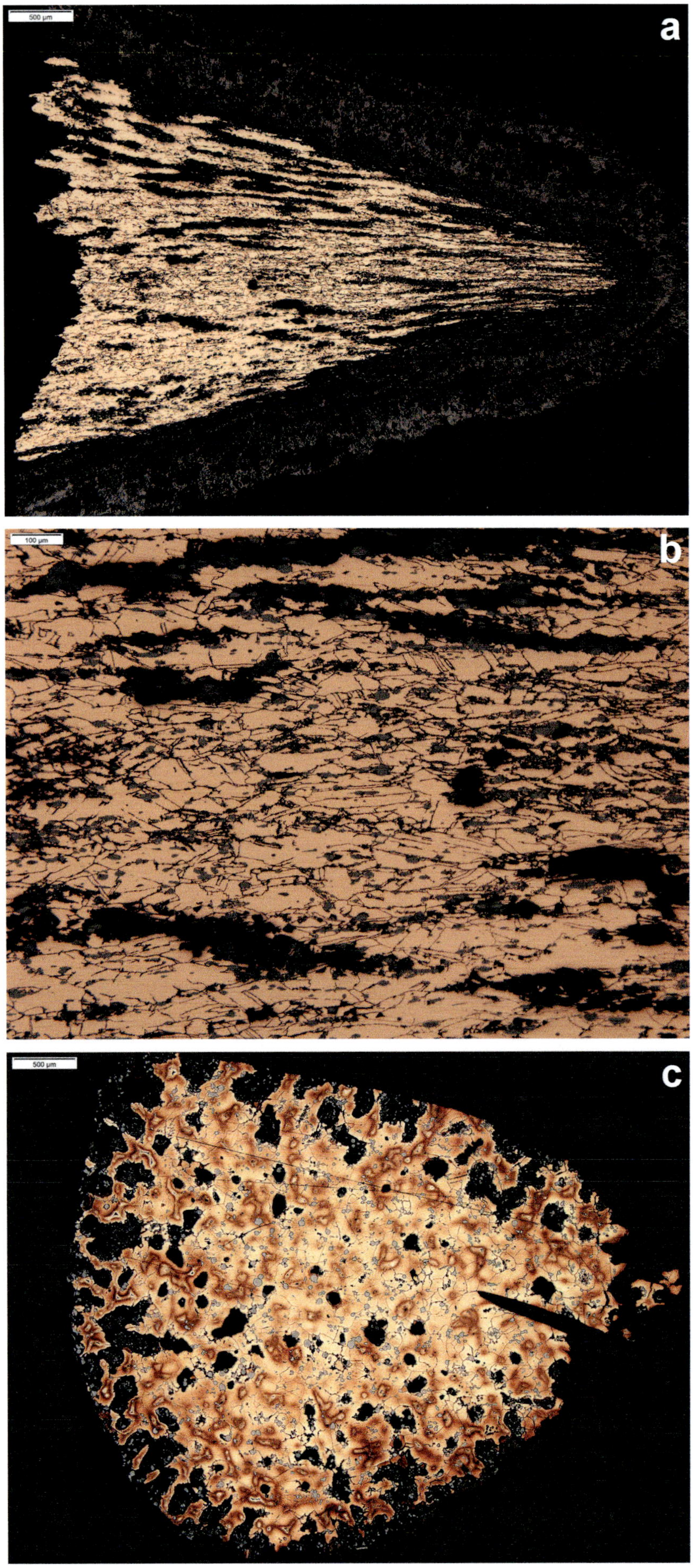

Fig. 376. Metallographs of the dagger blade sample 11-338 (a, b) and the production residue sample 12-013 (c). a) Transverse section of 11-338 showing differentially corroded laminar structure indicative of heavy forging; b) a magnified view of 11-338 showing annealing twins revealed by intra-granular corrosion, indicative of heating after forging; c) Section of amorphous lump 12-013, etched in ferric chloride, showing an as-cast structure and coring of the alloy during solidification.

5. The composition of copper-based artefacts and metal-working residues from Tell F3 and Tell F6

by Lloyd Weeks, Sarah Morriss, Eddy Faber, and Emma Watt

Introduction

This chapter presents a summary of the metallurgical analyses undertaken on material from the excavations at Tell F3 and Tell F6, including material from the initial Danish excavations in both tells in the period from 1958-1963, as well as more recent excavations on Tell F6 from 2008-2012 (Højlund & Abu-Laban 2016).

The metallurgical analyses explore the elemental composition of copper-base artefacts from the site, as well as residues from copper working, and provide insight into the nature and sources of the raw materials used on Failaka and the technologies employed in working with this material. The comparison of these data with existing metallurgical evidence from the region contributes to a better understanding of the site's connections with the wider world of the Bronze Age Persian Gulf, particularly the copper-supplying areas in the modern-day U.A.E. and Oman – ancient *Makkan* – that is not mentioned as copper supplier in Mesopotamian written sources after the Ur III period. The long silence from Mesopotamia belies a very active exchange system in the Persian Gulf during the second millennium BCE, one that is amenable to reconstruction through the close analysis of its material residues, abundant at sites such as Failaka Island.

This chapter presents a summary of the compositional studies of Failaka material, a sub-set of the very large amount of data generated by the wider archaeometallurgical study. The primary compositional data are to be presented elsewhere, as part of an integrated analysis and interpretation of the full results of this research.

The sampled assemblage

The metal artefacts and metallurgical production residues from the Danish excavations on Failaka are presented and macroscopically described in chapters 3 and 4 (this volume) and in Højlund (2016a, 2021). The assemblage is substantial in scale and diversity, amounting to several hundreds of complete and fragmentary artefacts and amorphous materials that can be identified as production residues, i.e. the waste material from a range of metallurgical activities that included melting, refining, alloying, and casting of copper-base artefacts. As Højlund notes (above p. 15), this is currently "the largest collection of copper objects known from the land of Dilmun".

Number and nature of archaeometallurgical samples collected

The Failaka metal assemblage was studied and sampled by SM, working on Failaka Island in 2010, 2011 and 2012 as a member of the Kuwait-Danish excavation team, and with access to most excavated materials. The archaeometallurgical analysis of this large and diverse assemblage could not hope to be comprehensive. Therefore, a sampling protocol was developed, based on macroscopic observations, to identify key items for detailed material investigation, with the major considerations being: 1) a representative selection of finished artefact and metallurgical residue types; 2) sampling of all components of the metallurgical production sequence at the site; and 3) where possible (and where data were available), a selection that represented the full chronological and spatial range of material from the excavated sites.

The archaeometallurgical sampling was also guided by the preservation state of the copper-base material. The burial environment on Failaka Island, which combines sediments rich in soluble salts, especially chlorides, with dramatic daily, seasonal, and annual variations in humidity and soil water content, is typically highly corrosive of copper-base materials (e.g., Oudbashi 2018. Schorsch 2014). Many of the Bronze Age artefacts and residues from excavations on the island are completely or nearly completely corroded (Højlund 2016a p. 207), with little or none of the original metal surviving for analysis. As the presence of original, uncorroded metal is fundamental to the generation of reliable archaeometallurgical data on composition, fabrication, and provenance (see p. 57-59), the archaeometallurgical sampling programme closely considered the preservation of materials. Often, assessing preservation was challenging based only on macroscopic exterior analysis. Virtually all copper-base material remains presented a thick exterior corrosion crust of green(-blue) hydrated copper carbonates and chlorides, as well as adhering sand and soil particles from the burial environment. Waste residues from metal refining and casting were sometimes differentiated not only by gross morphology – typified by amorphous, sub-rounded shapes – but also by a higher proportion of iron, apparent through the development of a rusty red component on the exterior corrosion layer.

As all materials presented strong surface corrosion, the relative density of material remains was a key consideration in sampling for materials analysis. Less corroded materials are heavier, per volume, than fully-corroded remains, and were preferentially targeted for analysis. This strategy was viable for identifying many categories of metal artefacts and residues, although metallurgical residues that were non-metallic at their time of their initial production – such as 'dross' (fully oxidised metal) formed in copper melting and casting crucibles – might be under-represented in such a sampling strategy.

Inevitably, however, due to uncertainties regarding their preservation, numerous fully-corroded copper-base remains were inadvertently sampled. This meant that more samples were collected than were eventually subject to material analyses, with assessment of preservation in polished metallographic specimens – where preservation could be examined microscopically across a full section of the artefact – being critical for decision making about further analysis.

Analysed artefacts and residues: Type, context, period

The analysed specimens were typically taken from fragmentary artefacts. The major types sampled reflect those that were frequent in the overall assemblage. This includes rod-shaped artefacts (n=40, 14 square-sectioned, 8 round-sectioned), sheet or vessel fragments (n=15), bladed tools and weapons including spears, axes, chisels and knives (n=9), nails (n=4), awls/needles (n=4), and hooks (n=3), alongside other rare types.

Also studied for their composition were a range of residues from metallurgical processes including refining and casting, comprising amorphous prills and droplets of impurities and oxidised metal (dross). Specimens from these samples (n=22) were usually taken from complete pieces, which are identified in the analytical tables as 'nodules' or 'lumps'. Even though heavily corroded in most cases, these residues can generally be differentiated from fragmentary finished artefacts by their macroscopic morphology and corrosion characteristics and by their microstructure, which typically displays an unmodified 'as-cast' structure as opposed to the evidence for heating and forging that characterises the microstructures of fragmentary finished artefacts (fig. 376).

In terms of spatial and chronological representation, of the 104 specimens analysed and discussed in this presentation, 41 come from Tell F3 (all deriving from the 1958-1963 excavations), while 57 come from Tell F6 (9 from the 1958-1963 excavations and 48 from the 2008-2012 excavations). Five of the analysed artefacts have an unknown excavation provenance. Although these samples span all the occupation phases documented by excavation, the representation of periods varies somewhat by provenance. The Tell F6 material from the 2008-2012 excavations is weighted towards the late third and especially early second millennium BCE, including 12 samples from Phases 1-3 (Ur III to Isin-Larsa Periods), 21 from Phases 4-5 (Isin-Larsa to early Old Babylonian Periods) and 8 from Phases 6-8 (Kassite Period). The remaining F6 samples (n=7) are undated or from disturbed contexts. Of the dateable finds from the 1958-1963 excavations in Tell F3, the opposite pattern is observed: most samples date to uncertain contexts across the Old Babylonian or Kassite Periods (16 samples from mixed Periods 3A-4) or to the Kassite Period (6 samples from Periods 4A and 4B), with only two samples from clear Isin-Larsa Period contexts (Period 2). Many of the analysed samples (n=17) from the 1958-1963 excavations at Tell F3 are of unknown date, as are all of the Tell F6 materials from the 1958-1963 fieldwork.

Sampling and analysis methods

Sample collection and preparation

Samples were collected in Kuwait by SM, using a fine jeweller's saw to cut sub-samples from metal artefacts and production residues that had been macroscopically examined and classified (see p. 55-56). Subsequent stages of sample preparation, examination and analyses were undertaken by the authors in the laboratories of the University of Nottingham, and the University of New England, Australia. Cut samples were mounted in 25 mm diameter moulds in cold-setting epoxy resin and ground and polished using standard metallographic preparation techniques, finishing with 1 micron diamond polish and, in some cases, 0.05 micron colloidal silica. Polished specimens were studied under reflected light on an optical microscope (Olympus BX51) fitted with a digital camera. Compositional analyses were undertaken on the polished surfaces of the prepared specimens in the resin blocks, using EPMA-WDS and SEM-EDS as described below.

Electron microprobe with wavelength-dispersive spectrometry (EPMA-WDS)

EPMA analyses were undertaken by SM and EF on 48 samples with preserved metal suitable for analysis. These samples were exclusively from the recent Danish excavations on Tell F6 (Højlund & Abu-Laban 2016). The samples were coated with a thin film of carbon prior to electron microprobe analyses, which were undertaken on a JEOL JXA-8200 electron microprobe (Department of Archaeology, University of Nottingham) following the protocols presented in Weeks et al. (in press). For copper alloys the following 19 elements were measured as weight percentage: O, Si, S, Cl, Ti, Cr, Mn, Fe, Co, Ni, Cu, Zn, As, Ag, Sn, Sb, Ba, Au, Pb. The detection limits for the analysis of copper alloys and precious metals vary from c. 90 ppm for Co to c. 900 ppm for As. For each sample, the results of multiple (typically ~5) point analyses were averaged to produce an overall composition. Backscattered electron (BSE compositional) images taken on the microprobe show relative differences in the average atomic weight of the elements present, thus areas composed of heavier elements appear brighter than areas composed of lighter elements. These images were used, alongside optical microscope images, to identify the different phases for analysis. The microprobe allowed for the targeting of areas of preserved metal in partially or heavily corroded specimens, as can be seen from the fact that the concentrations of O, Si and Cl are at trace levels or below detection limits in most samples.

Scanning electron microscopy with Energy-Dispersive Spectrometry (SEM-EDS)

SEM-EDS compositional analyses were undertaken by EW and LW on a JEOL6100 SEM (University of New England). In total, 62 samples were analysed from the 1958-1963 excavations on Failaka, including material from Tell F3 and Tell F6; 56 of these showed areas of metal preservation suitable for compositional analyses. Combinations of the following elements were measured: O, S, Cl, Fe, Co, Ni, Cu, Zn, As, Se, Ag, Sn, Sb, Te, Pb. For each sample, BSE compositional imaging was used to identify areas of best preservation that were then analysed by an EDS area scan. Quantifications of the EDS spectra were undertaken using standardless ZAF corrections in the analytical software. Typically, two area scans were conducted per sample and the results averaged to determine bulk composition. In addition, point analyses of the main metal phase(s) and inclusions were also undertaken for most samples. The detection limit for this technique is c. 0.1 wt% for the elements of interest. Weight percentages near or below this limit, although sometimes produced by the analytical software, are unreliable.

Compositional analyses and preservation

The preservation of the metal samples is strongly correlated with the reliability of the compositional data generated from their analysis. Where samples are only lightly corroded, all relevant phases and components can be seen in the polished metallographic specimen and captured in the analysis, allowing an accurate quantification of the original overall or 'bulk' composition of the sample. However, corrosion does not typically proceed evenly through a heterogeneous sample; rather, individual metallurgical phases or components tend to be preferentially corroded in advance of others. For example, many Bronze Age copper-base artefacts from Failaka display preferential corrosion of the interdendritic phases in cast alloys (fig. 377). To the extent that these phases were

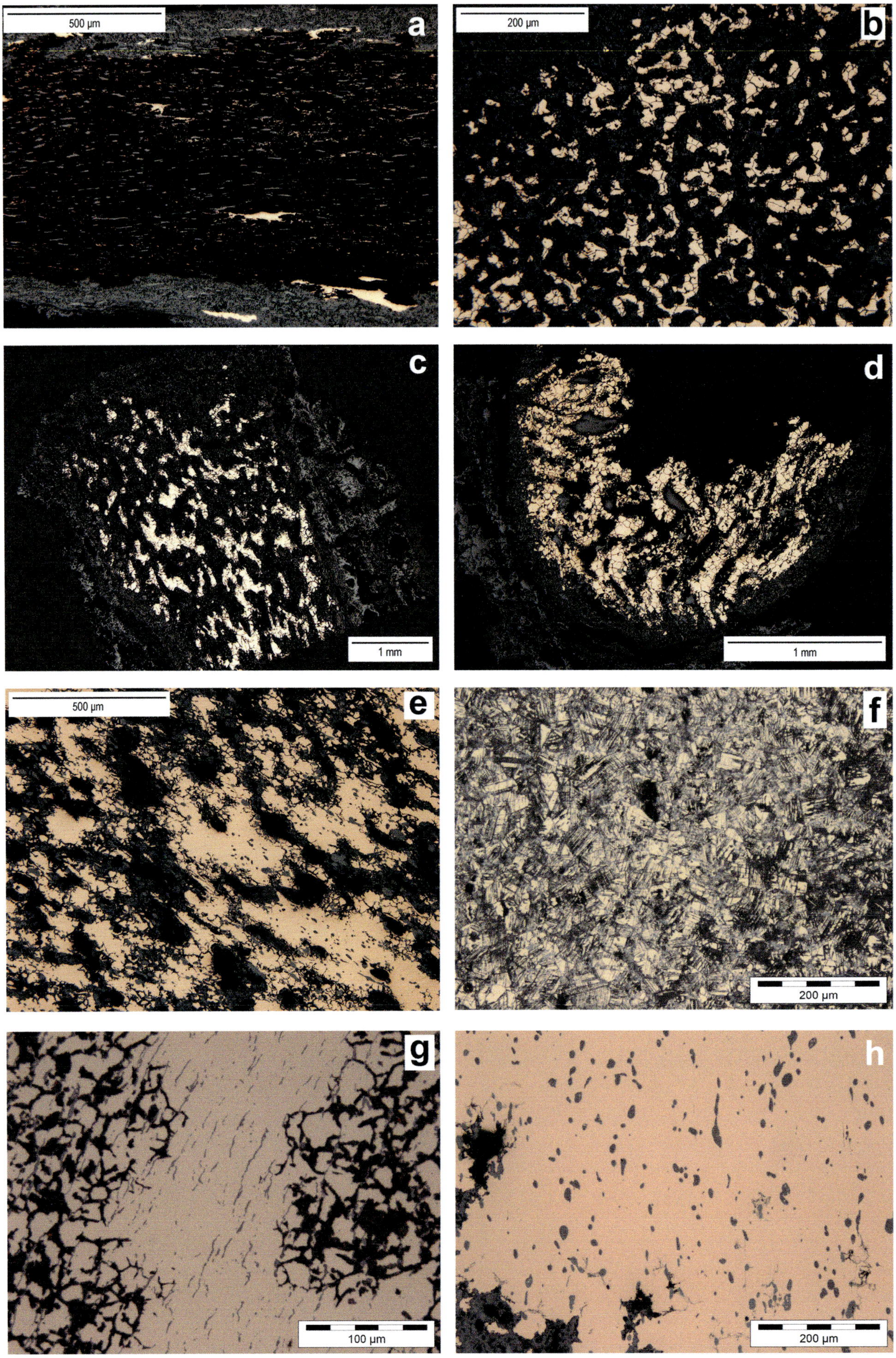
500 µm
a
200 µm
b
c
1 mm
d
1 mm
500 µm
e
f
200 µm
g
100 µm
h
200 µm

◀ Fig. 377. Metallographs of samples from Failaka showing various states of preservation and corrosion patterns. a) 10-139, almost entirely corroded with only small, isolated islands of metal remaining, with abundant, well-preserved, elongated sulphide inclusions; b) 11-385 with small islands of metal preserved across the section, but total corrosion of inter-dendritic spaces; c) 11-316, showing larger islands of preserved metal in a pervasively corroded section; d) 11-062, showing a significant proportion of preserved metal, and preferential corrosion highlighting a banded structure from heavy forging; e) 10-248, showing strong preferential corrosion of inter-dendritic spaces and corrosion along grain-boundaries in better preserved areas; f) 11-387, showing extensive intra-granular corrosion along slip lines; g) 11-401, showing coherent areas of well-preserved metal with frequent inclusions; and h) 11-405, showing substantial areas of well-preserved metal with frequent inclusions.

compositionally distinct from the dendrite core – a fundamental feature of cast alloys – the original bulk composition of the artefacts cannot be reconstructed based only on analysis of surviving uncorroded areas in the dendrite core. Thus, good preservation supports more reliable quantification of bulk composition, and in such cases the SEM-EDS area scans satisfactorily represent bulk composition. SEM-EDS point analyses, where undertaken, provide additional insights into the composition of specific phases and components, typically the main metal phase and non-metallic inclusions (the latter of which are very common in the Failaka assemblage). The averaged EPMA-WDS point analyses are also presented here as a proxy for the bulk alloy composition (Table 1: fig. 378). However, they are weighted heavily towards the composition of the metal component of the alloy rather than the inclusions and should be regarded as a less robust measure of bulk composition than the SEM-EDS area scans.

In Table 1 below (fig. 378), the preservation status of each specimen is rated according to a scale from 0 (most heavily corroded) to 4 (least corroded), as follows: 0 = no remaining metal in section; 1 = small, disconnected 'islands' of metal in section, likely not preserving all original phases; 2 = substantial islands of metal in section, but not necessarily preserving all original phases; 3 = coherent areas of surviving metal in section, likely preserving all original phases; 4 = well-preserved metal in section with large, coherent areas preserving all original phases. Samples with a preservation status of 3 or 4 should provide reliable data on bulk composition. The reliability of bulk composition calculations for samples with a preservation status of 1 or 2 is lower.

A summary of the analyses of the finished artefacts is given in Table 1 (fig. 378).

Results

In this section, the results of the compositional analyses are presented in relation to three main categories: 'impurities' of sulphur and iron; trace and minor elements, which considers the presence of cobalt, arsenic, antimony, silver, and nickel; and the common alloying elements tin, lead and zinc. These categories are somewhat arbitrary, as alloying elements, especially if appearing in low concentrations, may represent 'impurities' in the copper metal that derive from the ores that were chosen for smelting, rather than intentional addition. Equally, elements such as arsenic and nickel may be present at higher concentrations through processes of intentional raw material selection and pyrotechnological choices that can be considered as a variety of alloying practice. Nevertheless, the categories serve to introduce compositional variation in the Failaka assemblage, and the nuances of interpretation surrounding technology and intentionality are elaborated in the subsequent discussion (See p. 62-66).

Impurities of sulphur and iron

The artefacts from Failaka are made of copper-base metal with significant levels of impurities, particularly sulphur (S) and iron (Fe) (fig. 379). There are no significant differences in these characteristics according to the provenance of the analysed specimens or their chronology; high levels of sulphur and iron impurities characterise samples from both tells across all periods of occupation.

Based on SEM-EDS bulk compositional analyses, sulphur concentrations range from <0.1-1.4wt% S, with an average of 0.60±0.37wt% S. Sulphur concentrations are significantly lower in the EPMA-WDS analyses, as these are point analyses focused predominantly on the metallic component of the artefact, and sulphur is strongly concentrated into copper-(iron-)sulphide inclusions in the metal, which occur in virtually all samples and can be very abundant (fig. 380). Bulk SEM-EDS iron concentrations range from <0.1-2.79wt% Fe, with an average of 0.39±0.49wt% Fe. EPMA-WDS analyses of iron concentrations show a similar range from <0.01-3.1wt% Fe, with a somewhat higher average of 0.72±0.89wt% Fe.

▶ Fig. 378. Table 1. Samples from Failaka analysed in the present study.

Sample No.	Fig. No.	Field No.	Type	Context	Phase	Preservation	Technique	FLAME group (no.)*	Alloy Type**
10-010		C108-X309	Sheet	Trench C, layer 108	Disturbed	3	EPMA-WDS	CuAsNi (11)	Cu
10-013		C126-X339	Nodule	Trench C, layer 126	1	4	EPMA-WDS	CuNi (5)	CuNi
10-016		A163-X279	Rod	Trench A, layer 163	4	2	EPMA-WDS	CuAsNi (11)	CuSn
10-017		A163-X379	Rod	Trench A, layer 163	4	1	EPMA-WDS	CuAsNi (11)	Cu
10-018		A117-X448	Rod	Trench A, layer 117	?	3	EPMA-WDS	CuAsNi (11)	CuNi
10-019		A136-X340	Fragment	Trench A, layer 136	6	4	EPMA-WDS	CuAsNi (11)	CuSnNi
10-045		A196-X563	Nodule	Trench A, layer 196	4	1	EPMA-WDS	CuAsNi (11)	Cu
10-047		A152-X313	Rod	Trench A, layer 152	4	1	EPMA-WDS	CuAsNi (11)	Cu
10-049		A178-X640	Rod	Trench A, layer 178	4	3	EPMA-WDS	CuAsNi (11)	Cu
10-050		A209-X644	Sheet	Trench A, layer 209	3	2	EPMA-WDS	CuAsNi (11)	CuNi
10-051		A144-X291	Nodule	Trench A, layer 144	5	2	EPMA-WDS	CuAsNi (11)	CuAs
10-057		A120-X432	Nodule	Trench A, layer 120	4	4	EPMA-WDS	CuNi (5)	Cu
10-059		A134-X243	Nodule	Trench A, layer 134	6	2	EPMA-WDS	CuNi (5)	CuSn
10-061		A139-X272	Sheet	Trench A, layer 139	6	3	EPMA-WDS	CuAsNi (11)	CuNi
10-065		A131-X222	Nodule	Trench A, layer 131	6	4	EPMA-WDS	CuNi (5)	CuNi
10-066		A169-X386	Sheet	Trench A, layer 169	4	2	EPMA-WDS	CuAsNi (11)	CuNi
10-074		A180-X492	Nodule	Trench A, layer 180	4	4	EPMA-WDS	CuNi (5)	Cu
10-075		A180-X492	Nodule	Trench A, layer 180	4	3	EPMA-WDS	CuAsNi (11)	CuAsNi
10-077		A136-X254	Rod	Trench A, layer 136	6	3	EPMA-WDS	CuAsNi (11)	CuNi
10-099		A224-X714	Nodule	Trench A, layer 224	2	4	EPMA-WDS	CuAsNi (11)	Cu
10-112		A226-X796	Nodule	Trench A, layer 226	2	3	EPMA-WDS	CuNi (5)	Cu
10-116		A215-X709	Sheet	Trench A, layer 215	2	3	EPMA-WDS	CuAsNi (11)	CuNi
10-118		A215-X709	Sheet	Trench A, layer 215	2	1	EPMA-WDS	CuAsNi (11)	CuAs
10-121		A175-X439	Rod	Trench A, layer 175	4	1	EPMA-WDS	CuAsNi (11)	CuSnAsNi
10-125		A175-X439	Nodule	Trench A, layer 175	4	4	EPMA-WDS	CuAsNi (11)	CuNi
10-137		A175-X459	Rod	Trench A, layer 175	4	3	EPMA-WDS	CuAsNi (11)	CuNi
10-139		A220-X784	Sheet	Trench A, layer 220	2	1	EPMA-WDS	CuAsNi (11)	Cu
10-162		C112-X252	Nodule	Trench C, layer 112	Disturbed	2	EPMA-WDS	CuAsNi (11)	Cu
10-178		E75-X336	Rod	Trench E, layer 75	8	4	EPMA-WDS	CuAsNi (11)	Cu
10-185		E81-X340	Nodule	Trench E, layer 81	6	4	EPMA-WDS	CuAsNi (11)	CuNi
10-191				Tell F6		2	EPMA-WDS	CuNi (5)	Cu
10-200A		E99-X430	Nodule	Trench E, layer 99	6	3	EPMA-WDS	CuAsNi (11)	CuNi
10-200B				Tell F6		4	EPMA-WDS	CuAsNi (11)	CuNi
10-204		E104-X454	Rod	Trench E, layer 104	5	3	EPMA-WDS	CuAsNi (11)	CuNi
10-211		E109-X510	Rod	Trench E, layer 109	5	2	EPMA-WDS	CuAsNi (11)	CuAsNi
10-226		E130-X580	Nodule	Trench E, layer 130	4	3	EPMA-WDS	CuAsNi (11)	CuAs
10-245		E137-X653	Rod	Trench E, layer 137	4	2	EPMA-WDS	CuAsNi (11)	Cu
10-248		E134-X636	Sheet	Trench E, layer 134	5	2	EPMA-WDS	CuAsNi (11)	CuNi
10-249		E137-X641	Nodule	Trench E, layer 137	4	3	EPMA-WDS	CuAsNi (11)	CuNi
10-263		E165-X728	Rod	Trench E, layer 165	4	3	EPMA-WDS	CuAsNi (11)	CuAsNi
10-269		E171-X823	Sheet	Trench E, layer 171	3	2	EPMA-WDS	CuAsNi (11)	CuAsNi
10-270		E171-X823	Nodule	Trench E, layer 171	3	2	EPMA-WDS	CuNi (5)	Cu
10-284A		C128-X359	Nodule	Trench C, layer 128	Disturbed	3	EPMA-WDS	CuAsNi (11)	CuAsNi
11-060		E188-X871	Rod	Trench E, layer 188	3	3	EPMA-WDS	CuAsNi (11)	Cu
11-062		E118-X871	Rod	Trench E, layer 118	5	2	EPMA-WDS	CuAsNi (11)	CuAsNi
11-133		E246-X1123	sheet	Trench E, layer 246	2	2	EPMA-WDS	CuAsNi (11)	CuNi
11-138		E254-X1052	Rod	Trench E, layer 254	3/4	1	EPMA-WDS	CuAsNi (11)	CuAsNi
11-365				Tell F6		1	EPMA-WDS	CuAsAg (9)	Cu
12-013		C223-X812	lump	Trench C, layer 223	Disturbed	3	SEM-EDS	CuAsNi (11)	CuNi
					Period				
10-284B		F6	nodule			3	SEM-EDS	CuAsNi (11)	CuAsNi
11-303	296	881.SD	sheet, scrap	Trench RM, 42-52 N, level 6.79-6.35		3	SEM-EDS	CuAsNi (11)	Cu
11-307	340	F6.264	sheet, box	Trench SN 11-13 N, 0-1.5 E, level -0.69		2	SEM-EDS	CuAsNi (11)	CuSnAs
11-315	373	F6.1035	lump	Trench N2, level 0.78		3	SEM-EDS	CuAsNi (11)	CuAsNi
11-316	74	F3.bfc	hoe	Trench J, 76 N, 3E, level 6.42	2	2	SEM-EDS	CuAsNi (11)	Cu
11-317	355	F6.1020A	cleaver	Trench F1, 1-3 N, 4-8 W, level -1.41		3	SEM-EDS	CuAsNi (11)	CuNi
11-319		F3.72	rod, square section	Trench RM, 32.8 N, 0.6 W, level c. 8.20		4	SEM-EDS	CuNi (5)	CuNi

11-322		F3.bo	rod, square section	Trench B, sieve		3	SEM-EDS	CuAsNi (11)	CuNi
11-325		F3.te	dagger blade	Trenches Æ and Ø, sieve		3	SEM-EDS	CuAsNi (11)	CuNi
11-332		F3.rt	rod, square section	Trench Æ, sieve		3	SEM-EDS	CuAsSbNi (14)	Cu
11-333	368	F3.rt	lump	Trench Æ, sieve		4	SEM-EDS	CuAsNi (11)	CuNi
11-338	52	F3.bej.B	dagger blade	Trench AA, level 6.52-6.43	2	2	SEM-EDS	CuAsNi (11)	Cu
11-348	98	F3.baf	knife	Trench AO, level 7.63-6.63	4A/B?	1	SEM-EDS	CuAsNi (11)	CuNi
11-357		F3.bdr	awl	Trench Y, level 5.36	2	4	SEM-EDS	CuAsNi (11)	CuSn
11-358	82	F3.bbc	axe	Trench AO, 63.25 N, 5 W, level 6.65	4A/B?	3	SEM-EDS	CuAsNi (11)	Cu
11-360		F3.bab	rod, square section	F3, sieve		3	SEM-EDS	CuAsNi (11)	CuNi
11-361		F6.1194	rod, round section	Trench F1, 4-5 N, 6-7 W, level -1.94	1	2	SEM-EDS	CuAsNi (11)	Cu
11-373	69	F6.1205	arrowhead	Trench M1, 1-2 N, 8-10 W, level -1.28.		4	SEM-EDS	CuAsNi (11)	CuNi
11-385		F3.ajo	rod, square section	Trenches C-D, G-H or K-L		2	SEM-EDS	CuAgNi (8)	CuSn
11-386		F3.xk	rod, square section	Trenches Æ-X, level 9.60-8.15	3B/4B	3	SEM-EDS	CuAsNi (11)	CuSn
11-387		F3.ajo	rod, square section	Trenches C-D, G-H or K-L		2	SEM-EDS	CuAsNi (11)	CuSn
11-388		F3.xk	rod, square section	Trenches Æ-X, level 9.60-8.15.	3B/4B	2	SEM-EDS	CuAsNi (11)	CuNi
11-389		F3.ajo	rod, square section	Trenches C-D, G-H or K-L		2	SEM-EDS	CuAsNi (11)	Cu
11-390	127	F6.58	chisel	Trench SS 21.6 S, 1.4 E, level -1.80.		4	SEM-EDS	CuAsNi (11)	CuNi
11-391		F3.ajo	rod, square section	Trenches C-D, G-H or K-L		2	SEM-EDS	CuAsNi (11)	Cu
11-398	255	F3.xw	nail	Trench AG, level 9.35-8.03	3B?	3	SEM-EDS	CuAsNi (11)	CuNi
11-400	262	F6.655.1	nail	Trench F2, 17-18 N, 5-6 W, level -0.57.		2	SEM-EDS	CuAsNi (11)	Cu
11-401	254	F3.xk	nail	Trenches Æ-X, level 9.60-8.15.	3B/4B	2	SEM-EDS	CuAsSbNi (14)	CuAsNi
11-402	253	F3.xk.B	nail	Trenches Æ-X, level 9.60-8.15.	3B/4B	3	SEM-EDS	CuAsNi (11)	CuNi
11-404		F3.49	rod, round section	Trench RM, 20.8 N, 3.45 W, 1.2 below surface		4	SEM-EDS	CuAsNi (11)	CuNi
11-405		881.RS	rod, square section	Trench RM, 45-50 N, level c. 6.85-6.35		4	SEM-EDS	CuAsNi (11)	CuNi
11-406	97	F3.qt	knife?	Trenches X-Z, sieve		4	SEM-EDS	CuAsNi (11)	Cu
11-413	47	F3.øm.C	blade	Trench AE, sieve		3	SEM-EDS	CuAsNi (11)	Cu
11-410	46	F3.ømB	dagger blade	Trench AE, sieve		2	SEM-EDS	CuAsSbNi (14)	CuAsNi
11-417	297	F3.xk	sheet, scrap	Trenches Æ-X, level 9.60-8.15	3B/4B	2	SEM-EDS	CuAsSbNi (14)	Cu
11-418	277	F3.qn	vessel, rim	Trench Z, level 8.35-7.36	3B/4	3	SEM-EDS	CuAsNi (11)	Cu
11-419		F6.518	vessel, rim	Trench D1, 1-10 N, 1-4 W, level -1.08		2	SEM-EDS	CuAsAgNi (15)	CuSn
11-432	107	F3.ro	chisel/drill	Trench Y, 64 N, 1.5 W, level 7.06	4B	2	SEM-EDS	CuNi (5)	Cu
11-434	176	F3.dt	needle	Trench F, 40.80 N, 5.10 E		4	SEM-EDS	CuNi (5)	Cu
11-435	185	F3.yt	needle	Trench AI, level 8.69-8.30	4A	4	SEM-EDS	CuAsNi (11)	Cu
11-436		F3.xk	rod, round section	Trenches Æ-X, level 9.60-8.15.	3B/4B	2	SEM-EDS	CuAsNi (11)	Cu
11-442		F3.ajp	rod, round section	Trench C-D, G-H, or K-L		2	SEM-EDS	CuAsNi (11)	CuSn
11-443		F3.ajo	rod, square section	Trenches C-D, G-H or K-L		1	SEM-EDS	CuAsNi (11)	CuNi
11-448			rod, square section			4	SEM-EDS	CuAsNi (11)	Cu
11-460		F3.xk	rod, round section	Trenches Æ-X, level 9.60-8.15.	3B/4B	4	SEM-EDS	CuAsNi (11)	CuNi
11-461		F3.xk	rod, square section	Trenches Æ-X, level 9.60-8.15.	3B/4B	2	SEM-EDS	CuAsNi (11)	CuSnNi
11-462		F3.ajo	rod, round section	Trenches C-D, G-H or K-L		3	SEM-EDS	CuNi (5)	Cu
11-464		F3.zc	rod, round section	Trench AI, level 8.16-7.85	3B, 4	2	SEM-EDS	CuAsNi (11)	Cu
11-465		F6.855	rod, round section	Trench M2, sieve		2	SEM-EDS	CuAsNi (11)	CuNi
11-470		881.SX	rod, curved	Trench RM, sieve		2	SEM-EDS	CuAsNi (11)	CuAsNi
11-473	187	F3.abø	needle	Trench C, level c. 7.95-7.65	3A/4B	4	SEM-EDS	CuAsNi (11)	CuNi
11-479		F3.xk	rod, square section	Trenches Æ-X, level 9.60-8.15	3B/4B	3	SEM-EDS	CuAsNi (11)	CuNi
11-491	217	F3.115	hook	Trench RM, 3-15 N, 1-2.45 m depth.		2	SEM-EDS	CuAsNi (11)	Cu
11-494	236	F6.803	hook	Trench M2, sieve from above level -1.07		2	SEM-EDS	CuAsNi (11)	Cu
11-500	202	F3.j	hook	Trench A, 28.72 N, 3.82 E, level 8.23	3B	2	SEM-EDS	CuAsSbNi (14)	Cu

* FLAME group and group number indicate the presence of elements (As, Sb, Ag, Ni) at ≥0.1 wt% following Pollard (2018: p. 86; see text for details).
** Alloy type incorporates elements (Ni, As, Sn, Pb and/or Zn) present at ≥1 wt%.

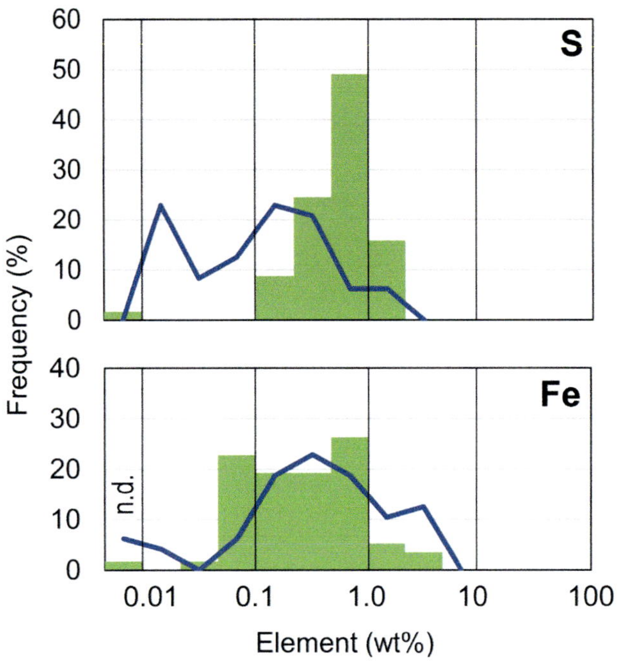

Fig. 379. Frequency histograms of the concentrations in weight percent (wt%) of sulphur (S) and iron (Fe) in the analysed samples from Failaka. Green blocks represent data from SEM-EDS analyses (n=56) while dark blue lines represent data from EPMA-WDS analyses (n=48). The leftmost column of each chart presents values that fall below the detection limits for each technique: 'n.d.' means 'not detected'.

Point analyses (SEM-EDS and EPMA-WDS) of the sulphide inclusions indicates that they are close to chalcocite (Cu_2S) in composition, occasionally containing up to c. 8wt% Fe. The copper-iron-sulphide inclusions sometimes incorporate minor to low-major concentrations of selenium (up to 2.6wt% Se) and tellurium (up to 0.57wt% Te), as determined by SEM-EDS point analyses; this is a typical characteristic of copper sulphide inclusions in ancient artefacts (Rehren & Northover 1991) and reflects trace elements carried over from the original sulphide ores. Se and Te concentrations in excess of 1% have been noted to exhibit distinct ratios within metal groups, which may be indicative of their source. However, more analyses of sulphide inclusions in copper from the Persian Gulf region are required to explore this issue with confidence.

Nickel, arsenic, cobalt, silver, and antimony

The metal artefacts from Failaka display a significant degree of homogeneity in their minor (0.1-1.0wt%) and trace element (<0.1wt%) characteristics (fig. 381). Both SEM-EDS and EPMA-WDS analyses indicate the commonplace occurrence of nickel (Ni) and arsenic (As) at minor to low-major concentrations, alongside cobalt (Co) at high-trace to minor concentrations. Other elements such as silver (Ag), and antimony (Sb), typically occur at concentrations near or below the analytical detection limits. There are no significant differences in these characteristics according to the provenance of the analysed specimens – from Tell F3 or Tell F6 – or according to their chronology within the Failaka sequence. Material from both tells is compositionally similar across all periods of occupation.

Ni, As and Co concentrations (fig. 381) show strongly normal distributions, indicative of a relatively homogeneous metal composition. This may indicate the dominance of a single or a very limited number of copper sources, but can theoretically be explained also by commonplace recycling and mixing of metal from different sources. The concentration ranges and averages of these elements reported in the EPMA-WDS analyses are similar to those derived from the SEM-EDS data, although Ni and As EPMA-WDS concentrations are skewed somewhat higher by the fact that they tend to concentrate in the metallic phase rather than in the copper-sulphide inclusions. Based on SEM-EDS analyses, Ni concentrations range from 0.39-5.24wt% Ni, with an average of 1.10 ± 0.69wt% Ni; EPMA-WDS analyses indicate a range from 0.09-5.1wt% Ni with an average of 1.29 ± 1.06wt% Ni. SEM-EDS As concentrations range from <0.1-1.9wt%As, with an average of 0.51 ± 0.41wt% As; EPMA-WDS analyses indicate a range from <0.01-2.5wt% As with an average of 0.63 ± 0.57wt% As. SEM-EDS Co concentrations range from <0.1-0.95wt% Co, with an average of 0.17 ± 0.16wt% Co; EPMA-WDS analyses indicate a range from <0.01-0.85wt% Co with an average of 0.12 ± 0.14wt% Co.

The concentrations of As, Ni, and Co are generally inter-correlated with each other, and with Fe. The strongest correlation is between iron and cobalt, seen clearly in both the SEM-EDS and EPMA-WDS analyses; perhaps a quarter to a half of the compositional variation in these elements can be ascribed to correlation. Iron and nickel are correlated in the SEM-EDS area analyses and in SEM-EDS point analyses of the preserved metal component, although not in the EPMA-WDS dataset. As and Ni are more weakly correlated; with less than ~20% of the variation in these element

▸ Fig. 380. Metallographs of metallurgical production residue samples 10-013 (top, unetched) and 11-315 (bottom, etched with ferric chloride), showing abundant blue-grey copper-(iron-)sulphide inclusions in the copper-base metal matrix. The etched specimen 11-315 also exhibits darker and lighter areas indicative of variations in As and Ni concentrations due to coring of the alloy during solidification.

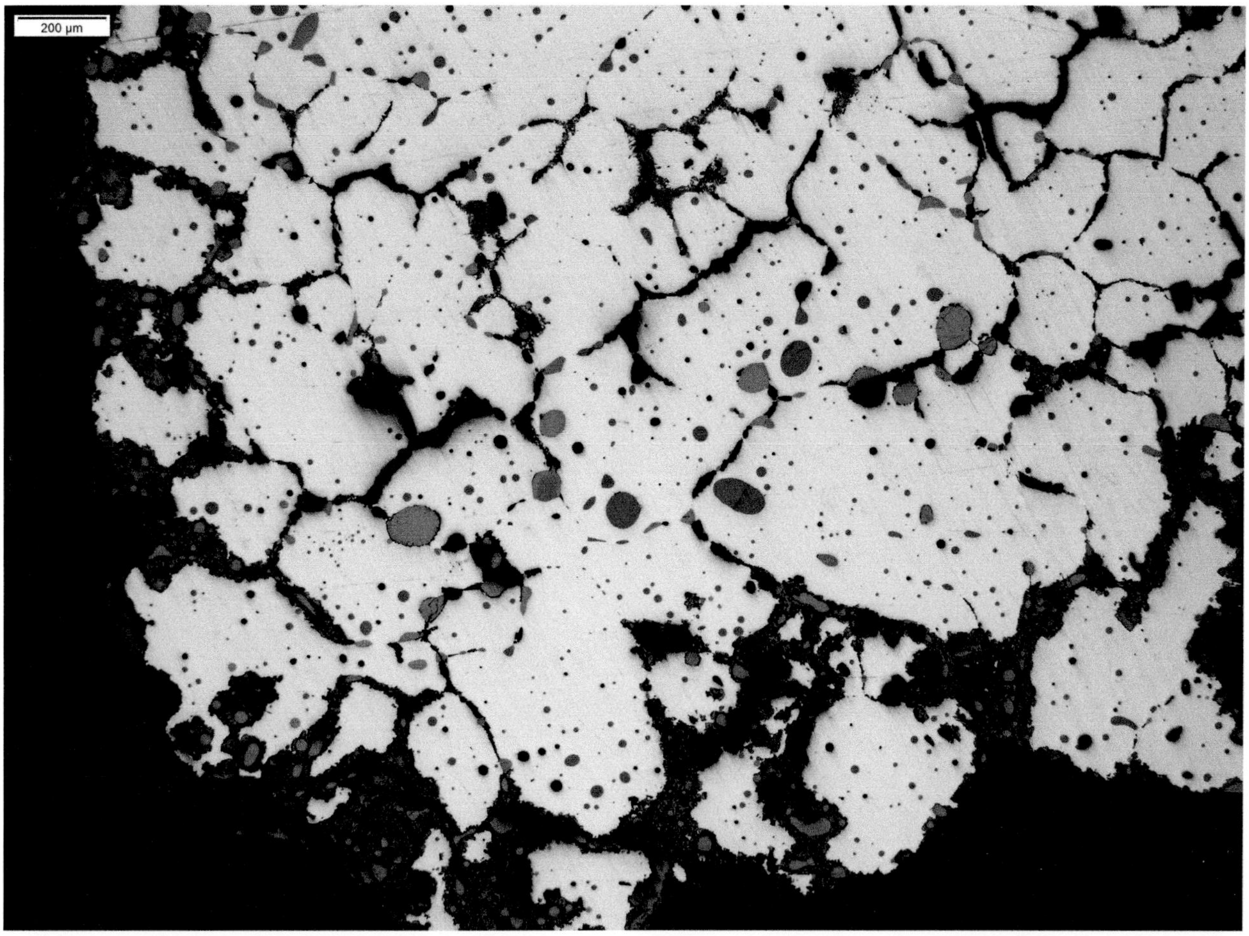
200 µm

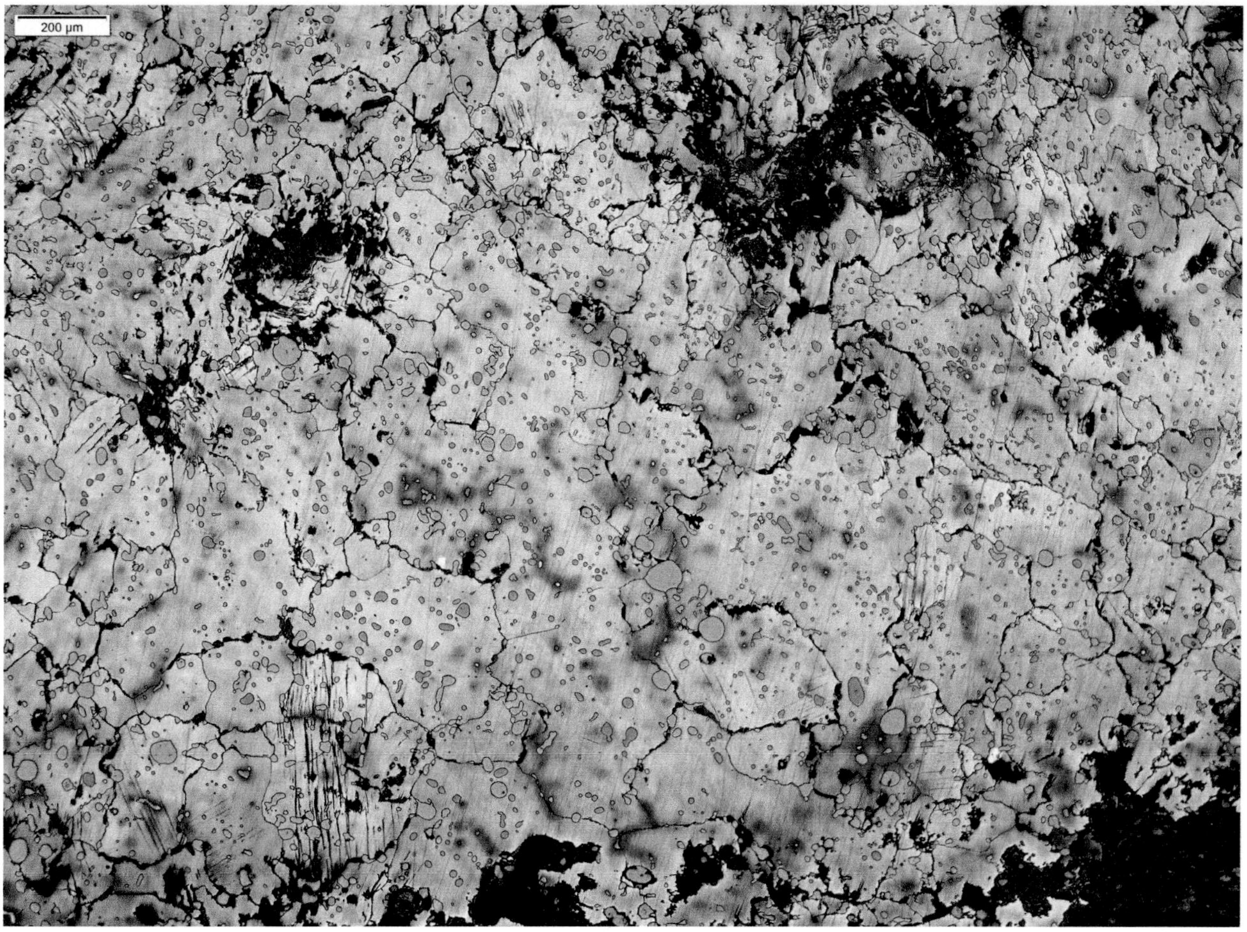
200 µm

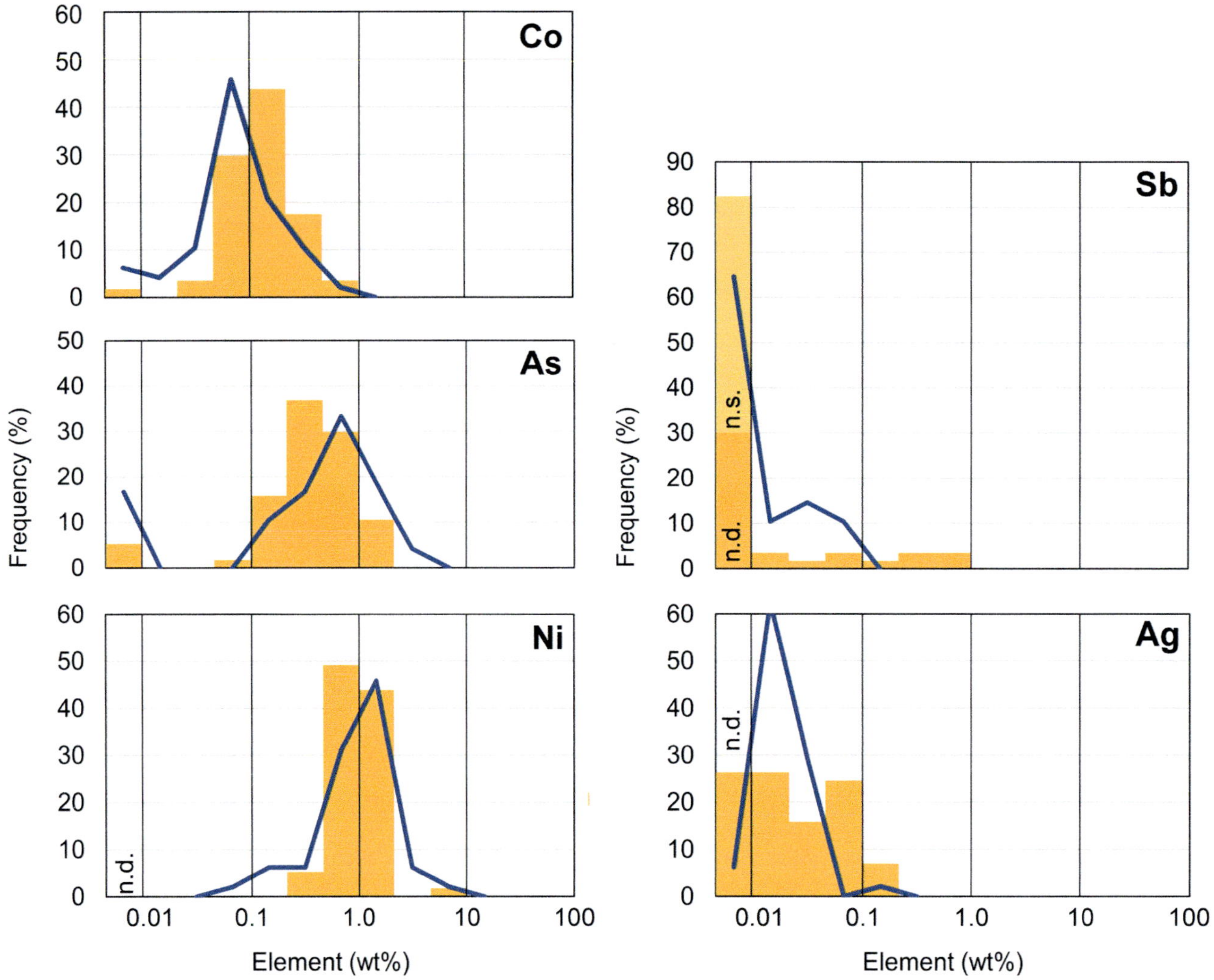

Fig. 381. Frequency histograms of the concentrations in weight percent (wt%) of cobalt (Co), arsenic (As), antimony (Sb), silver (Ag) and nickel (Ni) in the analysed samples from Failaka. Yellow blocks represent data from SEM-EDS analyses (n=56) while dark blue lines represent data from EPMA-WDS analyses (n=48). The leftmost column of each chart presents values that fall below the detection limits for each technique: 'n.d.' means 'not detected'. For Sb, 'n.s.' means 'not sought'.

compositions attributable to correlation. Nevertheless, correlations between As, Ni and Co concentrations are pervasive in metallurgical assemblages from the Persian Gulf region, particularly in eastern Arabia (Begemann et al. 2010). This consistent pattern likely reflects the prevalence of metal (and the mineralogy of ores) from a specific source region, most probably SE Arabia.

As indicated in fig. 381, most Ag and Sb concentrations fall below 0.1wt%; indeed, Sb was not sought in the majority of SEM-EDS analyses, due to the absence of relevant peaks in the visual observation of the EDS spectra. A minor exception to this pattern is provided by five Failaka samples analysed by SEM-EDS, for which possible Sb peaks were visually identified in the EDS spectra; re-analysis of these samples indicated that they contained between c. 0.1-0.5% Sb. In general, the concentrations of Ag and Sb in the Failaka assemblage strongly accord with previous analyses of Bronze Age copper-base artefacts and ingots from the Persian Gulf region (e.g., Begemann et al. 2010 figs. 2a, 2c).

Tin, zinc and lead

Tin, zinc, and lead are the three elements predominantly employed for alloying in the developed metallurgical industries of ancient Western Asia. Their concentrations in such alloys can be highly variable, but a value of >1wt% is commonly used as a differentiation point between alloys and non-alloys. There are considerable difficulties in the identification of the 'intentional' alloy production in the Bronze Age and earlier, as further discussed below in p. 70-73. The presence of tin, zinc and lead in the analysed samples from Failaka is illustrated in fig. 382. In general, there are no discernible differences in tin, zinc and lead levels between the two tells or across the various phases of occupation.

Tin concentrations in the Failaka assemblage are broad, ranging from less than the analytical detection limits to c. 13wt% Sn. Both the SEM-EDS and EPMA-WDS analyses show that two-thirds of samples (37 of 56; 33 of 48) have trace tin concentrations (<0.1wt% Sn). A further ~20% of the analysed specimens (12 of 56; 11 of 48) show concentrations from c. 0.1-0.9wt% Sn. These likely reflect the presence of small amounts of Sn from other metal sources introduced during recycling and remelting activities. Only around 10% of the analysed assemblage (8 of 56; 4 of 48) have Sn concentrations >1wt% and can therefore be classified as bronze alloys. Six of these have low concentrations of c. 1-3 wt% Sn that likely reflect the dilution of tin concentrations by mixing bronze with unalloyed copper stock during metal recycling. In contrast, six artefacts show more substantial tin concentrations from c. 5-13 wt% Sn that match typical bronze alloys as known from many regions of SW Asia at this time. Although the bronzes in the Failaka assemblage tend to have slightly lower average concentrations of S, Fe, Co, Ni and As than the remainder of the analysed assemblage, and slightly higher concentrations of Pb, these distinctions are not strong, and the bronzes fall into the same metal compositional groups (see p. 67-70) that dominate the Failaka metals.

Some variation can be seen in bronze use on Failaka according to artefact typology. In particular, rods and awls appear to comprise a higher proportion of bronzes (8 of 12 recorded bronzes) than other analysed categories such as sheet or vessel fragments (two examples) or amorphous lumps (one example). The low proportion of bronze among the analysed metalworking debris may suggest that bronze working on Failaka was comparatively limited in comparison to the processing of copper-base metal without tin, although the absolute numbers of bronzes analysed are too small to offer this hypothesis with any great certainty.

In contrast to tin, the artefacts from Failaka show no evidence for intentional alloying with zinc or lead. Zinc concentrations in the Failaka samples are typically below the reliable SEM-EDS detection limit of 0.1wt%; the more sensitive EPMA-WDS analyses exhibit a similar pattern, with concentrations ranging from <0.01-0.13wt% Zn and an average of 0.07±0.02wt% Zn. Lead concentrations are similarly low. SEM-EDS analyses indicate that most samples have Pb concentrations below the reliable EDS detection limit of c. 0.1wt%. Around a quarter of the analysed specimens show higher Pb concentrations between c. 0.1-0.3wt% Pb, with a single outlier at 0.59% Pb.

It is possible that concentrations at or around the detection limit are artefacts of the analytical quantification software. However, as Pb is virtually insoluble in copper, any Pb in copper-base metal artefacts tends to be present as distinct Pb-rich metallic inclusions within the metal matrix or incorporated into copper-sulphide inclusions. The analyses of the sulphide inclusions in the Failaka copper artefacts do not show any reliable evidence for the presence of Pb at measurable concentrations, but high atomic-weight metallic inclusions are observed in a small proportion of the specimens from Failaka (fig. 383) and have been confirmed as Pb-rich by SEM-EDS and EPMA-WDS

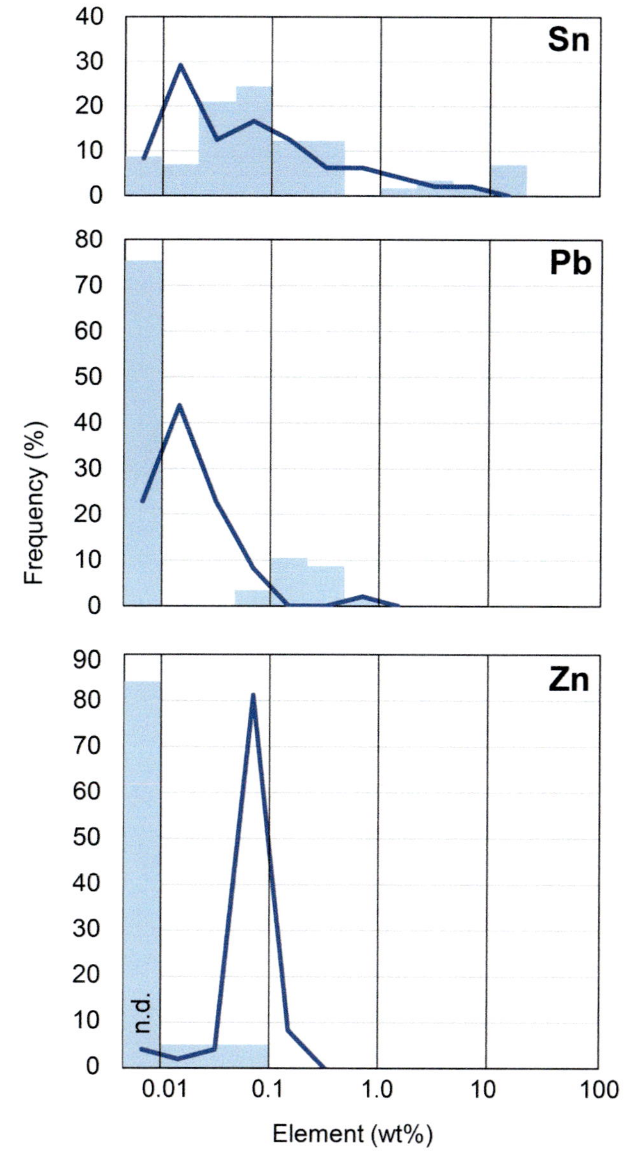

Fig. 382. Frequency histograms of the concentrations in weight percent (wt%) of tin (Sn), lead (Pb), and zinc (Zn) in the analysed samples from Failaka. Light blue blocks represent data from SEM-EDS analyses (n=56) while dark blue lines represent data from EPMA-WDS analyses (n=48). The leftmost column of each chart presents values that fall below the detection limits for each technique: 'n.d.' means 'not detected'.

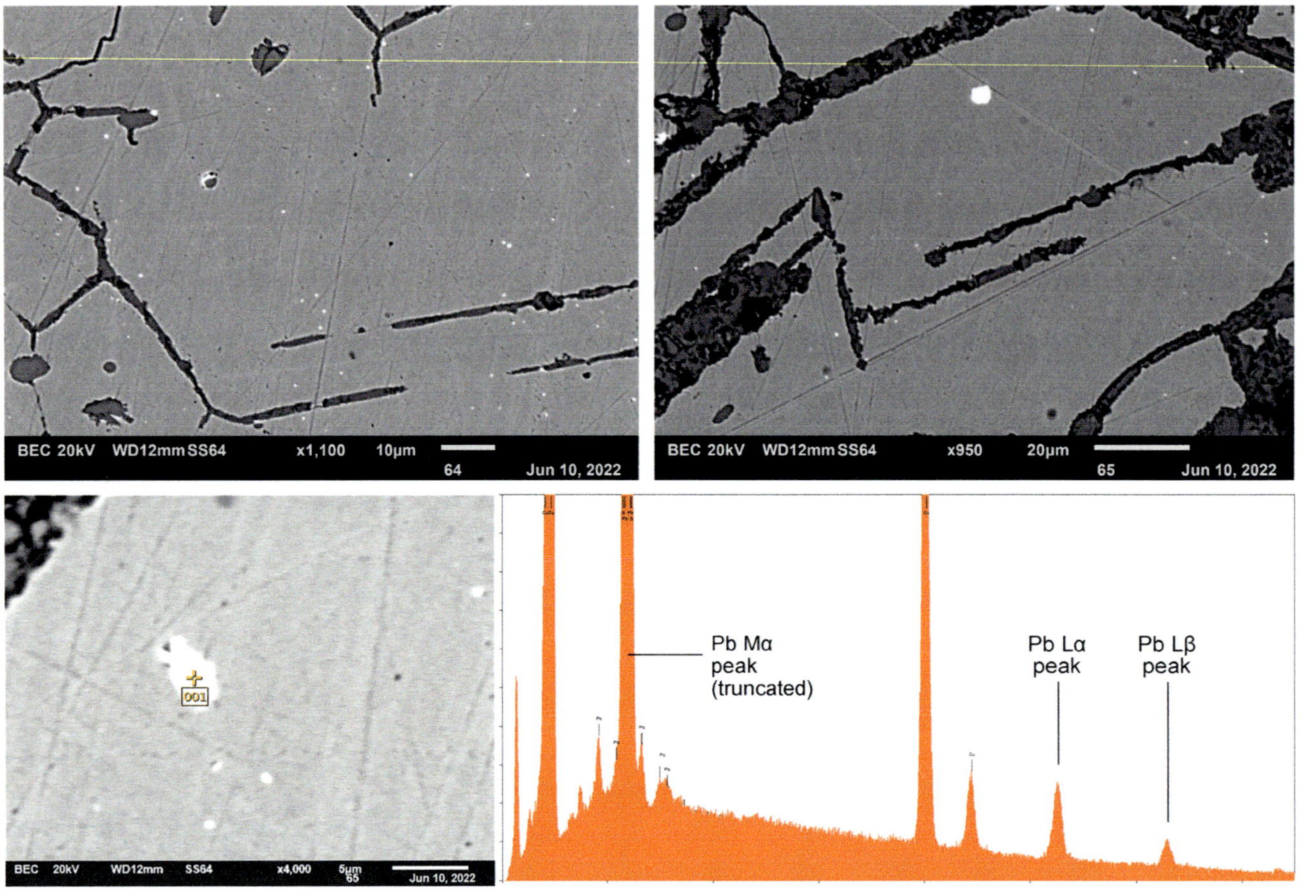

Fig. 383. Lead (Pb) inclusions in the sample 11-316, a cleaver or hoe, with c. 0.07wt% Pb, just below the reliable detection limit of 0.1wt%. The inclusions stand out as small bright/white points on the SEM using BSE compositional imaging mode. The EDS spectrum (lower right) for a point analysis of one of the bright inclusions in 11-316 shows clear peaks for Pb.

point analyses. Given the general impoverishment of Pb concentrations in copper metal circulating in the Persian Gulf (e.g., Prange 2001), the few instances of measurable and/or observable Pb in the Failaka artefacts likely reflect the inadvertent incorporation of small amounts of Pb from 'scrap' metal, probably of non-Omani origin, during workshop processes such as recycling and remelting.

Discussion

Metallurgical activities on Failaka

The material assemblage from the Danish excavations on Failaka provides abundant evidence that testifies to secondary metalworking activities on the island during the Bronze Age. A significant number of crucible fragments (infra p. 49-50, Højlund 2021 p. 130-131) – not yet scientifically studied – as well as rare mould fragments, and abundant metalworking residues from Tell F3 and Tell F6 indicate that raw metal imported into the island in ingot form was melted (in the process being somewhat further refined) and cast, possibly after the addition of recycled scrap metal or alloying components, in order to produce a range of tools and artefacts that Højlund (above p. 15) accurately describes as "a simple, utilitarian repertoire". Excavations document the ubiquity of such remains, even if true metallurgical workshops are yet to be definitively identified within the excavated areas of Tell F3 or Tell F6. They also indicate that metallurgical activities were a feature of all periods of occupation documented at these sites, including not only the early second millennium BCE when the large-scale exchange of copper in the Persian Gulf is well known from Mesopotamian written sources, but also the deposits of the later Old Babylonian and Kassite Periods, when the Mesopotamian sources are silent on metal from the south. In fact, the recent excavations at Tell F3 document an apparent expansion in metalworking in the later phases of occupation at the site (Højlund 2021 p. 130).

The archaeometallurgical studies of a subset of this assemblage further support this reconstruction of craft practices on Bronze Age Failaka. Although the lack of analysis of the crucibles and their residues remains a significant lacuna in our understanding of metalworking on the island, the analyses of many examples of finished artefacts and metal residues presented here has allowed the identification of their shared compositional characteristics and supports the identification of many of the residues as casting spills. Preliminary metallographic analyses of the assemblage identify the expected 'as cast' microstructures among these residues, and ongoing studies will further confirm and better quantify these initial observations.

Raw copper and refining practices in the Persian Gulf Region

The compositional analyses identify prevalent impurities of sulphur and iron in the copper-base metal from Failaka, principally present as copper-(iron-) sulphide inclusions. Although such impurities can be relatively easily removed from copper in a 'fire refining' stage prior to artefact manufacture, and iron levels can be reduced unintentionally by simply remelting the metal (Craddock & Meeks 1987 p. 192. Merkel 1990), the practice on Failaka appears to have been to use metal that was relatively unrefined. This tradition can also be seen in artefacts from second millennium BCE sites in the greater Persian Gulf region, such as Qarn al-Harf in the U.A.E. (Weeks et al. in press), Haft Tepe in Khuzestan (Oudbashi et al. 2019 fig. 4. Oudbashi et al. 2014 p. 169, fig. 10), and Kaftari period Tal-e Malyan in Fars (Pigott et al. 2003 p. 170ff., figs. 14.11b, 14.13a, 14.15a, b) which include abundant sulphide inclusions, sometimes heavily deformed during the process of artefact fabrication through forging. Based on their ubiquity, such impurities do not appear to have had a significantly deleterious effect on the workability of the metal or the viability of the artefacts produced from it.

Copper-iron-sulphide impurities in the artefacts reflect the presence of these impurities in the raw metal that reached Failaka through the Persian Gulf exchange system (cf. Howarth 2018 p. 276 ff. on iron impurities in eastern Arabia and southern Mesopotamia). Analyses of broadly contemporary ingots from Saar on Bahrain (Weeks & Collerson 2005) indicate that they contain abundant sulphide inclusions. Likewise, second millennium BCE copper-base ingots from Haft Tepe, Iran (Oudbashi et al. 2019) contain numerous copper-sulphide inclusions and other impurities such as (hydrated) iron oxides. Their presence in the raw metal traded in the greater Persian Gulf region indicates that sulphur-rich copper ores comprised at least a component of the furnace

FLAME Group	SEM-EDS	EPMA-WDS	EDS+WDS
Cu (1)	0	0	0
CuAs (2)	0	0	0
CuSb (3)	0	0	0
CuAg (4)	0	0	0
CuNi (5)	4 (7.1%)	8 (16.7%)	12 (11.5%)
CuAsSb (6)	0	0	0
CuSbAg (7)	0	0	0
CuAgNi (8)	1 (1.8%)	0	1 (1.0%)
CuAsAg (9)	0	1 (2.1%)	1 (1.0%)
CuSbNi (10)	0	0	0
CuAsNi (11)	45 (80.4%)	39 (81.3%)	84 (80.8%)
CuAsSbAg (12)	0	0	0
CuSbAgNi (13)	0	0	0
CuAsSbNi (14)	5 (8.9%)	0	5 (4.8%)
CuAsAgNi (15)	1 (1.8%)	0	1 (1.0%)
CuAsSbAgNi (16)	0	0	0
	n=56	n=48	n=104

Fig. 384. Table 2. Occurrence of FLAME metal groups in the Failaka assemblage.

charge at the primary smelting sites (e.g., Rostoker et al. 1989). However, a predominant focus on sulphide smelting at this time cannot be assumed, as oxidised ores and the metal smelted from them can sometimes be characterised by significant sulphur content due to the casual/unintentional smelting of oxide and sulphide ores that commonly co-occur in mineral deposits (e.g., Leese et al. 1986 p. 103. Tylecote et al. 1977. Hauptmann 2014 p. 104). The elemental and lead isotope composition of the ingots from Saar (Weeks & Collerson 2005) supports a provenance from south-eastern Arabia, Bronze Age *Makkan*, however the presence of abundant copper sulphide inclusions in the Failaka metals cannot alone be taken as indicative of any specific provenance.

Compositional groups in the Failaka Assemblage in regional perspective

The compositional characteristics of the Failaka metals can be usefully compared against wider regional patterns of metallurgy using the methodology developed by the FLAME project (Flow of Ancient Metal in Eurasia; Pollard 2018), sometimes called the Oxford approach (e.g., Bray et al. 2015). This methodology focuses on the concentrations of four elements – arsenic (As), antimony (Sb), silver (Ag) and nickel (Ni) – and particularly whether they are present above or below a threshold composition; this threshold can vary but is typically set at 0.1wt%, calculated after compositional data are normalised after the removal

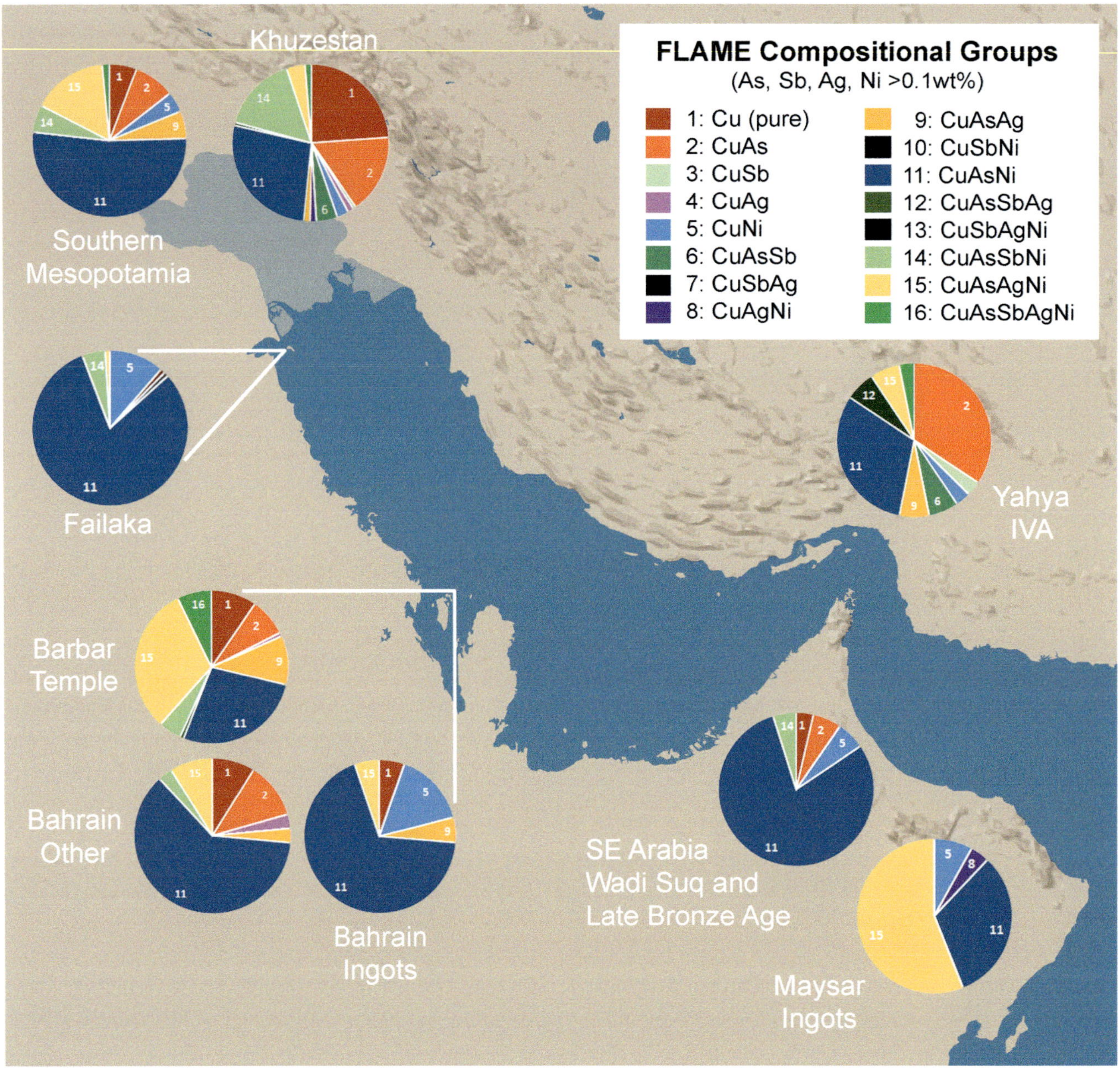

Fig. 385. A map of copper groups in 2nd millennium BCE (and earlier) metal assemblages from the greater Persian Gulf region, following the FLAME methodology (see text for details). Assemblage and analytical information as follows: 'Failaka' comprises artefacts presented in the present study (N=104, EPMA-WDS and SEM-EDS analyses); 'Barbar Temple' comprises Early Dilmun artefacts from the Barbar Temple (Sangmeister 2003. Heskel 2003. N=125, OES and spectrographic analyses); 'Bahrain Ingots' comprises Early Dilmun copper ingot samples from Nasaria, Qala'at al-Bahrain, Saar and unspecified locations on Bahrain (Prange 2001. Weeks and Collerson 2005. N=19, SEM-EDS, PIXE, and ICP-OES analyses); 'Bahrain Other' comprises Early Dilmun artefacts from Qala'at al-Bahrain, Saar, Ali, Diraz and Hamad Town (Prange 2001. Weeks and Collerson 2005. N=34, ICP-OES, SEM-EDS, and PIXE analyses); 'SE Arabia' comprises Wadi Suq period and Late Bronze Age artefacts from Qarn al-Harf, Al-Wasit, Bait Kshob, Akhdar, Masirah, al-Suwaiq, Nizwa and Samad (Weeks et al. in press. Prange 2001. N=84, EPMA-WDS and ICP-OES analyses); 'Maysar Ingots' comprises Umm an-Nar period copper ingots from Maysar, Oman (Prange 2001. N=25, ICP-OES analyses); 'Mesopotamia' comprises 2nd millennium BCE artefacts of the Isin-Larsa, Old Babylonian, and Kassite Periods from Ur, Uruk, Tello and Nippur (compiled in Cuenod 2013. N=69; XRF analyses); 'Khuzestan' comprises early- to mid-2nd millennium BCE artefacts from Susa and Haft Tepe (Malfoy & Menu 1987. Cuenod 2013. Oudbashi et al. 2012, 2019. Rafiei Alavi 2015. N=159, OES, UV-Emission Spectrometry, micro-PIXE, SEM-EDS and EPMA-WDS analyses); 'Yahya IVA' comprises artefacts from Tepe Yahya period IVA, c. 2000-1600 BCE (Thornton et al. 2002. N=32, ICP-MS and EPMA-WDS analyses).

of possible intentional alloying elements (Sn, Zn, Pb at concentrations of >1wt%). Characterisation using the FLAME methodology allows the identification of the presence and proportions in any assemblage of 16 possible metal compositional groups (Pollard 2018 p. 86, Tab. 1). The assessment of the patterns generated by the FLAME characterisation can then be considered alongside other evidence, including the average and range of specific elemental compositions and the presence of alloy types, as a way of understanding broad patterns of metal 'flow' within interconnected systems of metal production, exchange, and use.

The FLAME compositional groups identified in the Failaka metal artefacts are presented in Table 1 (fig. 378) and summarised in Table 2 (fig. 384). There is very close agreement between the SEM-EDS area scans and the averaged EPMA-WDS point analyses; both show a dominance of metal group 11 (CuAsNi), comprising about 80% of the assemblage, with a minor proportion of group 5 (CuNi). The SEM-EDS analyses also suggest the minor presence of metal group 14 (CuAsSbNi), which was not observed in the EPMA-WDS analyses. Other metal group types are rare, occurring only singly in the combined datasets. In general, the prevalence of Ni-containing metal groups in the Failaka assemblage is clear.

The FLAME compositional groups identified at Failaka can be compared with patterns from neighbouring areas in the greater Persian Gulf region – including SE Arabia, Bahrain, southern Mesopotamia and southern Iran – to explore regional patterns of metal circulation (fig. 385). Such comparisons benefit from the comprehensive, trans-regional research on metal compositions in the PhD studies of Cuenod (2012. Cuenod et al. 2015) and Howarth (2018). Of these, the most directly comparable is the work of Howarth, as it uses the same threshold of 0.1 wt% to assess the presence/absence of As, Sb, Ag and Ni.

The proportions of the FLAME compositional groups in the Failaka assemblage show broad similarities with contemporary assemblages from the Persian Gulf region, suggesting a shared participation in circuits of metal exchange. In particular, the high proportion of group 11 (CuAsNi) metal closely mirrors the composition of second millennium BCE assemblages from SE Arabia, including Qarn al-Harf (Weeks et al. in press) and al-Wasit (Yule & Weisgerber 2015. Prange 2001). The Late Bronze Age al-Wasit assemblage, specifically, is overwhelmingly comprised of group 11 metal, which certainly represents the dominant composition of locally-produced SE Arabian copper of that period. This composition also dominates the assemblage of analysed plano-convex copper ingots known from Bahrain Island, including material from Qala'at al-Bahrain (6 ingots and ingot fragments), Saar (3 ingots), and Nasariyah (10 ingots). In addition to group 11, group 5 (CuNi) metal also emerges from the regional analysis as a likely product of SE Arabia that reached sites in the Persian Gulf region: group 5 is a small but consistent component of SE Arabian second millennium BCE metal assemblages, copper ingots from Bahrain, and the Failaka assemblage.

The prevalence of group 11 (and group 5) metal throughout the greater Persian Gulf region can therefore be considered a likely – but not conclusive – reflection of the common use of SE Arabian copper in Mesopotamia and SW Iran. Although the FLAME compositional groups cannot be simplistically correlated with metal provenance and the group 11 metal may have been produced in multiple source regions, in the present case study the arguments for a SE Arabian provenance for much of the group 11 metal found in the wider region are strong. The FLAME analyses are reinforced by the evidence from Mesopotamian written sources on the Dilmun copper trade from the early second millennium BCE (e.g., Laursen & Steinkeller 2017 p. 63-70) and previous assessments of the archaeometallurgical evidence from key sites (e.g., Malfoy & Menu 1987. Begemann et al. 2010. Helwing 2021). Such a reconstruction receives further support from the studies of Howarth (2018 p. 171, Tab. 14), who identifies copper group 11 as the most prevalent component of southern Mesopotamian metal assemblages from the late-3rd through mid-2nd millennium BCE, comprising up to half of the metal in circulation in the early 2nd millennium BCE. Group 11 metal is also prominent in SW Iran at Susa and Haft Tepe. Group 5 metal is present, but typically in lower proportions, in assemblages from Mesopotamia and SW Iran, although it is more prominent at Haft Tepe (Oudbashi et al. 2012. Oudbashi et al. 2019). Significantly, the Failaka analyses suggest the continuation of the Persian Gulf copper trade into the post-Old Babylonian period, when Mesopotamian sources become silent on the supply of copper from Makkan via Dilmun – a point to which we return in the conclusion.

The FLAME compositional patterns are somewhat different to the patterns observed for plano-convex copper ingots from the Umm an-Nar period copper smelting site of Maysar in Oman (Prange 2001), and to the analyses of material from the Barbar Temple on Bahrain. While the Maysar ingots show the presence of group 5 and group 11 metal, nearly two-thirds of

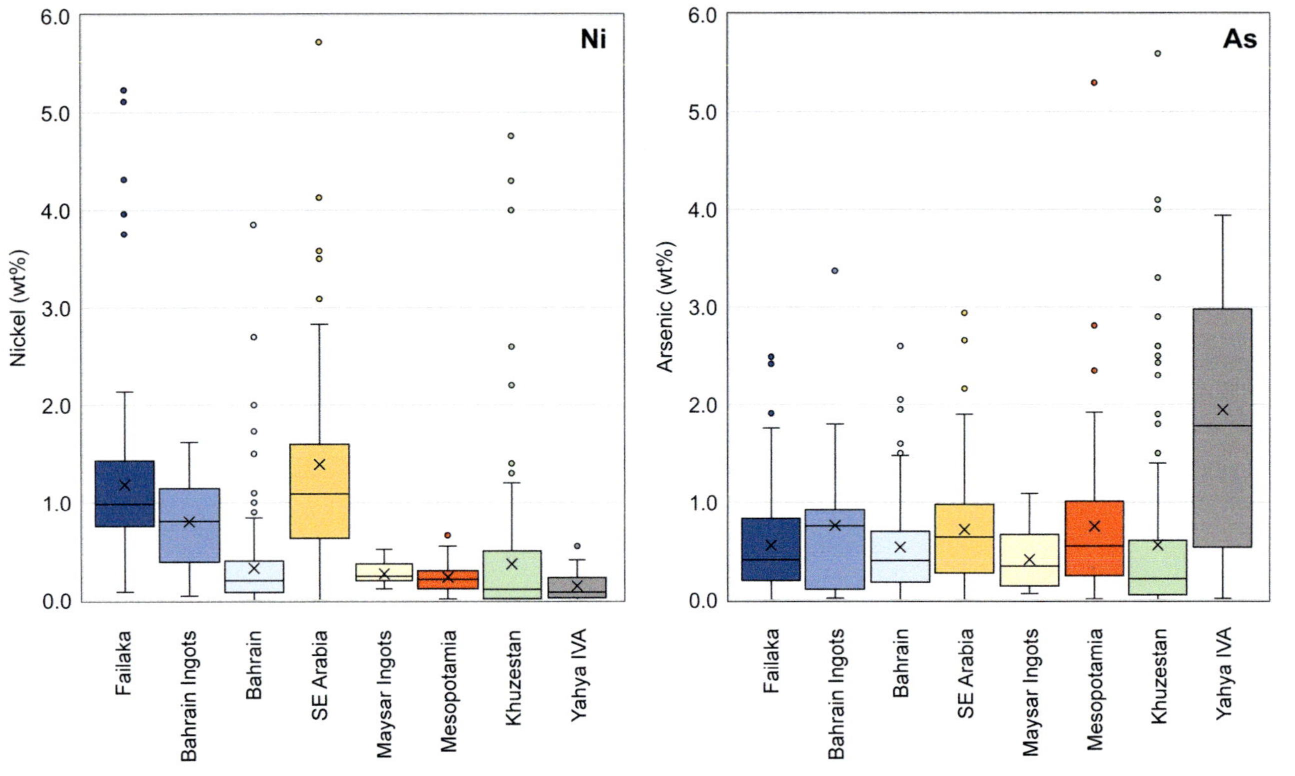

Fig. 386. Box-and-whisker plot of nickel and arsenic concentrations in metal assemblages from the greater Persian Gulf region, primarily dating to the second millennium BCE. Assemblage details follow fig. 385, other than 'Bahrain' (n=159), which groups the assemblages 'Barbar Temple' and 'Bahrain Other' from fig. 385.

the ingots show a noticeable concentration of silver, predominantly in metal group 15 (CuAsAgNi). Metal of this composition is comparatively rare on Failaka and in the assemblage of ingots from Bahrain. This might be interpreted as a 'chronological' signature, as high Ag concentrations seem more characteristic of third millennium BCE metal assemblages in the greater Persian Gulf region, as opposed to those of the second millennium BCE (Begemann et al. 2010 p. 156, fig. 2c). Howarth (2018 p. 173, fig. 62) similarly notes the prevalence of high-Ag metal in southern Mesopotamia in the mid- to late-third millennium BCE.

The pattern of compositional variation in the Barbar Temple assemblage is somewhat divergent from other sites in eastern Arabia and shows a greater degree of internal variety. The observed pattern is consistent across the two different analytical programmes and analytical techniques applied to the assemblage, including the OES analyses by the SAM project (Sangmeister 2003) and the spark-source mass spectrometry undertaken by Heskel (2003), suggesting that the results are robust and not an artefact of particular analytical techniques, although the proportions of different metal groups vary somewhat across these two studies.

The connection between the Failaka assemblage and SE Arabia identified from the FLAME group analysis is further confirmed by a comparison of the concentrations of Ni, and to a lesser extent As, in artefacts from the greater Persian Gulf region (fig. 386). While As concentrations strongly differentiate the metallurgy of Tepe Yahya in SE Iran from other regional traditions, the Ni concentrations in artefacts from Failaka, ingots from Early Dilmun Bahrain, and Wadi Suq to Late Bronze Age artefacts from SE Arabia are highly comparable to one another, and distinct from other regional assemblages.

Alloying practices in regional perspective

The identification of 'intentional' alloying practices can sometimes be challenging in the case of ancient metal artefacts. Artefact compositions may reflect complex interactions between ore sources and selection, pyrotechnological processes, and refining practices and recycling shaped by empirical knowledge and understanding, which are further affected by historically-contingent developments in exchange systems. This means that folk taxonomies (ethno-cat-

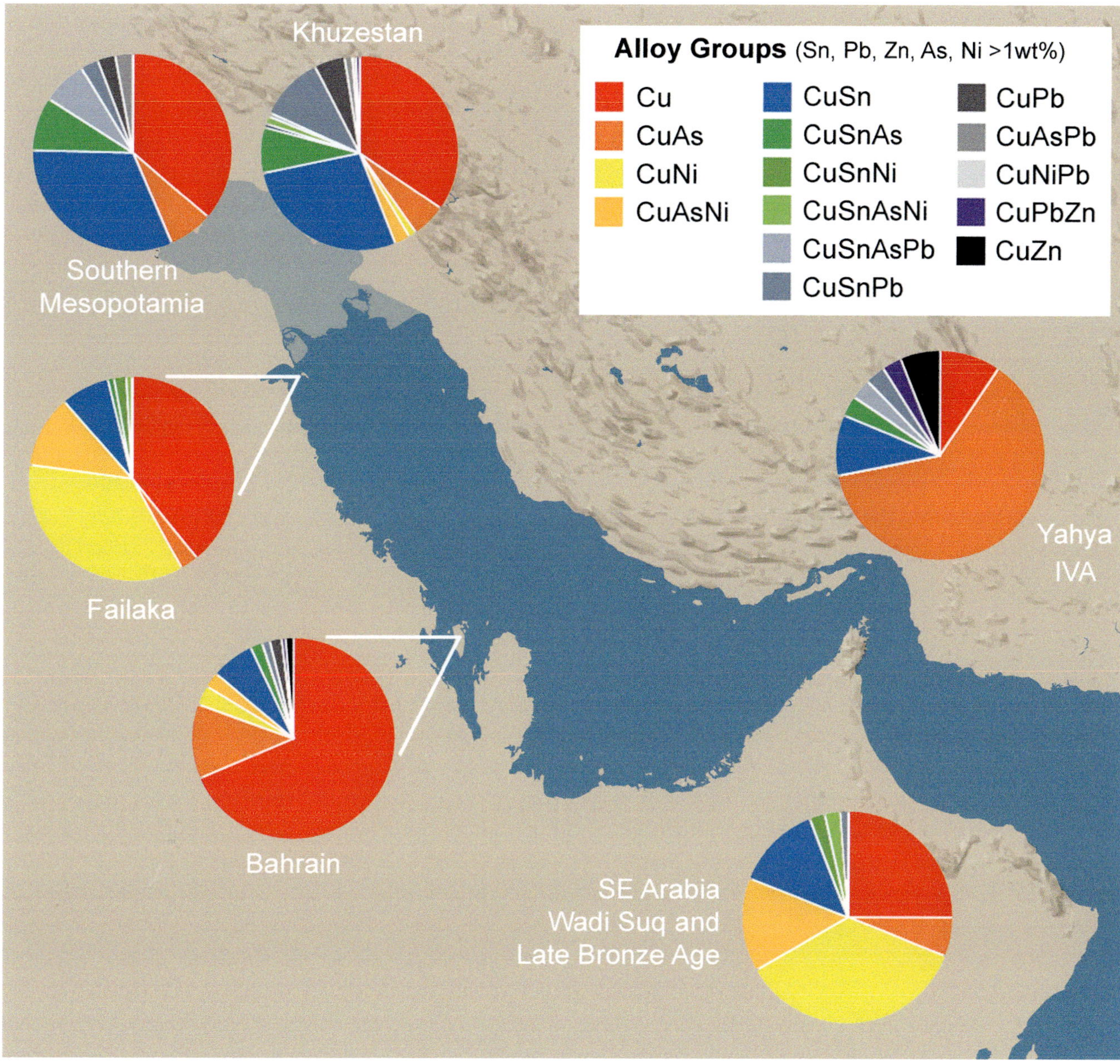

Fig. 387. A map of alloy types in 2nd millennium BCE metal assemblages from the greater Persian Gulf region. Assemblage details follow fig. 385, other than 'Bahrain' (n=159), which groups the assemblages 'Barbar Temple' and 'Bahrain Other' from fig. 385.

egories) and practices related to ancient metalworking – which we can gain some insight into through ancient written sources from Mesopotamia (e.g., Waetzoldt 1981. Waetzoldt & Bachmann 1984. Limet 1985. Limet 1993. Archi 1993. Begemann & Schmitt-Strecker 2009) – may be differently constructed than modern categories derived from the scientific understanding of materials and pyrotechnologies (e.g., Martinon-Torres 2023 p. 940-941). This is not to argue that the intentional alloying of copper and tin to produce bronze, for example, was not widely known and practiced in Bronze Age SW Asia – a range of written sources document such practices from the mid-third millennium BCE onwards – but that other avenues to alloy-like compositions are possible (e.g., Berger et al. 2022), with the composition of finished artefacts reflecting complex, culturally-specific, thoughts and practices.

If we define an 'alloy' on simple compositional grounds as characterised by the presence of >1wt% of As, Ni, Sn, Pb or Zn – an arbitrary but commonly employed boundary – the most prevalent metal on Failaka was unalloyed copper, comprising 39% of the assemblage. This metal was not particularly 'pure', being characterised by significant amounts of sulphur and iron (see p. 59-62). Unalloyed copper was marginally more common than copper-nickel 'alloy', which comprised about 35% of the analysed samples. These patterns are very similar to those observed at second millennium BCE sites in SE Arabia, including artefacts from Qarn al-Harf, Al-Wasit, al-Suwaiq, Al-Akhdar and Masirah Island – a pattern that has been previously documented for sites in Dilmun (Prange 2001. Begemann et al. 2010 p. 156).

In reality, unalloyed copper and copper-nickel alloys represent a compositional continuum in the Failaka assemblage, one that also includes copper-arsenic-nickel 'alloys' that make up about 11% of the assemblage (fig. 387). Histograms (fig. 381) demonstrate that both Ni and As concentrations are approximately normal and span the arbitrary 'alloy' boundary at 1wt%. This strongly suggests that they are present as a component of the raw copper metal, reflecting the composition of the exploited ores and the smelting technology that was employed in their extraction. Thus, the copper-nickel(-arsenic) alloys do not appear to have been 'intentional' as this term is traditionally understood – drawing on modern alloying practice in which metallic components such as copper and tin are melted together in predetermined ratios. However, this does not preclude the possibility that raw Cu-Ni(-As) 'alloys' were identified by ancient metalworkers in eastern Arabia as distinct from unalloyed copper, based on their appearance and/or mechanical properties, and intentionally selected as a preferred material for the production of (some kinds of) artefacts.

As shown in fig. 387, the use of bronze (defined here as an alloy containing >1wt% Sn) is comparatively infrequent in the second millennium BCE metallurgy of eastern Arabia. Typically, in this region, only 10-20% of artefacts might be classified as bronzes. A similar pattern is observed for the early second millennium BCE material from Tepe Yahya period IVA. These patterns differ substantially from alloying practices in southern Mesopotamia and Khuzestan, where around half of the analysed copper-base artefacts are bronzes (sometimes including other alloying elements such as Pb). In addition to identifying the general compositional diversity and variety of metal used in the developed metallurgical workshops of Babylonia and Elam – a not unexpected aspect of industries that relied entirely on the import of raw materials from multiple source regions, and one that is also visible in the FLAME group analyses presented above – such a pattern has implications for the exchange of tin and bronze in the early to mid-second millennium BCE. Specifically, it indicates that tin was more consistently accessible in Mesopotamia and Elam than in eastern Arabia or SE Iran and suggests that the use of bronze in Dilmun and SE Arabia most likely depended on exchange relations with these northern regions. This suggestion aligns directly with the well-known evidence from early second millennium BCE written sources that document the overland, east-to-west trade of tin through Elam to Mari and further west (e.g., Joannes 1991. Potts 1999 p. 169, tab. 6.2. Montero Fenollos 2019) and through Assur to Kanesh/Kultepe in Anatolia (e.g., Barjamovic 2018). Steinkeller (2016 p. 128) has suggested a transition from a primarily Gulf-oriented, maritime transport of exotic eastern materials to Mesopotamia in the 3rd millennium BCE towards an overland route through the Zagros and northern Iranian Plateau in the early second millennium BCE, relating this development to the emergence of the Bactrian camel as a pack animal and the control of the tin trade by a newly-emergent Shimashki dynasty in Iran. The ultimate sources of this fundamental Bronze Age raw material remain difficult to identify with certainty, but exchange routes likely stretched as far as mines in steppe Central Asia (Garner 2015. Pigott 2021. Helwing 2021. Berger et al. 2022). Recent analytical programmes exploiting Pb and Sn isotope analyses of Late Bronze Age tin ingots from the eastern Mediterranean (Powell et al. 2021, 2022. Berger et al. 2019) highlight the truly pan-continental scale of the movement of tin by this time, which appears to have come from sources as distant as Central Asia and Britain. For metalworkers on Failaka, direct connections with the Elamite world through Susa – well documented in the form of Dilmunite materials found there (e.g., Potts 1999 p. 178-180. Neumann 2013 p. 85-86. Laursen 2018 p. 217) – would have facilitated access to eastern tin and/or bronze, although indirect contact through southern Mesopotamia is also likely. Moreover, given the evidence for Dilmunite materials at Liyan on the Bushire Peninsula (Laursen & Steinkeller 2017 p. 65), and that site's close material connections with Kaftari period Tal-e Malyan, where bronze use is clearly documented (Pigott et al. 2003), other avenues for obtaining this alloy can also be envisaged.

As outlined on p. 65, zinc concentrations are very low in the Failaka assemblage and no artefacts made of brass (defined here as containing >1wt% Zn) were recorded, a situation that characterises most metal assemblages from Bronze Age eastern Arabia. However, rare exceptions to this pattern are recorded from second millennium BCE sites in the greater Persian Gulf region (fig. 387), including Tepe Yahya period IVA (Thornton et al. 2002 tab. 1), where three samples with c. 16-20% Zn were recorded, and from Haft Tepe (Oudbashi et al. 2012, one example with c. 1.1%

Zn). Several examples of artefacts with >5% Zn are also known from the Barbar Temple (Heskel 2003), sometimes characterised by the additional presence of Sn and Pb at >1wt% (see below). The Barbar examples have been suggested to date to the Islamic period based on their high Zn concentrations (Heskel 2003 p. 28) and the abundance of Sasanian and Islamic pottery recovered from the layers overlying the Barbar Temple (Andersen & Kennet 2003). However, the Iranian, Mesopotamian and Arabian examples of high-Zn alloys from Bronze Age contexts collated by Thornton (2007) and Howarth (2018 p. 289-294) allow the possibility that such alloys are of Bronze Age date.

The low Pb concentrations observed in the Failaka assemblage are typical for much copper in the Persian Gulf exchange system. This is particularly the case for the raw copper produced in SE Arabia, which generally has concentrations of less than a few hundred ppm Pb (Prange 2001. Begemann et al. 2010). Alloys incorporating the probable intentional addition of Pb (defined here as Pb >1wt%) are very rare at sites in eastern Arabia. A difference can be seen between most Arabian artefacts and assemblages and those from further to the north, in Mesopotamia and lowland SW Iran (fig. 387), where average Pb concentrations are higher than those in the Persian Gulf, and a significant minority of copper alloys contain >1wt% Pb (often alongside the presence of tin). Within the area of greater Dilmun, the only site that evinces the presence of Pb-bearing alloys is the Barbar Temple, with two Cu-Pb alloys (including an 'ingot fragment'), two Cu-Sn-Pb alloys (including a bronze bead with >5wt% Pb and a bronze flat axe with 2% Pb), and a Cu-Sn-Pb-Zn 'rod' (Heskel 2003. Sangmeister 2003).

Conclusions and further work

The analyses of the metallurgical remains from Tell F3 and Tell F6 serve to situate the inhabitants of Bronze Age Failaka within several overlapping spheres of technological/craft knowledge, economic exchange, and cultural interaction. The raw copper exploited on the island is compositionally quite homogeneous, and of a type widely utilised in the greater Persian Gulf region in the second millennium BCE, from SE Arabia to southern Babylonia and Elam. Identifiable by its concentrations of arsenic, nickel, cobalt and iron, and by abundant copper-iron-sulphide inclusions, this metal was likely exploited in its unalloyed state, although the common occurrence of >1wt% of Ni and As suggests that it might have been macroscopically identifiable as a distinctive 'type' of metal, perhaps associated by its users with particular material properties and/or with a particular source region. As expected from available ancient textual sources and strongly indicated by the compositional analyses, such material appears to have largely been a product of copper extraction in SE Arabia. The ways in which this raw material was processed into artefacts on Failaka find strong parallels in the contemporary metallurgical evidence from wider Dilmun, e.g. from Qala'at al-Bahrain and Saar, where a developed but comparatively small-scale tradition of secondary metallurgy can be identified, built around the crucible melting of plano-convex copper ingots, the occasional alloying of this metal and addition of recycled scrap, and the casting and forging of a range of mostly mundane finished tools, weapons, vessels and other items.

Significantly, however, while the identification of the use of SE Arabian copper in second millennium BCE Failaka (and neighbouring regions) aligns with the surviving textual evidence from Mesopotamia, clear archaeological evidence for contemporary copper smelting in SE Arabia itself is almost entirely lacking (Weeks 2003 p. 33-36, 40-42). Based on the fieldwork of the German Mining Museum, Hauptmann (1985 Abb. 1) suggested a reduction in the scale of Omani copper production during the second millennium BCE. Although possible smelting and mining sites of this period have been identified in Oman (Weisgerber 1991 p. 327. 2007 p. 195. 2020 p. 434), they remain little explored and entirely unanalysed. Scholars considering the sources of copper used in southern Babylonia and Elam at this time have treated the Arabian evidence in markedly different ways. Steinkeller (2016 p. 130), for example, has suggested that by c. 1750 BCE, the "Omani mines were completely abandoned, apparently as a result of the shift of commercial focus to Cyprus, where better and much cheaper copper was now in ample supply." In contrast, Helwing (2021 para 67), writing of Elam, has stated that "throughout the 2nd millennium BCE, copper supply seems to have come continuously from the Persian Gulf".

The problem in identifying early second millennium BCE copper smelting in SE Arabia derives in part from the poor chronological control of 'Bronze Age' smelting sites; very few such sites have reliable absolute dates, and it is likely that at least some of them date to the early second millennium BCE (Weeks 2003 p. 41-42), although proof of this remains in the future. At present, however, the best evidence for continued SE Arabian copper extraction in the second millennium BCE comes from the consideration of finished artefacts. Wadi Suq period and Late Bronze Age tomb assemblages from SE Arabia have produced significant assemblages of copper-base artefacts that document the persistence, even expansion, of copper-base artefact production and deposition in SE Arabia across the second millennium BCE (e.g., Weisgerber 1991. Yule 2015). Traditionally, such evidence has been used as circumstantial support for the continued local smelting of copper at this time (Weisgerber 1988 p. 285. Weisgerber 2020: 343). Recently, such arguments have gained considerably in strength with the growing demonstration that the copper used in SE Arabia across the second millennium BCE is compositionally distinct from that of the earlier Umm an-Nar period, particularly in terms of its higher Ni and lower As and Ag concentrations (e.g., Prange 2001. Begemann et al. 2010. Weeks et al. in press). Critically, this pattern of compositional change cannot reflect the simple recycling of earlier Umm an-Nar period metal artefacts, even allowing for the differential removal of more volatile elements such as As and Sb (cf. Pollard 2018) and does not appear to represent the wholesale import of raw metal from an external source (Prange 2001. Begemann et al. 2010). That such metal is found with abundance on Failaka and in greater Dilmun is now our best testament to continued primary copper production in contemporary SE Arabia and the long-distance movement of this material within the Persian Gulf exchange system, even if the smelting sites themselves are not yet well known or properly characterised. Weisgerber's (1988 p. 285) now decades-old suggestion that copper production in SE Arabia "seems to have been at least as important during the second millennium as during the previous one" appears to be confirmed, even if it is acknowledged that the absolute scale of primary production may have been smaller at this time.

Moving onto a separate matter, the compositional analyses indicate that bronze alloys comprised only a small proportion of the Failaka assemblage, including a few 'good' bronzes (c. 5-13wt% Sn) and a handful of samples with low Sn concentrations (1-3wt% Sn) that likely indicate the recycling and mixing of bronze and raw copper on Failaka. Other possible alloys, with >1wt% lead or zinc, were not recorded at all in the Failaka Bronze Age assemblage and are very rare across Dilmun and SE Arabia more generally, although a handful of examples are known from the Barbar Temple. This pattern of alloy usage contrasts strongly with contemporary metal assemblages in southern Babylonia and Elam, where bronzes and lead-bearing alloys are much more common. As outlined above, this pattern suggests that the tin and bronze that were reaching the Gulf and eastern Arabian communities at this time most likely came through exchanges with their northern neighbours in Babylonia and especially Elam, a suggestion that maps onto contemporary textual sources and emerging archaeological evidence regarding the early- to mid-second millennium BCE tin trade.

Finally, in concluding this chapter, it must be emphasised that the results of the archaeometallurgical research are still preliminary; additional analyses will eventually expand the insights that can be drawn from such studies. For example, although numerous crucible fragments are known from excavations (infra p. 50, Højlund 2021), these have not yet been scientifically studied. The crucibles have the potential to provide critical information on the nature of high-temperature metalworking activities on Failaka and on the composition of the metal being processed, providing an essential connection point between the study of finished artefacts and production residues. Additionally, small numbers of metallurgical residues from recent excavations at Tell F3 identified as 'slag' stand out from other residues from the site due to their larger dimensions (e.g., Højlund 2021 p. 131, noting several lumps of slag 2-5 cm across and a slag piece of 6.5 x 7 x 10 cm). A closer examination of such remains will broaden the evidence for metallurgical practices on Failaka. More generally, the full publication of the quantitative data from Failaka and its integration with metallographic analyses of fabrication practices offers the prospect of a more coherent understanding of the nature of Bronze Age metalworking activities on the island, and of the technological knowledge and capacities of Failaka's craftspeople. Likewise, the addition of lead isotope analyses for the exploration of provenance will help to clarify some of the insights deriving from the study of FLAME compositional groups. This work is in progress.

Acknowledgements

We thank the Kuwait National Council for Culture, Arts and Letters, as well as Flemming Højlund, Moesgaard Museum, and the Kuwaiti-Danish team members for support during SM's fieldwork. We acknowledge the University of Nottingham and the University of New England for the provision of direct and in-kind support and facilities that underpinned this research.

6. The cuneiform texts from Failaka

by Gianni Marchesi

Many artifacts bearing cuneiform inscriptions were discovered by the various missions that carried out archaeological research on Failaka island since 1958. These inscriptions have all been assigned a new identifying *siglum*—CFa (= Cuneiform [text from] Failaka)—which, we hope, will henceforth serve as the standard designator for cuneiform texts from Failaka. All of these documents are edited herein. The material has been divided into two groups: 1) Early campaigns: the findings of the Danish expedition of 1958-1963; 2) Other archaeological missions and occasional finds (not attributable to any specific archaeological mission). In addition, each group is further divided into the following object-based typological classes: stamp seals; cylinder seals; stone vessels; metal vessels; pottery; tablets; other.

The following symbols (with their respective meanings) are used in the transliteration and transcription of texts:

′	symbol marking line numbers after a gap (1′, 2′, 3′, …)
$^{!}$	corrected reading (the sign should read as indicated but the text shows something different)
$^{?}$	uncertain reading
[ ]	sign or text broken (the text between square brackets is a reconstruction)
[(…)]	the original presence of additional text in the break is uncertain
⌜ ⌝	partially broken sign
‹ ›	addition (the text between angle brackets is not present but is required by the context)
{ }	erroneous addition (the text between curly brackets was written by mistake and should thus be ignored)
^{m}	*Personenkeil* (a single wedge indicating a male personal name)
^{f}	female determinative (a cuneiform sign indicating a female personal name)
^{d}	divine determinative (a cuneiform sign indicating a divine name)
^{ki}	place determinative (a cuneiform sign indicating a geographical name)

I would like to thank Flemming Højlund for involving me in the study of the Failaka materials and sharing with me his vast knowledge of Gulf archaeology; and Steffen Terp Laursen, the head of the Oriental Department at the Moesgaard Museum, for welcoming me to the Museum's team, whose pioneering excavations on Bahrain and Failaka in the 1950s and early 1960s paved the way for modern archaeological research in the Gulf region. I am honored and pleased to be part of this glorious scientific enterprise.

My sincerest gratitude goes to the authorities of the National Council for Culture, Arts and Letters and to the authorities of the Kuwait National Museum, who made my study stay at the museum in November 2022 possible. At the Kuwait National Museum, I greatly benefited from the kind assistance of Ms. Hadeel Al-Shammari and Mr. Abdullah Al-Ansari.

I am also grateful to Lucia Benediková and the Kuwaiti-Slovak Archaeological Mission 2004-2009 for kindly sharing their images and information relating to the inscribed vessel KM8810.

In addition, my heartfelt thanks go to Helle Strehle (Moesgaard Museum), who provided me with her superbly made seal impressions and photos of the stamp seal KM1657; Michael P. Streck (Universität Leipzig), who offered several valuable suggestions concerning the analysis and interpretation of Amorite personal names; Glenn Magid, who helped me a lot in the final drafting of this work with his thoughtful feedback and careful editorial assistance; and, last but not least, Palmiro Notizia (University of Bologna), who processed some of the images and proofed the manuscript.

Finally, I would like to mention Dr. Hasan Ashkanani (Kuwait University), who made my sojourn in Kuwait a wonderful journey into Kuwaiti culture and history.

Early campaigns: the findings of the Danish expedition of 1958-1963

Stamp seals

CFa 1 (fig. 388). Stamp seal fragment (F3.109; 881.GS; KM1657). D c. 2.2, Th 0.3 cm. Green-blue stone (Amazonite?). Inscription on one side and the other side broken. Trench RM, 1-15 N, 1-2.45 m depth, sieve.

Bibliography: van Dijk 1962 no. 6; Alster 1983 p. 42 (no. 3) with n. 28 (on p. 68); Howard-Carter 1980-1983 p. 394 § 5.4.2 *a*; Glassner 1984 no. 2; Nashef 1984 p. 17 (no. 17); Gharbia et al. 1990 p. 44-45; Glassner 2008 no. 2; Marchesi 2017 p. 431 n. 38. By mistake not included in Kjærum 1983.

Text (collated):

1.	E$_{2}$.GAL G[U].‹LA›	Ekallum Ra[b]‹ûm› (/Rab[ī]‹tum›)
2.	^{m}*sa-mu-a* I[R$_{3/11}$]	Samu'a w[arad]
3.	⸢d⸣*in*-⸢*za*⸣-[*ak*]	Inza[k]
4.	[*ša*$_{2}$ *a*-GA-AŠ]	[ša Agaš$^{?}$]
5.	[*i*/*u*$_{2}$-... (?)]	[i/u... (?)]

(1)(Property of) "The Gr[e]‹at› Palace". (2)Samu'a, the s[ervant of] (3)Inza[k (4)of Agaš$^{?}$, (5)presented (it) (?)].

Remarks: Although the inscription is carved in the negative, as is customary on seals, this seal is most likely a votive seal (cf. Gelb 1977 p. 109; 120-121 *sub* XX; Collon 1987 p. 131-134; Braun-Holzinger 1991 p. 350-359); in fact, the inscription appears to be structurally identical to CFa 69 (which is probably a votive vessel; cf. also CFa 38 and 40 below).

Commentary:
Line **1**: There is not enough space at the end of this line to restore the expected LA sign. For E$_{2}$.GAL GU.LA, see CFa 49 below, comm. to I-II. For the use of the phrase E$_{2}$.GAL + modifier to characterize an object as belonging to a particular place, see *CAD* E s.v. *ekallu* 2; and Marchesi 2017 p. 425-429 with n 21.

Line **2a**: Note the unusual shape of the MU sign in line 2, with its two oblique wedges that cross the central long wedge (cf. Fossey 1926 nos. 3949, 3955, and 3967). Samu'a—which is not otherwise attested—is presumably a hypocoristic form of an Amorite personal name of the type Samu-X, "Descendent/Offspring of So-and-so" (cf. Streck 2000 p. 350 § 5.74 s.v. *śamīya*). Since Samu'a cannot be in genitival relation with what precedes it (otherwise the text would have read *E$_{2}$.GAL GU.LA *ša*$_{2}$ ^{m}*sa-mu-a* = *Ekallum Rabûm/Rabītum ša Samu'a*), it can only be the name of the donor as in CFa 69.

Lines **2b-4**: For *warad*(IR$_{3/11}$) ^{d}*in-za-ak ša*$_{2}$ *a*-GA-AŠ, "the servant of Inzak of Agaš$^{?}$", as the title of the kings of Dilmun, see Marchesi 2017 p. 428-430. Regarding the alleged toponym *a*-GA-AŠ, traditionally read as *a-ga-rum*, see, most recently, Marchesi 2017 p. 430-433. To summarize, supplement, and (partially) correct that source, the following points can be noted:

a) *a*-GA-AŠ, which is exclusively attested in association with the DN Inzak, occurs in inscriptions from both Failaka (see CFa 4, 31, and 49, below) and Bahrain (Marchesi 2017 p. 425-428), a fact that makes an interpretation of *a*-GA-AŠ—read as *a-ka*$_{3}$*-rum*—as the original name of Failaka and the etymon of Hellenistic Ikaros unlikely (contra Marchesi 2017 p. 432-433).

b) Alternative proposals to identify *a*-GA-AŠ—read as *a-ga-rum*—with the geographical names Hagar (an Arab kingdom of uncertain location in the Seleucid period) and Hağar (an ancient name of Hofūf and its oasis in the Eastern Province of Saudi Arabia) are difficult in many respects (Marchesi 2017 p. 430-431).

c) The same is true of the proposed connection with the Ḥağar mountains of Oman and the Emirates, which is not supported by any evidence (Marchesi 2017 p. 432).

d) The readings of *a*-GA-AŠ found in previous scholarship, i.e. *a-ga-rum* and *a-ka*$_{3}$*-rum*, are arbitrary and lacking in supporting evidence. In fact, the GA sign can be read as either *ga, ka*$_{3}$, or *qa*$_{2}$ (see von Soden & Röllig 1991 p. 32 *sub* 170; cf. *pa-qa*$_{2}$*-da* and *ka*$_{3}$*-ku-ul* in CFa 5 and 42, respectively), while AŠ can be read as either *aš, rum, ru*$_{3}$, or *rim*$_{5}$ (the last two values being, however, very rare; see von Soden & Röllig 1991 p. 1 *sub* 1; cf. Lieberman 1977 p. 107 with n. 310 and 316; p. 111 n. 348). This provides us with twelve different combinations and possible readings. In the absence of stronger evidence, the provisionally preferred reading is *a-ga-aš*. Since the precise nature of the consonant of the GA sign cannot be determined, it is only reasonable to take the sign at its face value, reading it as *ga*. In addition, in the case of a reading of *a*-GA-AŠ as *a-ga-rum* or *a-ga-rim*$_{5}$, one would expect that this word would sometimes be written alternatively as **a-ga-ru*(*-um*) or **a-ga-ri*(*-im*) (even more so if one considers the reluctance of Dilmunite scribes to use CVC values). Finally, *aš* is a more probable reading than *ru*$_{3}$ since the latter is attested much more rarely.

e) It is not even certain that *a*-GA-AŠ is a geographical name; the systematic absence of the semantic classifier (so-called "determinative") for place names in the writing of the word seems to speak against such an interpretation.

f) It is still possible that *a*-GA-AŠ, used as a qualifier of the DN Inzak, refers to Inzak's original place of worship; if so, we should think of a place—either a settlement or a cultic place, rather than a region (*pace* Denton 1997 p. 179; and Laursen 2017 p. 390)—located in either Bahrain (Qala'at al-Bahrain? The Barbar Temple?) or Eastern Arabia (cf. Marchesi 2017 p. 430), but not on Failaka (the Dilmun settlement on the island not being earlier than the 19th century BC; see F. Højlund in Højlund & Abu-Laban 2016 p. 252).

Line **5**: A verb of offering such as *iqīš* (CFa 41: 2), *išruq* (CFa 13: 1′), or *ušēli* (CFa 29: 7[-8]) is expected here.

CFa 2 (fig. 389). Stamp seal (F3.aoc; 881.AYO; KM1650). D 3, Th 0.8 cm. Black stone. Bifacial (Style III). Unspecified trench, sieve (contra Kjærum 1983 p. 142 [no. 350]).

Bibliography: Anonymous 1964 fig. 82: 5; Glob 1968 p. 133 and 210; Kjærum 1980 p. 46 and fig. 11 (on p. 51); Howard-Carter 1980-1983 p. 395 § 6.1.2 a; Alster 1983 p. 42 (no. 4) with n. 29 (on p. 68); Kjærum 1983 no. 350; Glassner 1984 no. 5; Nashef 1984 p. 17 (no. 16); Gharbia et al. 1990 p. 54-55; Denton 1997 p. 181; Peyronel 1997 p. 425 (with erroneous reference to fig. 5a instead of 5b) with n. 77-78 and fig. 5b (on p. 435); Calvet 2005 p. 50-51 (cat. 1); Glassner 2008 no. 6; Stiehler-Alegria 2011-2012 p. 21-22 and fig. 10; Hilton 2014 p. 105-106 and figs. 275 and 280; van Soldt 2021 p. 1047.

Text on side A (collated):

1. *a-na* DINGIR.MAḪ	ana Bēlet-ilī
2. NIN.A.NI.{IR}	bēltīšu
3. ^{m}*ri-ip*$^{?}$*-qa*$_2$*-tum/tu*$_4$	Ripqatu(m)$^{?}$

(1)To Bēlet-ilī, (2)his lady. (3)(From) Ripqatu(m)$^{?}$.

Remarks: Votive seal (cf. above, remarks on CFa 1). This may explain why the inscription is carved in the positive: perhaps it was intended to be read on the seal itself (not on its reversed impression). The only known *comparandum* for the inscription type (*ana* DN [= offeree] PN [= offerer], without a verb of offering) is found on a Kassite votive bead (Arnaud 1998 p. 199-201 no. 2). A few things should also be noted about the paleography of this text. As Glassner (1984 p. 35) already observed, the form of the GA (= *qa*$_2$) sign here differs from the one found on other stamp seals (see CFa 4: 4; CFa 5: 2′; and CFa 49 III 4)—a fact with possible chronological implications. But no definitive conclusions can be drawn on the basis of such tenuous evidence. What is certain is that both GA and TUM have forms that in the first half of the 2nd millennium BC, the period to which the Style III seals are dated (for the chronology of the stamp seals from Failaka, see, most recently, Højlund & Hilton 2021 p. 28 fig. 50; and F. Højlund, ibid. p. 84-88 and 162-165), typically appear in writing on clay (see Fossey 1926 p. 590-592 and 469-473, respectively). In Mesopotamia, these forms of GA and TUM (see also CFa 62 below) first occur in writing on stone only toward the end of the 2nd millennium and in the early 1st millennium BC (see Fossey 1926 nos. 19469 [Nebuchadnezzar I] and 15497 [Nabû-apla-iddina], respectively; for GA, see also Sassmannshausen 2008 p. 327 table 1b). In addition, the unusual shapes of the IB sign (which ends in two wedges; IB usually ends in a single wedge) and the MAḪ sign are also worth noting.

Commentary:

Line **1**: Glassner's rendering as "pour la Grande Déesse" (1984 p. 33; 2008 p. 175; see also id. 1996 p. 240) is erroneous, since it requires the spelling DINGIR$^{tim/ti(-im)}$ (DINGIR alone is nowhere attested as a logogram for *iltu(m)*, "goddess"; see *CAD* I/J s.v. *iltu*). DINGIR.MAḪ should rather be understood as representing Bēlet-ilī ("Lady of the Gods"), the Akkadian name of the mother goddess (see Borger 2003 p. 249; Frayne & Stuckey 2021 p. 58).

Line **2**: For the pleonastic use of the Sumerian dative in the writing of the phrase "to DN, his lord/lady" (also in CFa 29 and 70), see Glassner 2002 p. 343. The same phenomenon occurs in Kassite inscriptions (Bartelmus 2016 p. 246).

Line **3**: This personal name could derive from a root RPQ, "to support", otherwise attested in Hebrew (suggestion courtesy of M. Streck; cf. *HALOT* p. 1279 s.v. רפק). If this interpretation is correct, then Ripqatu(m) could be a hypocoristic form of an Amorite name of the type *Ripqī-DN, "(the deity) So-and-so Is My Support" (cf. Streck 2000 p. 315-316 § 4.9).

CFa 3 (fig. 390). Stamp seal fragment (F5.nw; KM1502). D 1.7, Th 0.8 cm. Green jasper. Unifacial (Style III). The boss is partially preserved and has part of a circle.

Bibliography: Glassner 1984 no. 1; Gharbia et al. 1990

p. 50-51; Glassner 2008 no. 1. By mistake not included in Kjærum 1983.

Text:
1. […]-^{d}*in-za-‹ak›* […]-Inza‹k›

Remarks: The inscription appears to consist of a single line.

Commentary:
Line **1**: Probably an acephalous personal name with the theophoric element Inzak, such as *ia$_{8}$-tar$_{2}$-in-za-ak*, "Inzak Is Surpassingly Great" (Scheil 1939 no. 550: 7); *ku-un-in-za-ak*, "Be Firm, o Inzak" (ibid. no. 423: 8; cf. Streck 2000 p. 273 § 3.20 with n. 1); etc.

CFa 4 (fig. 391). Stamp seal (F6.183; 1129.FH; KM1050). D 1.8, Th 0.5 cm. Lapis lazuli. Bifacial. Trench SS0-9, 3.45 S, 1.8 E, level +0.49.

Bibliography: Howard-Carter 1980-1983 p. 394 § 5.4.1 *a*; Alster 1983 p. 42 (no. 7) with n. 32 (on p. 68); Kjærum 1983 no. 366; Glassner 1984 no. 6; Nashef 1984 p. 17 (no. 15); Gharbia et al. 1990 p. 42-43; Denton 1997 p. 181; Glassner 2008 no. 5; David-Cuny & Neyme 2016 p. 132; Marchesi 2017 p. 428-429; van Soldt 2021 p. 1047.

Text on side A (collated):

1.	$^{[f]}$*u$_{2}$-la-^{d}pa-ni-pa*	'Ūla-Panipa
2.	DUMU.MUNUS	mārat
	^{m}*su-mu-le*-DINGIR	Sumu-lêl
3.	[I]R$_{11}$ ^{d}*in-za-ak*	[wa]rad Inzak
4.	*ša$_{2}$ a*-GA-AŠ	ša Agaš$^{?}$

(1)'Ūla-Panipa, (2)daughter of Sumu-lêl, (3)the [ser]vant of Inzak (4)of Agaš$^{?}$.

Remarks: According to Kjærum (1983 p. 152), "both sides [were] inscribed in cuneiform" but side B shows no traces of cuneiform writing (cf. David-Cuny & Neyme 2016 p. 132).

Commentary:
Line **1**: The reading here supersedes the one—[*la*]-*ú-la*-^{d}*pa-ni-pa* (= Lā'û-la-Panipa)—in Marchesi 2017 p. 429. In fact, it is very likely that the lost sign at the beginning of this line was the feminine determinative (i.e., ^{geme2}, here transliterated as ^{f}). This reconstruction also solves the problem of the gender incongruence between the elements *lā'û* (which is morphologically masculine) and Panipa (which is the name of a goddess). The female PN 'Ūla-Panipa can be interpreted as "Panipa Is Strength" (cf. Pagan 1998 p. 92 s.v. 'wl; for the goddess Panipa, see below, CFa 49 with remarks and comm. to III 1).

Lines **2-4**: See Marchesi 2017 p. 429 and above, comm. to CFa 1: 2b-4. Note that King Sumu-lêl also occurs in CFa 69 below.

CFa 5 (fig. 392). Stamp seal fragment (KM962). D 2.4, Th 1 cm. Green soft stone. Unifacial, with a boss on the reverse and transverse perforation; no circles or lines are preserved (but they may have been on the part of the seal that broke off). Unknown provenience (the excavation number F3.109 that is attributed to this seal in Kjærum 1983 p. 12 [no. 311] is erroneous).

Bibliography: Kjærum 1983 no. 311; Glassner 1984 no. 4; Nashef 1984 p. 17 (no. 14); Gharbia et al. 1990 p. 40-41; Glassner 2008 no. 4; van Soldt 2021 p. 1047.

Text (collated):
Lacuna (two lines?)

1'.	*sa-ri-tam-b*[*i*$^{?}$]	Sārī-Tamb$^{?}$
2'.	*u$_{3}$ pa-qa$_{2}$-da*	u Paqada

[…] (1')Sārī-Tamb$^{?}$ (2')and Paqada.

Commentary:
Lines **1'-2'**: These lines probably contain two Amorite personal names, despite the lack of determinatives. In line 1', *sa-ri-tam-b*[*i*$^{?}$] can be understood as a two-element name consisting of the active participle *sārī* (< *sāriy*) (suggestion courtesy of M. Streck; cf. Golinets 2018 p. 455 s.v. ŚRY) and the Dilmunite DN (?) Tamb, which also occurs in the PN *i-ṣi$_{2}$-ta-am-bu* (= 'Iṣī-Tamb, "Tamb Has Appeared") on a cuneiform tablet from Bahrain (Eidem 1994 p. 302-303; cf. Streck 2004 p. 329 with n. 28; note that the vowel in the last syllabogram of *tam-bi*/*ta-am-bu* is presumably a dummy one due to the fact that in a syllabic writing system, a final consonantal cluster cannot be written without using a word-final CV sign). Thus: Sārī-Tamb$^{?}$, "Tamb$^{?}$ Is One Who Protects" (or, with Streck [pers. comm.], "… Is Protecting"; for other Amorite personal names with the same structure [active participle + theophoric element], see Streck 2000 p. 329 § 5.24 and 5.25). In line 2', *pa-qa$_{2}$-da* may be an Amorite female name—"Handed over" (or the like)—based on the root PQD, "to hand over, to entrust" (cf. Streck 2000 p. 311-313 § 4.2-6; Golinets 2018 p. 154-156 § 10.1.7; and p. 428 s.v. PQD). We can tentatively restore the inscription (originally consisting of, presumably, four lines) as follows: "[(1)PN, (2)the …, servant (?) of] (3)Sārī-Tamb$^{?}$ and (4)Paqada". It should be noted, however,

Fig. 388. 2:1.

Fig. 389. 2:1.

Fig. 390. 2:1.

Fig. 391. 2:1.

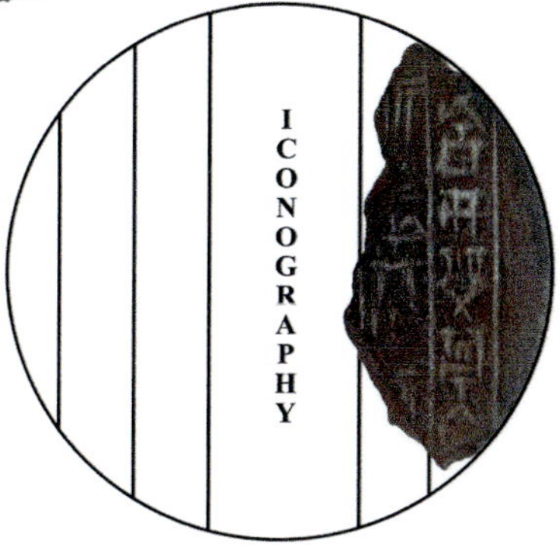

Fig. 392. 2:1.

that the paired reference to both a man and a woman is atypical. Were these the king and the queen of Dilmun? In this connection, note the unique mention of a queen of Dilmun in an Early Dynastic text from Lagash (Marchesi 2011).

Cylinder seals

CFa 6 (fig. 393). MB cylinder seal (F3.ka; 881.AEU; KM1653). L 3.1, D 1.3 cm. Blackish-grey soft stone. Trench I, 69 N, 1.25 E, level 5.97. Associated pottery: Period 2.

Bibliography: Howard-Carter 1980-1983 p. 394 § 5.4.1 *c*; Kjærum 1983 no. 407; Glassner 1984 no. 22; Nashef 1984 p. 19 (no. 28); Gharbia et al. 1990 p. 104-105; Stiehler-Alegria 1996 no. 245b; Glassner 2008 no. 24; Potts 2010 no. 65; van Soldt 2021 p. 1047.

Text (collated):

1. ^{d}EN.KI$^{!}$(Text: DI)	Ea
2. *be-lu*-GEŠTU ḪI IGI	bēl uzni …
3. AD AD.⌜ḪAL$^{?}$⌝	abi pirišti$^{?}$
4. DINGIR GAR GIDRU *a-nu*	ilu šakin ḫaṭṭi Anu
5. *za-ra-qum/qu*	Zaraqu(m)
6. DUMU *ba-an-na-ḫa*	mār Bannaḫa

(1)O Ea, (2)lord of wisdom …, (3)father of secret lore (?), (4)the god equipped with the scepter of Anu. (5)(This is) Zaraqu(m), (6)son of Bannaḫa.

Remarks: The inscription, which is carved in the positive, is displayed correctly on the seal but appears in reverse on the impression.

Commentary:
Line **2**: Note the sandhi writing *be-lu-uzni*(GEŠTU) instead of expected **be-el uzni*. Cf. *bēl uzni ḫasīsi*, "lord of wisdom (and) understanding" (Ea's epithet: Galter 1983 p. 38; translation modified).

Line **3**: Cf. Ea's epithet *bēl pirištim*, "lord of secret lore" (Galter 1983 p. 37; translation modified).

Line **5**: Amorite or West Semitic personal name, unattested elsewhere. Cf. Gelb 1980 p. 35 s.v. ZRQ; and the Aramaic PN (or nickname) *Zrq'*, "Blue(-Eyed One)", at Hatra (Hoftijzer & Jongeling 1995 p. 342 s.v. zrq_2; suggestion courtesy of M. Streck).

Line **6**: Personal name of unknown linguistic affiliation, unattested elsewhere.

CFa 7 (fig. 394). MB cylinder seal (F3.vr; 881.BNB; KM1274). L 3.4, D 1.5 cm. Faience. Mitannian Style. Trench AB, 70.60 N, 5.5 W, level 7.63. Associated pottery: Period 4B.

Bibliography: Kjærum 1983 no. 376; Glassner 1984 no. 9; Nashef 1984 p. 18 (no. 20); Gharbia et al. 1990 p. 76-77; Glassner 2008 no. 11; Potts 2010 no. 21.

Text:

1. *re-me-ni*	rēmēni
2. ^{d}AMAR.UTU	Marduk
3. *mu-ba-l*[*i-i*]*ṭ*	muball[i]ṭ
4. *kur-ba-šu*	kurbāšu

(1)Merciful is (2)Marduk. (3)He is the one who gives life—(4)worship him!

Remarks: The arrangement of the cases of the inscription is from left to right (as opposed to the customary right-to-left arrangement).

CFa 8 (fig. 395). Cylinder seal fragment (F3.yz; 881.BQV; KM1501). L 0.8, D 1.1 cm. Lazulite. Trench AF, sieve.

Bibliography: Kjærum 1983 no. 424; Glassner 1984 no. 28; Gharbia et al. 1990 p. 64-65; Glassner 2008 no. 30; Potts 2010 no. 98.

Remarks: Remains of two lines of an inscription (mostly illegible).

CFa 9 (fig. 396). Cylinder seal fragment (F3.æg; 881.BSK; KM1656). L 1.8, D 1.4 cm. Dark-grey stone. Trench AB or AF, sieve.

Bibliography: Kjærum 1983 no. 423; Glassner 1984 no. 26; Gharbia et al. 1990 p. 106-107; Glassner 2008 no. 28; Potts 2010 no. 97.

Remarks: The text is mostly illegible. Glassner's (1984 p. 38; 2008 p. 183) reading of the name of the god Enki in line 1 cannot be confirmed.

CFa 10 (fig. 397). MB cylinder seal (F3.åå; 881.BVS; KM1459). L 2.6, D 1.2 cm. Faience. Mitannian Style. Trench AI, sieve.

Bibliography: Kjærum 1983 no. 379; Glassner 1984 no. 10; Nashef 1984 p. 18 (no. 21); Gharbia et al. 1990 p. 84-85; Stiehler-Alegria 1996 no. 104a; Glassner 2008 no. 12; Potts 2010 no. 24.

Text (collated):

1. *re-me-ni*	rēmēni
2. ^{d}*e*$_2$-*a*$^{!}$(KU)	Ea$^{!}$
3. *za-qi*$_2$-*ip*$^{!}$(KISAL)	zāqip$^{!}$
4. *kur-ba-šu*	kurbāšu

(1)Merciful is (2)Ea. (3)He is the one who sets upright—(4)worship him!

Remarks: The arrangement of the cases of the inscription is from left to right (as opposed to the customary right-to-left arrangement).

CFa 11 (fig. 398). MB cylinder seal (F3.aaø; 881.AKZ; KM1461). L 3.5, D 1.7 cm. Glass. Trench D, northwest corner, level 8.65. Associated pottery: Period 4A.

Bibliography: Kjærum 1983 no. 406; Glassner 1984 no. 21; Nashef 1984 p. 19 (no. 26); Gharbia et al. 1990 p. 86-87; Glassner 2008 no. 23; Potts 2010 no. 64.

Remarks: The text is mostly illegible.

"CFa 12" (fig. 399). MB cylinder seal (F3.acu; 881.AMJ; KM1262). L 2.5, D 1.1 cm. Green, black-spotted soft stone. Trench D, level 8.00-7.70, sieve. Associated pottery: Period 4A.

Bibliography: Kjærum 1983 no. 403; Glassner 1984 no. 19; id. 2008 no. 21; Potts 2010 no. 61.

Remarks: The "text"—a pseudo-epigraph—is an attempt to imitate a cuneiform inscription. Cf. "CFa 15", "CFa 24", and "CFa 59".

CFa 13 (fig. 400). MB cylinder seal fragment (F3.aem; 881.ANS; KM1272). L 2.3, D 1.8 cm. Banded agate. Trench G, sieve from level 9.25-8.75. Associated pottery: Period 4A.

Bibliography: Kjærum 1983 no. 397; Glassner 1984 no. 13; Nashef 1984 p. 18 (no. 22); Gharbia et al. 1990 p. 68-69; Stiehler-Alegria 1996 no. 173a; Glassner 2008 no. 15; Potts 2010 no. 55; van Soldt 2021 p. 1047.

Text:

Lacuna

1′. [*iš*]-*ru-uk* [iš]ruk

[PN, …, (1′)pres]ented (it) [to …].

Remarks: Votive seal (see remarks on CFa 1, above). Cf. Stiehler-Alegria 1996 no. 268a (= Picchioni 1987-1988).

CFa 14 (fig. 401). MB cylinder seal fragment (F3.agr; 881.APO; KM1291). L 1.6, D 1.2 cm. Faience. Mitannian Style. Trench K, sieve from level 9.25-8.95. Associated pottery: Period 4A.

Bibliography: Kjærum 1983 no. 380; Glassner 1984 no. 11; Gharbia et al. 1990 p. 82-83; Glassner 2008 no. 13; Potts 2010 no. 25.

Text:

1. ^{d}[…]	[…]
2. IR$_3$ […]	arad […]
3. ⸢UGULA⸣ *me*-[*at*]	akil me[at]

(1)[PN], (2)servant of [PN], (3)the captai[n].

Commentary:

Line **3**: Lit. "commander of a hundred (men)"; cf. *CAD* M/2 s.v. *meat*. If the reading and the proposed interpretation are correct, then this is the first attestation of this military title outside of lexical sources.

"CFa 15". MB cylinder seal (F3.akj; 881.ATJ; KM1281). L 2.3, D 1.1 cm. Faience. Mitannian Style. Trench C or G, sieve.

Bibliography: Kjærum 1983 no. 387; Potts 2010 no. 32.

Remarks: Pseudo-cuneiform inscription. Cf. "CFa 12", "CFa 24", and "CFa 59".

CFa 16 (fig. 402). MB cylinder seal (F3.apx; 881.BAJ; KM1464). L 2.6, D 1.3 cm. Glass. Trench D, 36 N, 9.5 W, level 7.26. Associated pottery: Period 4A.

Bibliography: Kjærum 1983 no. 400; Glassner 1984 no. 16; Gharbia et al. 1990 p. 90-91; Glassner 2008 no. 18; Potts 2010 no. 58; van Soldt 2021 p. 1047.

Remarks: The text is mostly illegible.

CFa 17 (fig. 403). MB cylinder seal (F3.axk; 881.BZM; KM1652). L 3.1, D 1.2 cm. Carnelian. Trench AO, 63.30 N, 5.20 W, level 8.36. Associated pottery: Period 4A/4B (?).

Bibliography: Howard-Carter 1980-1983 p. 395 § 6.1.2 *c*; Kjærum 1983 no. 408; Glassner 1984 no. 23; Nashef

1984 p. 19 (no. 27); Gharbia et al. 1990 p. 66-67; Stiehler-Alegria 1996 no. 245a; Glassner 2008 no. 25; Potts 2010 no. 66; van Soldt 2021 p. 1047.

Text:

1. ^{d}IŠKUR *be-lu* GAL	Adad bēlu rabû
2. DINGIR *re-me-nu-u*$_2$	ilu rēmēnû
3. *tab-ni u tur*$_2$*-tiš*$_2$	tabni u turtīš
4. *šu-ul-li*$_2$*-im*	šullim
5. IR$_3$ *pa-li*$_2$*-iḫ-ka*	arda pāliḫka
6. *na-im-ru*	Na/imru
7. DUMU *ke-eš*-GAL	mār Keš-rabi

(1)O Adad, great lord, (2)merciful god, (3)you created and brought joy; (4)safeguard (5)the servant who reveres you, (6)(namely) Na/imru, (7)son of Keš-rabi.

Commentary:
Line **6**: Either Namru, "The Shining One", or Nimru, "Light": both are attested in the Akkadian onomasticon of this period (see Hölscher 1996 p. 146 and 151).

Line **7**: The PN Keš-rabi, "Keš Is Great", refers to the ancient cult center of the great Mesopotamian mother goddess Ninḫursaĝa/Bēlet-ilī. For other MB personal names incorporating the TN Keš, see Nashef 1982 p. 166.

CFa 18 (fig. 404). MB cylinder seal (F3.azk; 881.CBN; KM1462). L 3.4, D 1.4 cm. Glass (?). Trench AO, 60.50 N, 2.2 W, level 6.51. Associated pottery: Period 2, 3B/4A (?).

Bibliography: Kjærum 1983 no. 405; Glassner 1984 no. 20; Nashef 1984 p. 18 (no. 25); Gharbia et al. 1990 p. 88-89; Stiehler-Alegria 1996 no. 256b; Glassner 2008 no. 22; Potts 2010 no. 63.

Text:
1. ^{d}mes umun ⸢bulug$_3$⸣
2. ⸢dingir ša$_3$⸣-la$_2$-[su$_3$]

3-4. ⸢...⸣ (traces of signs, mostly illegible)

(1)O "Vigorous One" (= Marduk), supreme lord, (2)merci[ful] god, (3-4)...

Remarks: Sumerian language. Cf. CFa 21 below.

CFa 19 MB cylinder seal (F3.azs; 881.CBU; KM1655). L 3.4, D 1.4 cm. Glass. Trench AO, 61 N, 3 W, level 6.55. Associated pottery: Period 2, 3B/4A (?).

Bibliography: Kjærum 1983 no. 401; Glassner 1984 no. 17; Nashef 1984 p. 18 (no. 24); Gharbia et al. 1990 p. 96-97; Glassner 2008 no. 19; Potts 2010 no. 59.

Remarks: The text is mostly illegible.

CFa 20 (fig. 405). MB cylinder seal fragment (F3.bbu; 881.CDZ; KM1264). L 2, D 1.3 cm. Faience. Trench AN, 72.5 N, 6 E, level 6.62. Associated pottery: Period 2.

Bibliography: Kjærum 1983 no. 398; Glassner 1984 no. 14; Gharbia et al. 1990 p. 72-73; Glassner 2008 no. 16; Potts 2010 no. 56.

Remarks: The text is mostly illegible.

CFa 21 (fig. 406). MB cylinder seal (F3.ben; 881.CGS; KM1267). L 3, D 1.3 cm. Glass. Trench AN, upper layer, sieve.

Bibliography: Kjærum 1983 no. 399; Glassner 1984 no. 15; Nashef 1984 p. 18 (no. 23); Gharbia et al. 1990 p. 74-75; Stiehler-Alegria 1996 no. 112b; Glassner 2008 no. 17; Potts 2010 no. 57.

Text:
1. ^{d}mes umun bulug$_3$
2. dingir ša$_3$-la$_2$-su$_3$
3. sag an-ki
4. [ar]ḫuš tuku-a

(1)O "Vigorous One" (= Marduk), supreme lord, (2)merciful god, (3)the pre-eminent one of heaven and earth, (4)have [pi]ty!

Remarks: Sumerian language.

Commentary:
Line **1**: For the meaning of the Sumerian term mes, here used as a byname or epithet of Marduk, see Marchesi 2004 p. 191-193.

CFa 22. MB cylinder seal (F3.bez; 881.CHF; KM1465). L 3.3, D 1.5 cm. Glass or faience. Trench J, level 6.47. Associated pottery: Period 2.

Bibliography: Kjærum 1983 no. 402; Glassner 1984 no. 18; Gharbia et al. 1990 p. 92-93; Glassner 2008 no. 20; Potts 2010 no. 60.

Remarks: The text is illegible.

CFa 23 (fig. 407). OB cylinder seal (KM46[?]/1235; see remarks below). L 2.8, D 1.3 cm. Black stone. From Tell F3.

Bibliography: Anonymous 1964 fig. 46; Kjærum 1983 no. 370; Glassner 1984 no. 8; Nashef 1984 p. 18 (no. 19); Gharbia et al. 1990 p. 100-101; Glassner 2008 no. 10; Potts 2010 no. 13.

Text (collated):

1. ^{d}EN.KI	Ea
2. ^{d}DAM.GAL.NUN.NA	Damkina

(1)Ea (2)(and) Damkina.

Remarks: The museum number is recorded as KM46 in Glassner 1984 but as KM1235 in Glassner 2008. Though it may be the case that the number actually was changed, one suspects, instead, that the number KM46 is an error arising from the fact that the first publication of a photo of this seal in Anonymous 1964 was as "fig. 46" of said volume.

Commentary:
Lines **1-2**: The fact that a seal with this legend was found on Failaka cannot be taken as evidence for an identification, in Dilmun, of the divine couple of Eridu—Enki/Ea and Damgalnuna/Damkina— with the divine couple of Dilmun, as Nashef (1984 p. 2 and 7) advocated. In fact, several additional seals bearing the same inscription (sometimes with the addition of the conjunction *u*$_3$, "and", between the two divine names) are known; see, e.g., Buchanan 1981 nos. 784, 785, 873; and Collon 1986 nos. 67, 92, 516 (additional references in Galter 1983 p. 214 n. 3). In general, seals bearing only the names of one or more deities are commonly attested in the OB period (see Collon 1986 p. 17 *sub* a and c); according to Collon (1987 p. 131), they were "personal seals under the protection of the deities concerned".

"CFa 24" (fig. 408). MB cylinder seal (F6.393; 1129.NP; KM1654). L 3.1, D 1.3 cm. Faience. Trench D2, 14-15 N, 3.5-4 W, level -0.96.

Bibliography: Kjærum 1983 no. 418; Glassner 1984 no. 24; Gharbia et al. 1990 p. 94-95; Glassner 2008 no. 26; Potts 2010 no. 76.

Remarks: In this pseudo-epigraphic inscription, a single pseudo-cuneiform sign is repeated many times. Cf. "CFa 12", "CFa 15", and "CFa 59".

CFa 25 (fig. 409). Ur III cylinder seal (F6.902; 1129.AJU; KM1280). L 2.7, D 1.4 cm. Soft stone. Trench F2, 14.5 N, 6.5 W, level -1.98. Associated pottery: Period 1.

Bibliography: Anonymous 1964 fig. 64; Kjærum 1980 p. 45 and fig. 1 (on p. 50); id. 1983 no. 368; Glassner 1984 no. 7; Nashef 1984 p. 17-18 (no. 18); Gharbia et al. 1990 p. 102-103; Potts 1990 p. 286; Glassner 2008 no. 7; Potts 2010 no. 7; David-Cuny & Neyme 2016 p. 54.

Text (collated):
1. nam-ḫa-ne$_2$
2. dumu ka-ku$_3$

(1)Namḫanne, (2)son of Kaku(g)

Remarks: Sumerian language and Sumerian personal names.

Commentary:
Line **1**: For the transcription of this name as Namḫanne, rather than Namḫani, see Marchesi & Marchetti 2011 p. 157 n. 19; and note the more accurate spelling nam-ḫa-an-ne$_2$ (Figulla & Martin 1953 no. 165 rev. 3; Charpin 1980 p. 205 TS 7: 19; etc.). Both nam-ḫa-ne$_2$ and nam-ḫa-an-ne$_2$ are "phonetic" spellings of the Sumerian PN whose standard writing is nam-maḫ(-a/ḫa)-ne$_2$, representing its actual pronunciation (see Marchesi & Marchetti 2011 p. 158 n. 24). The name in question means "His/Her Magnificence" and is the abbreviation of a longer name—*nam-maḫ(-a/ḫa)-ne$_2$(-i$_3$)-du$_{10}$—that means "His/Her (i.e., the deity's) Magnificence Is Good".

Line **2**: The KA sign in the writing of this personal name (which is often erroneously read as inim-ku$_3$) has the value ka, "mouth", not inim, "word": the name in question is, in fact, an abbreviation of *ka-ku$_3$-ga-ne$_2$-mu(-un)-ba/bad, "He/She (= the deity) Has Opened His/Her Holy Mouth" (see Balke 2017 p. 216).

CFa 26 (fig. 410). MB cylinder seal (F6.986; 1129.AOA; KM1286). L 3.2, D 1.4 cm. Faience. Trench F1, 3 N, 6 W, level -0.30.

Bibliography: Kjærum 1983 no. 419; Glassner 1984 no. 25; Gharbia et al. 1990 p. 80-81; Stiehler-Alegria 1996 no. 24a; Glassner 2008 no. 27; Potts 2010 no. 77; David-Cuny & Neyme 2016 p. 55.

Text:
1. ⌜d⌝mes ⌜x⌝ […]

Fig. 393. 2:1.

Mirror image of the impression.

Fig. 394. 2:1.

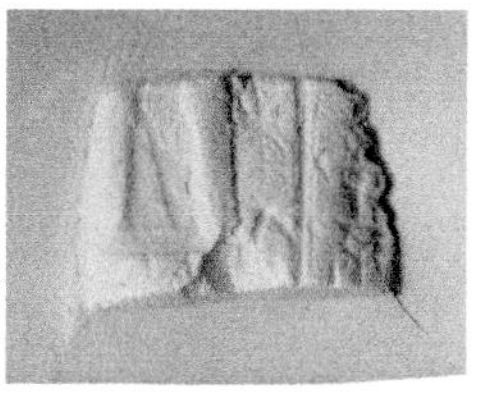

Fig. 395. 2:1.

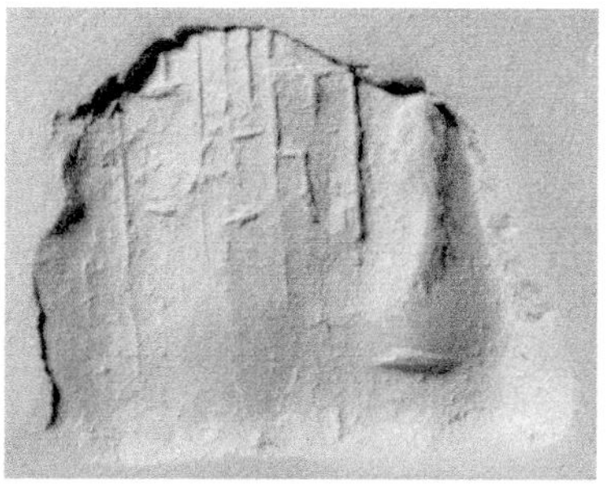

Fig. 396. 2:1.

Fig. 397. 2:1.

Fig. 398. 2:1.

Fig. 399. 2:1.

Fig. 400. 2:1.

Fig. 401. 2:1.

Fig. 402. 2:1.

Fig. 403. 2:1.

Fig. 404. 2:1.

Fig. 405. 2:1.

Fig. 406. 2:1.

Fig. 407. 2:1.

Fig. 408. 2:1.

Fig. 409. 2:1.

Fig. 410. 2:1.

2-3. ⌜…⌝ (mostly broken and illegible)

(1)O "Vigorous One" (= Marduk), … […], (2-3)…

Remarks: Sumerian language. Cf. CFa 21 above.

CFa 27. MB cylinder seal (KM1277). L 2.6, D 1.2 cm. Faience or glass. From Tell F3, Tell F5, or Tell F6.

Bibliography: Kjærum 1983 no. 421; Glassner 1984 no. 27; Gharbia et al. 1990 p. 78-79; Glassner 2008 no. 29; Potts 2010 no. 79.

Remarks: The text is almost completely illegible.

Stone vessels

CFa 28 (fig. 411). Rim fragment (F3.8; 881.CP; KM3529). 6 × 2.5 × 1.3 cm. Reconstructed diameter 16 cm. Soft stone. Trench RM, c. 17 m N, unknown depth.

Bibliography: van Dijk 1962 no. 1; Glob 1968 p. 134; Alster 1983 p. 42 (no. 5) with n. 30 (on p. 68); Glassner 1984 no. 39; Gharbia et al. 1990 p. 160-161; Glassner 2008 no. 41; Hilton 2014 p. 49, 148 (fig. 360), and 181.

Text (collated):

1. […] GAL
2. […]-*ḫu* SANGA?/UMBISAG?
3. […] ⌜x x⌝
4. […] NI
5. [(…) d*en*/*in*]-*za*-⌜*ak*⌝
6. […] ⌜x⌝ […]

Lacuna

Too broken to translate.

Remarks: The horizontal arrangement of the writing implies a late date (end of the 2nd millennium or 1st millennium BC; cf. CFa 41 below). Too little of the original text is preserved to get a sense of its contents. Only the DN Enzak or Inzak (in line 5) and, perhaps, a professional title (line 2; either SANGA = *šangû*, "temple administrator", or UMBISAG = *tupšarru*, "scribe") are recognizable.

Commentary:

Line **2**: The reading EN DILMUNki ("lord of Dilmun"), first proposed by van Dijk, should definitely be abandoned (see above, *sub* Remarks).

Line **5**: For a possible restoration [d*en*]-*za*-⌜*ak*⌝, rather than [d*in*]-*za*-⌜*ak*⌝, note the occurrence of a by-form Enzak—variously written as d*en-zak* (see, e.g., comm. to CFa 41: 1, below), (d)*en-za-ak* (in the fPN f*ba-al-ti-en-za-ak*; Clay 1912 p. 62), or d*en-zak*x(SAG) (see, e.g., Eidem 1997 p. 80 fig. 322)—of the divine name Inzak in the MB period and later.

CFa 29 (fig. 412). Shallow bowl fragment (F3.87B; 881.FV; KM3528). 5.4 × 4.5 × 0.6 cm. Reconstructed diameter 20 cm. Soft stone. Trench RM, 11.95 N, 2.70 W, 1.76 m below surface.

Bibliography: van Dijk 1962 no. 2; Alster 1983 p. 42 (no. 6) with n. 31 (on p. 68); Glassner 1984 no. 38; Gharbia et al. 1990 p. 158-159; Glassner 2008 no. 40; Hilton 2014 p. 49, 157 (fig. 409), and 191; van Soldt 2021 p. 1047.

Text (collated):

1.	[*a-na*] ⌜^{d}⌝EN.⌜KI⌝	[ana] Ea
2.	[LU]GAL.A.NI$^{!}$(IR).{I‹R›}	[bē]līšu
3.	[$^{(m)}$*a*$^{?}$]-*ba-si-di-a*	['A]ba$^{?}$-Sidi'a
4.	[NAR$^{?}$].GAL ^{d}*in-*	[nar]gal$^{?}$ In=
5.	[*za-‹ak›* D]UMU *ḫa-din*-DING‹IR›	[za‹k› m]ār 'Adin-'e‹l›
6.	[…] ^{d}*in-za-*	[…] Inza=
7.	[*ak*] BUR *ú-še-*	[k] pūra(m) ušē=
8 (?).	[*li*]	[li]

$^{(1)}$[To] Ea, $^{(2)}$his [lo]rd, $^{(3)}$['A]ba$^{?}$-Sidi'a, $^{(4)}$the chief [musician (?)] of In= $^{(5)}$[za‹k›, s]on of 'Adin-e‹l›, $^{(6)}$[the …] of Inza= $^{(7)}$[k], present= $^{(8)}$[ed] $^{(7)}$the stone vessel.

Remarks: van Dijk (1962 *ad* no. 2) noted that "le récipient a été réparé et a même subi un remaniement de sa forme, de sorte que les fins des lignes, incomplètes également au commencement, ont été effacées", while according to Glassner (2008 p. 187), it is an "œuvre d'un lapicide maladroit qui, arrivé en fin de lignes, abrège les noms et laisse des signes d'écriture inachevés". As my reconstruction of this text implies, from line 4 onward the engraver miscalculated the space for the inscription and divided several words between two successive lines.

Commentary:
Line **1**: Note that the occurrence of Enki/Ea and Inzak* in the same text (lines 1, 4/5*, and 6/7*) weighs against Nashef's (1984 p. 6-7 and 10) hypothesis of an identification of these two deities in Dilmun.

Line **2**: See above, comm. to CFa 2: 2.

Line **3**: Restoration suggested by M. Streck (pers. comm.). If this restoration is correct, we can tentatively reconstruct the personal name as 'Aba-Sidi'a and interpret it as "Sidi'a (= DN?) Is the Father" (cf. Streck 2000 p. 281; 283 § 3.43; and 331 § 5.31).

Line **4**: The context requires a professional title borrowed from a Sumerian word of the type x(= profession)-gal. In addition, the term in question should already be attested in the 2nd millennium BC and occur in association with qualifying divine names ("the chief … of DN"). There is only one term I know of that meets these conditions: *nargallu(m)*, "chief musician" (but cf. Eidem 1997 p. 77 no. 7: 3-5; and p. 80 *ad loc.*; I consider Eidem's suggestion to read ENGAR.GAL ^{d}niraḫ, "chief farmer of (the god) Niraḫ", in this passage unlikely. For occurrences of nar-gal/*nargallum* in association with qualifying divine names, see Huber Vuillet 2010 p. 146 Ni. 2426 ii 19-23 and 149 Ni. 2436 iii 10-13—both from OB Nippur, reign of Rīm-Sîn I).

Line **5**: Cf. ^{m}*ḫa-din-*^{d}*i-ba-nu-u*[*m*], name of a Dilmunite merchant in YBC 5547: 5 (Hallo 1965 p. 200-202). The onomastic element *ḫa-din* is almost certainly from the Amorite root 'DN (Streck 2000 p. 322 § 5.8 n. 1; Golinets 2018 p. 366 s.v.; see also Durand 2023 p. 165 n. 1). Thus *ḫa-din*-DINGIR could be interpreted as 'Adin-'el, "The God Is Pleasant" (for *qatil*-adjectives used predicatively in nominal sentence names in Amorite, see Golinets 2018 p. 159-160).

Line(s) **7(-8)**: Or: *ú-še-‹li›*, with the text ending at line 7. The use of the verb *elû(m)* (in the Š stem) is rather unexpected. Occurrences of dedicatory formulas with *elû(m)* Š are very rare, and none of them is attested in texts from southern Mesopotamia (see *CAD* E s.v. *elû* 9c); on the contrary, this usage is well attested in OB Mari (ibid.; see also Charpin 1984 no. 1 rev. 14'; no. 2: 14; and Frayne 1990 E4.6.11.1: 15). One might wonder whether this common feature in the dedicatory formulas of Failaka and Mari is related to the fact that contacts were established between Dilmun, Mari, and Assyria during the reign of Šamši-Adad in the 18th century BC (see Groneberg 1992; Eidem & Højlund 1993 and 1997; van Koppen 1997; Ziegler 2008).

CFa 30 (fig. 413). Decorated vessel fragment (F3.138; 881.HU). Soft stone. Failaka Figurative Style. Trench RM, 40-60 N, level c. 8.25-9.10. Lost.

Bibliography: van Dijk 1962 no. 3; Bibby 1969 pl. 20 (lower left); Howard-Carter 1980-1983 p. 393 § 4.7 no. 2; Alster 1983 p. 42 (no. 1) with n. 26 (on p. 68); Glassner 1984 no. 37; Nashef 1984 p. 16 (no. 7); Glassner 2008 no. 39; Hilton 2014 p. 49, 117 (fig. 242), and 190.

Text:

1.	[… NAR$^{?}$].GAL ^{d}*in-za-ak*	[… nar]gal$^{?}$ Inzak

$^{(1)}$[PN], the chief [musician (?)] of Inzak.

Remarks: Cf. CFa 29 above (same offerer?).

CFa 31 (fig. 414). Flat base vessel fragment (F3.ir; 881.ADK; KM1518). 7 × 5.5 × 1 cm. Reconstructed diameter

10 cm. Soft stone. Trench E, sieve from level c. 7.00-6.00. Associated pottery: Period 2.

Bibliography: van Dijk 1962 no. 5; Glassner 1984 no. 32; Gharbia et al. 1990 p. 150-151; Glassner 2008 no. 34; Hilton 2014 p. 48-49, 149 (fig. 365), and 187; van Soldt 2021 p. 1047.

Text (collated):
1. […]
2. […] ⌜x⌝
3. [… ^{d}*in-z*]*a-ak*
4. [*ša*$_2$ *a*-GA]-AŠ

… [(3)][(…) of Inz]ak [(4)][of Ag]aš$^?$.

Commentary:
Lines **3-4**: See above, comm. to CFa 1: 2b-4.

CFa 32 (fig. 415). Rim fragment (F3.xø; 881.BPR; KM1296). 7.2 × 4 × 1.1 cm. Reconstructed diameter 36 cm. Soft stone. Trench Z, 44.8 N, 9.30 E, level 8.26. Associated pottery: Period 4.

Bibliography: Anonymous 1964 fig. 53; Howard-Carter 1980-1983 p. 395 § 6.2 *b.*; Glassner 1984 no. 29; Nashef 1984 p. 16 (no. 10); Gharbia et al. 1990 p. 144-145; Glassner 2008 no. 31; Hilton 2014 p. 48, 147 (fig. 354), and 182; Ashkanani 2021 p. 83; van Soldt 2021 p. 1047.

Text:
Lacuna

1′. […] ^{m}DUMU-[… (…)]	[…] Mār-[… (…)]
2′. […] ^{m}*ia-mi*-⌜*u*$_2$⌝ […]	[…] Yaḫmī'u […]
3′. […] ŠA TA ⌜x⌝ […]	[…] … […]

[(1′)][…] Mār-[… (…) [(2′)]…] Yaḫmī'u [… [(3′)]…] … […].

Remarks: The inscription is placed upside down in relation to the vessel (see Hilton 2014 fig. 354). The horizontal writing points to a late 2nd millennium BC or later dating (cf. CFa 41 below).

Commentary:
Line **1′**: Akkadian personal name of the type "Son of …" (Stamm 1968 p. 260 and 269). Cf. ^{m}DUMU-*u*$_2$-*zi-bi*, (= Mār-Uzibi, "Son of Uzibi") and DUMU-U$_4$.20.KAM (= Mār-ešrē, "Son of the Twentieth Day") in early Kassite texts from Bahrain (see André-Salvini & Cavigneaux forth. QA 94.49: 5 and QA 96.157: 3, respectively).

Line **2′**: Amorite personal name (hypocoristic; cf. Golinets 2018 p. 76-80 § 6.5.1.2), probably from the root ḪMY, "to protect" (*DRS* 6 p. 880 s.v.). Cf. the Amorite PN *ia-mi-i-la* (= Yaḫmī-'ila), "The God Has Protected (the family)" (Gelb 1980 nos. 3351 and 3871; for a different interpretation, see Streck 2000 p. 274 § 3.22).

CFa 33 (fig. 416). Vessel fragment (F3.øå; 881.BUO; KM1522). 2.7 × 1.7 × 1 cm. Soft stone. Trench AE, sieve.

Bibliography: Glassner 1984 no. 34; Gharbia et al. 1990 p. 154-155; Glassner 2008 no. 36; Hilton 2014 p. 49, 157 (fig. 408, showing the sherd upside down), and 191.

Remarks: Remains of two lines of an inscription with only three signs fully (2) or partially (1) preserved.

CFa 34 (?) (fig. 417). Rim fragment (F3.anå; 881.AYL; KM1649). 7.2 × 5.7 × 2.1 cm. Reconstructed diameter 42 cm. Soft stone. Trench O, level c. 7.20-6.90 (but the daybook mentions only pottery from this lot).

Bibliography: Hilton 2014 p. 49, 156 (fig. 406), and 181.

Remarks: According to Hilton (2014 p. 49), there are some undecipherable cuneiform signs on the rim.

CFa 35. Vessel fragment (F3.axi; 881.BZK; KM1728). 4.6 × 3.5 × 1.2 cm. Reconstructed diameter 13 cm. Calcite. Found in Trench AN, 77.8 N, 6 E, level 7.21.

Bibliography: Hilton 2014 p. 49, 68 (fig. 92), and 191.

Remarks: Remains of an inscription but no identifiable signs (collated).

CFa 36 (?). Decorated vessel—body fragment (F3.yo, 881.BQK, KM3051). 8.4 × 5.8 × 0.9 cm. Chlorite (Hilton 2014 fig. 17). Failaka Figurative Style. Trench AH, 58.50 N, 4.4 E, level 8.40. Associated pottery: Period 4?

Decorated vessel—rim fragment (KM3082). 4 × 3.2 × 0.6 cm. Reconstructed diameter 20 cm. Chlorite. Failaka Figurative Style. From Tell F3.

Decorated vessel—base fragment (FH1012; KM1394). 8 × 7.5 × 1.8 cm. Chlorite. Failaka Figurative Style. From the Johns Hopkins University excavations at Tell F5, area of the "Hellenistic Fortress": Trench FH6, Level 3, Floor 2 (at 1.70 m).

Bibliography: Howard-Carter 1984 folio 49; Hilton 2014 p. 49, 110 (fig. 218), and 182.

Remarks: According to Hilton (2014 p. 49), "a few undecipherable cuneiform signs" are incised on this vessel (cf. Hilton's drawing, ibid., fig. 218).

CFa 37 (fig. 418). Spouted bowl—rim fragment (883. AKD; KM1517). 6.2 × 5.8 × 0.6 cm. Reconstructed diameter 14 cm. Soft stone. From Tell F5, under the Hellenistic fortress (Nashef 1984 p. 17).

Bibliography: Anonymous 1964 fig. 32; Howard-Carter 1980-1983 p. 395 § 6.2 *a*; Glassner 1984 no. 31; Nashef 1984 p. 16-17 (no. 12); Gharbia et al. 1990 p. 148-149; Glassner 2008 no. 33; Hilton 2014 p. 48, 108 (fig. 215), and 179 (Hilton's "1962.AKP" is erroneous); Ashkanani 2021 p. 127; van Soldt 2021 p. 1047.

Text:
1. [… …]-*mu-um* AN ⸢E⸣ IGI TA […]
2. […] ⸢x⸣ SI e$_2$-kar$^{!}$(TE.‹A›)-ra […]
3. [… …]-*am ina pa-ni*(-)[(…) …]
4. […] *ta-am-bi* […]
5. […] ⸢AN⸣ […]
Lacuna

Too broken to translate.

Remarks: The horizontal writing suggests that the inscription is late MB or later (cf. CFa 41 below).

Commentary:
Line **1**: AN and E could represent *šamê*(AN)^{e}, "heaven, sky", but without the context (all the other elements of this line are obscure) we cannot be sure.

Line **2**: For the Ekara-temple, see below, comm. to CFa 41: 1.

Line **3**: *ina pa-ni*(-)[…] could stand for either *ina pāni* […], "before [… (someone/something)]", or *ina pānī*[*šu*], "before [him/it]", or *ina pānī*[*ti*], "previou[sly]".

Line **4**: *tambi* is the third person feminine singular or the second person masculine singular of the verb *nabû(m)*, "to name, nominate, decree".

CFa 38 (fig. 419). Decorated vessel—rim fragment (883.ALA; KM1520). 5.2 × 3.6 × 1 cm. Reconstructed diameter 28 cm. Soft stone. Failaka Figurative Style. From Tell F5.

Bibliography: Glassner 1984 no. 33; Gharbia et al. 1990 p. 152-153; Glassner 2008 no. 35; Hilton 2014 p. 49, 109 (fig. 216), and 181.

Text (collated):

1. [E$_2$].GAL GU.LA	[E]kallum Rabûm(/Rabītum)
2. ^{m}⸢x⸣-[…]	…[…]

Lacuna

(1)(Property of) "The Great [Pa]lace". (2)P[N, (3+x)…].

Remarks: The interpretation offered here assumes that the vertical line after [E$_2$].GAL GU.LA is a dividing line that was meant to separate two consecutive cases of the inscription. Alternatively, the line in question could have the function of signaling the start and end point of the text, which is written counterclockwise in the round on the top of the rim; if so, we would have an inscription beginning with a personal name—^{m}⸢x⸣-[…]—and ending with E$_2$.GAL GU.LA, "The Great Palace". It should be noted, however, that E$_2$.GAL GU.LA followed by a personal name also occurs at the beginning of other inscriptions (see CFa 1 and 69; cf. also CFa 40 below), which supports the former interpretation.

Commentary:
Lines **1-2**: See comm. to CFa 1: 1 and 2a; and CFa 49 I-II.

Lines **3+x**: Cf. CFa 1 and 69.

CFa 39 (fig. 420). Rim fragment (KM1645). 5 × 4.1 × 1 cm. Reconstructed diameter 25 cm. Dark grey-greenish, hard stone (probably dolerite). Found in 1958 by Imran Abdo, a Museum employee, on the surface of Tell F6 (Kjærum, pers. comm. to F. Højlund).

Bibliography: Glassner 1984 no. 36; Gharbia et al. 1990 p. 156-157; Glassner 2008 no. 38; Hilton 2014 p. 49, 130 (fig. 302), and 178.

Text (collated):

1. ^{m}BA-$^{\{m\}d}$[…]	Iqīš-[…]

Commentary:
Line **1**: Probably an Akkadian personal name of the type Iqīš-DN, "(the deity) So-and-so Has Presented (the child)".

CFa 40 (fig. 421). Plate—rim fragment (KM1642). 5.2 × 2.5 × 0.8 cm. Reconstructed D 36 cm. Dark grey-greenish, hard stone (probably dolerite).

Bibliography: Glassner 1984 no. 35; Gharbia et al. 1990 p. 166-167; Glassner 2008 no. 37; Hilton et al. 2012 no. 11; Hilton 2014 p. 49, 155 (fig. 402), and 181.

Text (collated):
1. […] GAL […]
2. […]-*din*/*tin*-DINGIR/^{d}[…]
Lacuna?

Too broken to translate.

Remarks: No chronological significance can be attached to the horizontal writing (which is probably due to the form of the vessel).

Commentary:
Line **1**: Hilton et al. (2012 col. 416) suggested to restore [E$_2$].GAL [GU.LA]. For inscriptions beginning with E$_2$.GAL GU.LA, see CFa 1, 38 (?), and 69.

Line **2**: The DIN/TIN and AN/DINGIR signs are almost certainly part of the writing of a personal name, but several alternative reconstructions are possible, e.g., [*ḫa*]-*din*-DINGIR/^{d}[…] (= 'Adin-'el/DN, "The God/DN Is Pleasant"; see above, CFa 29: 5 with comm.); [*ia*$_{(8)}$-(*an*/*at*)]-*tin*-DINGIR/^{d}[…] (= Yan/ttin-'el/DN, "The God/DN Has Given (the child)"); [*id*/*i*]-*din*-DINGIR/^{d}[…] (= Iddin-ilum/DN; Akkadian, same meanings); etc.

Metal vessels

CFa 41 (figs. 282 and 422). Rim fragment (F3.avw; 881.BXQ; KM1298). 10.1 × 3.9 × 0.2 cm. Copper or bronze. Found in Trench AI (according to Kjærum [pers. comm. to F. Højlund], from the sieve; most of the pottery from Trench AI dates to Period 3A or 4A).

Bibliography: Glassner 1984 no. 46; Gharbia et al. 1990 p. 118-119; Glassner 2008 no. 45.

Text (collated):
1. [*a-na* ^{d}EN.KI L]UGAL ABZU(ZU:AB) *a-šib* e$_2$-kar-ra *be-l*[*i*$_2$-*šu* …]
2. [… ^{d}IŠKUR]-⸢MU⸣-URU$_3$ LUGAL KIŠ *a-na* TI.LA ⸢^{d}⸣[IŠKUR-MU-URU$_3$ … *i-qi*$_2$-*iš*]

1. [ana Ea b]ēl apsî āšib Ekara bēl[īšu …]
2. [… Adad]-⸢šuma⸣-uṣur šar kiššati ana balāṭ [Adad-šuma-uṣur (…) iqīš]

1. [To Ea, the l]ord of the *apsû*, who dwells in the Ekara(-temple), [his] lord, [PN(, …)],
2. [the … of Adad]-šuma-uṣur, king of the world, for the life of [Adad-šuma-uṣur (…) presented (it)].

Remarks: This inscription was interpreted by Glassner as a dedication to the Akkadian sun-god Šamaš by Nebuchadnezzar II, but neither that god nor that king are named in the text. What was previously misread as UD.AB and misinterpreted as the logogram for the name of one of the sun-god's cities—Larsa—should actually be read as ZU.AB, the customary writing of the term *apsû*, which denotes the realm of the lord of subterranean water, the god Enki/Ea. As regards the name of the king that occurs in this inscription, apart from paleographic considerations (which point to a MB period dating), the presence of the MU sign (which is clearly visible on the photo) before URU$_3$ rules out the possibility of this king being Nebuchadnezzar II. It can only be either Adad-šuma-uṣur or Illil-šuma-uṣur (conventionally, "Enlil-nādin-aḫi", but see Marchesi forth.), respectively the fifth-to-last and the last rulers of the Kassite Dynasty. Both of these kings bore the title *šar kiššati*, "king of the world" (see Seux 1967 p. 311; Paulus 2014 p. 366 AŠU 1 i 8; and p. 485 ENAh 1 i 7′). However, additional paleographic considerations support the reconstruction of the royal name Adad-šuma-uṣur in this text. Note, especially, the graphic shapes of the signs MU and URU$_3$ in the only known monumental inscription—the kudurru BM 113891—that mentions Illil-šuma-uṣur (see Cifola 1988 pl. 33b i 6′ and 10′): they are considerably different from the MU and the URU$_3$ in our inscription. For the same signs in inscriptions of Adad-šuma-uṣur (with forms more similar to those on our vessel), see Steele 1951 pl. VIIa [on p. 25] 4; Dossin 1962 pl. XIII no. 1: 1 and pl. XIV no. 2: 1; Seidl 1989 pl. 5c i 8.

Commentary:
Line **1**: The Ekara, "House of the Quay" or "House of the Harbor", is also known from Mesopotamian sources; see, especially, Schroeder 1920 no. 84 A 7′-8′: e$_2$-kar-ra *bīt*(E$_2$) ^{d}⸢x⸣.[x] / [*ša*$_2$] *til-mun*^{ki} …, "Ekara, the house of (the god) […] in (lit. of) Dilmun. …"; George (1993 p. 56) restored this as *bīt* ^{d}*e*[*n-zak*], "the house of E[nzak]", but in view of our text, one is tempted to emend George's restoration to E$_2$ ^{d}E[N.KI], that is, "the house of E[a]". On the other hand, in the so-called "Syncretistic Hymn to Nanaya", one reads (lines 13-14): [*ina*] e$_2$-kar-ra ^{d}*šu-luḫ-ḫi-tu*$_4$ *al-ti* ^{d}*en-zak u* ^{d}*mes-ki-l*[*ak*] / […]-⸢x⸣ *ša*$_2$ *til*-⸢*mun*⸣ *i-qab-bu-u-ni* ⸢*ana*⸣-[*ku-ma*] ^{d}*na-n*[*a-ia*], "[in] the Ekara, they call me Šuluḫḫītu, the wife of Enzak, and Meskil[ak, the …] of Dilmun—[I], Nan[aya]" (Oshima 2020 p. 372-373; transliteration

Fig. 411. 2:1.

Mirror image of the impression.

Fig. 412. 2:1.

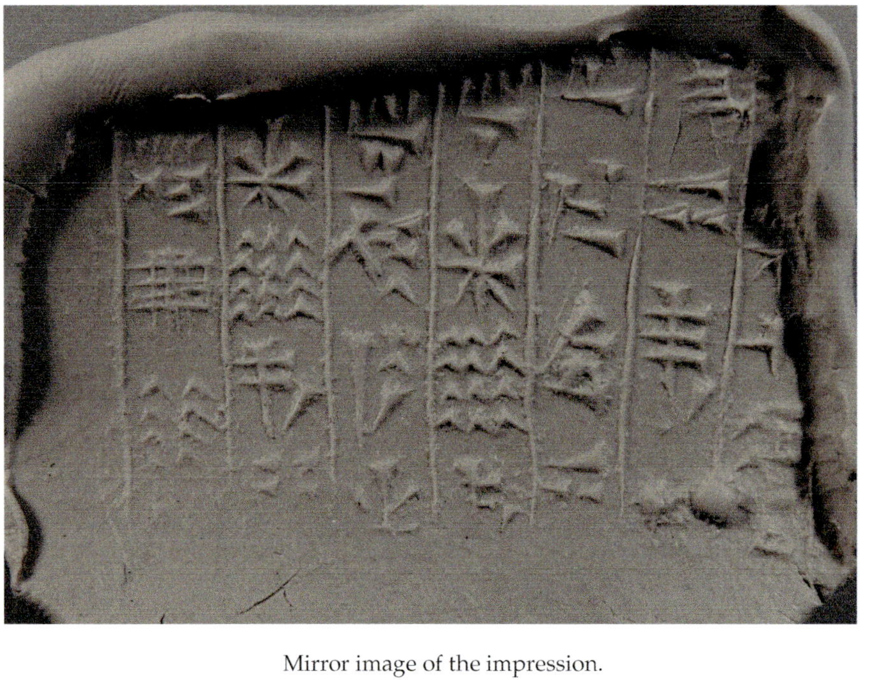

Mirror image of the impression.

Fig. 413. 1:1.

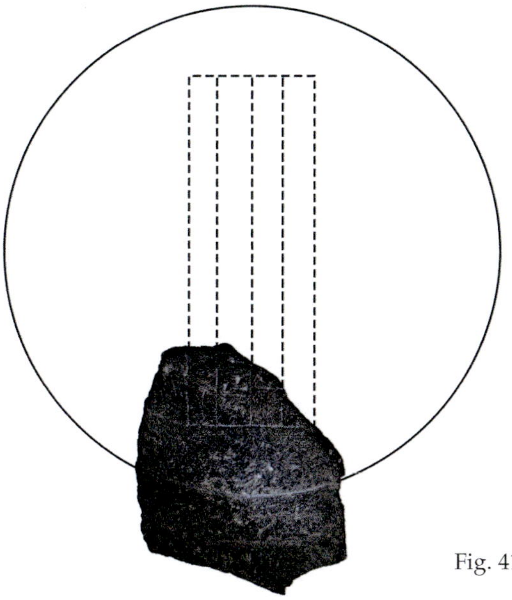

Fig. 414. 1:2 and 1:1.

Fig. 415. 1:1.

Flipped mirror image of the impression.

Fig. 416. 2:1.

Fig. 417. 1:1.

Mirror image of the impression.

Fig. 418. 1:1.

Mirror image of the impression.

and translation slightly modified here). Was the Ekara-temple of Failaka a "collective" shrine devoted to a mix of Dilmunite and Mesopotamian deities?

Line **2a**: If one assumes, as is typical of horizontal inscriptions, that all the lines of the text start from the same imaginary vertical line on the left, then there is too much space at the beginning of line 2 to restore only ^{d}IŠKUR. The same is true of ^{d}EN.LIL$_{2}$, if one were instead to attribute the inscription to Illil-šuma-uṣur (see above, *sub* Remarks). This combined with the fact that TI.LA is not followed by the suffix -*šu* ("his") but rather by a sign that begins with a central horizontal wedge makes it all but certain that this text is not a royal inscription but is rather the private inscription of a high-ranking official who made a votive offering for the benefit (lit. "for the life") of his sovereign (cf., e.g., Becker 1993 p. 59 no. 791). It could very well be a Kassite governor of Dilmun (cf. Potts 1990 p. 307-310; Brinkman 1993; Sassmannshausen 2008 p. 317-320; Clayden 2020 p. 96 n. 20) or some other Kassite notable who was on Failaka island.

Line **2b**: For restoring *iqīš* at the end of the inscription, it should be noted that *iqīš* is the standard verb of offering in Kassite votive inscriptions (both private

Fig. 419. 2:1.

Fig. 420. 2:1.

Fig. 421. 2:1.

and royal); see Scheil 1917 p. 91 (line 12); Stein 2000 p. 130-148 passim; etc. For rare attestations of *išruk*, see CFa 13 above and Stiehler-Alegria 1996 no. 268a (= Picchioni 1987-1988).

Pottery

CFa 42 (fig. 423). Potsherd—rim fragment (F3.cp; 881. XR). 10.5 × 5.8 cm. Trench I, from the surface level in 9.56 to 9.06. Associated pottery: Period 4B.

Bibliography: Knudsen 1982 p. 16-17 *sub* 1799a and 3878a/6280a; Nashef 1984 p. 19 (no. 29); Eidem 1987 p. 179 and fig. 718; Gharbia et al. 1990 p. 140-141; Glassner 1990 p. 123 (*ICF* 49); id. 2008 no. 48.

Text:

1. 1 *ka*$_3$-*ku-ul*	ištiāt kakkul
2. ^{m}*ia*$_8$-*ta-ra-*[*tim*/(*a*-)*ia*$_8$]	Yatara[tim]/ Yatarā[ya]
3. DUMU *gu-ur-d*[*a-an*]	mār Gurd[ān]

(1)One fermentation vat (2)of Yatara[tim]/Yatarā[ya], (3)son of Gurd[ān].

Commentary:
Line **1**: For this type of vessel, see Eidem 1987 p. 179.

Line **2**: The name of the vessel owner was either Yataratum or Yatarāya: both are hypocoristic forms of the Amorite name types X-yatra and Yatar-x, "So-and-so Is Surpassingly Great" (see Streck 2000 p. 315-316 § 4.9; 354 § 5.83; Golinets 2018 p. 252-253 *sub* YTR).

Line **3**: Cf. *gu-ur-da-an*, Amorite personal name at Mari (Gelb 1980 no. 1799).

CFa 43. Potsherd—rim fragment (F3.ho; 881.ACJ; KM1302). 9.1 × 7.6 × 1.1 cm. Trench E, 33.5-35.5 N, level 6.65-5.95. Associated pottery: Period 2.

Bibliography: van Dijk 1962 no. 4; Howard-Carter 1980-1983 p. 394 § 5.4.3 *a*; Alster 1983 p. 42 (no. 2) with n. 27 (on p. 68); Glassner 1984 no. 40; Nashef 1984 p. 16 (no. 6); Eidem 1987 p. 179 and fig. 719 (on p. 180); Gharbia et al. 1990 p. 136-137; Eidem 1997 p. 80 *sub* 11; Glassner 2008 no. 46; van Soldt 2021 p. 1047.

Text (collated):
1. ^{m}NI-⸢x⸣-[… … (…-)^{d}*i*]*n-za-ak*

(1)P[N … (…-)I]nzak.

Remarks: The interpretation offered here assumes that the original inscription extended counterclockwise along the entire perimeter of the rim, and that the beginning and end are preserved.

Commentary:
Line **1**: Inzak may also be part of a personal name. Cf. CFa 3 above with comm.

CFa 44 (fig. 424). Potsherd (F6.995.B1; 1129.AOO; KM1663). 3.2 × 2.8 × 0.6 cm. Trench F1, level -0.85.

Bibliography: Glassner 1984 no. 41; Eidem 1987 p. 180 and fig. 720; Gharbia et al. 1990 p. 138-139; Glassner 2008 no. 47.

Text (collated):
Lacuna

1′. […] ⸢x x⸣ […]	[…] … […]
2′. [^{m}…]-⸢*ma*?⸣-*ta-nu* UGULA […]	[…]matanu? akil […]
3′. ⸢*ar*?⸣-*du ša*$_2$ ^{d}ištara[n]	ardu? ša Ištara[n]
4′. [DUMU]	[mār]
⸢^{m}⸣*ia-am-ru*$_3$-^{d}nin-[…]	Yamrū-Nin[…]

… (2′)[…]matanu?, the chief/overseer of […], (3′)servant (?) of (the god) Ištara[n], (4′)[son] of Yamrū-Nin[…].

Remarks: Based on the horizontal writing and paleography, the text is late MB or later (cf. Eidem 1987 p. 180).

Commentary:
Line **2′**: Cf. the Aramaic PN Masamatānu (^{m}*ma-sa-ma-ta-nu*), "Obedient" (*PNA* 2/2 p. 743 s.v.).

Line **4′**: ^{m}*ia-am-ru*$_3$-^{d}nin-[…] provides evidence for a new Amorite name type Yamrū-DN, based on the root MR′ or MRY/W (cf. Gelb 1980 p. 25 s.v. MR′?; Golinets 2018 p. 305-307 § 23.1.1-2).

Tablets

CFa 45 (fig. 425). Tablet fragment (F3.110; 881.GT; KM1297). 4.4 × 3.5 × 2.1 cm. Grey core, brown surface. Partially baked. Trench RM, 1-15 N, 1-2.45 m below surface, sieve.

Bibliography: van Dijk 1962 no. 8; Glassner 1984 no. 42; Eidem 1987 p. 180 n. 1; Gharbia et al. 1990 p. 126-127; Eidem 1997 p. 77 comm. to 2: 2; Calvet 2005 p. 56 (cat. 8); Glassner 2008 no. 49; van Soldt 2021 p. 1042.

Text (collated):
Obv. (?) i′
Lacuna
1′. […^{d}]nin-sikil-l[a…]
2′. […-*ḫ*]*u-um* ^{m}*la-ap-p*[*a*-…]
3′. [^{m}]*ṣi*$_2$-*il*$_5$-*ḫu-um* ^{m}KI-*im-ma*-[…]
4′. 1 *i-na aban*(NA$_4$) *ab-di-im a-na* ^{m}[…]
5′. ^{m}*zi-ra-ḫu-um* ^{m}PA-*ta*-[…]
6′. ⸢^{m}⸣*ṣa-ap-nu-um i-na aban*(NA$_4$) *ab*-[*di-im*]
7′. [*a*]-*na r*[*i*]-*mu-t*[*im*]/*t*[*i*(-*im*)]

(1′)[…]Ninsikil[a…]; (2′)[… ḫ]um, Lapp[a…], (3′)Ṣilḫum, (and) K/Qimma[…]; (4′)1 (unit of weight) by the weight stone of the *abdûm* to […], (5′)Ḏirāʻum, PA-ta[…], (6′)(and) Ṣapnum. (Weighed out) by the weight stone of the *ab*[*dûm*] (7′)[a]s a g[i]f[t].

Rev. (?) i′
1. […] PA […]
2. NA$_4$ *al*-⸢x⸣(-)[…]
3. *a-na* ^{m}⸢x⸣-[…]
4. ^{m}⸢*ši*⸣-*mu*-[*ut*-…]
Lacuna (text almost completely broken)

(1)… (2)the weight stone …[…] (3)to P[N], (4)Šimu[t?-…] (= PN), (5+x)[…].

Rev. (?) ii′ is almost completely broken.

Remarks: The only part of the tablet that retains textual contents appears to record deliveries of some good (possibly silver or gold) to various people as gifts. This document probably dates to the (early?) MB period, despite the occurrence of mimation (final /m/) in the writing of the term *abdûm* (cf. van Soldt 2021 p. 1051 and 1053). In fact, this word is otherwise attested only in MB sources (see below, comm. to obv. i 4′).

Commentary:
Obv. (?) **i′ 1′**: For this Dilmunite (?) deity, see Krebernik 1993-1997. In our text, Ninsikila is probably the theophoric element of a personal name in which either the beginning or the ending is broken (i.e., either x-Ninsikila or Ninsikila-x).

Obv. (?) **i′ 3′**: For mZI-EL-*ḫu-um* = Ṣilḫum, "Success" (otherwise unattested Amorite or West Semitic personal name), cf. *HALOT* p. 1025-1026 s.v. צלח (interpretation and reference courtesy of M. Streck). Also cf. the Phoenician PN *Ṣlḥ* (Benz 1972 p. 400 s.v. ṢLḤ). As regards the other personal name in this line, Glassner read and interpreted it as m*ṭe-em-ma*-[…] = Ṭēm-ma[…], but note that the first sign is not DI = *ṭe* (cf. the form of the DI sign in the following line in the writing of *abdîm*).

Obv. (?) **i′ 4′**: The rare term *abdû(m)*, which also occurs on a cuneiform tablet from Bahrain, appears to denote a high-ranking official in Dilmun during the MB period (Eidem 1997 p. 77). This role was not exclusive to Dilmun, however: a certain Šagarakti-Illil *abdû* is known from a Nippur text dating to the reign of Burna-Buriyaš II (see Hölscher 1996 p. 199 s.v. Šagarakti-Enlil).

Obv. (?) **i′ 5′**: Following a suggestion by M. Streck (pers. comm.), I assume that m*zi-ra-ḫu-um* stands for Ḏirā'um, "Arm, Strength" (otherwise unattested Amorite or West Semitic personal name). Cf. Arabic *ḏirā'* (with the same stem) and Ugaritic *ḏr'*, both meaning "arm"(see *DRS* p. 341 s.v. ÐRƐ). For the other personal name, read, perhaps, m*ḫat-ta*-[…].

Obv. (?) **i′ 6′**: I assume that ⸢m⸣ZA-AB-*nu-um* stands for Ṣapnum, "Sheltered, Protégé" (otherwise unattested Amorite or West Semitic personal name). Cf. *HALOT* p. 1049 s.v. צפן.

Rev. (?) **i′ 4**: Possibly a personal name beginning with the Elamite DN Šimut; cf. Zadok 1984 p. 39-40; and Dalley 2013 p. 181.

CFa 46 (fig. 426). Tablet fragment (F3.mb; 881.AHD; KM1568). 3.5 × 3.3 x 1.4 cm. Trench M, 50.5 N, 1.6 E, level 5.75. Associated pottery: Period 2. Found on a clayey floor or a clay-saturated layer.

Bibliography: Glassner 1984 no. 43; Gharbia et al. 1990 p. 128-129; Glassner 2008 no. 50; van Soldt 2021 p. 1042.

Remarks: Administrative tablet. Too little is preserved to attempt an interpretation.

CFa 47 (fig. 427). Tablet fragment (F3.qp, 881.BIK, KM1664). 4.1 × 2.6 × 0.9 cm. Trench X, 50 N, 5.50 E, level 8.07. Associated pottery: Period 3B/4B.

Bibliography: Howard-Carter 1980-1983 p. 395 § 6.1.2 *b*; Glassner 1984 no. 45; Gharbia et al. 1990 p. 132-133; Glassner 2008 no. 52.

Remarks: Too little is preserved to attempt an interpretation.

CFa 48 (fig. 428). Tablet fragment (F3.no number; KM1569). 2.7 × 2.1 x 1.3 cm.

Bibliography: Glassner 1984 no. 44; Gharbia et al. 1990 p. 130-131; Glassner 2008 no. 51; van Soldt 2021 p. 1042.

Remarks: Administrative tablet. Too little is preserved to attempt an interpretation.

Other archaeological missions and occasional finds

Stamp seals

CFa 49 (fig. 429). Stamp seal (KM2453). D 2.2, Th 0.5 cm. Carnelian. Bifacial (Style III). Findspot unknown. Found on Failaka after 1975 (Kjærum, pers. comm. to F. Højlund). According to the object card of the Kuwait National Museum, it was registered on 6/3/1976. Calvet (2005 p. 52) attributed it to the "mission de l'uni-

Fig. 422. 1:1.

Fig. 423. 1:1.

Fig. 424. 2:1.

Fig. 425. 2:1.

Fig. 426. 2:1.

Fig. 427. 2:1.

Fig. 428. 2:1.

versité Johns-Hopkins (Baltimore), 1976", but the JHU Expedition took place in 1973-1974 and no mention of this seal was made by Howard-Carter either in her later treatment of the epigraphic material from Failaka (Howard-Carter 1980-1983 p. 394-395) or in her unpublished 1984 report (Howard-Carter 1984).

Bibliography: Glassner 1984 no. 3; Gharbia et al. 1990 p. 46-47; Calvet 2005 p. 52 (cat. 2); Glassner 2008 no. 3; Marchesi 2017 p. 431-432; Ashkanani 2021 p. 119.

Side A
Inscr. I

1. E$_2$.GAL GU.LA	Ekallum Rabûm(/Rabītum)

Inscr. II

1. ^{d}*in-za-ak*	Inzak

Side B
Inscr. III

1. ^{d}*pa-ni-pa*	Panipa
2. *mu-da-at* NUMUN	mūdât zēr
3. ^{d}*in-za-ak*	Inzak
4. *ša*$_2$ *a*-GA-AŠ	ša Agaš$^{?}$

Inscr. I: $^{(1)}$"The Great Palace".
Inscr. II: $^{(1)}$Inzak.
Inscr. III: $^{(1)}$Panipa, $^{(2)}$she who knows the seed $^{(3)}$of Inzak $^{(4)}$of Agaš$^{?}$.

Remarks: The text seems to consist of three different inscriptions. The first two, on side A, simply note, respectively, what is presumably a temple name and the divine name Inzak; the third one, which is more articulated, names the goddess Panipa. Clearly, there was some relationship among these three subjects. What the three inscriptions on this seal seem to tell us is that Panipa was related to Inzak—presumably as his consort—and that both were related to "The Great Palace", which was presumably Inzak's temple, in which Panipa was worshipped as well (for the designation of this temple as "palace", see Marchesi 2017 p. 429 with n. 23). The special emphasis on the goddess Panipa here may be due to the fact that the seal in question belonged to Panipa's high priest or high priestess.

Commentary:
Inscr. **I-II**: In the inscriptions from Failaka, E$_2$.GAL(.)GU.LA is traditionally interpreted as the name—Egalgula—of Failaka's Inzak temple (see, among others, Glassner 1984 p. 48; George 1993 p. 87; Glassner 1996 p. 241; Marchesi 2017 p. 431-432). It should be noted, however, that the E$_2$.GAL(.)GU.LA is nowhere explicitly said to be "the temple of Inzak" (**bīt*(E$_2$) ^{d}*in-za-ak*) or to belong to this god. In this connection, note that the translation of side A as "Egalgula of Inzak" in Marchesi 2017 p. 432 should be reconsidered. If E$_2$.GAL(.)GU.LA is understood as being in genitival relation with Inzak, then a problem arises: as a non-Akkadian name, Inzak cannot take a genitive ending. The only way a genitival relation between E$_2$.GAL(.)GU.LA and Inzak could have been expressed would have been through the use of the determinative pronoun. In other words, if the relation is a genitival one, we should expect the text to read *E$_2$.GAL(.)GU.LA *ša*$_2$ ^{d}*in-za-ak*. Unless we assume that E$_2$.GAL(.)GU.LA is not a temple name, but rather part of an Akkadian genitive phrase meaning "the great palace of Inzak". In that event, however, we would expect the text to have been worded as *E$_2$.GAL ^{d}*in-za-ak* GU.LA (= **ekal Inzak rabûm*/*rabītum*), because of the syntactical rules of the Akkadian "status constructus" construction; or as *E$_2$.GAL GU.LA *ša*$_2$ ^{d}*in-za-ak* (= **ekallum rabûm*/*rabītum ša Inzak*). Side A should thus be interpreted as containing two separate inscriptions: E$_2$.GAL(.)GU.LA (= Inscr. I) and ^{d}*in-za-ak* (= Inscr. II). On the other hand, the three inscriptions on this seal seem to imply that the E$_2$.GAL(.)GU.LA was the name or designation of a temple (cf. CFa1, 38, 40, and 69) in which Dilmun's divine couple, Inzak and Panipa, was worshipped (see above, *sub* Remarks). Even so, it is unlikely that a Dilmunite temple that existed before the Mesopotamian dominations—by the Sealand I and Kassite dynasties—was given a Sumerian name (following the Mesopotamian tradition of naming temples with Sumerian names). It is more likely that E$_2$.GAL(.)GU.LA represents an Akkadian expression—Akkadian being the language of this text and, in general, of all the Dilmunite cuneiform inscriptions that we know of—translating whatever the original name of this temple had been in the native language of Dilmun. In this connection, note the lexical entries [e$_2$-g]al g[u-l]a = *ekallum*(E$_2$.GAL) ⌜*ra*⌝-*b*[*u-u*]*m* in OB Kagal I ii 56 (Civil 1971 p. 229) and e$_2$-gal gu-la = *ekallu*(E$_2$.GAL) *rabītu*(GAL)^{tu} in MA Kagal II i 12 (Civil 2010 p. 39), which provide two Akkadian equivalents for Sumerian e$_2$-gal gu-la and the possible Akkadian readings of E$_2$.GAL GU.LA when used logographically in Akkadian texts.

Inscr. **III**, line **1**: For the goddess Panipa, see Krebernik 2003-2005b. Glassner (2002 p. 338) proposed the alternative reading ^{d}*pa-li*$_2$-*ḫat* (= Palīḫat, "Celle qui est vénérée"), but the use of the PA sign as the syllabogram *ḫat* is not attested before the MB period (for attestations of the DN Panipa in cuneiform sources from Bahrain that are certainly older, see Laursen et al. forth.). Panipa is likely a name of unknown linguistic affiliation, like Inzak (contra Marchesi 2014-2016 p. 51; and Laursen & Steinkeller 2017 p. 84 n. 22).

Inscr. **III**, lines **2-4**: See Marchesi 2017 p. 431-432 with n. 40.

Cylinder seals

CFa 50. MB cylinder seal (FH6; KM1345). L 2.6, D 1.2 cm. Agate. Johns Hopkins Expedition's Trench FH2 (topsoil) in Tell F3 (cf. Kjærum & Højlund 2013 fig. 2).

Bibliography: Ferrara 1977; Howard-Carter 1980-1983 p. 394 § 5.4.3 *b*; Glassner 1984 no. 12; Howard-Carter 1984 folio 44 (FH6); Gharbia et al. 1990 p. 62-63; Stiehler-Alegria 1996 no. 269; Glassner 2008 no. 14; Potts 2010 no. 54; van Soldt 2021 p. 1047.

Text:

1. *ša-ki-in-šu*	šakinšu
2. *li-ib-lu-uṭ*	libluṭ
3. *li-iš-li$_2$-im*	lišlim
4. *li-iḫ-ḫi-iš*	liḫḫiš
5. *li-me-er*	limmer
6. *li-di-iš*	līdiš
7. *li-bu-ur*	libūr

(1)He who is equipped with it (= this seal)—(2)may he live, (3)may he be healthy, (4)may he prosper, (5)may he shine (with joy), (6)may he be renewed, (7)may he last long!

CFa 51. Ur III/OB cylinder seal (F87.2119; KM 5346). L 2.3, D 1.1 cm. Grey soft stone. From the French excavations at Tell F6.

Bibliography: Gharbia et al. 1990 p. 108-109; Glassner 1990 p. 123 (*ICF* 51); id. 2008 no. 8; Potts 2010 no. 103.

Remarks: Only the NA sign at the end of the last line of the inscription remains.

CFa 52. Ur III/OB cylinder seal fragment (F88.2417; FFF400; KM5848). L 2, D 1.4 cm. Black stone. From the French excavations at Tell F6.

Bibliography: Glassner 1990 p. 124 (*ICF* 52); Pic 1990 p. 138-139 (no. 25); Gharbia et al. 1990 p. 110-111; Glassner 2008 no. 9; Potts 2010 no. 104.

Text:
1. ĝiri$_3$-ne$_2$-[…]
Lacuna

(1)Ĝirinne-[idab/isa(g), (2+x)…].

Commentary:
Line **1**: Probably to be restored as either ĝiri$_3$-ne$_2$-[i$_3$-dab$_5$], "[He Has Taken] His/Her (i.e., the deity's) Path"; or ĝiri$_3$-ne$_2$-[i$_3$-sa$_6$], "His/Her Path Is Good" (both Sumerian personal names). Cf. Limet 1968 p. 422-423; and CFa 55 below.

CFa 53. Ur III (?) cylinder seal (KM8198). L 3.4, D 1.9 cm. Soft stone. Tell F6, area of the "Palace", surface (found in 2007 by the Slovak Mission during a visit to the site).

Bibliography: David-Cuny & Neyme 2016 p. 62-63 (reading of the inscription by J.-J. Glassner); Eidem 2016 p. 162 (no. 4); Pittman 2016 p. 159 and fig. 755 (on p. 160).

Text:
1. *ri*!(ḪU)-*iš-ka-bar*
2. dumu/DUMU ur-dPA

(1)Rīš!-kabar, (2)son of Ur-…

Remarks: The language is possibly (but not definitively) Sumerian. Attributed to the Ur III period on stylistic grounds (Pittman 2016 p. 159), but the Akkadian-Amorite name of the seal owner (see below, comm. to line 1) may suggest a later date.

Commentary:
Line **1**: The ḪU and RI signs are similar and thus are often confused and interchanged. The name in question appears to be a hybrid Akkadian-Amorite name (cf. Streck 2000 p. 146 and 148 § 12.6) comprising the Akkadian verb *riāšu(m)*, in the stative, and the Amorite adjective *kabrum* in the "0-case", which is used here as a theophoric element (cf. ibid. p. 280-282 § 3.39-40); thus, Rīš!-kabar, "The Great One Is Celebrated". Note that the patronymic (line 2) is Sumerian.

Line **2**: Cf. Krebernik 2003-2005a.

CFa 54. Ur III cylinder seal (C125-X314). L 3.3, D 1.6 cm. Soft stone. Tell F6, Trench CE, layer C125 (Phase 1). Kuwaiti-Danish Archaeological Mission 2008-2012.

Bibliography: Eidem 2016 p. 162 (no. 1); Pittman 2016 p. 159 and fig. 752 (on p. 160).

Text:
1. lu_2-^{d}nin-subur
2. dub-sar
3. dumu al-ba-ni-du_{11}
4. nu-$banda_3$

(1)Lu-Ninsuburaka, (2)the scribe, (3)son of Albanni'du(g), (4)the colonel.

Remarks: Sumerian language and Sumerian personal names.

Commentary:
Line **3**: For the reconstruction of the morphological structure of this name as {al.ba.nni.'.du(g)}, note the variant spellings al-ba-an-ni-du_{11} (Limet 1968 p. 372; Yıldız & Gomi 1993 Um. 1829: 9) and al-ba-ni-a-du_{11} (Limet 1968 p. 372). The name in question is an abbreviation of a longer name, which is attested for instance in de Genouillac 1922 (= TCL 5) AO 5674 i 12: ti-il-al-ba-ni-du_{11}, that is, "I Petitioned Him/Her (= the deity) for (long) Life for Myself".

Line **4**: For this title in the Ur III period, see, most recently, Steinkeller 2017 p. 540 with n. 14.

CFa 55. Ur III cylinder seal (C198-X714, KM11184). L 3.2, D 1.6 cm. Soft stone. Tell F6, Trench CEE, layer C198 (Phase 1). Kuwaiti-Danish Archaeological Mission 2008-2012.

Bibliography: Eidem 2016 p. 162 (no. 2); Højlund 2016b fig. 5 (on p. 11); Pittman 2016 p. 159 and fig. 753 (on p. 160).

Text:
1. $\hat{g}iri_3$-ne_2-i_3-sa_6
2. dumu lu_2-^{d}zuen(EN.ZU)

(1)Ĝirinne-isa(g), (2)son of Lu-Zu'ena.

Remarks: Sumerian language and Sumerian personal names. The $GIRI_3$ and EN signs are flipped horizontally.

Commentary:
Line **1**: See above, comm. to CFa 52: 1.

CFa 56. Ur III cylinder seal (C208-X755, KM11194). L 3.2, D 1.5 cm. Soft stone. Tell F6, Trench CEE, layer C208 (Phase 1). Kuwaiti-Danish Archaeological Mission 2008-2012.

Bibliography: Eidem 2016 p. 162 (no. 3); Pittman 2016 p. 159 and fig. 754 (on p. 160).

Text:
1. lu_2-^{d}nanna
2. dumu ka-ka

(1)Lu-Nanna, (2)son of Kaka.

Remarks: Sumerian language and Sumerian personal names.

CFa 57. Ur III cylinder seal fragment (C117-X289, KM8508). Ca. 1 × 1 cm. Banded white quartz. Tell F6, Trench CE, layer C117 (Phase 1). Kuwaiti-Danish Archaeological Mission 2008-2012.

Bibliography: Eidem 2016 p. 162 (no. 5); Pittman 2016 p. 159 and fig. 756 (on p. 160).

Remarks: Remains of two cases of an inscription but too little is preserved to attempt a reconstruction.

CFa 58. Cylinder seal fragment (JA2-X12, KM11239). Ca. 1.8 × 0.9 cm. Banded agate. Tell F6, Trench JA, layer J2 (disturbed context). Kuwaiti-Danish Archaeological Mission 2008-2012.

Bibliography: Eidem 2016 p. 163 (no. 6); Pittman 2016 p. 159 and fig. 757 (on p. 160).

Text:
1. *nu-ur*$_2$-^{d}[...]
Lacuna

(1)Nūr-[..., (2+x)...]

Commentary:
Line **1**: Personal name of the type Nūr-DN, "Light of (the deity) So-and-so".

"CFa 59". MB Cylinder seal (E69-X252, KM8447). L 2.6, D 1.2 cm. Faience. Mitannian Style. Tell F6, Trench E, layer E69 (Phase 7). Kuwaiti-Danish Archaeological Mission 2008-2012.

Bibliography: Pittman 2016 p. 159 and fig. 760 (on p. 161).

Remarks: Pseudo-cuneiform inscription. Cf. "CFa 12", "CFa 15", and "CFa 24", above.

CFa 60. Ur III/Early OB cylinder seal (KM8667). L 3.8, D 1.9 cm. Dark green, grey-spotted soft stone. From Al-Khidr. Kuwaiti-Slovak Archaeological Mission 2004-2009 (found in 2004).

Bibliography: Barta et al. 2008 fig. 11 (on p. 133); F. Rahman apud Barta et al. 2008 p. 124; Benediková 2010 p. 55 (reading of the inscription by F. Rahman) and fig. 68a-f (on p. 81); Potts 2010 no. 9; David-Cuny & Azpeitia 2012 p. 32-33; Laursen & Steinkeller 2017 p. 111-112 (Seal 3) with fig. 12/3.

Text:
1. es_3-ge-na
2. lu_2 ma_2 gal-gal
3. dumu ur-ab-ba

(1)Esgenna, (2)master sailor (lit. "the man of big boats"), (3)son of Ur-ab(b)a.

Commentary:
Line **1**: Read as "ab-gi-na" by F. Rahman (see bibliography above), but the interpretation of the AB sign as es_3, "shrine", makes better sense ("The Shrine Is Firm/Stable") than ab, "sea". For the reading of the Sumerian word for "shrine" as es_3 (rather than $eš_3$) before the OB period, see Meyer-Laurin 2011 p. 67; cf. Attinger 2021 p. 362 with n. 899.

Line **2**: The professional title lu_2 ma_2 gal-gal(-la) seems to denote a specialist sailor for ships; see, most recently, Laursen & Steinkeller 2017 p. 104-106.

Stone vessels

CFa 61. Vessel fragment (FH66; KM1355). 7.1 x 5.3 x 2.2 cm. Soft stone. Johns Hopkins Expedition's Trench FH2 (Level 2) at Tell F3 (cf. Kjærum & Højlund 2013 fig. 2).

Bibliography: Glassner 1984 no. 30, fig. 8. Howard-Carter 1984 folio 47; Gharbia et al. 1990 p. 146-147; Glassner 2008 no. 32.

Remarks: Remains of five lines of an inscription, but only a few scattered signs are identifiable.

CFa 62 (fig. 430). Vessel fragment (KM…?). Soft stone. Discovered in 2020 by Hamid Al-Mutairi on the surface of Tell F3, west of Sheikh Ahmad's House.

Remarks: Only a single sign—TUM—is preserved; note that its form is exactly the same as the one that appears in CFa 2: 3 (see above, remarks on CFa 2).

CFa 63. Vessel fragment (F85.H191; FFF.161; KM4142). 2.5 × 1.6 × 0.7 cm. Lapis lazuli (?). From the French excavations at Tell F5 (1985's stratigraphic sounding, fill of Tell F5, mixed context).

Bibliography: Calvet & Glassner 1986; Gharbia et al. 1990 p. 122-123; Glassner 1990 p. 123 (*ICF* 48); id. 2008 no. 44.

Text:
Lacuna
1′. […] DIŠ […]
2′. [(…) ^{d}]EN.KI ⌜x⌝ […]
3′. […] LA NA […]
4′. […] ŠE U_3 NI […]
5′. […] *ša* ^{d}dumu-z[i …]
Lacuna?

Too broken to translate.

Remarks: Only the DNs Ea (written ^{d}EN.KI) and Dumuzi are recognizable. In line 2′, the x sign is possibly LUGAL (cf. CFa 41: 1, above).

CFa 64. Vessel fragment (F86.1648; KM 5166). Soft stone. From the French excavations at Tell F6.

Bibliography: Gharbia et al. 1990 p. 162-163; Glassner 1990 p. 123 (*ICF* 50); id. 2008 no. 42.

Text:
Lacuna
1′. […] GA UN
2′. […] ⌜x NI⌝
Lacuna

Too broken to translate.

Commentary:
Line **2′**: Perhaps […]-⌜i_3-li_2⌝, with *ilī*, "my god", as an element of an Akkadian personal name.

CFa 65. Vessel fragment (F88.2400; KM5846). Soft stone. From the French excavations at Tell F6.

Fig. 429. 2:1.

Fig. 430. 2:1.

Fig. 431. 2:1.

Fig. 432. 1:1.

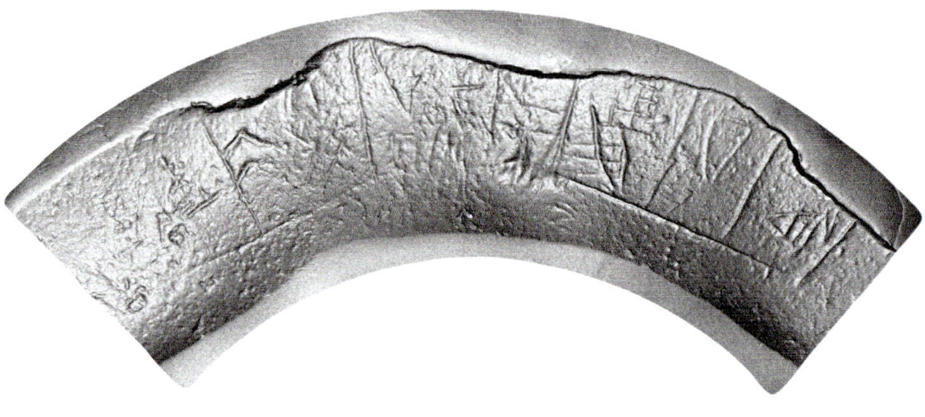

Fig. 433. 1:5.

Bibliography: Gharbia et al. 1990 p. 164-165; Glassner 1990 p. 124 (*ICF* 53); id. 2008 no. 43.

Remarks: Only the beginning of what is, presumably, an Akkadian personal name—*a-pil-*[…]—is preserved. Note that the preserved signs are flipped.

CFa 66. Plate—rim fragment (C104-X210; KM8381). 2.7 × 2 × 1.1 cm. Reconstructed diameter ca. 34 cm. Grey-greenish hard stone (dolerite?). Tell F6, Trench C, layer C104 (disturbed). Kuwaiti-Danish Archaeological Mission 2008-2012.

Bibliography: Hilton et al. 2012 no. 6; Eidem 2016 p. 163 (no. 7); Hilton 2016 p. 170 and fig. 811 (on p. 174).

Remarks: Only the AN sign is preserved (and only partially).

CFa 67. Plate—rim fragment (E73-X265; KM8449). 3.1 × 2.5 × 0.4 cm. Grey-greenish hard stone (dolerite?). Tell F6, Trench E, layer E73 (Phase 7; Failaka Period 4A). Kuwaiti-Danish Archaeological Mission 2008-2012.

Bibliography: Hilton et al. 2012 no. 10; Eidem 2016 p. 163 (no. 8); Hilton 2016 p. 168 and fig. 794 (on p. 173).

Text:
1. [… (…)](-)^{d}*in-za-*[*ak* …]
2. […] ⸢x⸣ […]
Lacuna?

Too broken to translate.

Remarks: The horizontal writing is probably due to the form of the vessel. Therefore, no chronological significance can be ascribed to it.

Commentary:
Line **1**: Inzak may also be part of a personal name. Cf. CFa 3 above with comm.

CFa 68 (?). Bowl—rim fragment (E110-X471, KM8463). 3.6 × 2.1 × 1 cm. Reconstructed diameter 20 cm. Red and white hard stone. Tell F6, Trench E, layer E110 (Phase 5). Kuwaiti-Danish Archaeological Mission 2008-2012.

Bibliography: Eidem 2016 p. 163 (no. 9); Hilton 2016 p. 167 and fig. 786 (on p. 172).

Remarks: There are engravings but their interpretation as remains of cuneiform signs is questionable.

CFa 69 (fig. 431). Vessel fragment (KM…?). 3.8 × 2.2 × 0.7 cm. Soft stone (Hilton's [2014] type 3). Found in 2019 by F. Højlund, north of the Temple in Tell F6, in spoils from the French excavations of the 1980s.

1.	[E$_2$].GAL GU.⸢LA⸣	[E]kallum Rabûm(/Rabītum)
2.	[*s*]*u-mu-le*-[DINGIR]	[S]umu-lê[l]
3.	[IR$_{3/11}$] ⸢^{d}*in*⸣-[*za-ak*]	[warad] In[zak]
4.	[*ša*$_2$ *a*-GA-AŠ]	[ša Agaš$^?$]
5.	[*i*/*u*$_2$-… (?)]	[i/u… (?)]

(1)(Property of) "The Great [P]alace". (2)[S]umu-lê[l, (3) the servant of] In[zak (4)of Agaš$^?$, (5)presented (it) (?)].

Remarks: Cf. CFa 1, 38, and 40.

Commentary:
Line **1**: See above, comm. to CFa 1: 1 and CFa 49 I-II.

Line **2**: See above, comm. to CFa 1: 2a. For the Amorite PN Sumu-lêl, "Truly Offspring of the God", see Streck 2000 p. 165-166 (§ 2.29), 237 (§ 2.152), and 304 (§ 3.70). For this Sumu-lêl as a king of Dilmun, see Marchesi 2017 p. 428-430.

Lines **3-4**: See above, comm. to CFa 1: 2b-4.

Line **5**: See above, comm. to CFa 1: 5.

CFa 70 (fig. 432). Vessel fragment (196.04; KM8810). 6.3 × 3.5 × 0.4 cm. Soft stone. From Al-Khidr. Trench 23, feature 13, square 6/b W, elevation 4.7 m a.s.l. (uppermost horizon of Bronze Age architectural remains; see Benediková 2010 fig. 28c) in the central part of Mound KH-1 (information courtesy of the Kuwaiti-Slovak Archaeological Mission 2004-2009).

Bibliography: Benediková 2010 fig. 89a-d (on p. 102).

Remarks: Remains of a seven-line cuneiform inscription (collated), but most of the signs, mostly only partially preserved, are difficult to identify. However, it is possible to recognize, in the first two lines, a dedication to the god Ea: [*a-na* ^{d}E]N.KI / [LUGAL.A.N]I.{IR}, "[To E]a, [hi]s [lord]" (cf. CFa 29 above).

Tablets

CFa 71. MB tablet fragment (BE4-X22, KM11388). 3 × 1.8 × 1.3 cm. Hard-fired, dark clay. Tell F3, Trench BE, layer 4 (Phase 5). Associated pottery: Period 4A. Kuwaiti-Danish Archaeological Mission 2012-2017.

Bibliography: Eidem 2021.

Remarks: Possibly a letter. See Eidem 2021.

Other

CFa 72 (fig. 433). Paving stone (KM1479). 54.5 × 54.5 × 11.5 cm. Fine, hard, whitish limestone. The upper side is worn and smooth. Found in 1953 in the foundation of a modern farmhouse near Tell F3 (Ferrara 1975 p. 231).

Bibliography: Ferrara 1975; Howard-Carter 1980-1983 p. 395 § 6.2 *c*; Glassner 1984 no. 47; id. 2008 no. 53.

Text (collated):
1. E$_2$.GAL ^{d}AK-*ku*-⸢*dur*$_2$-*ri*⸣-URU$_3$ LUGAL TIN.TIR^{ki}

1. ekal Nabû-kudurrī-uṣur šar Bābili

1. Palace of Nebuchadnezzar, king of Babylon.

Remarks: The object on which this text was inscribed has been designated as a "door sill" (Howard-Carter) or a "threshold" (Glassner), but it is too small in size for that. Comparanda such as Koldewey 1913 p. 156 fig. 99 (reference courtesy of Nicolò Marchetti) make it clear that it should rather be understood as a paving stone (see also Ferrara 1975 p. 231). Ferrara (1975 p. 232) speculated that the stone in question, which possibly comes from Oman or elsewhere further east, ended up on Failaka when it was en route to Babylon for use in one of the palaces of Nebuchadnezzar II (see also Howard-Carter 1987 p. 112). Glassner (1984 p. 49-50; 2008 p. 193) hypothesized, on the contrary, that the stone originated in Babylon: Glassner speculated that the stone was secondarily used as ballast for a ship and was then abandoned on the Gulf island by the ship's seamen. Finally, Kjærum (apud Nashef 1984 p. 16) believed that "the stone originated on Failaka itself, possibly belonging to a small governor's palace on the island from the NB period" (see also Elayi 2023). However, all of these hypotheses are either far-fetched or implausible. For instance, it is implausible to suppose that a piece of stone that was traveling in the Gulf had already been shaped and inscribed long before it reached Babylon. It is equally unlikely that a "small governor's palace" would have been called the "Palace of Nebuchadnezzar (II), king of Babylon". We should, instead, consider the possibility that a monumental building belonging to the Babylonian king may have existed on the island at the time of Nebuchadnezzar II (after all, Dilmun was one of the provinces of the Neo-Babylonian Empire and a governor of Dilmun is attested under Nabonidus; see Potts 1990 p. 349-350). In this connection, it should be noted that at least two very large buildings made of stone ashlars have been almost completely removed from Failaka: the Dilmun temple in Tell F6, which was built with white oolitic limestone, and which was leveled to its foundation in antiquity (Højlund & Abu-Laban 2016 p. 258); and a big building that was built with large beach-rock ashlars and whose remains have been discovered in the upper layers of Tell F6, post-dating the Kassite layers (see Højlund & Abu-Laban 2016 p. 59-60). The proximity of those structures to the beach would have facilitated the efficient transporting of limestone or beach-rock slabs elsewhere by boat. The same thing, one may speculate, may have happened to Nebuchadnezzar's palace: it is entirely possible that there once had been a large building belonging to Nebuchadnezzar II on Failaka, even if only a single paving stone from it survives. On the other hand, it should be noted that Babylonian sources are completely silent about the existence of Nebuchadnezzar II's palaces outside the city of Babylon (see, most recently, Beaulieau 2017 p. 9-10), whereas sources do record the construction of a palace at Tayma, in Arabia, by Nabonidus (Schaudig 2001 p. 568 and 575). Moreover, this inscription of Nebuchadnezzar II is the only cuneiform text from Failaka that can definitively be dated to the 1st millennium BC (another inscription that was previously attributed to the same ruler actually dates to an earlier period; see CFa 41). Indeed, no other cuneiform texts from Failaka can be dated with certainty to the 1st millennium BC—a fact which supports the view that the island experienced a phase of decline and marginalization during the first half of the 1st millennium BC, and which would hardly square with the hypothesis that a Babylonian royal palace existed there at that time.

Commentary:
Line **1**: For the writing TIN.TIR^{ki} for Babylon, see Beaulieu 2019 p. 30-31.

Indexes

Personal names

Titles and professions

Divine names

Temple names

Geographical names

The cuneiform texts from Failaka—an assessment

Most of the texts edited here are difficult to understand because of their poor state of preservation (most are simply fragments), the occurrence of unusual sign forms (which, in several cases, make the signs in question difficult to identify), and the lack of parallels that can be used for comparison. Moreover, in many cases, it is difficult to assign them a precise dating—most of these texts having been written in "that timeless Babylonian style used for inscriptions on stone from the Akkad period up to the Neo-Babylonian", to borrow the words of A. Leo Oppenheim (1954 p. 16 n. 27).

Despite this, the texts in question provide important historical and cultural information. For instance, the presence among these artifacts of several Ur III seals—some of them bearing legends that reveal the names of their owners (see, e.g., CFa 25, 54-56, and 60; cf. also CFa 52-53)—shows that the island was frequented by people from southern Mesopotamia in the 21st century BC. Thanks to ceramic artifacts, archaeologists were able to identify an Ur III settlement dating to this period in the lower layers of Tell F6 (see F. Højlund in Højlund & Abu-Laban 2016 p. 15-30 and 251-252). This was probably a way station for merchants and/or seamen who routinely sailed to the coast of the Emirates, the ancient land of Magan (or Makkan), to procure Omani copper and other maritime trade products from those trading posts.

Subsequently, in the first half of the 2nd millennium BC, Failaka became part of the kingdom of Dilmun, which centered on the island of Bahrain (Failaka Periods 1-2 and 3B). The names of two kings of Dilmun (Samu'a and Sumu-lêl) and of a Dilmunite princess ('Ula-Panipa) are recorded in the written sources of Failaka (CFa 1, 4, 69); these add to the names of Dilmunite kings—Ri'mum and Yaglī-'el—that are known from the Bahrain sources (see Marchesi 2017 p. 425-428). Two additional royal figures—a king and a queen of Dilmun—are possibly named on a stamp seal from Failaka whose owner's name is lost (see above, CFa 5, with comm. to lines 1′-2′).

All of these royal names can be interpreted as Amorite (or West Semitic) based on lexical and/or morphological considerations. This is also true of almost all of the personal names that are attested in the Failaka sources from this period. Only later, in the MB documentation, do we find, as expected, a certain number of Akkadian personal names. It should be noted, however, that most of the Amorite personal names from the Gulf region (including the onomastic material of the contemporary texts from Bahrain, for which see Eidem 1994 p. 302; Streck 2004 p. 329; Marchesi 2017 p. 425-428) are not attested in the Amorite onomastica of Mesopotamia and Syria. Moreover, the peculiar Amorite onomastic tradition of the Gulf also survives in later times as evidenced by the attestation of such personal names as Yaḥmī'u (CFa 32) and Yamrū-DN (CFa 44) in texts from the MB period or later (see also CFa 6 and 45).

A few inscribed Style III stamp seals, as well as inscribed vessels of the iconographically (and chronologically) related Failaka Figurative Style (Hilton 2014 p. 105-107), should be attributed to the final phase of Dilmun's authority over the island (Failaka Period 3B; 16th century BC), before the conquest by the Sealand Dynasty (see, most recently, F. Højlund in Højlund & Hilton 2021 p. 163-164). A particularly notable piece from this period is the bifacial seal mentioning the goddess Panipa as "she who knows the seed of Inzak" (CFa 49), which may have belonged to a priestly officer of this goddess. In addition, two vessel epigraphs (CFa 29 and 30) name the "chief musician of (the god) Inzak", who must have been another important figure of that time.

Cuneiform sources from Bahrain attest to the control of this island (and thus of Failaka) by the last king of the Sealand, Ea-gāmil, and successively by the early Kassite rulers (André-Salvini & Cavigneaux forth.; see also van Koppen 2017 p. 74-76; and Boivin 2018 p. 84-85). In this regard, Dalley (2013 p. 178-182) suggested that the conquest of Dilmun by the Sealand may have happened as early as the reign of Aya-daragalamma. According to Dalley, the title "king of the world" (Akkadian *šar kiššati*) in an alleged inscription of Aya-daragalamma from Tell en-Nasbeh, in Palestine, might have been justified, in part, by Aya-daragalamma's control of Dilmun. It should be noted, however, that Dalley's interpretation of the inscription in question and her attribution of it to Aya-daragalamma are highly questionable (see Boivin 2018 p. 35-36 with n. 42). It is true that one of this ruler's year-names is "Year in which Enlil established the rule (lit., shepherdship) over the whole earth for Aya-daragalamma, the king" (ibid. p. 248 Aa G; cf. Dalley 2013 p. 178), but we know that such statements were often simply rhetorical. In point of fact, Aya-daragalamma's successor, the third-to-last ruler of the dynasty, Akurdu-ana, styles himself simply as "king of E-Uriku ('House of Holy Ur'), king of Sumer and Akkad" on his seal (*CDLI*: P455982; see Gabbay & Boivin 2018 p. 35-36 n. 25), with no indication that he exerted any control over extra-Mesopotamian territories. Since the tablet from Bahrain that dates to the reign of Ea-gāmil, the last king of the dynasty, refers to the fourth regnal year of this ruler (Boivin 2018 p. 250 Eg 4), it is likely that Ea-gāmil inherited the control of Dilmun from his predecessor, the obscure Melem-kurkura. From these scanty data, we may perhaps infer that the conqueror of Dilmun was either Akurdu-ana (in the final years of his reign) or Melem-kurkura. The latter's name—"Divine Splendor of All Lands"—may even betray the aspiration, on his part, for universal dominance.

The Babylonian dominion over the northern and central Gulf region is also attested much later, in the 6th century BC, when Dilmun became a province of the Neo-Babylonian Empire. A paving stone from Failaka with an inscription of the famous Nebuchadnezzar II (CFa 72) may testify to this phase and attest to the existence of a palace of the king of Babylon on the island in that period, but this document remains isolated, and its interpretation and implications are controversial (see above, remarks on CFa 72).

Another inscription (CFa 41), which previously had been attributed to Nebuchadnezzar II, turned out, upon closer inspection, to be much older; it mentions the Kassite ruler Adad-šuma-uṣur. This text—which is probably not a royal epigraph but rather the private inscription of a high-ranking official in the service of the Kassite king—is important because it attests to the continued control of the island by the Kassites until at least the reign of Adad-šuma-uṣur (late 13th and early 12th centuries BC).

As regards gods and cults, the following information can be gathered from the texts. Inzak appears to have been the most important deity. Certainly, Inzak is the most frequently attested god in the Failaka sources (see index of divine names, above). In one of these texts (CFa 49), he occurs together with the goddess Panipa, who appears to have been his divine consort. It should be noted, however, that neither Inzak nor Panipa are attested as recipients of votive offerings. In contrast, votive offerings are attested for the Mesopotamian deities Enki/Ea (CFa 29, 41, and 70; see also CFa 63) and Ninḫursaĝa/Bēlet-ilī (CFa 2)—the latter being Inzak's mother, according to the Sumerian myth "Enki and Ninḫursaĝa" (Attinger 1984 p. 26-31 lines 250ff.). As for Ea, his cult on Failaka appears to be attested at least since the 16th century BC (CFa 29). It is quite possible that this cult was introduced to the island in this period, when the relations between Failaka and southern Mesopotamia intensified, and various Babylonian cultural elements penetrated the island and its local Dilmunite culture (cf. F. Højlund in Højlund & Hilton 2021 p. 163-164).

One of the three votive inscriptions dedicated to Ea (CFa 41) reveals that Ea was worshipped in a temple called Ekara, "House of the Quay/Harbor" (which was previously misattributed to the sun-god Šamaš), while another alleged Sumerian temple name—Egalgula—is better interpreted as the Akkadian translation—either *Ekallum Rabûm* or *Ekallum Rabītum*, "The Great Palace"—of whatever was the original Dilmunite language designation of the temple in question (see above, comm. to CFa 49 I-II).

"The Great Palace" may well have been the great Dilmun Temple of Tell F6. A vessel fragment with a royal inscription mentioning "The Great Palace" (CFa 69), which has recently been found near the Dilmun Temple among the spoils of the 1980s' French excavations in that area, supports this identification. By the same token, a votive stamp seal from Tell F3 (CFa 2), with its dedication to Bēlet-ilī, suggests that the open-air shrine in Tell F3 may have been devoted to the cult of this goddess (although a seal is perhaps too small and too "mobile" an object to ensure the validity of such an identification).

Admittedly, a vessel dedicated to Ea "who dwells in the Ekara" (CFa 41) also comes from Tell F3, but in no way can the Tell F3 open-air shrine be identified with the Ekara. First, the word for "temple"—Sumerian e_2, Akkadian *bītu(m)*—primarily means "house" (temples having been conceptualized as houses of the gods). There are, however, other Sumerian and Akkadian terms that could have been used to refer to open-air cultic installations: for instance, Sumerian es_3/$eš_3$, "shrine", or Akkadian *māḫāzu(m)*, "sacred place". The name Ekara, "House of the Quay/Harbor", points to a "house", that is, a building. Moreover, the Ekara is known to have been in use at the time of Adad-šuma-uṣur (see CFa 41 above), that is, much later than the period in which the Tell F3 open-air shrine was in use. In fact, the three use phases that have been identified for the latter shrine all fall within the Failaka Period 3B (ca. 16th century BC; see F. Højlund in Højlund & Hilton 2021 p. 151).

Nor, on similar chronological grounds, can the Ekara be identified with the recently discovered North-east Temple in Tell F6 (Højlund & Hagelquist 2019). In fact, the pottery found in the Northeast Temple, which belongs almost exclusively to the Barbar tradition (ibid. p. 176), suggests that the use of this cultic building was limited to the 19th and 18th centuries BC.

Finally, it should be noted that Ekara is a Sumerian temple name and as such attests to the Mesopotamian tradition of naming temples with Sumerian names. One does not expect to find this Mesopotamian tradition on Failaka before the 15th century BC, that is, before the Mesopotamian dominations of the island. It is thus probable that the Ekara was built, or at least named this way, only in the second half of the 2nd millennium BC. The name itself, "House of the Quay/Harbor", could refer to either the bay extending south of Tell F3 and Tell F6 or the bay of Al-Khidr in the northwest (both bays provide safe landing places as well as protection from the region's main winds). Be that as it may, the Ekara site is still awaiting discovery.

Nor are we better informed about the indigenous Dilmunite toponymy. While the GN Dilmun, or Tilmun, continues to be unattested in the written documentation from both Failaka and Bahrain, the hypothesis that Agarum or Akarum was the ancient name of Failaka and the etymon of Ikaros, the name by which the island was known in Hellenistic times, can no longer be maintained. The name in question is best read as Agaš and it may refer to a place located in either Bahrein or Eastern Arabia (see above, comm. to CFa 1: 2b-4).

7. Miniature sculptures

Evidence of life-size statues of animals were uncovered at the Barbar temple on both sides of the staircases leading up from the well chambers of Temple II and III (Andersen & Højlund 2003, vol. 1, figs. 203-217, 242-245, p. 167-171, 326-327). They were constructed of wood and clad with copper plate and their eyes were probably inlaid with shell and lapis lazuli (Andersen & Højlund 2003, vol. 1, figs. 819 and 829). Furthermore, a pair of sculptured rams in stone were found in a well shaft at the Umm as-Sujur temple (Andersen & Højlund 2003 vol. 2 p. 43, figs. 14-16). Nothing similar was found at the temple in Tell F6, but certain observations may indicate that there was a cult figure inside the building, at the back wall (Højlund & Abu-Laban 2016 p. 259, fig. 91:3). In addition, an eye-shaped object in yellow-white limestone with central depression to receive an inlay of the iris was found in Tell F3 (fig. 566) (cf. from Qala'at al-Bahrain, Højlund & Andersen 1994 fig. 2063). However, a small number of miniature sculptures may be described, of which the miniature rams stand out, perhaps as evidence of some kind of domestic worship. In this context reference should be made to the incineration of the remains of sacrificial animals, among them goats, probably male, in an oven behind the temple in Tell F6 (Højlund & Abu-Laban 2016 p. 39).

Frog in copper, weight 48.25 g (fig. 434, Ashkanani 2021 p. 107) (F3.pv). Trench X, 53.15 N, 5.50 E, level 8.44, that is, above the last floor of the open-air shrine. Weights were sometimes made in the shape of frogs in Mesopotamia (Black & Green 1992 p. 85). Associated pottery: Period 3B/4B.

Right hand in copper with all fingers including thumb outstretched and of anatomically correct length (fig. 435, Ashkanani 2021 p. 111) (F3.att), that is, different from the pottery hands described below which are clenched. Trench P, 25.70 N, 9.60 W, level 8.51. Associated pottery: Period 4A. Compare the human figures with hands in prayer position illustrated on soft stone vessels (Hilton 2014 fig. 223), stamp seals (Kjærum 1983 nos. 49 and 350), and Mesopotamian cylinder seals (Kjærum 1983 no. 369).

Hind leg of animal? in copper (fig. 436) (F3.ze). Trench AD, level 8.85-7.55. Associated pottery: Period 3A, 3B, 4A.

Hind leg of animal? in copper (fig. 437, Ashkanani 2021 p. 97) (F3.æj). Trench AD, level 8.86-6.86. Associated pottery: Period 3A, 3B, 4A.

Fragment of bull's hind leg in a black asphaltic rock, the joint between the tibia and metatarsal bones with the protruding calcaneous bone (the hock) (fig. 438) (F6.904). Trench F2, 14-15 N, 6 W, - 1.98. Associated pottery: Period 1. The lower part of the leg with the hoof is broken off and the upper part ends in a protruding tenon. The piece is perforated transversely. Originally the tenon was probably longer and secured in a mortice with a perforation (as in the French-exca-

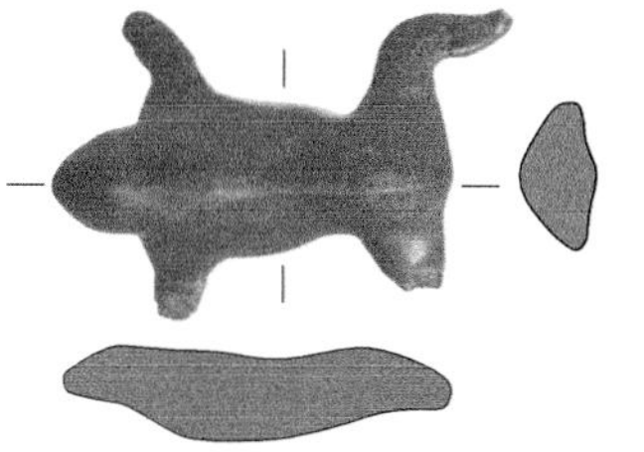

Fig. 434. 1:2.

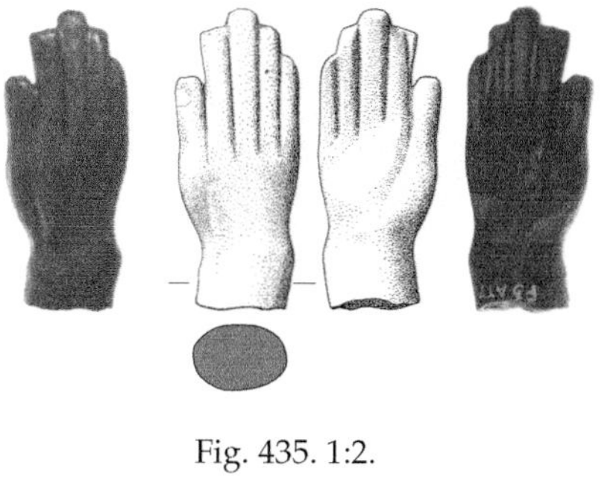

Fig. 435. 1:2.

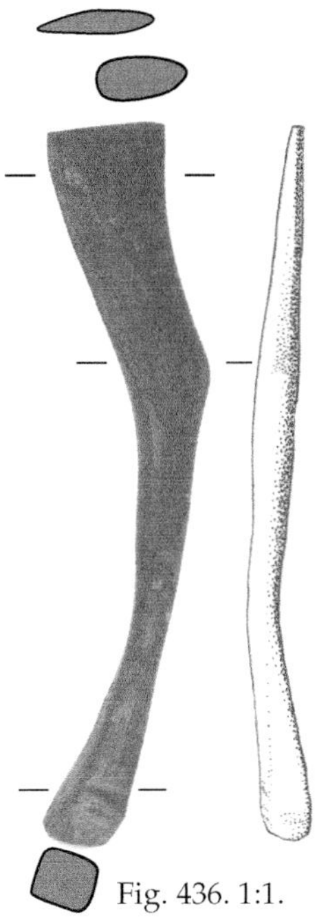

Fig. 436. 1:1.

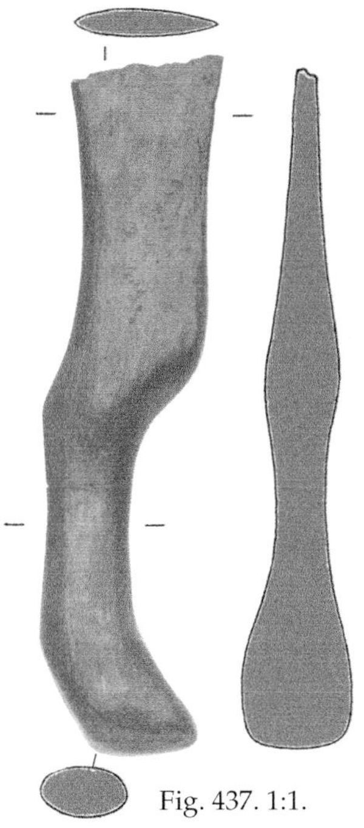

Fig. 437. 1:1.

vated piece described below), but after being damaged a new perforation was created so that it could be tied to the first perforation with a cord.

A similar object was found in the French excavations of the temple in Tell F6, in many details identical to the one described here. Rather than a tenon, this one had a mortise cut in the top and a corresponding perforation to keep the tenon in place (Calvet & Pic 1986 fig. 31).

Both examples are decorated with incised, double lines accentuating the Achilles tendon, and on the right side, two hanging tongues which are not easily explained with reference to the anatomy of the animal. Perhaps they were meant to represent tufts of hair? They may have been decorative attributes attached to a sacrificial animal.

Two close parallels dating to the first half of the 2nd millennium BC are known from Susa. They have similar shapes and incised decoration – note that in the illustration the tongues are on the left side of the leg (Connan & Deschesne 1996 nos. 224-225).

A similar bull's leg in black stone is found on the website of an auction house, a piece without provenience (Phoenix Ancient Art S.A., provenance Monique de Sancey serial no. 5752). It shows the same part of the hindleg but is preserved inclusive of the hoof. On this piece the same two hanging tongues are seen on the right side of the leg.

Notably, both fragments from Tell F6 have the tongues on the same side, that is, the right. Had they derived from the same animal sculpture one would expect one fragment to have been a left hindleg and to have had the tongues on the visible left side. Therefore, it is perhaps more likely that the legs were mounted with the legs pointing in the same direction on some kind of object like the offering tables with bull hooves of Syro-Cappadocian origin known from Dilmun stamp seals (Peyronel 2008 p. 245, Kjærum 1986b p. 272). See also the three-footed bowl with ibex from a burial at Susa (Amiet 1966 no. 210).

The two bull's legs are probably made of a natural bituminous rock (bitumen mastic), deriving east of Susa in Elam (Connan 2012 p. 157-177). A fragment, possibly of the same material, is worth mentioning here: 1.1 x 1.6 x 2 cm, with shiny, obsidian-like breakage (F3.nf, 811.AII). Trench Q, level 6.15. Associated pottery: Period 2.

Fig. 438. 1:1.

Statuette of a bearded man

by David Mulder & Holly Pittman

Tell F3, Trench H, sieve from between level c. 8.65 and c. 6.50. Soft black stone, height 5.5 cm (fig. 439) (F3.aqe, KM56).

The overall pose and garment of this figure show strong ties to Mesopotamian royal statuary of the late third and early second millennia BCE, although certain details of the figure's dress and features are without any clear parallels. The man depicted steps forward onto his left foot and clasps his hands in front of his torso. Such a clasped-hands gesture is extremely common in Mesopotamian sculpture, beginning in the Early Dynastic period and continuing well into the second millennium BCE, with some of the best-known exemplars found in the statues of Gudea of Lagash (ca. 2150 BCE) from Tello (ancient Girsu) The somewhat irresolute nature of the carving of the Failaka statuette leaves uncertain the precise positions of the hands, but it appears that the figure's proper right hand lies nearly flat over the balled fist of the left. This gesture would closely parallel the hand positions of two deities in a Gudea-period relief fragment in Berlin and in an unprovenanced Gudea statue in Detroit (Hansen 1988 p. 15 and 17, fig. 17).

The pose of the legs with one stepping forward, however, is unlike that of Gudea's sculptures in the round. Its only direct parallel in Mesopotamian statuary of the late third-early second millennium is to be found in a sculpture dedicated by Shulgi of Ur (2094-2047 BCE) to the god Igalim, also excavated at Tello (Suter 1991-1993 p. 63-70). This piece appears to be the sole surviving translation into three dimensions of a figure type commonly seen in Isin-Larsa/Old Babylonian presentation scene seals, wherein the king, bearing an animal offering in one or both arms, approaches and greets a deity (Ibid., fig. 6).[1] The long mantle worn by the king in these seals and in the Shulgi statue is of Strommenger's *Togagewand* type (Strommenger 1971, p. 37-55), which was prevalent in the Neo-Sumerian and Old Babylonian periods. When the forward stride of these figures parts the garment beneath the left arm, we see that the longer robe is worn over a short kilt that falls just above the knee.[2] The Failaka statuette's garb broadly conforms to the same pattern, but with some notable variations. The outer robe appears very narrow at the front but widens dramatically at the back into a long cape. Compared to the Mesopotamian examples, in which the garment typically passes across the upper chest to just below

Fig. 439. 2:1.

the right armpit, the Failaka figure's robe falls at a steeper angle across the torso and wraps around the right side at a much lower point on the hip, thus exposing the waistline and upper corner of the kilt below. The hem of the garment that should run up the right side and be tucked into the diagonal fold along the torso, as seen in the Shulgi statue, is not indicated in the work from Failaka. As it is depicted, the latter figure's outer garment appears to be a continuous ring of cloth of variable width, draped over the shoulder like a sash. However, given the work's overall similarity to the Mesopotamian royal type, we must assume that this piece of clothing is simply an abbreviated and schematized rendering of the toga-style wrap worn by the supplicant Shulgi.

The Failaka statuette's straight-sided headgear has fewer Mesopotamian parallels. It bears no resemblance to the brimmed cap worn by Neo-Sumerian and Old Babylonian rulers. Some analogies might be drawn to the flat cap of certain combatants in Akkadian-period contest scene seals (Boehmer 1965, Taf. 6.53-64, etc.) and by the central figure on the seal of Kalki (Ibid., Taf. 61.717. See also Aruz & Wallenfels 2003, p. 220, no. 150), but these often appear shorter and possibly less structured than the one on the Failaka figure. One terracotta plaque mold from Kish depicts a man in a long garment with a short, pointed beard whose headgear is described by Barrelet as a cylindrical toque (Barrelet 1968, p. 336-338, no. 639a-b).[3] This figure's identity is difficult to determine, but he holds a closed jar in what appears to be an offering gesture. Tall, cylindrical headdresses with feathers (?) appear in depictions of entertainers in Old Babylonian terracottas, which may or may not be related to the later use of this item of clothing as a royal and divine crown (Ibid., no. 829; Hill, Jacobsen & Delougaz 1990, Ish. 34:41, pl. 35b; Woolley & Mallowan 1976, pl. 75, nos. 110-111; Huot (ed.) 2003, p. 376, no. 14 (L.70.47). It is only in the mid to late second millennium (Kassite period and after) that such a head covering appears as a common attribute of royal and divine figures in Babylonia, as on the *kudurrus* of Melishipak, Nebuchadnezzar I, and Marduk-nadin-ahhe (Seidl 1989 nos. 23, 67, and 76, respectively).

The tapering beard of the Failaka figure also distinguishes it from most of its Mesopotamian counterparts of the Ur III through Old Babylonian eras, which tend to favor a squared beard. The tapering beard may hearken back to the Akkadian style seen, for example, in the Pir Hussein and Susa stelae of Naram-Sin (Aruz & Wallenfels 2003 p. 196, fig. 59, and p. 203, no. 130). A similar beard is worn by the anonymous head with brimmed cap from Adab (Bismaya) (Ibid., p. 435, no. 309), and a more rounded version is visible in a sculpture of Ur-Ningirsu of Lagash (Ibid., p. 434, no. 308). The tapered points of the beards of the sculptures Iddin-ilum and Puzur-Eshtar of Mari have also been interpreted as deliberate emulations of an Akkadian convention (Eppihimer 2019 p. 117-121, figs. 4.16 and 4.17).

Two final aspects of the figure's rendering deserve comment. The first is the depiction of the spine as a straight groove running down the back and neck. This is not unusual in Mesopotamian and Susian sculpture of the third and early second millennia, although it distances the Failaka statue from the Gudea sculptures in which the skeletal and muscular structure of the back are smoothed over by the wrapped garment. Similarly emphatic portrayals of the spinal groove can be found in Early Dynastic sculpture and in the Akkadian-period statues of Eshpum from Susa (Braun-Holzinger 2007, AKK 11, Taf. 44) and of an unnamed ruler from Mari (Ibid., AKK 13, Taf. 45). The second striking feature of the Failaka statuette is the enormity of the ears, which put even the famously "broad-eared" Gudea to shame (Winter 2009 p. 151-165). It is uncertain whether this exaggeration should be read as deliberate on the part of the sculptor or as an unintentional stylistic peculiarity.

The strong resemblance of the Failaka statuette to the Shulgi sculpture cited above indicates a date of manufacture during or shortly after the period of the Third Dynasty of Ur (ca. 2112-2004 BCE), despite certain dissimilarities to other Mesopotamian statuary of the Neo-Sumerian and Old Babylonian eras. The figure represented is likely a ruler, and his attitude is appropriate to a worshiper or supplicant before a deity, as seen in the presentation scenes of Gudea and in the Old Babylonian seals. If the right hand is indeed meant to be viewed as lying flat over the fist of the left, this detail would indicate a strong link with certain artworks connected to Gudea. The pointed beard and the rendering of the outer garment are somewhat unusual but not entirely inexplicable, whereas the everted cylindrical headdress has few obvious parallels in Mesopotamia, Elam, or the Gulf in the late third and early second millennia.

1. A seal of this type from Failaka is published in Calvet & Pic 2008, p. 197, pl. 3.10. For other examples see Collon 1986 no. 395, which can be dated by its inscription to the reign of Erra-imitti of Isin (1868-1861 BCE); and ibid., no. 345, which mentions Ibiq-Adad of Eshnunna (ca. 1825 BCE).
2. A similar garment with one leg exposed is worn by the libating figure on the right of a stamp seal also from Failaka (Tell F5), Hilton 2014 fig. 279.
3. Two figures with similar "toques" from Kish (Barrelet 1968 nos. 640a-b and 641a-b) show the caps tapering towards the top like fezzes, very different from the everted shape of the Failaka figure's.

Ram figures

A few figures of rams sculpted in the round in soft stone are of approximately the same size, less than 5 cm in length, and have the same recumbent posture with the legs tucked under the body. The same posture is seen in the two rams found in the Umm as-Sujur temple in Bahrain (Andersen & Højlund 2003, vol. 2, p. 43, figs. 14-16). They may be symbols of a god or depictions of sacrificial animals. Bones of, probably male, goats were identified in the oven behind the great temple in Tell F6 where the remains of the sacrifices were incinerated (Højlund & Abu-Laban 2016 p. 253-254).

Ram's head in greenish-black soft stone, neck broken, face/nose worn off, 1.7 x 2.4 cm. The curved horns are finely engraved, and the surface is smooth and shiny (fig. 440) (F6.963). Trench F1, sieve from above level -0.15.

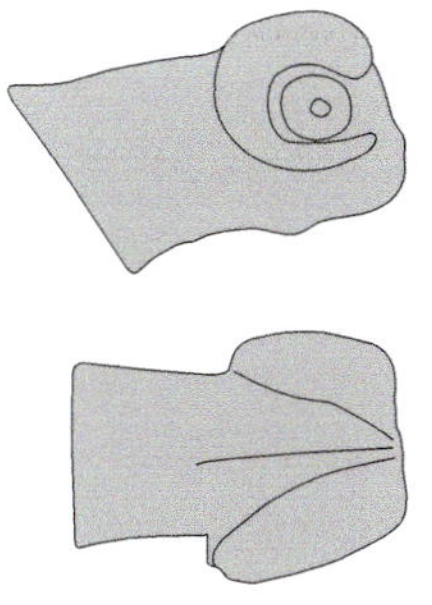

Fig. 440. 1:1.

A rather close parallel was found in the French excavations of a Hellenistic sanctuary (B6) on Failaka, in this case a complete, recumbent ram, 3.8 cm high, with curved horns and prominent dewlap (KM3459); the excavators suggested it may have been an old, reused piece (Caubet & Salles 1984 figs. 38 and 67, no. 134, p. 128, note 8. Salles 2005 p. 84. Ashkanani 2021 p. 84). On the registration card in the Kuwait National Museum, it is described by Caubet and Salles as having an "elegant fleece pattern across back and rear". Another close parallel, excavated by the French in Tell F5, again a recumbent ram cut in soft stone, 4 cm high, with curved horns and marked dewlap; the hind part has been cut off and was probably used for something else (KM5216) (Ashkanani 2021 p. 155). Compare also a possible head/neck of ram in soft stone found in Tell F5 (below p. 180, fig. 701).

Plaster cast of probably soft stone fragment (now disappeared) of the forepart of recumbent quadruped, 3.5 cm high, with the right foreleg folded below the body, part of the neck is preserved, turned slightly to the right, surface covered in carefully carved, small dots imitating fur, possibly a ram as in the two preceding entries (fig. 441) (no number, possibly Tell F3).

Soft stone fragment with two faces preserved, one covered in small dots like the previous item, 2.7 x 2.9 x 3 cm, possibly hind part of ram (fig. 442) (KM3088).

Fig. 441. 2:1.

Fig. 442. 2:1.

Male faces

Male face in relief in oolitic limestone, thickness 2.8 cm, pointed oval eyes, wedge-shaped nose continuing in eyebrows and small mouth with indication of beard. There may be a certain resemblance to 1st millennium sculpture from Saudi Arabia (Al-Ghabban et al. 2010 p. 257 no. 105 and p. 280, no. 114). On the upper side a protruding part is equipped with a small depression, perhaps for burning incense, though no darkening could be attested. Unable to stand on base, which appears damaged (fig. 443, Ashkanani 2021 p. 122) (F3.5). Trench RM, 16.45 N, 5 W, 0.92 m below surface.

Terracotta plaque with a broad, frontal face in relief (fig. 444) (F3.nb), with wide, grinning mouth and bared teeth, depicting the demon Humbaba (Kawami & Olbrantz 2013 p. 93, pl. 11. Gasche & Pons 2014 pl. 49). The backside and the edge are smoothed. Trench F, from sieve. The image of Humbaba was believed to be effective as a magical force to combat evil (Black & Green 1992 p. 58).

Terracotta pendant finely decorated in relief with male, bearded face with bushy eyebrows. The edge around the plaque is smoothed, but the upper part is broken off, leaving half of a piercing made for hanging (fig. 445) (KM1492). Tell F3. The face looks like faces depicted on two stamp seals in Style III (Kjærum 1983 nos. 345 and 347) and on a unique soft stone vessel in 2nd Millennium Figurative Failaka Style (Hilton 2014 p. 106, figs. 256-263).

Fig. 443. 1:1.

Fig. 444. 2:1.

Fig. 445 . 1:1.

8. Stone objects

Square stone vessels

In one case a square stone vessel was found in relation to a so-called "kitchen table" dating to Period 3A. The remaining vessels found out of context seem to date to the late part of the Failaka sequence. Cf. from Saar Settlement, Killick & Moon 2005 p. 232.

Square stone vessel, beach-rock, height 16.5 cm, depth of depression 10.5 cm, half-full of hard plaster, probably secondary (fig. 446) (F3.82). Trench RM, 33.73 N, 1.7 W, level 7.97.

Square stone vessel, beach-rock, complete (figs. 447-448) (F3.ax). Trench B, 36.80 N, 1.90 E, level 8.01, rested on flat stone slab. Associated pottery: Period 3A/3B.

Fragment of square stone vessel, oolitic limestone (fig. 449) (F3.xa). Trench AB, level 8.28-7.28. Associated pottery: Period 4B.

Square stone vessel, undetermined type of stone. Height 4.5 cm, length 6.9 cm, width 5.3 cm, depth of depression 2 cm (F3.xt). Trench AE, level 6.75-6.35. Associated pottery: Period 3A.

Square stone vessel, beach-rock (figs. 450-451) (F3.aoy). Trench G, level 7.09. Associated pottery: Period 3A. The vessel stood on a stone slab east of the "kitchen table", beside a complete pottery bowl (Højlund 1987 figs. 294-295 and 617. Kjærum & Højlund 2013 fig. 49). A larger, square stone block with a shallow depression stood up against the east side of the same "kitchen table" (Kjærum & Højlund 2013 figs. 45 and 49).

Fragment of square, stone vessel, oolitic limestone (fig. 452) (F3.aph). Trench O, 33 N, 20.70 W, level 6.70. Associated pottery: Period 3A/4A.

Fragment of square stone vessel, oolitic limestone (fig. 453) (F3.apj). South part of Trench O, level c. 7.50-6.70. Associated pottery: Period 3A/4A.

Two fragments of square stone vessel, one has a hole through the side, oolitic limestone (figs. 454-455) (F3.apn.1-2). Trench O, level c. 7.20-6.80. Associated pottery: Period 3A/4A.

Fragment of square stone vessel, probably beach-rock (fig. 456) (F3.asi). Trench K, level 7.00-6.50. Associated pottery: Period 3A.

Square stone vessel (fig. 457) (F3.axq). Trench AP, 65 N, 11 E, level 8.99.

Square stone vessel, beach-rock. Height 7.8 cm, length 16, width 15 cm, depth of depression 4.3 cm, thickness of wall 2 cm (F6.1148.A). Trench N1, 5-7 N, 13-15 W, level -0.82.

Three fragments of quadrangular stone vessel with repair holes, covered with bitumen, height 8 cm, wall thickness 2.3 cm, preserved length 26 cm, oolitic limestone (F3.ac). Trench B, 37.40 N, 2.3 E, level 7.92. Associated pottery: Period 3A/3B.

Grindstones

The grinding stones may have been used for grinding grain for baking bread (cf. the tannurs, the flat baking plates and the three-legged baking plates, Højlund 1987 types 38, 43-44).

Fragment of rounded-rectangular slab of stone with a 9 cm deep, concave grinding surface, restored with gypsum, 38 cm wide, 19 cm high, and a preserved length of 24 cm (F3.xx). Trench AF, 75.20 N, 4.50 W, level 6.95. Associated pottery: Period 2.

Rounded-rectangular quern with three feet in beach-rock (fig. 458) (F6.906). Length 39.5 cm, width 33 cm, height 8.5 cm, depth of depression 5.5 cm. Trench E2, 11 N, 1-2 E, level -1.70. Associated pottery: Period 1.

Rounded-rectangular grindstone of sandstone or fine beach-rock with smooth, convex grinding surface (F6.906.3), 8.7 x 13.5 x 5 cm. Trench E2, 11 N, 1-2 E, level -1.70. Associated pottery: Period 1.

Rounded-rectangular grindstone of sandstone or fine beach-rock with slightly convex, smooth workface (fig. 459) (F6.1126.A). Length 31.5 cm, width 16.2 cm, height 4.3 cm. Trench F1, level +0.62.

Rounded-rectangular grindstone of beach-rock with slightly convex, uneven, rough workface (F6.1126.B). Length 33 cm, width 13 cm, height 7 cm. Trench M1, level + 0.62.

Fragment of rounded-rectangular grinding slab, length 20 cm, width 14.3 cm, height 5 cm, beach-rock, slightly convex, very smooth workface (KM6403).

Fragment of rounded-rectangular quern in hard, compact beach-rock, preserved length 21 cm, width 31 cm, thickness 8.5 cm. One round foot with a diameter of 9 cm is preserved (KM6398).

Hammer stones

All hammer stones are made of hard stone, normally a dark, fine-grained rock, that do not occur naturally on the island of Failaka and must have been imported.

Irregular hammer stone with crushing traces on protruding edges, 5.5 x 6.5 cm (F3.ad). Trench B, level c. 8.90-8.50. Associated pottery: Period 3A/3B.

Two oval hard stones, 4.8 x 7.1 x 8.9 cm and 4.5 x 6.8 x 9.5 cm, with crushing traces at both ends (F3.bø). Trench B, middle of the trench, level 7.90-7.46. Associated pottery: Period 3A/3B.

Fragment of spherical hammer stone, originally at least 10 cm in diameter, with crushing traces all over excepting a 4 x 5 cm portion that is smooth and even (F3.fc). Trench F, north part, level 7.19-6.89. Associated pottery: Period 2, 3A, 3B.

Spherical hammer stone, 6 cm in diameter (F3.hz). Trench N, level 8.66-8.27. Associated pottery: Period 3B/4.

Fragment of spherical hammer stone, 7 cm in diameter, with crushing traces all over (F3.nr). Trench B, level 6.60-6.35. Associated pottery: Period 2.

A square block, 5 x 6 x 6.5 cm, with crushing traces all over except one side, which is smooth (F3.pf). Trenches E and A, outside oven.

Spherical/oval hammer stone, 4 x 7 x 8 cm, with crushing traces all over (F3.vv). Trench Ø, level 7.04-6.79. Associated pottery: Period 2.

Six hammer stones, 1) spherical, 7 cm in diameter, with crushing traces all over, 2) oval, 6 x 11 cm with traces of crushing at the ends, 3) irregular oval, 6 x 7 x 10 cm, with traces of crushing at the ends, 4) spherical/oval, 3.5 x 6 cm, smooth with crushing traces at one end, 5) irregular, 6 x 6.5 cm, with traces of crushing and one 3-4 cm smooth part and 6) fragment of irregular stone, at least 6 x 10 cm, smooth with traces of crushing at one end (F3.åe). Trench AL, level 6.85-5.98. Associated pottery: Period 2, 3B.

Egg-shaped stone, smooth all over, 5 x 6.4 cm (F3.åi). Trench AC.

An egg-shaped hammer stone, 5.2 x 6 x 7.6 cm, with crushing traces all over. A natural hard stone nodule, 5.5 x 7.1 x 7.4 cm, with crushing traces at one end (F3.afm). Trench D, level c. 6.77.

Fragment of spherical hammer stone, 6 cm in diameter, with crushing traces all over (F3.aqo). Trench O.

Oval, calcite, smooth except the end which has traces of crushing, 3.6 x 5.7 x 6.7 cm (F3.arb). Trench K, level c. 7.80-7.40. Associated pottery: Period 3A/4A.

Spherical/oval hammer stone, 6 x 9 x 10 cm, with crushing traces all over (F3.asæ). Trench K, level 6.50-7.00. Associated pottery: Period 3A.

Longish stone, black and fine-grained, with a broad, convex polished base, polished sides and a butt with crushing marks (fig. 460) (F3.avj). From the area west of Trench RM, level c. 6.80.

Fragment of round hammer stone with traces of crushing, preserved diameter 7.5 cm (F6.42). Trench A1, 0-9 S, 1-4 W, level +0.74.

Discus-shaped hammer stone with marks of crushing on the edges, 7.6 cm in diameter and 4.8 cm thick (F6.63). Trench SS 0-9 S, 0-1.5 W, level -0.52.

Fragment of oval hammer stone in calcite with traces of crushing all over, preserved length 6 cm, 7 cm wide, 4 cm thick (F6.227). Trench C1, level -0.32.

Spherical hammer stone with crushing traces all over, 7 cm in diameter (F6.366). Trench D2, 14-20 N, 1-4 W, level -0.55.

Spherical hammer stone with a band of crushing around the stone and opposing smooth areas (F6.497). Trench D1, level -0.79.

Twenty-nine hammer stones of different hard stones, with varying traces of crushing, ranging between 4 and 8 cm in diameter (F6.757). Trench F2, 12-15 N, 5-8 W, level -1.61, that is, probably below the first floor of the "Palace". Associated pottery: Period 1.

Five natural stone nodules, 5-7 cm across, with traces of crushing (F6.769). Trench E2, 12-13 N, 2-3 E, level -1.49.

Fragment of a spherical hammer stone with crushing traces all over, original diameter c. 9 cm (F6.856.A). Trench M2, level -1.31 to -2.12.

Spherical hammer stone with crushing traces all over, 5 cm in diameter (F6.876). Trench F2, 15-17 N, 5-6 W, -2.02. Associated pottery: Period 1.

Irregular hammer stone with traces of crushing (F6.891). Trench F2, 15.6-16.4 N, 6-7 W, level -2.59. Associated pottery: Period 1.

Smoothing stone

A discus-shaped stone, 3.3 x 6.3 cm, in calcite, shaped by crushing and then smoothed all over (F3.afm). Trench D, level c. 6.77.

Architectural elements

The house walls uncovered in Tell F3 and Tell F6 were generally built of undressed stones and, to a lesser extent, roughly ashlar-shaped stones (Kjærum & Højlund 2013 p. 11 and 101. Højlund & Abu-Laban 2016 p. 262, note 27). The 1960-1963 and subsequent 2008-2012 excavations of Tell F6 uncovered at least eighteen large, well-dressed ashlars in a fine beach-rock; they had no relation to the "Palace" but instead clearly derived from a later, post-Period 4A construction (Højlund & Abu-Laban 2016 p. 59-63).

During the 1958-1963 excavations of Tell F3, ashlars in fine beach-rock were encountered in two places. Firstly, in a pillared altar in the middle of the Period 3B open-air shrine. The altar was constructed of square pillars measuring c. 26 x 26 cm in cross section, with a height of c. 70 cm, standing on bases (Kjærum & Højlund 2013 p. 71, figs. 92, 94-95). Secondly, in House 30, dating to Period 4B (Kjærum & Højlund 2013 fig. 110), the south jamb of the door between rooms 1 and 2 consists of a large ashlar, 76 cm tall and 24 x 25 cm in cross section in a fine beach-rock. The upper end of this ashlar has a recess. In the corner immediately east of the door was a 1.47 m high pilaster consisting of four ashlars of whitish, coarse sandstone with fossils, on top of each other, the upper one 55 cm tall and 28 x 31 cm in cross section, possibly a roof-carrying pillar (Kjærum & Højlund 2013 figs. 18 and 116).

Furthermore, three similar, pillar-like ashlars were found lying loose in the north part of Trench I (fig. 461) which was disturbed by a large plundering hole extending below and destroying the floor in room 1 of House 30. Their original context is uncertain. They are described in the diary as c. 85 cm long and c. 30 x 30 cm in cross section.

Small, rectangular ashlar in oolitic limestone with a 1 x 2 cm rabbet cut along one side (fig. 462) (F3.xq). Trench AF, level 8.05-6.80. Associated pottery: Period 2, 4B.

Door anchor in oolitic limestone (fig. 463) (F3.ya). The head is 6.5 cm thick, the shaft 8.2 cm thick. Trench AF, 74.80 N, 6.30 W, level 7.22, in rubble north of the northwest corner of Period 4B House 30 (Kjærum & Højlund 2013 fig. 8). Associated pottery: Period 4B.

Ashlar in beach-rock with several square holes cut in two sides, 12.6 x 13.7 x 30 cm (F3, KM81).

Oolitic limestone block with concave cuttings on three sides, 14.5 x 16.5 x 28 cm (F6.75). Trench SS, 3 S, 0.80 E, level +0.55.

Oolitic limestone block with roughly cut runnel and carefully cut oblique lines on three sides which correspond to each other. Possibly a gutter from a roof, since the decoration was intended to be seen from below, perhaps imitating a pruned palm trunk (fig. 464) (F6.423). Length 27.5 cm, width 15 cm, height 12.5 cm, depth of runnel c. 5 cm, broken on both ends. Trench D2, level -1.11.

Fig. 446. 1:5.

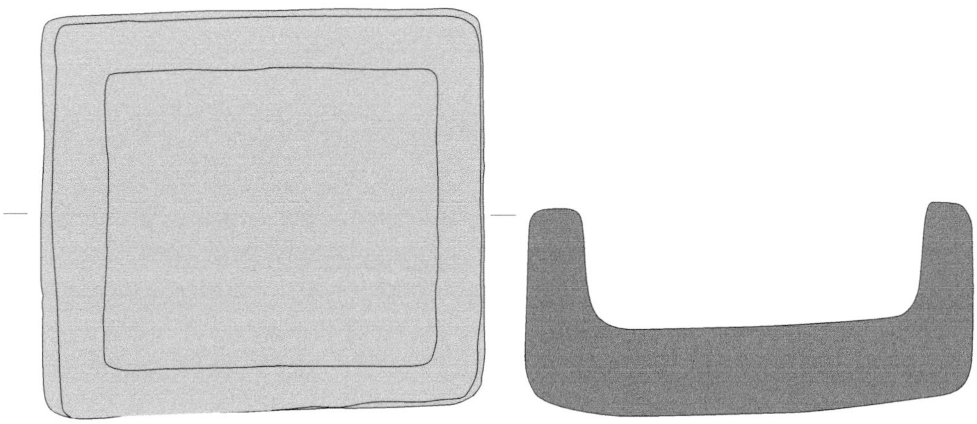

Fig. 447. 1:5.

Fig. 448. Stone vessel (= fig. 447), resting on flat stone in Trench B, Tell F3.

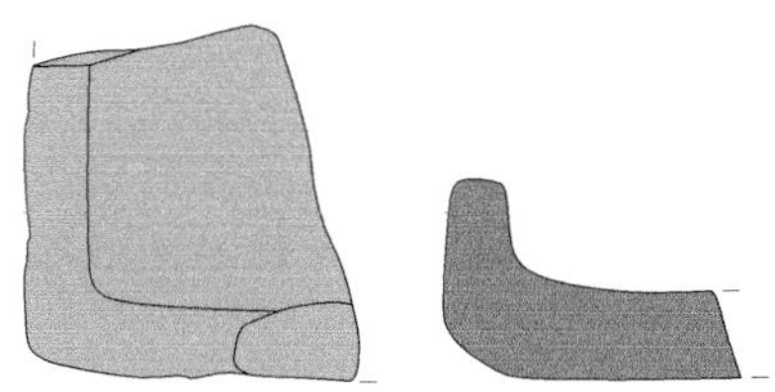

Fig. 449. 1:5.

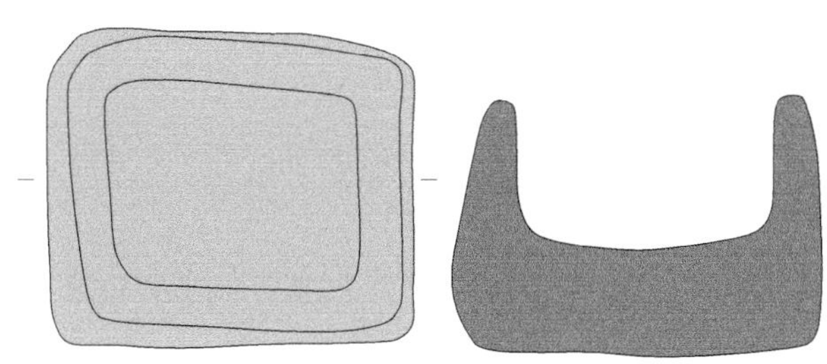

Fig. 450. 1:5.

Fig. 451. Stone vessel (= fig. 450) and pottery bowl at the "kitchen table" of House 6 in Trench G, Tell F3, looking SE.

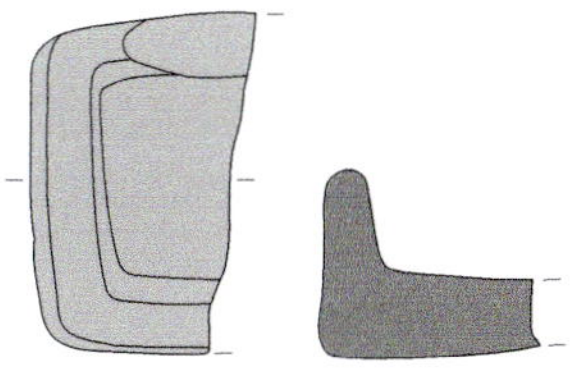

Fig. 453. 1:5.

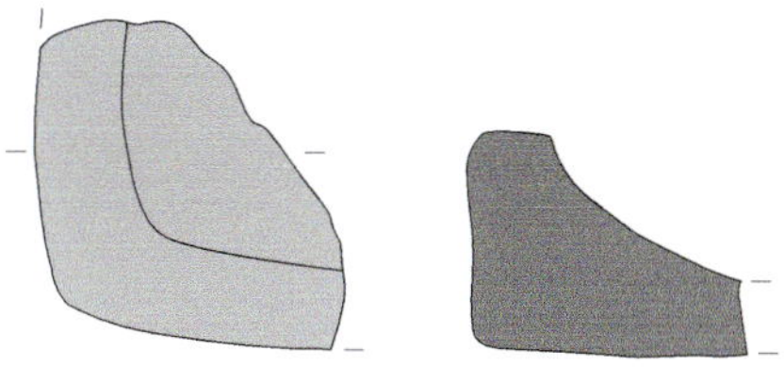

Fig. 454. 1:5.

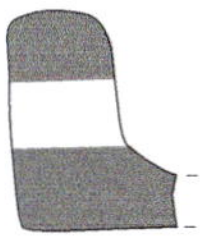

Fig. 455. 1:5.

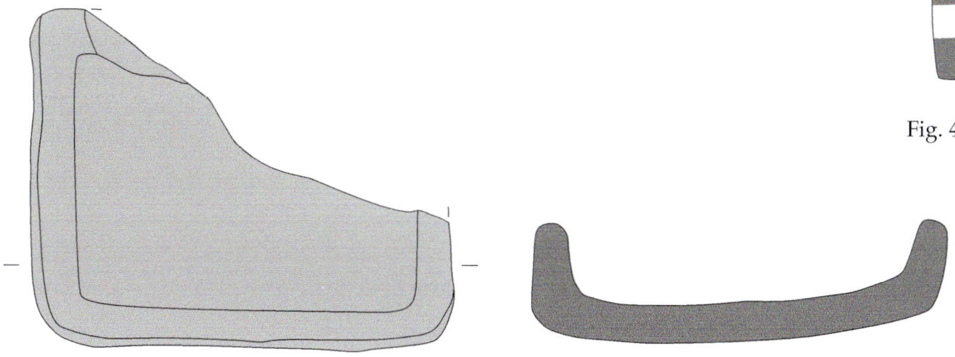

Fig. 452. 1:5.

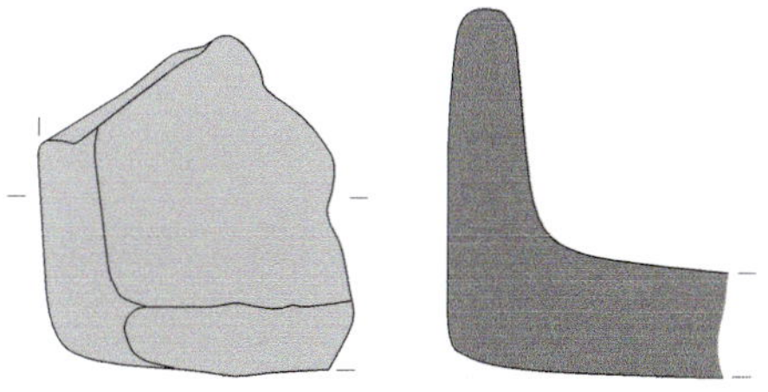

Fig. 456. 1:5.

Fig. 457. 1:5.

Fig. 458. 1:5.

Fig. 459. 1:5.

Fig. 460. 1:2.

Fig. 461. Ashlars lying loose in plundering pit through the floor of room 1 in House 30 in Trench I, Tell F3.

Fig. 462. 1:3.

Fig. 463. 1:5.

Fig. 464. 1:5.

Miniature altars

In the 2012-2017 excavations in Tell F3 a small cylinder in oolitic limestone with a longitudinal, furrowed ridge was found in Trench BH (Højlund & Hilton 2021 fig. 532). It was eroded all over, and no obvious function could be suggested. During the subsequent study of the finds presented in this volume, four similar, but better-preserved objects were identified which allow for their interpretation as miniature altars. They all have a protruding, longitudinal ridge furnished with a furrow. Two of the objects have a concave bowl-shaped top, and one is sufficiently well preserved to reveal that the bowl has an outlet into the furrow along the longitudinal ridge. A fifth small altar with a square cross section has a concave bowl-shaped top emptying into a furrow on the front, but without a ridge. The base of one of the altars is shaped as a tenon for insertion and has incised decoration on three sides.

The general shape of these objects is paralleled by several large, cylindrical altars from the Barbar Temple I-II (c. 2000 BC) which were furnished with a vertical projecting part, of which two had a concave front (Andersen & Højlund 2003 vol. 1, figs. 61-64, 164-166. Højlund et al. 2005 fig. 22). The rationale behind the shape may have been to direct sacrificial liquid (blood?) from the upper depression down the front of the altar. See also a spouted altar from Ain Abu Zaydan in Bahrain (Insoll et al. 2016 fig. 9 left).

Four of the miniature altars were found spread out in the southwest part of Tell F3 (Trenches RM, O, C, and BH). The one from Trench BH was found in Tell F3: Phase 2 layers dating to Period 3B, the three others came from uncertain contexts. No altars were found at Tell F6, adding weight to their interpretation as miniature altars engaged in private religious rituals conducted within the household.

Finely dressed, square with longitudinal furrowed ridge and concave upper side in oolitic limestone. Incised decoration on three sides. The base is shaped like a tenon for insertion and is partly covered with bitumen (fig. 465) (F3.44). Trench RM, 16.35 N, 5 W, 95 cm below surface.

Cylinder with concave upper side and longitudinal furrowed ridge in oolitic limestone; the surface is roughly executed (fig. 466) (F3.acj). Trench C, 34.7 N, 7.41 W, level 7.29. Associated pottery: Period 3A/4A?

Finely dressed cylinder with longitudinal, furrowed ridge in oolitic limestone. The upper surface is slightly concave, but damaged (fig. 467) (F3.ant). From Trench O, level c. 7.50-7.30. Associated pottery: Period 3A/4A.

Cylinder with longitudinal, furrowed ridge in unidentified type of stone (fig. 468) (F3.no number). Trench RM.

Square block of oolitic limestone with finely ground faces. On the upper side a low depression and a furrow on the front, the bottom side covered with secondary crushing marks (fig. 469) (F3.øe). Trench AK, level 6.69-6.18.

Rectangular, finely ground stones

Of special interest is a group of rectangular stones, carefully dressed and finely ground, normally in oolitic limestone but occasionally in beach-rock, a type of object that was also encountered during the 2012-2017 excavations in Tell F3 (cf. Højlund & Hilton 2021 figs. 531, 538, 539, 540, 541 and 544). Related to this group are rectangular stones with prongs.

Their function is unknown. They might be objects of veneration, house altars, and reference may be made to the central altar in the open-air shrine on Tell F3 which consists of stones of somewhat similar shape, though more square than rectangular in cross section, and much larger and without bulging sides (Kjærum & Højlund 2013 p. 71-73, figs. 88-98). Weights in stone and terracotta of similar shape are known from Dholavira, Gujarat (Bisht 2015 fig. 8.60), but they are much smaller, and the actual weights of the stones from Failaka, which are given below, do not seem to conform to any weight system (contra Højlund & Hilton 2021 p. 139).

Like the preceding type, the miniature altars, this type is only found in Tell F3 and not in Tell F6, neither from the 1958-1963 nor from the 2008-2012 excavations, which may support the notion that they had a private, domestic function, perhaps as house altars.

Ten of these rectangular stones, including those from the 2012-2017 excavations (Højlund & Hilton 2021 figs. 531, 538-541 and 544), were found scattered all over Tell F3, but the majority derive from the southern part of Trench RM, 0-20 m N, an area devoid of architecture with sloping layers of sand and refuse of all kinds, that is, they seem to have been discarded like trash. Their dating is uncertain.

Rectangular stone of unidentified type, 5 x 7 cm (fig. 470) (F3.14).

Fig. 465. 1:1.

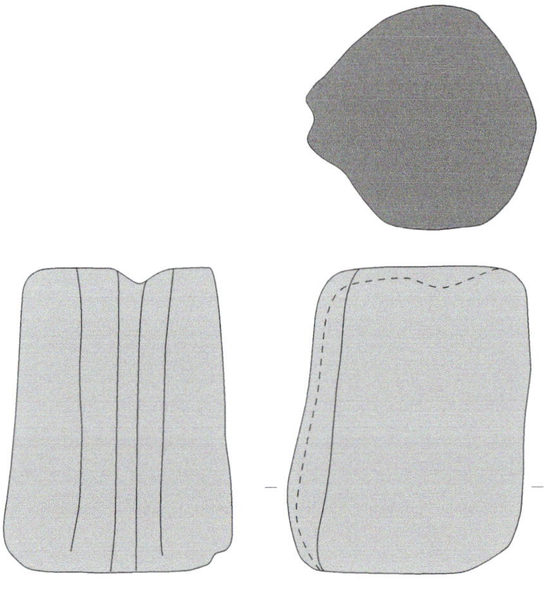

Fig. 466. 1:2.

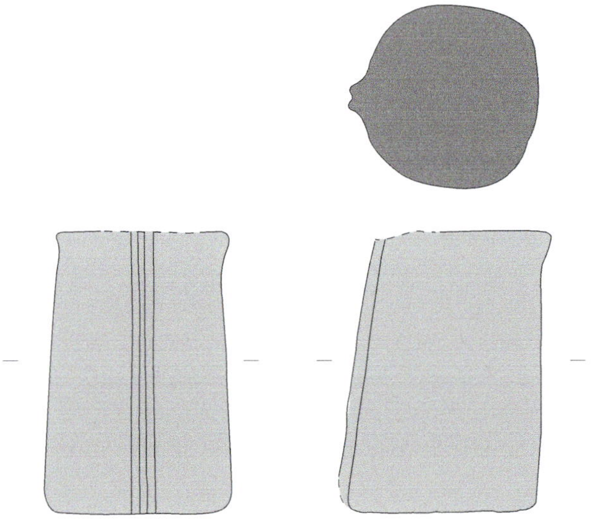

Fig. 467. 1:2.

Fig. 468. 1:1.

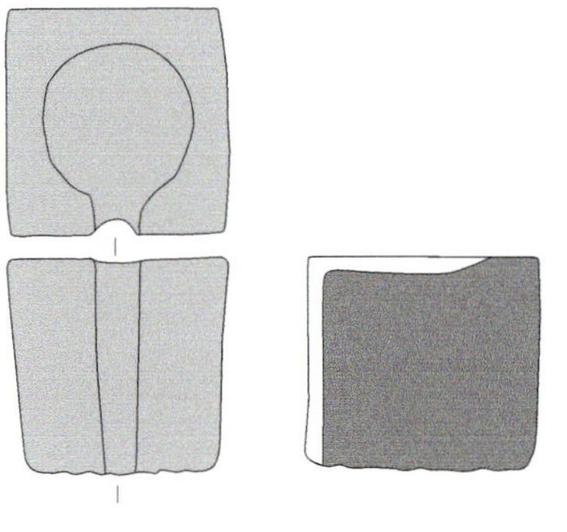

Fig. 469. 1:2.

Rectangular stone in fine beach-rock, 3.2 cm thick, 108 g (fig. 471) (F3.45). Trench RM, 16.35 N, 5 W, 0.95 below surface.

Rectangular stone in oolitic limestone, 2.6 x 4.7 x 6.7 cm (125 g) (881.AL?).

Twelve rectangular, finely ground stones of oolitic limestone, 3.2 x 4.7 x 6.4 cm (113 g), 2.2 x 4.7 x 6.8 cm (103 g), 2.5 x 4.6 x 5.2 cm (87 g), 2.3 x 2.9 x 3.4 cm (34 g), 2.6 x 4 x 5.2 cm (80 g), 2.6 x 3.8 x 7.1 cm (96 g), 2.3 x 5.3 x 7 cm (102 g), 2.7 x 5 x 6.1 cm (93 g), 3.7 x 7.4 x 11.8 cm (471 g), 3.2 x 6.5 x 9.1 cm (260 g), 3.4 x 4.9 x 7.6 cm (161 g), and one with transverse lines (86 g) (fig. 472) (881. QV). Trench RM, 0-20 N, above 1 m depth.

Rectangular stone in oolitic limestone with engravings on one side, 3 cm thick, weight 211 g (fig. 473) (881.RD).

Rectangular stone of oolitic limestone, 4.1 cm thick cm, weight 129 g (fig. 474) (881.SG). Trench RM, 50-60 N, above level c. 6.30.

Rectangular stone of oolitic limestone, 1.5 cm thick, weight 48 g (fig. 475) (881.SL). Trench RM.

Rectangular stone, oolitic limestone, weight 46 g (fig. 476) (F3.hs). Trench M north, level 7.09-6.73. Period 3A/3B?

Rectangular stone slab, finely ground faces, oolitic limestone, weight 465 g (fig. 477) (F3.kw). Trench I.

Rectangular stone slab with a tenon at the end, oolitic limestone, weight 284 g (fig. 478) (F3.læ). Trench W, 84 N, 2.50 E, level 7.95. Associated pottery: Period 4B.

Fragment of rectangular stone, 5.4 x 4.5 cm in cross section, 2.1 cm in preserved length, oolitic limestone (F3.th). Trench Q, level 5.35.

Rectangular stone, rough, possibly secondary depression in one face, oolitic limestone, weight 181 g (fig. 479) (F3.øg). Trench AL, level 9.63-8.96. Associated pottery: Period 4B.

Rectangular stone, oolitic limestone, weight 109 g (fig. 480) (F3.amv). Trenches K, P, or O, sieve.

Rectangular stone, all faces are carefully ground and slightly bulging, oolitic limestone, weight 630 g (fig. 481) (F3.aoq). Trench O, level c. 7.50-6.70. Associated pottery: Period 3A/4A.

Fragment of rectangular oolitic limestone, 3.1 x 5.2 cm in cross section, 2.1 cm in preserved length, one side secondarily crushed, weight 42 g (F3.ate). Trench O, level c. 9.00-6.60. Associated pottery: Period 3A/4A.

Rectangular stone, 1.7 cm thick, oolitic limestone (fig. 482) (F3.bjl). Sieve.

Rectangular stone with tenon for insertion (fig. 483) (881.RD?). Trench RM.

With prongs

Rectangular stone ending in three prongs in oolitic limestone with bitumen spots, 2.4 cm thick, 117 g (fig. 484) (F3.15). Trench RM, 13.8 N, 4 W, 0.9-1.1 m below surface.

Rectangular stone ending in three prongs in oolitic limestone, 2.5 cm thick, 71 g (fig. 485) (F3.41). Trench RM, 10 N, 2.5 W, 0.75-1 m below surface.

Rectangular stone ending in three prongs in oolitic limestone, 2.2 cm thick (fig. 486) (F3.128). Trench RM, 3-15 N, above 1 m depth.

Rectangular stone ending in two prongs in oolitic limestone, 2.1 cm thick, 68 g (fig. 487) (F3.316). Trench RM, 0-20 N, above 1.5 m depth.

Rectangular stone of oolitic limestone with two prongs and rectangular cross section, upper thickness 2.7 cm, lower thickness 3 cm (fig. 488) (881.QV). Trench RM, 0-20 N, above 1 m depth.

Rectangular stone with two prongs, 1.7 cm thick, oolitic limestone (fig. 489) (F3.bjl). Sieve.

Rectangular stone ending in three prongs in oolitic limestone, weight 40 g (fig. 490) (881).

Fig. 470. 1:2.

Fig. 471. 1:2.

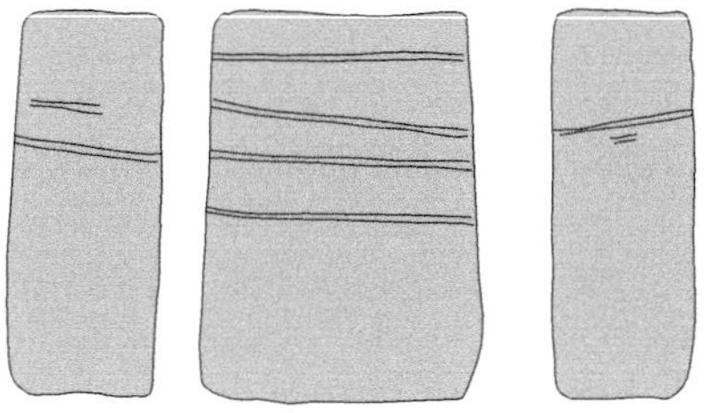

Fig. 472. 1:2.

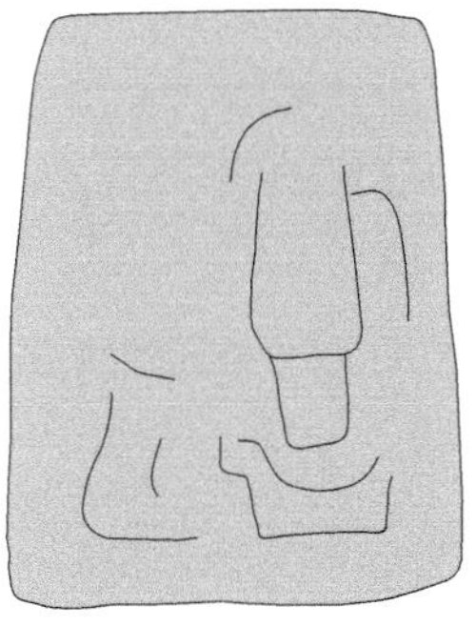

Fig. 473. 1:2.

Fig. 474. 1:2.

Fig. 475. 1:2.

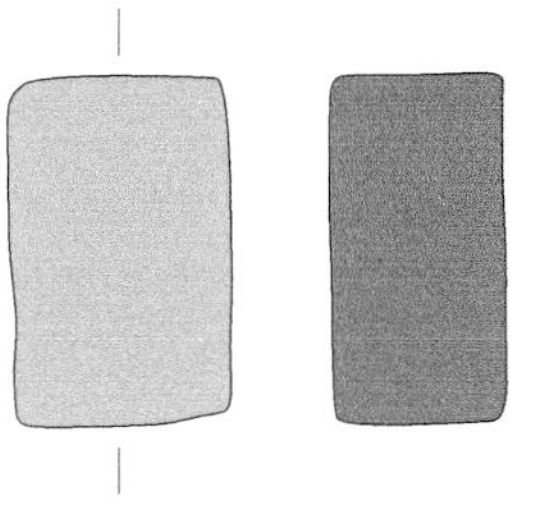

Fig. 476. 1:2.

Fig. 477. 1:2.

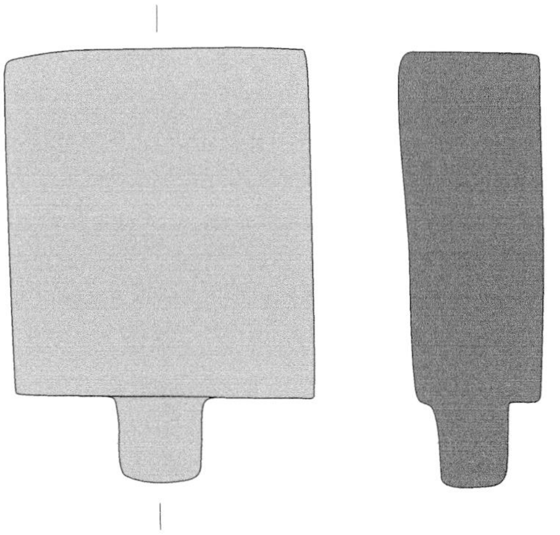

Fig. 478. 1:2.

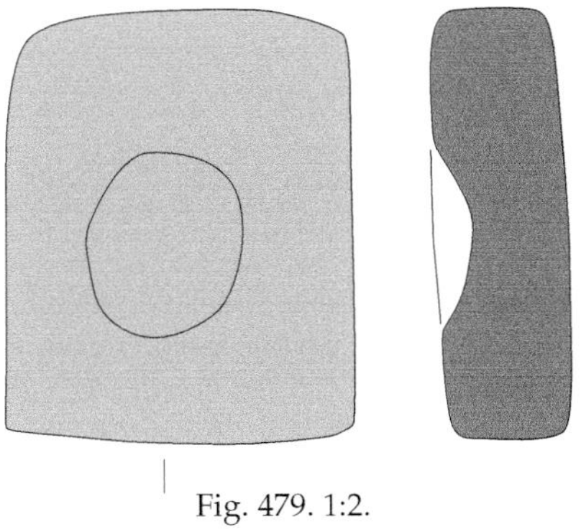

Fig. 479. 1:2.

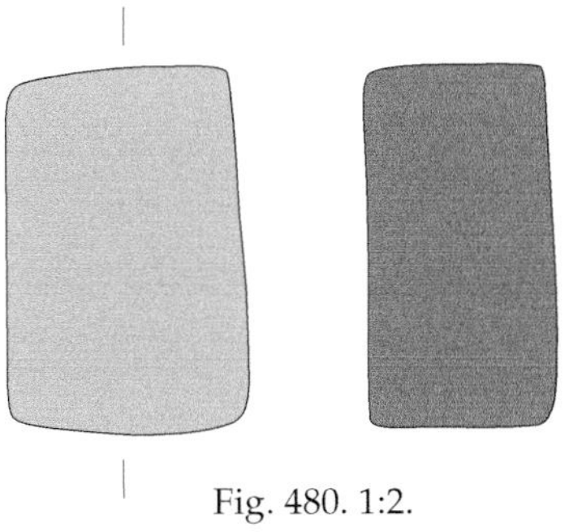

Fig. 480. 1:2.

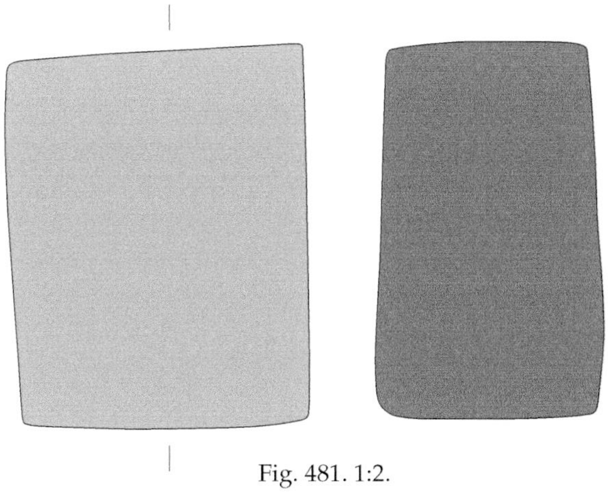

Fig. 481. 1:2.

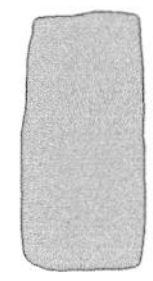

Fig. 482. 1:2.

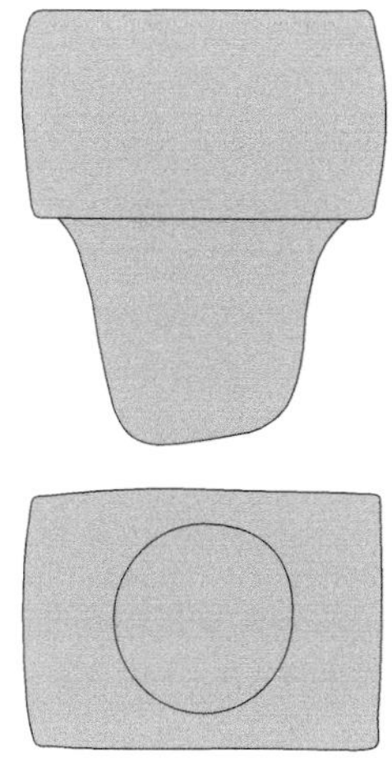

Fig. 483. 1:2.

Fig. 484. 1:2.

Fig. 485. 1:2.

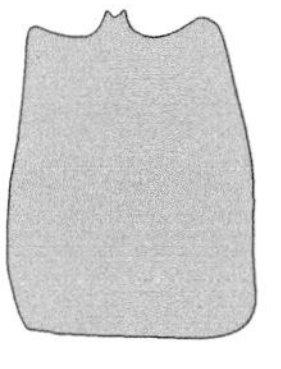

Fig. 486. 1:2.

Fig. 487. 1:2.

Fig. 488. 1:2.

Fig. 489. 1:2.

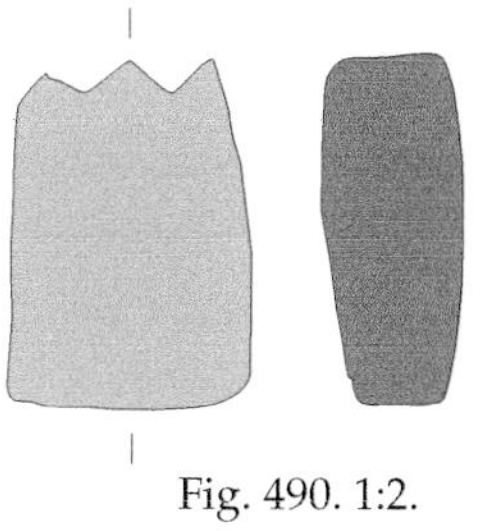

Fig. 490. 1:2.

Stoppers and lids

Pottery vessels, mostly in fragments, were the most common objects found in the excavations of Tell F3 and Tell F6. Many of the vessels were no doubt intended for storage, and there was a need to close them to prevent insects and rodents gaining access to their contents. This function was served by stone slabs (in several cases found in situ, e.g. Højlund 1987 figs. 57 and 325), but also by dedicated lids and stoppers made of stone, pottery, or plaster (cf. Højlund & Hilton 2021 figs. 519 and 522. Benediková 2010 fig. 118e-f. Killick & Moon 2005 fig. 5.21).

Stopper of oolitic limestone. Head 3.5 x 4.5 cm, shaft 3 x 3.6 cm (fig. 491) (F3.17). Trench RM, 14.20 N, 3.9 W, 1.2 m below surface.

Square stopper of oolitic limestone, head 3.2 x 3.5 cm, shaft 3 x 3.2 cm (fig. 492) (881.QV). Trench RM, 0-20 N, above 1 m depth.

Stopper of oolitic limestone (fig. 493) (881.RP). Trench RM, 40-50 N, level c. 8.25-7.75.

Lid in white limestone, round, 10.3 cm diameter, 2.5 cm thick, lower edge is flanged, incised V on the inner side? (F3.øo). Trench AI, level c. 6.20. Associated pottery: Period 3A.

Lid, oval, 11 x 12.50 cm, 5 cm thick, oolitic limestone (F3.ajw). Trench D, level c. 6.50-700.

Lid, 9.5 cm in diameter, 2.3 cm thick, fine-grained stone, quartz? (F3.alz). Trench K, level c. 7.00-6.80. Associated pottery: Period 3A.

Lid, 20 cm in diameter, 2.1 cm thick, beach-rock (F3.alk). Trench H, level c. 7.10-6.50.

Lid, upper part splays near top to convex face, oolitic limestone (fig. 494) (F3.arg). Trench K, level c. 7.90-7.40. Associated pottery: Period 3A/4A.

Lid of stone or plaster, 3.5 cm thick (fig. 495) (F3.bjf). Trench AM, level 6.85-6.35. Associated pottery: Period 3A?

Lid with handle in oolitic limestone (fig. 496) (F6.1106). Trench D1, 7 N, 0.5 W, level -1.37.

Stones with depression

Many stones have a depression on one side (cf. from Qala'at al-Bahrain, Højlund & Andersen 1994 figs. 2007-2011, and from Saar Settlement, Killick & Moon 2005 p. 232). Some may have been incense burners, like the one standing against the rectangular altar in the open-air shrine at Tell F3 (Kjærum & Højlund 2013 p. 72, figs. 88 and 96).

Cubic oolitic limestone, height 4.7 cm, with circular, 2 cm deep, depression in top, incense burner? (fig. 497) (F3.16). Trench RM, 17.1 N, 4.65 W, 0.95 m below surface.

Cubic shape in oolitic limestone with four-sided depression cut into one side and, secondarily, a circular depression cut into another side (fig. 498) (F3.ok). Trench I, level 5.65. Associated pottery: Period 2.

Four stones, 4-7 cm, with round depressions, in oolitic limestone (881.QV). Trench RM, 0-20 N, above 1 m depth.

Square stone with depression cut into one side, oolitic limestone (fig. 499) (F3.æo). Trench AD, level 7.22. Trench 3A-3B.

Fragment of square stone with depression with cutting or turning striations, oolitic limestone (fig. 500) (F3.aic). Trench G, level 8.17-6.98 in room 2 in House 6 (Kjærum & Højlund 2013 fig. 45). Associated pottery: Period 3A, 4A.

Incense burner of oolitic limestone with depression on upper surface, volutes on two sides, possibly imitating a human face with curly hair (fig. 501, Ashkanani 2021 p. 123) (F6.179). Trench A1, 1 S, 1-4 W, level -1.02 to -1.23.

Cylinder with a depression in the top, diameter 4.7-5.5 cm, depression 1.6 cm, possibly an incense burner (fig. 502) (F6.987). Trench F1, level -0.30.

Square stone with depression, oolitic limestone (fig. 503) (no number).

Round stone with depression, 14.5 x 15 cm, oolitic limestone (F3.ahø). Trench H, 39.5 N, 11.5 W, level 7.42. Associated pottery: Period 4A.

Cubic block in sandy oolitic limestone, 6.1 x 6.4 x 8.5 cm, with crushing marks on one end and crushed depressions on several faces (F3.aop). Trench P, level c. 7.00-6.20. Associated pottery: Period 3A.

Rectangular block of sandstone, 4.7 x 7 x 8.8 cm, with one smooth broad side and a crushed depression on the opposite (F3.vm), Trench AA, level 7.26-7.10. Associated pottery: Period 4.

Stone circles

Their function is uncertain, but they could perhaps be stands to carry round-bottomed pottery vessels or sacks of animal skins.

Fragment of stone circle, oolitic limestone (fig. 504) (F3.ajn). Trench G, from the "kitchen table" in room 2 in House 6 (cf. Kjærum & Højlund 2013 fig. 45). Associated pottery: Period 3A.

Fragment of stone circle decorated with two ridges on the external side, oolitic limestone (fig. 505) (F3.alz). Trench K, level c. 7.00-6.80. Associated pottery: Period 3A.

Stone circle, complete, oolitic limestone (fig. 506) (F3.aox). Trench G, standing on "kitchen table" at level 7.02 in room 2 in House 6 (Kjærum & Højlund 2013 figs. 45 and 49). Associated pottery: Period 3A.

Door sockets and potter's wheel

Door socket determined as amphibolite by Aage Jensen (University of Copenhagen), with remains of copper in the depression, probably from a sheathing of the doorpost (fig. 507, Ashkanani 2021 p. 115) (F6.930.A). Trench D1, 7.2 N, 2.8 W, level -1.32, that is, in room 1 in the "Palace" (Kjærum & Højlund 2013 fig. 138), immediately northeast of the main gate into the room, in the corner between the built-in pillar and the southeast wall of the room, found together with the following object.

Door socket or potter's wheel bearing of dark, fine-grained material with an extremely smooth, 2 cm deep, depression in one side with very clear circular traces of wear, the other sides are shaped by crushing (fig. 508) (F6.930.B). Found together with the previous object (cf. Calderbank 2018 p. 143, figs. 5.4 and 5.5. Rouault & Masetti-Rouault 1993 p. 269, cat.no. 132).

Rough block of soft stone with circular depression cut with a knife, broken; attempt to make a door socket? (fig. 509) (F3.arå). Trench K, level c. 7.00-6.50. Associated pottery: Period 3A.

Door socket or mortar, hole 11 cm deep (fig. 510) (F3.åu). Trench AL, 60.25 N, 0.50 W, level 6.86. Associated pottery: Period 3B.

Spindle-shaped haematite weights

Two spindle-shaped, haematite weights were found during the 1958-1963 excavations at Tell F3. A small number of similar weights conforming to the Mesopotamian weight standard have been found on sites within Dilmun, for example, Al-Khidr, Failaka (Benediková 2010 fig. 105: e), Qala'at al-Bahrain, Bahrain (Højlund & Andersen 1994 fig. 1990), Saar Settlement (Killick & Moon 2005 p. 5.36h-i), Al Hajjar cemetery (Lombard & Kervran 1989 no. 56), and from a Saar burial mound (Højlund 1990b. Vine 1993 p. 47. Lombard 1999 nos. 100-103). So far, the dating indications point to a dating to Qala'at al-Bahrain Periods IIb-c which is interesting as a number of Indus type weights found at Qala'at al-Bahrain date to the preceding Qala'at al-Bahrain Period IIa (Højlund & Andersen 1994 p. 395-397).

Spindle-shaped weight in haematite, dark grey with light spots, 1 x 2.8 cm, 5.55 g or approximately two thirds of a Mesopotamian shekel (fig. 511) (F3.235). Sieve.

Fragment of spindle-shaped weight in shiny black haematite, preserved length 1.2 cm, maximum diameter 0.6 cm, 0.95 g (fig. 512) (F3.309). Trench RM, 32.55 N, 1.05 W, level 6.88.

Fig. 491. 1:2.

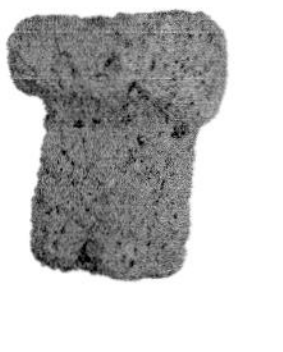

Fig. 492. 1:2.

Fig. 493. 1:2.

Fig. 495. 1:3.

Fig. 496. 1:3.

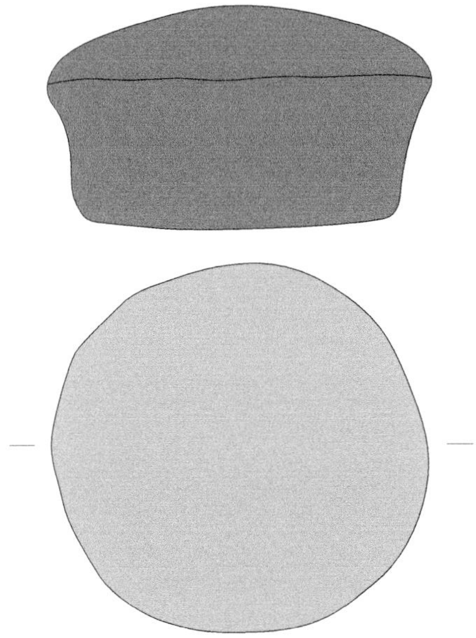

Fig. 494. 1:2.

Fig. 497. 1:2.

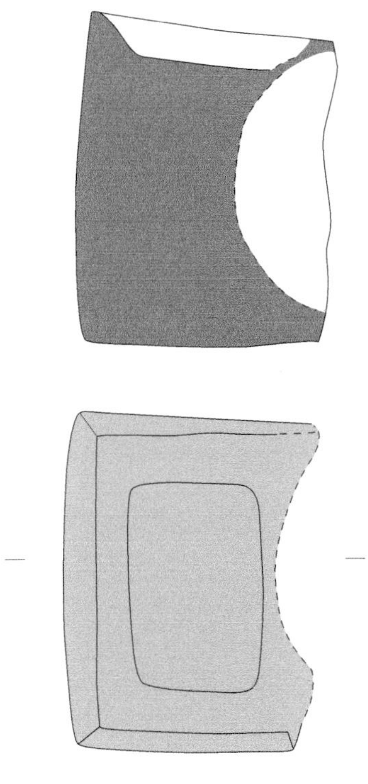

Fig. 498. 1:2.

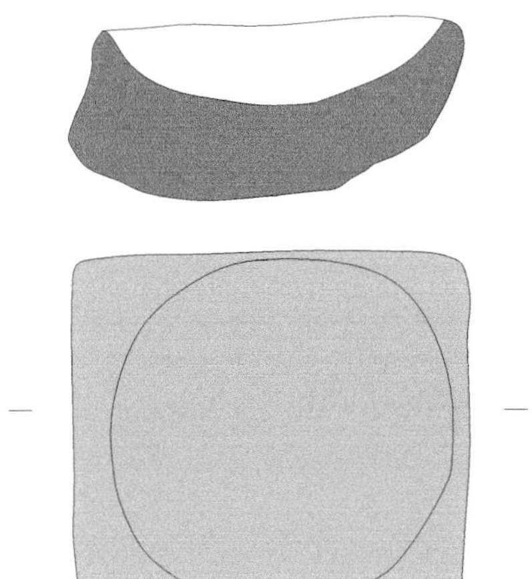

Fig. 499. 1:3.

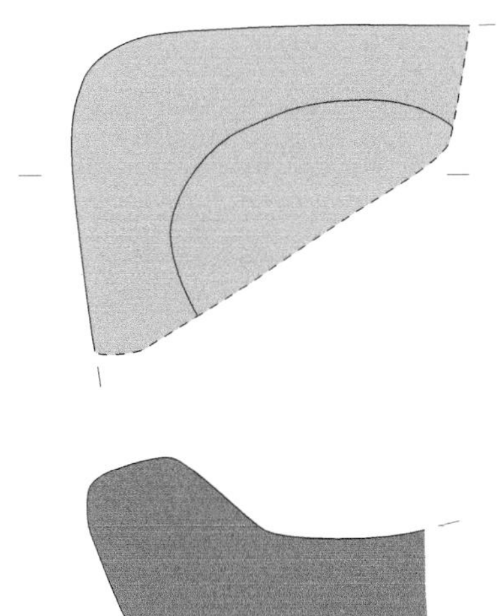

Fig. 500. 1:2.

Fig. 501. 1:3.

Fig. 502. 1:2.

Fig. 503. 1:2.

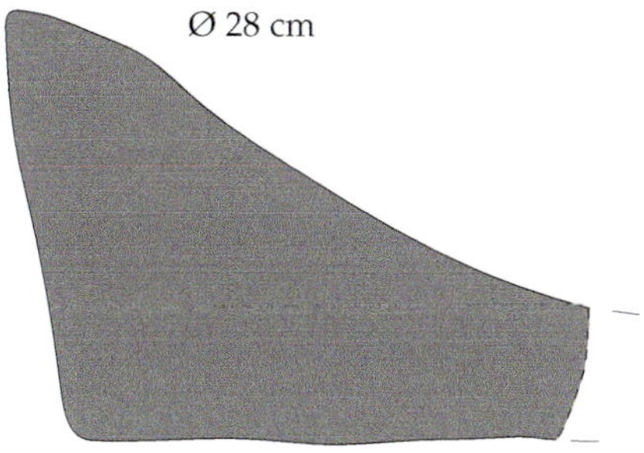

Fig. 504. 1:2.

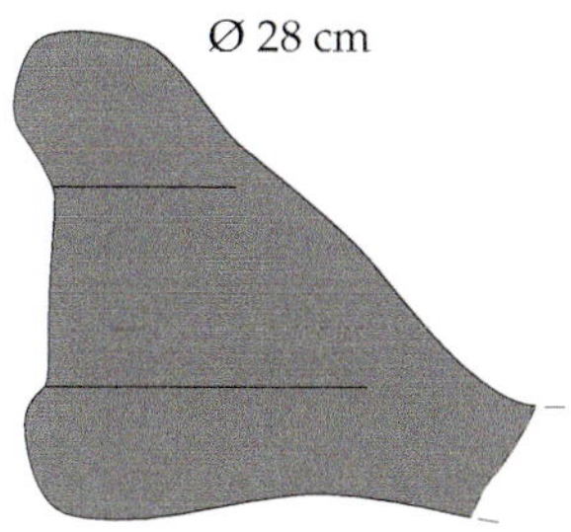

Fig. 505. 1:2.

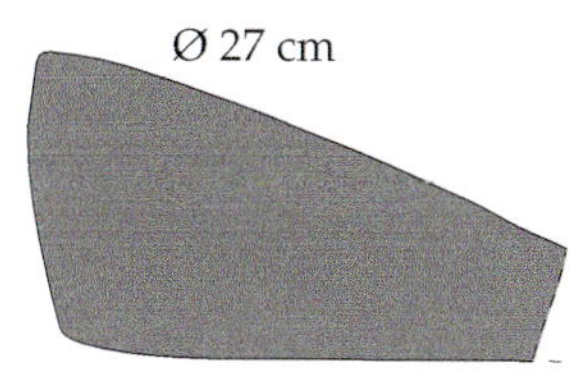

Fig. 506. 1:2.

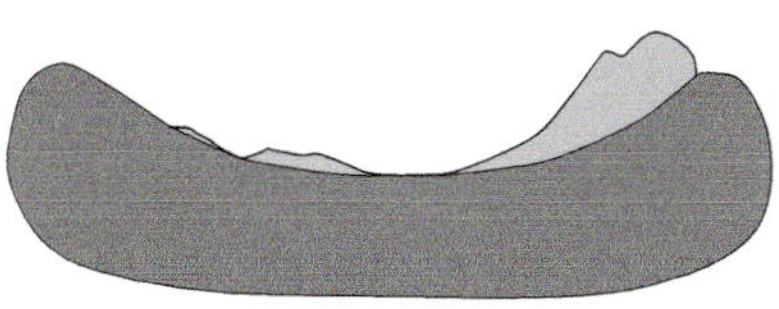

Fig. 507. 1:2.

Fig. 508. 1:2.

Fig. 509. 1:2.

Fig. 510. 1:10.

Fig. 511. 1:1.

Fig. 512. 1:1.

Pendants, spindle whorls, and other soft stone vessel reuse

by Anna Hilton

This section will present a selection of items cut from broken soft stone vessels into new objects, like pendants, spindle whorls, and blanks. These objects carry recognizable traits from their former vessel shape, or they retain decoration in one of the stone vessel styles that have previously been defined based on material from the 1958-1963 excavations on Failaka, that is, the Umm an-Nar Style, the Wadi Suq Style, the Figurative Failaka Style, the Plain Failaka Style, and the Late Bronze Age Style (Hilton 2014 p. 51ff). They also reveal marks from the reworking process and traces of secondary use unrelated to their initial use as vessels.

Reuse of soft stone vessel fragments has previously been dealt with by Ciarla (1985. 1990) and Hilton (2014 p. 163-166). The material was documented, drawn, and photographed in 2008-2009 by Anna Hilton Soria and Rune Soria. If available for inspection the type of stone has been classified according to Hilton (2014 p. 12).

In the 2014 study of the Failaka soft stone vessels it was found that 91 of the 387 diagnostic sherds or 30 % had traces of having been used as raw material for producing other objects (Hilton 2014 p. 163). The most common method to work the sherds was carving a furrow halfway into the sherd followed by breakage. The dislodged fragment was then further carved and ground into shape, a suspension hole was often drilled, and additional decoration was incised. Sometimes the object showed signs of wear, especially around the hole, probably because it was worn on a string.

On many objects the original stone vessel decoration is preserved, often various geometric patterns which derive from the Umm an-Nar, the Wadi Suq, or the Late Bronze Age Styles (Hilton 2014). In other cases, an element from the Failaka Figurative Style may be incorporated into the decoration, for example, a rosette, associated with worship, on a Figurative Failaka Style vessel (Hilton 2014 figs. 223-225).

Some objects were secondarily incised with motifs of possible symbolic meaning. There is one example of an arrow-in-box, a well-known motif incised on pottery (Højlund 1987 fig. 712:k-l) and stamp seals, possibly a reference to the temple institution or cult of Inzak (Laursen 2016 p. 5 and 16). A palm branch (fig. 530) may signal a relation to the god Inzak (Nashef 1986 p. 346 = Nashef 1984). This motif is seen also on stamp seals (Kjærum 1983 nos. 49 and 350) and on stone vessels in Failaka Figurative Style (Hilton 2014 figs. 213, 243 and 258). A worship scene (fig. 519) has parallels on stamp seals (Kjærum 1983 nos. 49, 345 and 350) and on Failaka Figurative Style vessels (Hilton 2014 figs. 213, 223 and 257).

One item is decorated with a boat (fig. 516), a motif that occurs on Dilmun stamp seals (Højlund & Hilton 2021 fig. 336) and grid patterns (figs. 514-515) may recall similar patterns on stamp seals (Kjærum 1983 nos. 303, 325, 327 and 364. Højlund & Hilton 2021 fig. 335).

Many items are sooted on the exterior, probably because they derive from vessels that were originally used for cooking.

Pendants, spindle whorls, and blanks were found almost exclusively in Tell F3. Of the 70 objects treated in this section only one comes from Tell F6. Considering that all phases of their production can be followed in the finds from Tell F3 and that the raw material for this production was available on the site there can be no doubt that the production of these objects took place on Tell F3. The presence of wear on some of the objects suggest that they were also used there, but it is equally likely that some of them were produced for export.

A small number of these objects made of re-used stone vessel sherds occur in layers where the associated pottery may give an indication of their dating and this dating has been appended to their description below. All periods revealed in Tell F3 seems to be represented.

Pendants

Pendants occur in various shapes, for example, rectangular, square, trapezoid, and round, and they were normally pierced in one end. Some pendants were pierced through the middle, and a few had a small knob to tie a string around. They are often decorated on both sides and very often also with a single line on the edges. Some of them have traces of wear on the surfaces or at the hole. They were probably worn as personal adornments or amulets (cf. Benediková 2010 fig. 90: e-f).

Pendant (fig. 513) (F3.101, 881.GK, KM3166_5). Tell F3, Trench RM, 0-10 N, sieve. It is square, pierced at one end, area around hole is worn. The edges and surfaces are secondarily decorated with geometric patterns. Obverse and reverse: Horizontal, vertical, and oblique lines. Size: L 2.6, W 2.4, Th 0.6, D hole 0.35 cm. Stone type 4.

Pendant (fig. 514) (F3.113, 881.GX, KM3166_2). Tell F3, Trench RM, 1-15 N, between 1-2.45 m below surface, sieve. It is trapezoid, pierced at one end, appears to have been exposed to heat after reshaping. Obverse: Original decoration of horizontal, vertical and oblique lines. Reverse: -. Size: L 3.3, W 2.7, Th 0.7, D hole 0.47 cm. Stone type 4.

Pendant (fig. 515) (F3.150, 881.IH, KM3166_1). Tell F3, Trench RM, 56 N, 3.7 W, between 0.95 and 1.25 m below surface. It is ovoid, pierced at one end, with a brownish hue, indicative of exposure to heat. Obverse: Vertical and horizontal lines in a grid pattern. Reverse: Horizontal, vertical, and oblique lines, herringbone pattern. Size: L 3.4, W 2.3, Th 0.65, D hole 0.34 cm. Stone type 4.

Pendant (Hilton 2014 fig. 444) (F3.162, 881.IT, KM3159_2). Tell F3, Trench RM, 40-60 N, above 1.90 m below surface. It is circular, pierced longitudinally. Obverse: Incised branch. Reverse: -. Size: L 2.6, W 2.55, Th 0.85, D hole 0.28 cm. Stone type 3.

Pendant (Hilton 2014 fig. 434) (F3.170, 881.JC, KM3163_1). Tell F3, Trench RM, 24.05 N, 1.8 W, level 7.37. It is rectangular, pierced at one end, signs from use-wear around hole. Obverse: Original Umm an-Nar Style decoration of horizontal lines and dots in single circles. Reverse: Horizontal and vertical lines. Size: L 3, W 2.22, Th 0.6-0.72, D hole 0.5 cm.

Pendant (fig. 516) (F3.183, 881.JP, KM3162_6). Tell F3, Trench RM, 48.1 N, 3.3 W, level 7.12. It is rectangular, broken in half, the part with the hole missing. The edges are incised with lines. Surfaces have indications of wear. Obverse: Incised with a boat, a person, a sun/star and a small cross in the lower left corner. Reverse: Horizontal and vertical lines. Size: L 2.1, W 1.8, Th 1 cm. Stone type 4.

Pendant (fig. 517) (F3.196, 881.KD, KM3165_9). Tell F3, Trench RM, 42.45 N, 3.15 W, level 7.64. It is ellipsoidal, pierced at one end, uppermost part broken, the edges are recut, polished, and decorated with incised lines. Obverse and reverse: Vertical, horizontal, and oblique lines. Size: L 3.6, W 1.65, Th 0.9, D hole 0.32 cm. Stone type 3.

Pendant (F3.273, 881.NG, KM3162_5). Tell F3, Trench RM, 1.65 m below surface. It is rectangular, broken in half, and the upper part including the hole is missing, edges reworked and incised with lines. Obverse and reverse: Horizontal and vertical lines. Size: L 1.8, W 1.7, Th 1.2 cm. Stone type 2.

Pendant (fig. 518) (F3.296, 881.OD, KM3164_1). Tell F3, Trench RM, sieve. It is ellipsoid, pierced. Obverse: Horizontal and vertical lines meeting in a cross. Reverse: Oblique lines. Size: L 3.8, W 2.62, Th 0.56-0.8, D hole 0.47 cm. Stone type 1.

Pendant (881.QY, KM3162_7). Tell F3, Trench RM, 1-10 N, 0.8-1 m below surface. It is trapezoid, broken in half, one side and the upper part including the hole is missing. Surfaces have indications of use-wear. Two outer edges are incised with lines. Obverse: Horizontal and vertical lines. Reverse: Horizontal, vertical, and oblique lines. Size: L 2.5, W 1.5, Th 0.6 cm. Stone type 4.

Pendant (fig. 519. Hilton 2014 fig. 443) (F3.nt, 881.AIS, KM1636). Tell F3, Trench I, level 5.85. Associated pottery: Period 2. It is trapezoid and slightly curved due to the shape of the original vessel. It is pierced at one end and has wear marks from hanging. Obverse: Two figures with their arms raised in devotion, one bears a flounced garment, the other has a plain dress, standing upon a grid-pattern. The edges of the pendant are incised with a single or double line. Reverse: Horizontal, vertical, and oblique lines. Size: L 3.95, W 2.9, Th 0.5, D hole 0.37 cm. Stone type 4.

Pendant (fig. 520) (F3.qæ, 881.BIU). Tell F3, Trench Z, sieve. Undecorated. Size: L 5.3, W 2.8, Th 1.5 cm.

Pendant (F3.tq, 881.BLX, KM3162_3). Tell F3, Trench Ø, level 7.23. It is ellipsoid, broken in half, pierced. The edge is incised with several lines. Obverse: Original design of horizontal lines and dot in circle. Reverse: Horizontal, vertical, and oblique lines. Size: L 4.2, W 2.3, D hole 0.24 cm.

Pendant (fig. 521) (F3.wb, 881.BNN, KM3162_2). Tell F3, Trench AB, level 7.55. Associated pottery: Period 4B. It is square and pierced longitudinally. The outer edges have not been secondarily polished/reworked. Obverse: Horizontal and vertical lines. Reverse: -. Size: L 5.5, W 2.4, Th 0.8, D hole 0.3 cm. Stone type 3.

Pendant (Hilton 2014 fig. 442) (F3.wø, 881.BON, KM3009). Tell F3, Trench AB, 64.20 N, 6.4 W, level 7.28. Associated pottery: Period 4B. It is circular with a small knob at the top to which a string may have been attached. Two edges have clear secondary cuts, whereas two other edges are polished. Obverse: The original design of a rosette with ten petals. Reverse: Vertical, horizontal, and oblique lines forming a tree-like motif. Size: L 2.6, W 2.2, Th 0.5-0.8 cm. Stone type 4.

Pendant (fig. 522) (F3.zu, 881.BRU, KM1639). Tell F3, Trench AC, level 6.75. Associated pottery: Period 3B. It is trapezoid. The edges are incised with a thin line. Obverse and reverse: Oblique, vertical, and horizontal lines. Size: L 3.23, W 3.4, Th 0.87-1, D hole 0.43 cm. Stone type 3.

Pendant (fig. 523) (F3.åz, 881.BVP, KM1640). Tell F3, Trench AI, sieve. It is square and pierced at one end. Obverse: Horizontal and oblique lines emerging from one point. Reverse: Oblique lines. Size: L 2.26, W 2.26, Th 0.4-0.56, D hole 0.26 cm. Stone type 4.

Pendant (fig. 524) (F3.asa, 881.BCQ). Tell F3, Trench H, sieve. It is circular, pierced near the edge and both sides are decorated with transverse lines. Size: D 2.2 cm.

Pendant (fig. 525) (F3.avj, 881.BXD). Tell F3, Trench RM, level 6.80. It is rectangular and pierced near the edge. Decorated with horizontal and vertical lines on both sides. Size: L 2.8, W 2.4, Th 0.9 cm.

Pendant (fig. 526) (F3.ayj, 881.CAL, KM3165_3). Tell F3, Trench AO, level 7.46. Associated pottery: Period 4A/B? It is rectangular, pierced at one end. Obverse: Vertical, horizontal, and oblique lines. Reverse: Vertical and horizontal lines. Size: L 3.75, W 2.2, Th 0.7, D hole 0.35 cm. Stone type 3.

Pendant (fig. 527) (F3.bch, 881.CEM, KM3165_6). Tell F3, Trench AN, level 6.23. Associated pottery: Period 2. It is trapezoid, pierced at one end, two edges incised with lines. Obverse: Horizontal and oblique lines. Reverse: Vertical, horizontal, and oblique lines. Size: L 2.6, W 2.9, Th 0.7, D hole 0.56 cm. Stone type 3.

Pendant (fig. 528) (F3.bcl, 881.CEQ, KM3157_2). Tell F3, Trench RM, level 6.78. It is circular and pierced, with clear use-wear, especially concentrated around the hole. The edges are incised with a single line. Obverse: Incised with one vertical and two horizontal lines. Reverse: Two oblique lines meeting in a cross. Size: L 2.84, W 2.75, Th 0.8, D hole 0.4 cm. Stone type 3.

Pendant (F3.bhs, 881.CKA, KM3165_2). Tell F3, Trench P, level 6.23. Associated pottery: Period 3A. It is ellipsoidal, pierced at one end, broken in half. Obverse: Geometric decoration including a cross, an 'A' and oblique lines. Reverse: Vertical, horizontal, and oblique lines. Size: L 4.5, W 1.45, Th 0.6, D hole 0.53 cm. Stone type 2.

Pendant (fig. 529) (F3.bek, 881.CGP, KM3166_4). Tell F3, Trenches I, AN, and AO, sieve. It is ovaloid, pierced at one end. Obverse: Horizontal, vertical, and oblique lines. Three deep circular carvings. Reverse: -. Size: L 3.4, W 3, Th 0.8, D hole 0.36-0.6 cm. Stone type 3.

Pendant (fig. 530, Hilton 2014 fig. 427) (F3.bia, 881.CKI, KM3083). Tell F3, sieve. It is triangular and all edges, except the original rim, have been smoothed. One edge displays a cut and an intentional break. One edge has part of a mending hole (D 0.54 cm) from its primary use. The exterior surface is sooted. Obverse: Several parallel lines, crudely incised, as well as a herringbone or branch pattern. Reverse: -. Size: L 7, W 3.8, Th 1.26-1.6 cm. Stone type 3.

Pendant (fig. 531) (F3.bib, 881.CKJ, KM3165_5). Tell F3, Trench AX, level 7.49. Associated pottery: Period 3B. It is rectangular, pierced at one end, the edges incised with lines. Obverse: Vertical, horizontal, and oblique lines. Reverse: Oblique lines meeting in a cross. Size: L 2.7, W 2.1, Th 0.9, D hole 0.4 cm. Stone type 3.

Pendant (F3.bif, 881.CKN, KM1633). Tell F3, Trench AV, sieve. It is irregularly square; one end is pierced. Obverse: Original design of three grooves incised on top of horizontal lines. Reverse: Four incised grooves. Size: L 2.3, W 2.2, Th 0.5, D hole 0.45 cm.

Pendant (fig. 532) (F3.big, 881.CKO, KM3165_8). Tell F3, Trench AA, level 5.66. Associated pottery: Period 2. It is ellipsoidal, pierced at one end, the edges decorated with incised lines. Obverse: Vertical and horizontal lines. Reverse: Horizontal line. Size: L 3.5, W 2.2, Th 1.2, D hole 0.32 cm. Stone type 3.

Pendant (fig. 533) (F3.biu, 881.CLD, KM3163_3). Tell F3, Trench AV, level 7.54. It is trapezoid, pierced, signs from use-wear around hole. Two edges incised with several lines. Obverse: Original Umm an-Nar or Wadi Suq Style decoration of horizontal and vertical lines and dots in circles. Reverse: Horizontal and oblique lines. Size: L 4.33, W 2.79, Th 0.6-1, D hole 0.5 cm.

Pendant (fig. 534) (F3.bje, 881.CLM, KM3164_2). Tell F3, Trench AV, level 7.00. It is trapezoid, one end round, the other square, pierced. Undecorated. Size: L 3.6, W 1.95, Th 0.78-0.88, D hole 0.43 cm. Stone type 4.

Pendant (F3.bjl, 881.CLS, KM3162_8). Tell F3, sieve. It is rectangular, broken in half with part of the upper end including the hole and one side missing. One edge is incised with lines. Obverse: Horizontal and vertical lines. Reverse: Oblique lines. Size: L 2.3, W 2, Th 0.4 cm. Stone type 2.

Pendant (fig. 535) (KM1648). It is trapezoid, pierced at one end, with traces of wear around the hole and on surfaces. The edges have been incised with a thin line. Obverse: The decoration includes four rows of herringbone pattern and below one of them is an arrow-in-box, and vertical and horizontal lines. Reverse: Oblique, vertical, and horizontal lines. The secondary decoration appears to have been applied after the hole-piercing, as some incised lines extend inside the hole. Size: L 4.44, W 2.68, Th 0.6-0.7, D hole 0.43-0.48 cm. Stone type 4.

Pendant (Hilton 2014 fig. 441) (KM3159_1). Tell F3. It is circular. Obverse: A vertical and four oblique lines were added to the original Umm an-Nar Style decoration of two horizontal lines and two dots in single circles. Two holes were never fully completed. Reverse: -. Size: L 2.2, W 2.25, Th 0.65, D hole 0.4 cm.

Pendant (fig. 536) (KM3162_4). It is trapezoid. The object is broken in half and the upper part, including the hole, is missing. All surfaces are worn. The edge incised with multiple lines. Obverse: Original Late Bronze Age Style decoration of horizontal, vertical, and oblique lines. Reverse: Horizontal and vertical lines. Size: L 2.8, W 2, Th 0.6 cm. Stone type 4.

Pendant (Hilton 2014 fig. 435) (KM3163_2). It is trapezoid, pierced at one end. Signs from use-wear around hole. Obverse: Original Umm an-Nar Style or Wadi Suq Style decoration of dots in double circles and straight lines. Reverse: Vertical lines. Size: L 3.2, W 2.5, Th 0.6-0.7, D hole 0.65 cm.

Pendant (fig. 537) (KM3165_7). It is triangular, pierced at one end, the edges are recut, polished, and decorated with incised lines. Obverse: Vertical, horizontal, and oblique lines. Reverse: Vertical and horizontal lines. Size: L 3.6, W 2.45, Th 0.5, D hole 0.28 cm. Stone type 3.

Pendant (fig. 538) (KM3166_3). It is square, pierced at one end, area around hole is worn, lowermost edge displays a secondary cut and break, one edge incised with lines. Obverse: Horizontal and vertical lines in a grid pattern, in addition to some oblique lines. Reverse: Horizontal, vertical, and oblique lines possibly forming a hut pattern. Size: L 3.3, W 3.4, Th 0.75, D hole 0.35-0.56 cm. Stone type 3.

Spindle whorls

The spindle whorls are either completely flat or slightly domed in section. The five that could be examined were made of soft stone type 3. One had original Wadi Suq Style decoration preserved. Spindle whorls made of pottery sherds are more common and, like the soft stone ones, are found almost exclusively in Tell F3 (infra p. 148).

Spindle whorl (fig. 539) (F3.la, 881.AGA). Tell F3, Trench J, 78 N, 3.6 E, level 5.77. Associated pottery: Period 2. It is circular, pierced in the centre and decorated with an incised triangle. Size: D 2.5 cm.

Spindle whorl (F3.ahg, 881.AQD). Tell F3, Trench G, level 7.19. Associated pottery: Period 3A. Circular and pierced in the centre. Size: D 3.7, Th 0.7, D hole 0.7 cm.

Spindle whorl (Hilton 2014 fig. 436) (F3.ayk, 881.CAM, KM3156_8). Tell F3, Trench AO, level 7.44. Associated pottery: Period 4A/B? It is slightly domed, pierced in the centre, only roughly shaped; the colour is reddish brown, probably due to exposure to heat. Size: D 2.80, Th 0.9-1, D hole 0.55-0.60 cm. Stone type 3.

Spindle whorl (F3.azi, 881.CBL). Tell F3, Trench AO, level 7.02. Associated pottery: Period 4A/B? Circular and pierced in the centre. Size: D 3.4, Th 0.7 cm.

Spindle whorl (Hilton 2014 fig. 445) (F3.bbj, 881.CDN, KM3157_3). Tell F3, Trench AB, level 6.54. Associated pottery: Period 2. It is slightly domed, pierced in the centre with traces of the original Wadi Suq Style decoration which includes dots in circles and parallel horizontal lines. Size: D 6.8, Th 1.08, D hole 0.9 cm. Stone type 3.

Spindle whorl pre-fabricate (fig. 540) (F3.bbv, 881.CEA, KM3160_10). Tell F3, Trench AN, level 6.80-6.62. Associated pottery: Period 2. It is circular. All sides are polished. Circular cavity at the centre of the obverse side (unfinished hole?). Size: D 6.2, Th 1.3, D hole 1.1 cm. Stone type 3.

Spindle whorl (fig. 541) (F3.bgi, 881.CIO, KM3156_16). Tell F3, Trench Y, level 5.60. Associated pottery: Period

2. It is flat, pierced in the centre. Size: D 4, Th 0.9 cm, D hole 0.65-0.8 cm. Stone type 3.

Spindle whorl (fig. 542) (KM1646). It is flat, pierced in the centre. Secondary cuts on both the obverse and reverse. Appears worn after reshaping. Size: D 2.4, Th 0.96-1.30, D hole 0.53-0.58 cm. Stone type 3.

Blanks

Some of the blanks appear to be pre-stages for pendants, whereas others seem to be pre-stages for other types of objects.

Blank (F3.*13, 881.M, KM3171_4). Tell F3, Trench BB. It is irregularly cubic. All sides are blank. Size: L 1.9, W 1.8, Th 1.3 cm. Stone type 4.

Blank (881.BV, KM3161_1). Tell F3, Trench BB. It is ellipsoidal, broken in half. Size: L 4, W 2.5, Th 0.96-1.02 cm. Stone type 4.

Blank (fig. 543) (F3.311, 881.OS, KM3171_7). Tell F3, Trench RM, sieve. It is ellipsoidal. Obverse: Original Wadi Suq or Geometric Failaka Style decoration is preserved including dots in single circles and two parallel lines. Size: L 1.7, W 1.3, Th 0.6 cm.

Blank (Hilton 2014 fig. 428) (881.SS, KM3168_1). Tell F3, Trench RM, sieve. It is rectangular, pierced with two holes, clear cutting mark, followed by a break, semi-rough surfaces. Size: L 3.16, W 1.6, Th 0.48, D hole 0.34-0.4 cm. Stone type 3.

Blank (881.SS, KM3171_6). Tell F3, Trench RM, sieve. It is rectangular. One part of the object may have broken off. An unfinished hole on one side. Size: L 1.7, W 1.1, Th 1, D hole 0.29 cm. Stone type 1.

Blank (fig. 544) (881.SZ, KM3162_1). Tell F3, Trench RM, surface find. It is squarish. Obverse: Horizontal and vertical lines. Reverse: Horizontal lines. Size: L 2.7, W 2.6, Th 0.8 cm. Stone type 4.

Blank (F3.mv, 881.AHU, KM3171_2). Tell F3, Trench B/M, above level 8.00. Associated pottery: Period 3A/B. It is circular, semi-rough surfaces. Size: D 1.9, Th 1 cm. Stone type 4.

Blank (F3.wr, 881.BOD, KM3161_2). Tell F3, Trench AC, level 6.00. Associated pottery: Period 3B. It is circular, made of a base sherd. Size: L 8.5, W 4.5, Th 0.6-0.7 cm. Stone type 2.

Blank (F3.xå, 881.BPS, KM3160_9). Tell F3, Trench AD, level 6.48. Associated pottery: Period 3A. It is circular. The obverse side is domed and the reverse flat. All sides are polished. D 5.4, Th 1.16-0.8 cm. Stone type 3.

Blank (Hilton 2014 fig. 433) (F3.æz, 881.BTE, KM3171_3). Tell F3, Trench AD, sieve. It is trapezoid, both sides display grinding marks. Size: L 3.6, W 2.8 cm. Stone type 2.

Blank (Hilton 2014 fig. 432) (F3.øa, 881.BTI, KM3160_7). Tell F3, Trench AK, level 6.38. It is circular. The exterior surface is sooted. Size: D 3.4-3.6, Th 1.2 cm. Stone type 3.

Blank (Ciarla 1985 fig. 8. Hilton 2014 fig. 440) (F3.bee, 881.CGJ, KM3122). Tell F3, Trench AT, level 6.60. It is rectangular, carved from a rim sherd. Obverse: Some incised crosshatches have been added to the original Umm an-Nar or Wadi Suq Style decoration of horizontal lines and dots in single circles. Reverse: -. Size: L 2.52, W 1.84, Th 0.35-0.72 cm. Stone type 4.

Blank (fig. 545) (F3.bhq, 881.CJY, KM6072_10). Tell F3, Trench AO, level 5.62. Associated pottery: Period 2. It is rectangular. Obverse: Original decoration of horizontal lines and dots in double circles. Size: L 4.2, W 1.7, Th 0.5-1 cm. Stone type 4.

Blank (fig. 546) (F6.578, 1129.VB, KM1638). Tell F6, Trenches D2/E2, level -0.03. It is roughly square. Probably unfinished since the edges are roughly carved and there are coarse grinding striations on all surfaces. Obverse: Oblique, vertical, and horizontal lines. Size: L 2.5, W 2.45, Th 0.92-1.05 cm.

Blank (Hilton 2014 fig. 430) (KM3147_2). It is squarish. All sides are blank. Size: L 4.2, W 3.69, Th 1.8-2 cm. Stone type 3.

Blank (Hilton 2014 fig. 431) (KM3160_8). It is irregularly round, sooted on the exterior face. Obverse: Horizontal and oblique lines from original Wadi Suq or Geometric Failaka Styles. Reverse: -. Size: L 4, W 3.5, Th 1.1 cm. Stone type 3.

Blank (fig. 547) (KM3165_1). It is rectangular and has a secondary cut in one side. The exterior surface is sooted. Obverse: Original Wadi Suq Style decoration

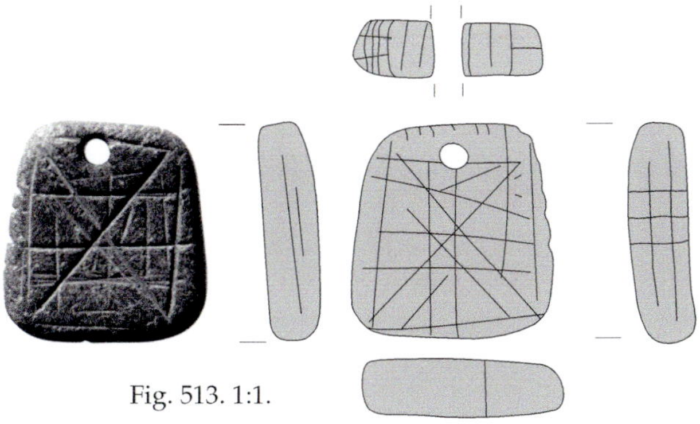

Fig. 513. 1:1.

Fig. 514 1:1.

Fig. 515 1:1.

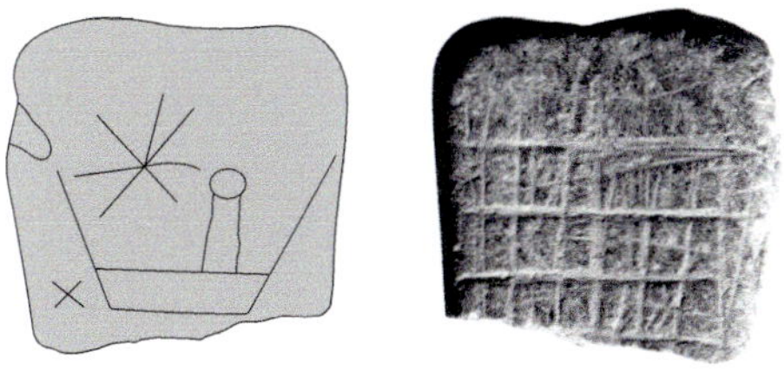

Fig. 516 1:1.

Fig. 517. 1:1.

Fig. 518. 1:1.

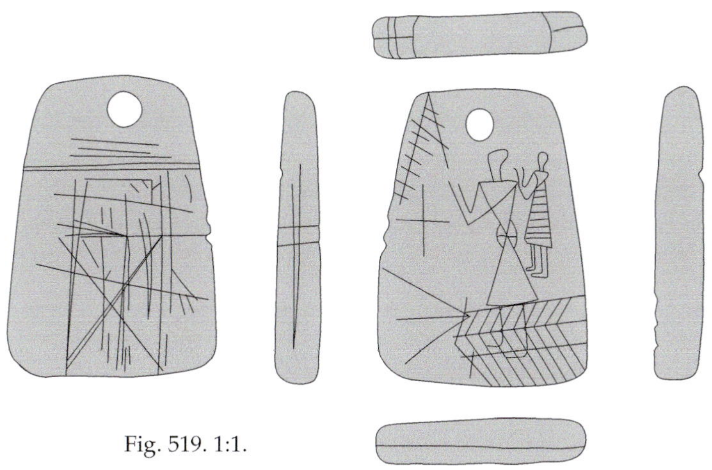

Fig. 519. 1:1.

Fig. 520. 1:1.

Fig. 521. 1:1.

Fig. 522. 1:1.

Fig. 523. 1:1.

Fig. 524. 1:1.

Fig. 525. 1:1.

Fig. 526. 1:1.

Fig. 527. 1:1.

Fig. 528. 1:1.

Fig. 529. 1:1.

Fig. 530. 1:1.

Fig. 531. 1:1.

Fig. 532. 1:1.

Fig. 533. 1:1.

Fig. 534. 1:1.

Fig. 535. 1:1.

Fig. 536. 1:1.

Fig. 537. 1:1.

Fig. 538. 1:1.

Fig. 539. 1:1.

Fig. 540. 1:1.

Fig. 541. 1:1.

Fig. 542. 1:1.

Fig. 543. 1:1.

Fig. 544. 1:1.

Fig. 545. 1:1.

Fig. 546. 1:1.

Fig. 547. 1:1.

of oblique lines meeting in an angle. Reverse: -. Size: L 3, W 1.7, Th 0.6 cm. Stone type 4.

Miscellaneous objects

Lid or seal blank of Indus type (cf. Joshi & Parpola 1987 p. 87: M-352) (fig. 548) (F3.1, 881.CI, KM3127_1). Tell F3, Trench RM, 12.40 N, 0.60 W, 0.64 m below surface. It is square with a central, square knob. There are no signs of wear. Size: L 3.57, W 3.46, Th 1.1, Knob 1.34 x 1.32, Th 2.2 cm. Stone type 3.

Gaming piece? (fig. 549) (F3.228, 881.LK, KM3127_2). Tell F3, Trench RM, 42.50 N, 2.10 W, level 6.74. It is square. Obverse: Possible remains from original design of dot in circle. Reverse: Faintly incised vertical, horizontal, and oblique lines crossing each other at the centre. Size: L 2.82 W 2.54 Th 0.81-0.87 cm. Stone type 1.

Rectangular soft stone object with extraordinarily intricate decoration on both sides (fig. 550) (F3.298) (cf. Kjærum 1983 no. 365). Trench RM, sieve.

Cube (fig. 551) (F3.f, 881.TR). Tell F3, Trench A, above c. level 8.60. Associated pottery: Period 3B. It is cubic with flat ground faces, one face is smooth and slightly concave indicating that the piece was made from a soft stone vessel sherd, stained black by bitumen on most faces. Size: L 3.0, W 1.9, Th 2.9 cm. Weight 38.6 g.

Triangular object (fig. 552) (F3.67, 881.FA, KM3168_2). Tell F3, Trench RM, 31.6 N, 0.70 W, 0.5 m below surface. It is broken, with two holes pierced from one side and thus with a greater diameter (0.48 cm) on the obverse side, and a smaller one on the reverse side (0.27 cm). Size: L 1.53, W 1.6, Th 0.48, D hole 0.48-0.27 cm.

Object of unknown purpose (fig. 553, Ciarla 1985 fig. 6) (F3.yk, 881.BQG, KM3121). Tell F3, Trench AD, level 6.42. Associated pottery: Period 3A. A side sherd from soft stone vessel, sooted on the outside, carved into a shovel-like tool. All edges were reshaped and display incised marks from the shaping process, especially on the "handle". The item has a concentration of secondary wear marks next to the "handle". Size: L 18, W 6.5, Th 0.5-0.95 cm. Approximate diameter of original vessel 35 cm.

Object of unknown purpose (fig. 554) (F3.zæ, 881.BSB, KM6108_6). Tell F3, Trench AH, level 8.25-7.25. Associated pottery: Period 3B. It is irregularly rectangular and has broken edges. All sides are sooted. Obverse: The object is incised with a grid pattern, and it has two circular depressions (D 0.7 cm). Reverse: -. Size: L 5.4, W 2.5-4, Th 2.4 cm. Stone type 3.

Circular object, button? (fig. 555) (F3.apz, 881.BAL, KM3157_1). Tell F3, Trench C, level 8.66. Associated pottery: Period 4A. All edges are smoothed. It has two pierced holes. Obverse: Three concentric stepped ridges remaining from the original vessel have been smoothed down in order to get a uniform surface (cf. Hilton 2014, Types 51A or 68A, figs. 369-374). Vertical and horizontal lines form a grid pattern. Reverse: -. Size: L 3.5, W 3.89, Th 0.44, D hole 0.36 cm. Stone type 4.

Pyramidal object (fig. 556) (F3.axu, 881.BZX, KM3171_1). Tell F3, Trench AO, level 8.23. Associated pottery: Period 4A/B? All sides are blank. Size: L 1.1, W 1.4, Th 1.3 cm. Stone type 4. Gaming piece, weight, stamp seal blank (Kjærum 1983 no. 317)? Cf. similar objects from Saruq al-Hadid (Karim et al. 2017).

Soft stone cylinders

Fragment of cylinder, broken in the drilled hole, dark soft stone, length 1.5, diameter 2.5 cm (KM1235:1).

Fragment of cylinder, grey soft stone (fig. 557) (F3.76, KM1235:2). Trench RM, 37 N, above 1 m below surface.

Fragment of cylinder, small depression in both ends, light grey soft stone (fig. 558) (KM1235:3).

Fragment of cylinder, small depression in one end, light grey soft stone (fig. 559) (KM1235:4).

Fragment of cylinder, light grey soft stone (fig. 560) (F3.awz, KM1235:5). Trench AM, level 8.12. Associated pottery: Period 4B.

Complete cylinder, light grey soft stone (fig. 561) (F3.bde, KM1235:6). Trenches AN-I, sieve.

Semi-precious and other stones

Lump of flint, 2.8 x 3.9 cm (881.QR). Trench RM, 48-49 N, level 7.00-6.60.

Chip of flint, 0.7 x 2.6 x 3 cm (F3.he). Trench M, level 7.60-7.09. Associated pottery: Period 3B.

Lump of green stone, 1.4 x 3.5 cm (F3.me). Sieve.

Block of flint, 7.2 x 10.6 x 13.2 cm (F3.ne). Trench M, level 5.80. Associated pottery: Period 2.

Flake in dark, fine-grained flint with a clear bulb of percussion (F3.qi). Trench Y.

Lump of carnelian, 2.4 x 5.5 cm, and block of flint, 3.2 x 3.9 cm (F3.ta). Trench Ø, level 8.97-8.46. Associated pottery: Period 4.

Lump of carnelian, 2.5 x 3.7 cm (F3.vq). Trench AA, level 7.10-6.94. Associated pottery: Period 2, 4.

Flake of carnelian, 1.1 x 3.8 x 4.8 cm (F3.wk). Trenches AE and AD, level 8.43-8.05. Associated pottery: Period 3A, 4A.

Lump of carnelian partially covered by cortex, 4 x 4.3 cm (F3.wå). Trench AE, level 8.05-7.75. Associated pottery: Period 3A.

Block of flint, 2.3 x 3 cm (F3.xw). Trench AG, level 9.35-8.03. Associated pottery: Period 3B.

Block of carnelian, 3.2 x 4.3 cm, and chip of calcite, 0.7 x 2.8 x 3.8 cm (F3.yk). Trench AD, level 6.48-6.17. Associated pottery: Period 3A.

Lump of green stone, 2.9 x 4.3 cm (F3.yx). Trench AI, level 8.84-8.16. Associated pottery: Period 4A.

Small block of carnelian, 2.1 x 3.2 cm (F3.zc). Trench AI, level 8.16-7.85. Associated pottery: Period 4A.

Flake of calcite, 1 x 3.1 x 5.3 cm, with cortex on one face (F3.zq). Trench AG, level 9.22-6.85. Associated pottery: Period 3B.

Lump of flint, 2 x 6 cm (F3.æi). Trench AE, level 8.77-6.22. Associated pottery: Period 3A.

Flake of carnelian 0.7 x 2.9 x 3.6 xm (F3.æx). Trench AI, level 7.30-6.31. Associated pottery: Period 3A.

Block of flint, 2 x 4.3 cm (F3.aeh). Trench C, level c. 7.00-6.50. Associated pottery: Period 3A.

Flake in undetermined hard stone, clear percussion bulb, 5.6 cm long, 4.2 cm wide and 1.4 cm thick (F6.79). Trench A3, level -0.05.

Other stone objects

Rectangular stone with rounded corners and engraved furrow, in oolitic limestone, 1.6 cm thick (fig. 562) (F3.3). Trench RM, 16.60 N, 3.95 W, 75 cm below surface.

Boat-shaped figure in oolitic limestone, 1.9-2.1 cm thick (fig. 563) (F3.7). Trench RM, c. 17 N, c. 4 W, c. 0.90 m below surface.

Phallus of stone (fig. 564) (F3.83). Trench RM, 17.60 N, 1.6 W, 1.6 m below surface.

Fragment of sieve in soft stone (fig. 565) (F3.218). Trench RM, 31.90 N, 4.5 W, level 7.00.

Eye-shaped object in yellow-white limestone with central depression to receive an inlay of the iris (fig. 566) (F3.226). Trench RM, 40-60 N, sieve. For similar objects in shell from Qala'at al-Bahrain and the Barbar Temple, cf. Højlund & Andersen 1994 fig. 2063 and Andersen & Højlund 2003, vol. 1, figs. 819 and 829.

Rectangular stone, oolitic limestone, perforated at one end, steatite of type 3 (Hilton 2014 p. 12) (fig. 567) (F3.281). Trench RM, 56.1 N, 1 m W, level 6.65.

Square block of oolitic limestone, 5.5 x 13 x 18 cm, perforated, hole diameter 4 cm (F3.ch). Trench F, from surface to level 8.92. Associated pottery: Period 3A/3B.

Finely polished, fine-grained, black stone shaped like an axe, crushing traces on butt and edge (fig. 568) (F3.he). Trench M, level 7.60-7.09. Associated pottery: Period 3B. A similar object was found beside a small mortar in a tomb in Al-Faw together with a Dilmun burial jar (Laursen & Al-Otaibi 2022 fig. 12: 27). Same type of stone and same surface treatment as oval stone from Tell F6 (Højlund & Abu-Laban 2016 fig. 1136).

Rectangular stone with projection at one end, and two perforations. On one side two small depressions (fig. 569) (F3.hi). Trench J, 75.50 N, 3.5 E, level 8.50. Associated pottery: Period 4B.

Perforated, black stone, 0.9 cm thick (fig. 570) (F3.ng). Sieve.

Triangular slab of finely ground, fine sandstone, weight 66 g (fig. 571) (F3.xm). Trench AD, level 7.30-7.05. Associated pottery: Period 3A-3B.

Rectangular block of oolitic limestone with finely ground faces and two drilled holes in one side (fig. 572) (F3.æh). Trench AI, level 8.94-6.49.

Whetstone of light greenish, fine sandstone, with longitudinal facets (fig. 573) (F3.ån). Trench AF, sieve.

Fragment of grid, oolitic limestone (fig. 574) (F3.agb). Trench G, level c. 8.43-7.93. Associated pottery: Period 4A.

Oval disc with a central depression in both faces, beach-rock (fig. 575) (F3.alh). Trench K, 34.02 N, 17.51 W, level 7.15. Associated pottery: Period 3A.

Cylinder, 8 cm tall, 8.4 cm in diameter, of oolitic limestone (F3.ali). Trench K, 34.02 N, 17.51 W, level 7.15. Associated pottery: Period 3A.

Fragment of stone grid with one hole preserved (fig. 576) (F3.ans). Trench P, level c. 8.00. Associated pottery: Period 4A.

Slab of fine sandstone, 4 x 11 x 11 cm, with circular depression, 2.5 cm in diameter (F3.asy). Trench K, level c. 9.40-7.90. Associated pottery: Period 4A.

Roughly square, 20 x 22 cm, 9.5 cm thick block of beach-rock with central hole, 6 cm in diameter (F3.ats). Trench H, level c. 8.35. Associated pottery: Period 4A.

Disc of stone or cement, 6.8 cm in diameter, 1.5 cm thick, perforated in the centre, hole diameter 1 cm, weight 67 g (F3.avf). Trench AC, below level 6.66. Associated pottery: Period 3B.

Cylinder in soft stone, pierced by two transverse holes (fig. 577) (F3.bal). Trench I, 63.50 N, 4.50 E, level 6.52. Associated pottery: Period 3A/3B.

Stone with perforation cut in one end, oolitic limestone (fig. 578) (F3.bhm). Trench AM.

Fragment of round stone with smooth upper side and a circular depression, 0.9 cm deep (fig. 579) (F3.bhu). Trench AH, in the northeast corner of the open-air shrine, between the second and third floors (cf. Kjærum & Højlund 2013 p. 71). Associated pottery: Period 3B.

Fragment of round sieve in stone, one complete hole is preserved and remains of three others. The surface of the sieve is rough, except the oblique underside, which is smooth and would probably have rested on the inner side of a storage vessel neck (fig. 580) (F3.bic). Trench AX, sieve.

Block of stone with ten holes, c. 2 cm deep, drilled into the flat surface, 10 x 27 x 29 cm, beach-rock (fig. 581, Ashkanani 2021 p. 128) (Tell F3, KM76).

Rim fragment in grey soft-stone (fig. 582) (F6.347). Trench SN, 18-20 N, 0-1.5 E, level -1.57. Associated pottery: Period 1.

Fragment of circular tube in oolitic limestone (fig. 583) (F6.432). From baulk between Trenches A2 and A3, level -1.29.

Conical soft stone cylinder with seal-like carving at the end (fig. 584) (F6.764). Trench F2, 15.8 N, 5 W, -1.69. Associated pottery: Period 1.

Barrel-shaped cylinder in black stone with light grey inclusions, height 2.2 cm, diameter 2.6 cm, weight 26.6 g (fig. 585) (F6.828). Trench M2, 17 N, 10 W, level -1.59. Associated pottery: Period 1.

Conical object of reddish-brown agate with white veins, pierced longitudinally, diameter of perforation 0.5 cm (fig. 586) (F6.968). Trench F1, 3 N, 4-5 W, level -0.79.

Fig. 548. 1:1.

Fig. 549. 1:1.

Fig. 550. 1:1.

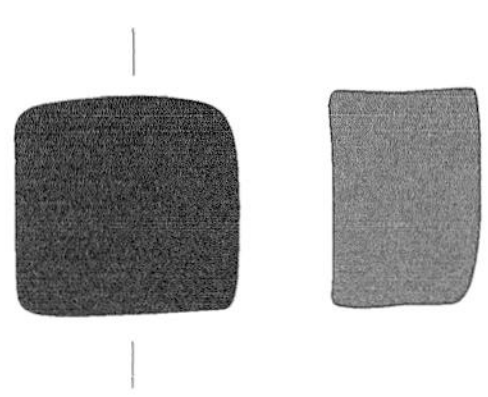

Fig. 551. 1:2.

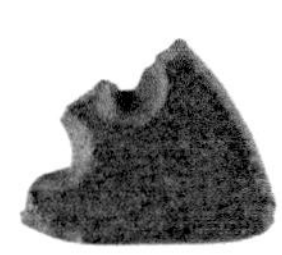

Fig. 552. 1:1.

Fig. 553. 1:3.

Fig. 554. 1:1.

Fig. 555. 1:1.

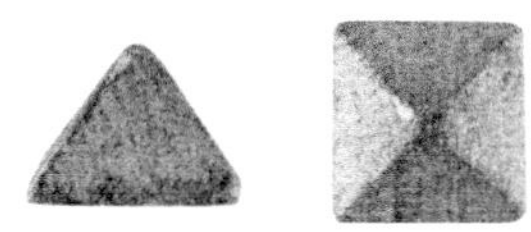

Fig. 556. 1:1.

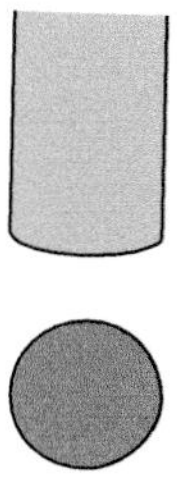
Fig. 557. 1:1.

Fig. 558. 1:1.

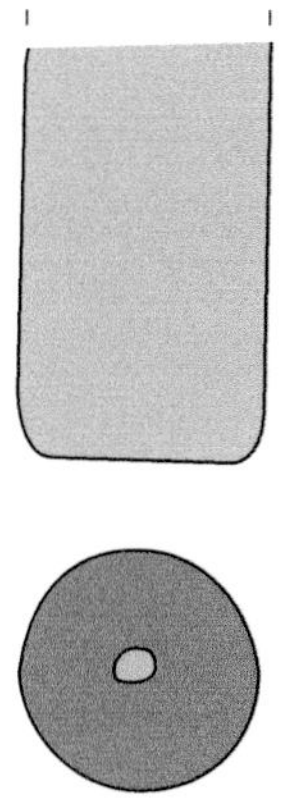
Fig. 559. 1:1.

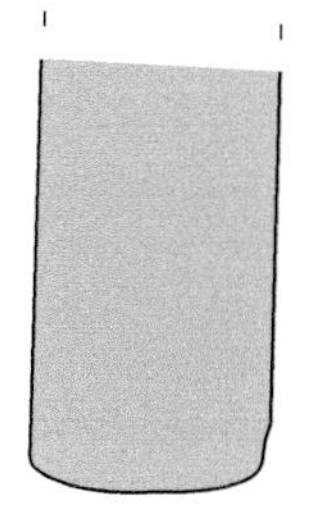
Fig. 560. 1:1.

Fig. 561. 1:1.

Fig. 562. 1:2.

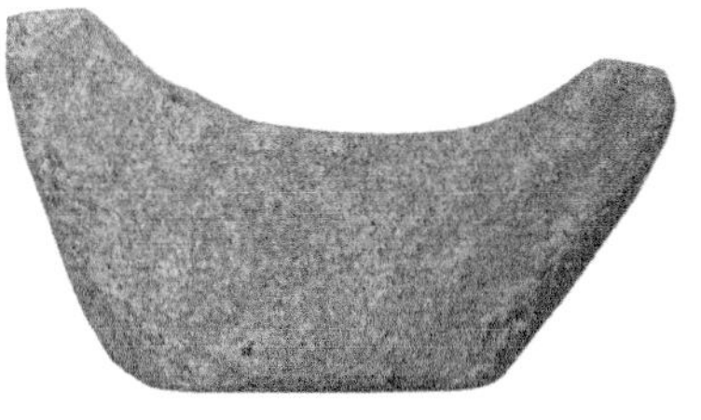
Fig. 563. 1:2.

Fig. 564. 1:2.

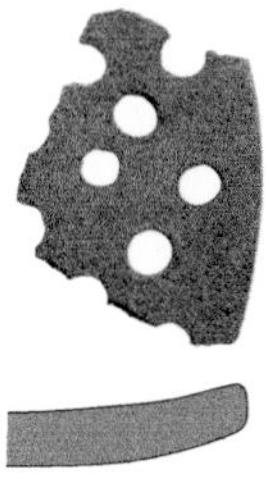
Fig. 565. 1:2.

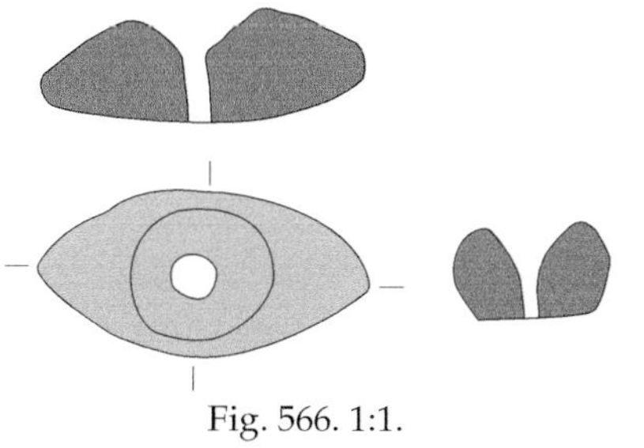
Fig. 566. 1:1.

Fig. 567. 1:2.

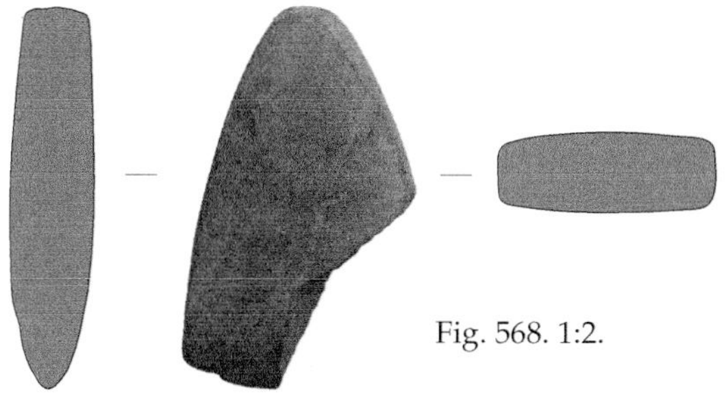
Fig. 568. 1:2.

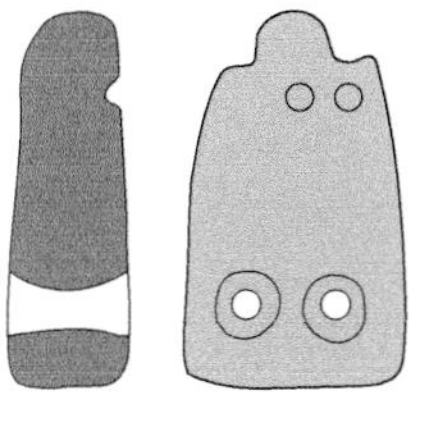
Fig. 569. 1:2.

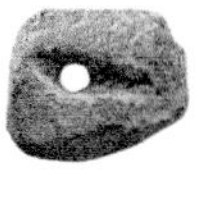
Fig. 570. 1:2.

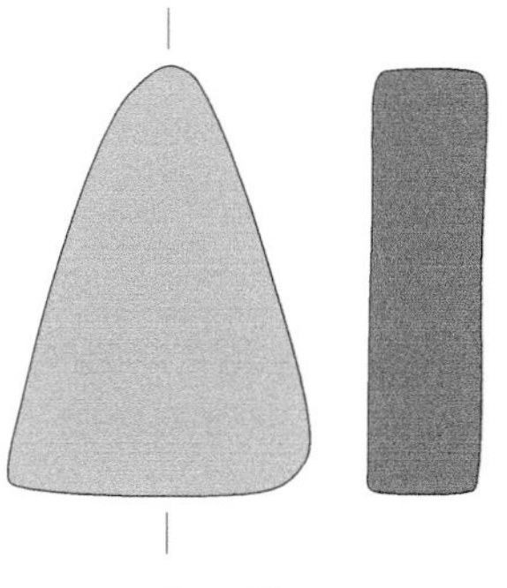
Fig. 571. 1:2.

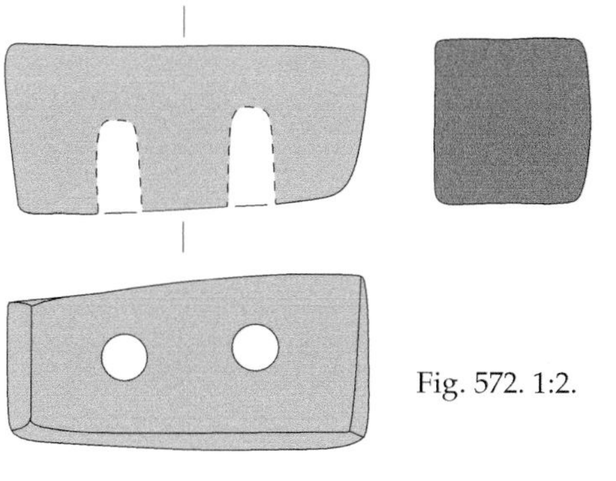
Fig. 572. 1:2.

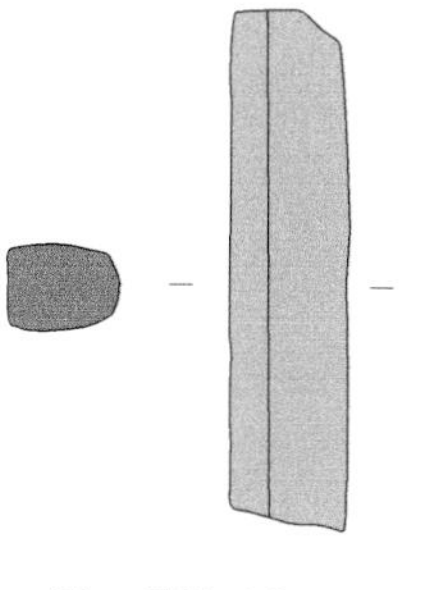
Fig. 573. 1:2.

Fig. 574. 1:2.

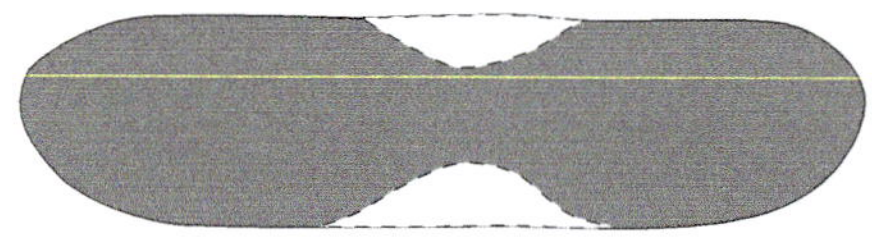

Fig. 575. 1:2.

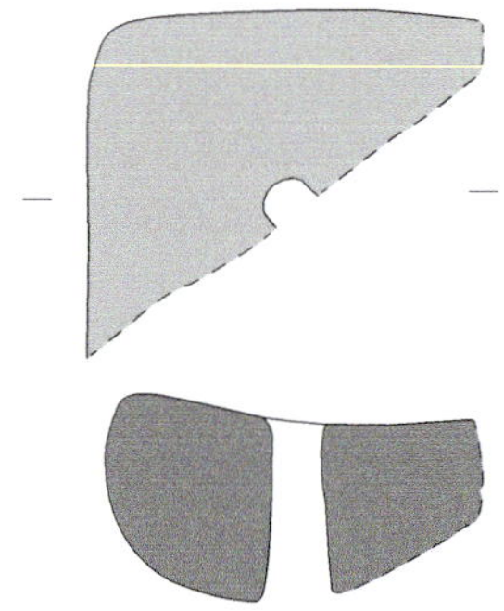

Fig. 576. 1:2.

Fig. 577. 1:1.

Fig. 578. 1:4.

Fig. 579. 1:3.

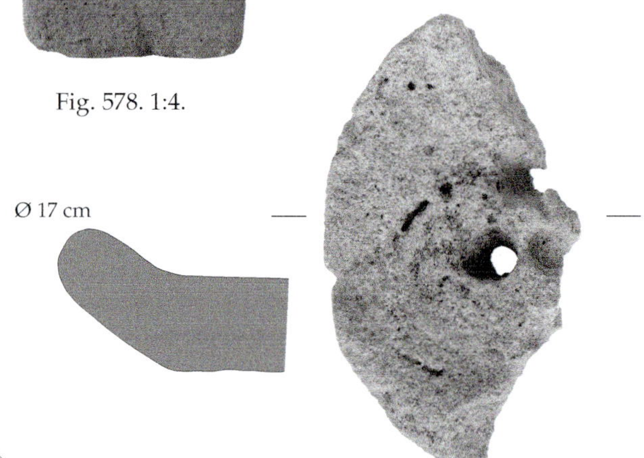

Fig. 580. 1:3 .

Fig. 581. 1:5.

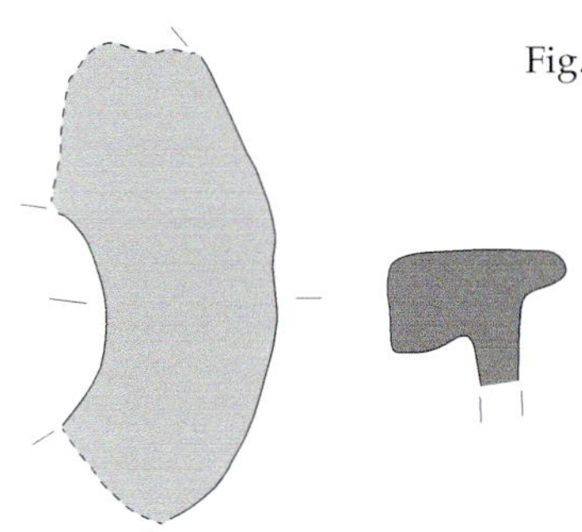

Fig. 582. 1:1.

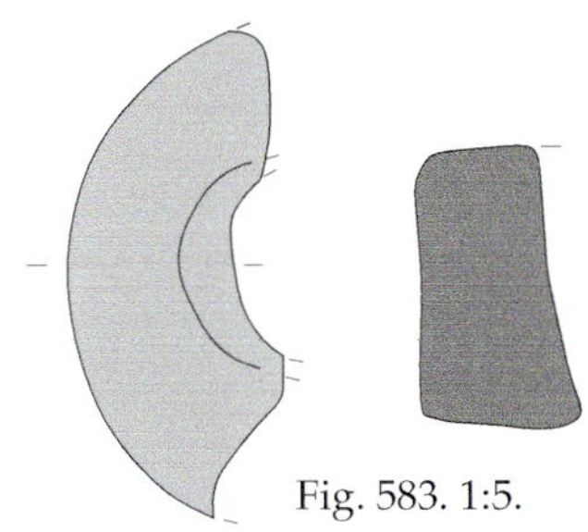

Fig. 583. 1:5.

Fig. 584. 1:2.

Fig. 585. 1:1.

Fig. 586. 1:1.

9. Pottery objects

Terracotta fists

Ten fists, right and left, in burnt clay were found in Tell F3 and Tell F6. They are lightly clenched with four fingers bent in towards the palm, the thumb extended against the side of the index finger, and with nails indicated; never tightly clenched with the thumb clamped over the middle phalanges, as is the position when boxing. When well-preserved, the end of the wrist can often be seen to be shaped as a tenon, for insertion into a kind of mortise, very likely also in clay, the interface smoothed over. Sometimes the wrist shows small cutting marks which may have been left by a rib used to smooth over the interface. It is uncertain what type of object was furnished with these hands, possibly a pottery vessel, and their meaning is unknown.

The hands are miniature in size, the width of the wrist varying between 1.9 and 3.5 cm.

The ware is light brown pinkish, lightly tempered with fine sand, resembling ware type C and E (Højlund 1987 p. 103-106), with a yellow surface that is covered in a pale red slip.

The fists were found in both Tell F3 and Tell F6; none of them in well-dated contexts. Their uniformity suggests that they derive from a limited period of time, but the sparse stratigraphical indications are inconclusive. The colour of their red slip is very similar to the colour of the horizontal bands found on storage vessels of type 57C-D in Periods 3B and 4A (Højlund 1987 p. 65-70. Højlund & Abu-Laban 2016 fig. 570. Højlund & Hilton 2021 figs. 235, 278-279).

A fragment of a similar clay hand was found during the 2012-2017 excavations in Tell F3, in a Period 4A context (Højlund & Hilton 2021 fig. 45). The type of object is not reported from Bahrain or further down the Gulf.

Two terracotta hands were found during the French excavations in Tell Khazneh on Failaka. They are different from the above-described terracotta hands in that they grasp an object and lack a red slip, and they also appear to belong to a later period (Salles 1986 p. 150, fig. 61: no. 202 and p. 196, fig. 72: nos. 202-203. Ashkanani 2021 p. 162, KM3717).

A hand in copper was found in Tell F3 (fig. 435), but in this case the fingers are stretched out and not clenched in a fist.

Terracotta hands are reported from Tall al-Hamidiya in the Khabur region in a secondary-use context in a palace attributed to the Mittanian period which should be dated to the 15th century BC (Soldi 2017 p. 17. Wäfler 1993 p. 195, 351 and 464, cat. No. 327). The specimen illustrated (Soldi 2017 fig. 13) is, however, very different from the Failaka hands and more like the glazed clay hands found in 9th-8th century Assyria (Soldi 2017 figs. 1, 5-8).

Left hand, three fingers are preserved with nails indicated, whereas two fingers including the thumb are broken off. Yellow-greenish pottery with a pale red slip (fig. 587, Ashkanani 2021 p. 110) (F3.163). Trench RM, 40-50 N, above level c. 7.35.

Left hand with nails indicated, tenon at wrist, red-slipped light-brown ware (fig. 588, Ashkanani 2021 p. 109) (KM54).

Left hand in red, fine sand-tempered ware with yellowish eroded surface. The wrist is shaped into a c. 0.9 cm long tenon with a 2.2 x 2.5 cm cross section, with a straight termination, as if it was set into the wall of a pottery vessel (fig. 589) (F3.aau). Trench C, 33.45 N, 8.40 W, level 8.12. Associated pottery: Period 4A.

Left hand with broken off fingers, tenon at wrist, pink, fine sand-tempered ware (fig. 590) (F3.apr). Found in sieve west of Trench RM.

Right hand, the fingertips including the thumb are broken off, and it is also broken at the wrist, pink, fine sand-tempered ware with yellowish surface and a pale red slip (fig. 591) (F6.477). Trench D2, level -1.58. Associated pottery: Period 1.

Right hand, the tips of four fingers and the thumb are broken off, and it is also broken at the wrist. Pink, fine sand-tempered ware with a yellowish surface and a pale red slip. Around the wrist are at least twelve small cutting marks (fig. 592) (F6.498). Trench E2, 11-13.5 N, 1.5-3 E, level -1.10.

Finger, broken-off, nail indicated with an incised line, fine sand-tempered ware with a yellow surface and a pale red slip (fig. 593) (F6.664). Trench F2, 18 N, 5 W, level -0.51.

Spindle whorls

Pieces of broken pottery make up the majority of finds from the excavations of Tell F3 and Tell F6. A small portion of sherds, a total of 28, have been chipped to a roughly round shape followed by a grinding of the edge and a central perforation. They are interpreted as spindle whorls, and they seem to occur in all periods in the Failaka sequence.

Their maximum diameter varies from 2.9 to 8.2 cm. Some are completely circular with a carefully ground perimeter (fig. 595), some are more irregular but still with the perimeter ground (fig. 594), and some are very irregular with no grinding at all.

It is notable that when ground, the edges are not ground to a rounded shape, but always to a flat edge at right angles to the faces of the sherd.

The hole is in the approximate centre of each sherd and appear to have been drilled, often from both sides, being double conic. The minimum diameter of the holes varies from 3 to 14 mm with the majority between 4 and 7 mm. This regularity may suggest that the size of the object inserted in the hole were of significance or perhaps that the drill used was of a rather constant size, like the copper drills described above (figs. 103-123).

A few spindle whorls were decorated with straight lines radiating from the central perforation, incised after firing.

All the spindle whorls were weighed and for the fragmented ones an estimate of the weight when in complete condition was made. Their weight varies from 4 to 64 g.

It is not possible to determine the function of these perforated sherds unequivocally, but they are known from all over the world and have often been interpreted as spindle whorls. Other possibilities are loom-weights and net-sinkers.

Strikingly, only two of the 28 spindle whorls were found at Tell F6, the rest were found at Tell F3. The same goes for the soft stone spindle whorls dealt with above (p. 137).

The spindle whorls could have been used to spin wool/hair from sheep and goat which was available to the Dilmunites, as well as plant fibres. Mesopotamian cuneiform sources indicate that huge quantities of textiles were exported from Mesopotamia down the Gulf (Laursen & Steinkeller 2017 p. 71), but a local production of thread, cord and rope as well as textiles is perfectly likely.

Similar objects are known from other Dilmun settlement sites, for example, Al-Khidr (Benediková 2010 figs. 114a-f, 115a-f), Qala'at al-Bahrain (Højlund & Andersen 1994 figs. 1807-1808), and Saar Settlement (Killick & Moon 2005 fig. 5.13:b-c).

Fragment of round potsherd with evenly ground edge, diameter 4.3 cm, thickness 1.2 cm, perforated centrally, hole diameter 5 mm, weight 17 g, estimated 20 g (F3.q). Trench B, level c. 8.95-8.55, sieve. Associated pottery: Period 3A/3B.

Fragment of roughly round potsherd with evenly ground edge, diameter 7 cm, thickness 1 cm, perforated centrally, hole diameter 7 mm, six incised diagonal lines on the inside, weight 19 g, estimated 50 g (F3.ip). Trench N, level 8.27-8.13. Associated pottery: Period 3B/4.

Round potsherd with evenly ground edge (string-cut base of bowl of Failaka type 88A, cf. Højlund 1987), diameter 5.3 cm, thickness 2.2 cm, perforated centrally, hole diameter 12 mm, weight 39 g (F3.km). Trench J, level 7.16-6.55. Associated pottery: Period 4B.

Round potsherd with evenly ground edge (string-cut base of bowl of Failaka type 88A, cf. Højlund 1987), diameter 5.2 cm, thickness 1.4 cm, perforated centrally, hole diameter 9 mm, weight 31 g (F3.om). Trench E, above level 7.03. Associated pottery: Period 2, 3A.

Fragment of round potsherd with evenly ground edge, diameter 4 cm, thickness 0.7 cm, perforated centrally, hole diameter c. 5 mm, weight 4 g, estimated 14 g (F3.vg). Trench AA, sieve.

Fragment of roughly round potsherd with evenly ground edge, diameter 7.5 cm, thickness 1 cm, perforated centrally, hole diameter 5 mm, weight 23 g, estimated 50 g (F3.vm). Trench AA, level 7.26-7.10. Associated pottery: Period 4.

Fragment of round potsherd with evenly ground edge, diameter 8 cm, thickness 1 cm, perforated centrally, hole diameter 5 mm, weight 25 g, estimated 60 g (F3.ze). Trench AD, level 8.85-7.55. Associated pottery: Period 3A, 3B, 4A.

A roughly round potsherd with unground edge, diameter 7.3 cm, thickness 1 cm, perforated centrally, hole diameter 3 mm, weight 56 g (F3.æe). Trench AA, level 9.66-6.91. Associated pottery: Period 2, 4.

A roughly round potsherd with evenly ground edge, diameter 4.5 cm, thickness 1 cm, perforated centrally, hole diameter 4 mm, weight 22 g (F3.æg). Trenches AB and AF, sieve.

Fragment of round potsherd with rough edge, diameter 6.3 cm, thickness 0.8 cm, perforated centrally, hole diameter 7 mm, weight 21 g, estimated 42 g (F3.øl). Trench AI, level 6.20. Associated pottery: Period 3A.

Roughly round potsherd with unground edge, centrally perforated, weight 61 g (fig. 594) (F3.øn). Trench AL, level 8.96-7.60. Associated pottery: Period 4B.

Fragment of round potsherd with evenly ground edge, diameter 5 cm, thickness 1 cm, perforated centrally, hole diameter 5 mm, weight 13 g, estimated 30 g (F3.ace). Trench D, level c. 7.07-6.77.

Fragment of round potsherd with the edge evenly ground to a conical shape, diameter 3.2 cm, thickness 1.3 cm, perforated centrally, hole diameter 4 mm, weight 8 g, estimated 10 g (F3.adt). Trench D, level c. 7.07-6.77.

Roughly round potsherd with evenly ground edge, diameter 5 cm, thickness 0.9 cm, perforated centrally, hole diameter 8 mm, weight 18 g (F3.agc). Trench G, level c. 9.43-7.93. Associated pottery: Period 4A.

Fragment of round potsherd with evenly ground edge, diameter 7 cm, thickness 1.1 cm, perforated centrally, hole diameter c. 5 mm, weight 17 g, estimated 44 g (F3.aih). Trench K, level c. 9.40-7.90. Associated pottery: Period 4A.

Fragment of round potsherd with evenly ground edge, diameter 7.7 cm, thickness 1 cm, perforated centrally, hole diameter 6 mm, weight 43 g, estimated 64 g (F3.ajt.1). Trench K, level c. 9.40-7.90. Associated pottery: Period 4A.

Fragment of round potsherd with evenly ground edge, diameter 5.7 cm, thickness 0.9 cm, perforated centrally, hole diameter 5 mm, weight 20 g, estimated 27 g (F3.ajt.2). Trench K, level c. 9.40-7.90. Associated pottery: Period 4A.

A roughly round potsherd with evenly ground edge, diameter 6.2 cm, thickness 1.2 cm, perforated centrally, hole diameter 6 mm, weight 45 g (F3.akx). Trench H.

Fragment of round potsherd with evenly ground edge, diameter 6 cm, thickness 0.5 cm, perforated centrally, hole diameter 5 mm, weight 8 g, estimated 22 g (F3.amt). Trench P, level c. 7.20-6.80. Associated pottery: Period 3A.

Round potsherd with evenly ground edge, perforated centrally, weight 43 g (fig. 595) (F3.anh). Trench O, level c. 9.00-7.50. Associated pottery: Period 3A-4A.

A roughly round potsherd with evenly ground edge, diameter 8.2 cm, thickness 1.1 cm, perforated centrally, hole diameter 7 mm, weight 63 g (F3.ank). Trench D, level c. 9.17-7.67. Associated pottery: Period 4A.

A roughly round potsherd with evenly ground edge, diameter 3.5 cm, thickness 0.6 cm, perforated centrally, hole diameter 4 mm, weight 8 g (F3.aod). Trench D.

Fragment of roughly round potsherd with partially ground edge, diameter 6.5 cm, thickness 0.9 cm, perforated centrally, hole diameter 1.4 cm, weight 34 g, estimated 44 g (F3.aqo). Trench O, 28.40 N, 23.60 W, level 7.39. Associated pottery: Period 3A, 4A.

Fragment of round potsherd with evenly ground edge, diameter 6 cm, thickness 1 cm, perforated centrally, perforation only partially preserved, with three diagonal incised lines, weight 18 g, estimated 64 g (F3.aqr.1). Trench D.

Round potsherd with evenly ground edge, diameter 3.2 cm, thickness 0.9 cm, perforated centrally, hole diameter 3 mm, weight 9 g (F3.aqr.2). Trench D.

Fragment of a roughly round potsherd with evenly ground edge, diameter 6.5 cm, thickness 0.8 cm, perforated centrally, hole diameter 1.1 cm, weight 21 g, estimated 40 g (F3.no number).

Round potsherd with evenly ground edge, diameter 3.8 cm, thickness 0.6 cm, perforated centrally, hole diameter 4 mm, weight 10 g (F6.280). Trench SN, 12.2 N, 1 E, level -0.99.

Round potsherd with evenly ground edge, diameter 2.9 cm, thickness 0.4 cm, perforated centrally, hole diameter 5 mm, weight 4 g (F6.358). Trench D2, 17.5-19.5 N, 1-4 W, level -0.13.

Wheels

The following two discs are almost identical and differ in their pointed oval cross sections from the spindle whorls described above. Unlike the spindle whorls made of broken pot sherds, these two discs were shaped in wet clay and fired. They are slightly asymmetrical, one side more flattened and one side flanged around the perforation. Possibly part of votive chariot or toy (cf. Starr 1937-1939 p. 415, pl. 98: I-J. Mackay 1943 pl. LVIII: 19-25).

Perforated disc with pointed oval cross section (fig. 596) (F3.li). Trench B, 38 N, 2 E, level 6.85. Associated pottery: Period 2.

Perforated disc with pointed oval cross section, 2.2 cm diameter, 0.8 cm thick, perforation diameter 0.4 cm (F3.asc). Trench H, sieve.

Chariot

A badly preserved, eroded, T-shaped pottery object, c. 4 x 7.5 cm, pierced transversely, may be part of a chariot (fig. 597) (no number) (cf. Starr 1937-39 pl. 99: E-K. Gasche & Pons 2014 pl. 69-71).

Gaming pieces

Some "gaming pieces" have the same dimensions and the same grinding of the edge as the previous group of spindle whorls, so they might be prefabricates intended to be perforated and become spindle whorls, though in view of the risk of breaking the sherd during drilling of the hole it is perhaps more likely that the final grinding of the round shape would have been done *after* the drilling. They seem to have a wide distribution in time. Parallels to this type are known from other Dilmun sites like Al-Khidr (Benediková 2010 figs. 116a-f, 117a-f), Qala'at al-Bahrain (Højlund & Andersen 1994 figs. 1792-1796), and Saar (Killick & Moon 2005 fig. 5.12:f). Similar objects found at the site of Dholavira in Gujarat are interpreted as weights (Bischt 2015 fig. 8.56).

A potsherd with evenly ground edge, roughly round with the edge chipped, diameter 4.6 cm, thickness 0.7 cm, weight 16 g, estimated 17 g (F3.js). Trench R, level 8.20-7.45. Associated pottery: Period 3A, 3B.

A round potsherd with evenly ground edge, diameter 6.2 cm, thickness 0.7 cm, weight 33 g (F3.lg). Trench B, 43 N, 0.6 E, level 6.99. Associated pottery: Period 2.

A round potsherd with evenly ground edge, diameter 1.9 cm, thickness 0.5 cm (F3.vo). Trench Ø, sieve.

Fragment of round potsherd with evenly ground edge, diameter estimated 5.1 cm, thickness 0.7 cm, weight 8 g, estimated 22 g (F3.æx). Trench AI, level 7.30-6.31. Associated pottery: Period 3A.

Fragment of round potsherd with evenly ground edge, diameter 4 cm, thickness 0.3 cm, weight 5 g (F3.aan). Trench C, 31.6 N, 6.60 W. Associated pottery: Period 3A.

A roughly round potsherd with evenly ground edge, diameter 3.8 cm, thickness 0.6 cm, weight 10 g (F3.afg). Trench H, level c. 9.65-9.15. Associated pottery: Period 4A.

A roughly round potsherd with evenly ground edge, weight 14 g (fig. 598) (F3.amv). Trenches K, P, or O, sieve.

A round potsherd with evenly ground edge and faces, weight 32 g (fig. 599) (F3.no number).

Fragment of round potsherd with evenly ground edge, diameter 5.7 cm, thickness 0.5 cm, weight 12 g, estimated 28 g (F3.apy). Trench D.

Fragment of roughly round potsherd with evenly ground edge, diameter 5.2 cm, thickness 0.8 cm, weight 14 g, estimated 28 g (F3.arå). Trench K, level c. 7.00-6.50. Associated pottery: Period 3A.

Dominoes

Half a domino with four spots and a straight line, diameter 2.8 cm, thickness 0.9 cm, yellow-brown pottery, traces of piercing in the breakage, reused potsherd (fig. 600) (Tell F3).

Domino with two crossed lines and five spots, pottery (fig. 601) (F3.ci). Trench E, 31 N, 6.3 E, level 8.32. Associated pottery: Period 3A.

Domino with crescent incised, thickness 1 cm, light brown pottery, reused potsherd or modelled (fig. 602) (F3.gd). Trench J, 78 N, 1.3 E, level 7.15. Associated pottery: Period 4B.

Domino with incised straight lines and one depression, 2.5 diameter, 1.4 cm thick, pottery (F3.akv). Trench H, 43.15 N, 12 W, level 7.41. Associated pottery: Period 4A.

Domino, peripherally perforated, 2.2 cm in diameter, 0.9 cm thick, on both sides faint traces of incised crossing lines and four spots, pottery (F3.asc). Trench H, sieve.

Domino with two crossed lines and four spots, thickness 1.2 cm, light brown pottery, reused potsherd (cf. Kjærum 1983 no. 324) (fig. 603) (F3.ayo). Trench AP, c. 7.98. Associated pottery: Period 4.

Domino with two crossed lines, three spots and a crescent, diameter 2.7 cm, thickness 0.8 cm, light brown pottery, reused potsherd (fig. 604) (F3.bjs). Trench AY, level 6.34.

Domino with two crossed lines and four spots, thickness 1.3 cm, light brown pottery, reused potsherd (fig. 605) (Tell F3, KM1570).

Sherds with incised decoration

Square potsherd with incised decoration, on external side two close, kneeling persons with outstretched arms and on the internal side an X-shaped figure (fig. 606) (F6.1135). Trench F1, level +23.

Other sherds with incised decoration have been dealt with by Højlund (1987 p. 165-170, figs. 712 and 716).

Other pottery objects

Two body sherds with a ridge in hard, grey pottery (stone ware) (F3.alø). Trench O, level c. 9.00- 7.50. Associated pottery: Period 3A, 4A.

Stopper made of sherd in red pottery (fig. 607) (F3.æh). Trench AI, level 8.94-6.49. Associated pottery: Period 3A, 4A.

Stopper in reddish clay (fig. 608) (F3.asd). Trench C, bottom layer.

Stopper of clay (fig. 609) (F3.aza). Trench AN, level 8.01-6.83. Associated pottery: Period 2, 4.

Fragment of sieve-bowl in Barbar ware type B (Cf. Højlund & Andersen 1997 fig. 99. Højlund & Andersen 1994 Type B33, figs. 168 and 655) (fig. 610) (F3.zi). Trench Ø, level 8.12-6.80. Associated pottery: Period 2, 3B.

The prow of a ship in red sand- and lime-tempered pottery, with a straight, horizontal keel, a high sheer bow or stern, and a hole for the anchor rope (fig. 611) (F3.ek). Trench F, level 7.19-6.88. Associated pottery: Period 2, 3A, 3B. Two close, contemporary parallels are known from Qala'at al-Bahrain (Højlund & Andersen 1994 figs. 1812-1813).

Fragment of four-sided tray with hole in one corner, in straw-tempered pottery stained with bitumen (fig. 612) (F3.bdi). Trench AT, level 8.09 -7.82. Associated pottery: Period 4.

Incised-grey ware sherd from straight-sided beaker with herringbone decoration, 4.5 mm thick (fig. 613) (F3.aog). Trench P, level c. 7.00-6.20. Associated pottery: Period 3A. A similar sherd was found in the 2008-2012 excavations in Tell F6. They may ultimately derive from SE Iran nor SW Pakistan (Højlund & Abu-Laban 2016 fig. 271).

Rim sherd in incised-grey ware, rim diameter c. 10 cm (fig. 614) (F3.på). Trench Y, level 8.50. Associated pottery: Period 4B. Cf. previous item, fig. 613.

Fragment of round potsherd with evenly ground edge, diameter 5 cm, thickness 0.9 cm, two peripheral holes, hole diameter 0.5 cm, weight 7 g, estimated 16 g (F3.nr). Trench B, level 6.60-6.35. Associated pottery: Period 2.

A roughly round potsherd with evenly ground edge, diameter 3.8 cm, thickness 0.7 cm, peripherally perforated, hole diameter 0.2 cm, but with the beginning of a drilled hole in the centre, weight 10 g (F3.yå). Trench AF, sieve.

Roughly round potsherd with evenly ground edge, diameter 5.5 cm, thickness 0.7 cm, twice perforated centrally, hole diameters 0.5 cm, weight 16 g, estimated 19 g (F3.adæ). Trench C, level c. 7.35-7.05. Associated pottery: Period 3A/4A?

A roughly round potsherd with evenly ground edge and four drilled holes, weight 55 g (fig. 615) (F3.apk). Trench S, level c. 7.80-8.80. Used for tablet weaving? (cf. Højlund & Andersen 1994 fig. 1806).

Fig. 587. 1:2.

Fig. 588. 1:2.

Fig. 589. 1:2.

Fig. 590. 1:2.

Fig. 591. 1:2.

Fig. 592. 1:2.

Fig. 593. 1:2.

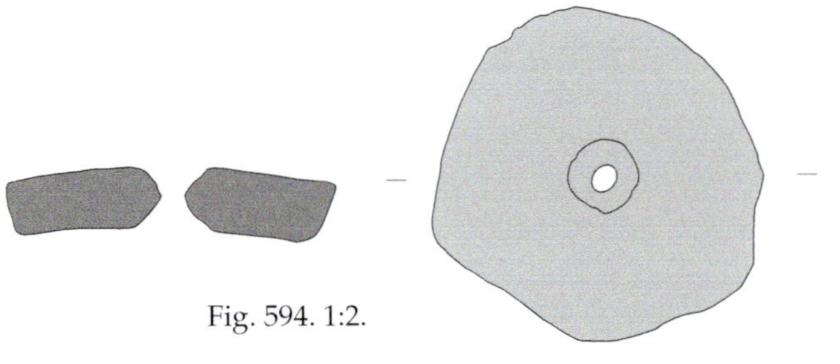
Fig. 594. 1:2.

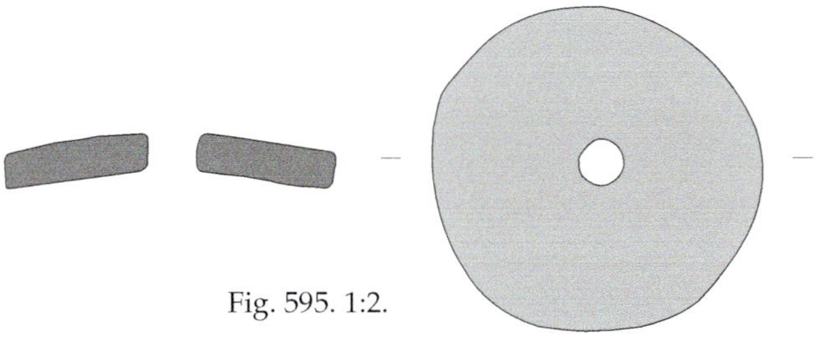
Fig. 595. 1:2.

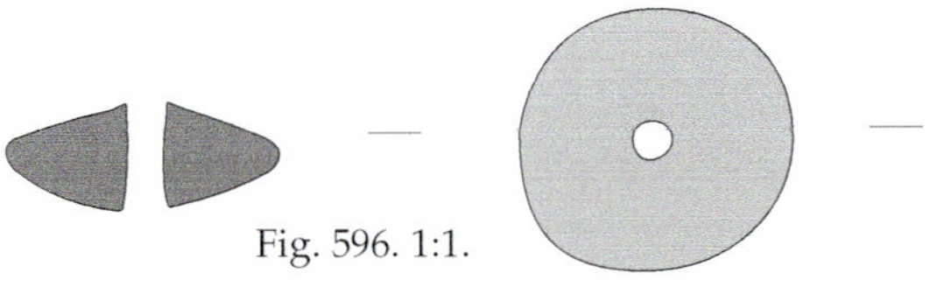
Fig. 596. 1:1.

Fig. 597. 1:2.

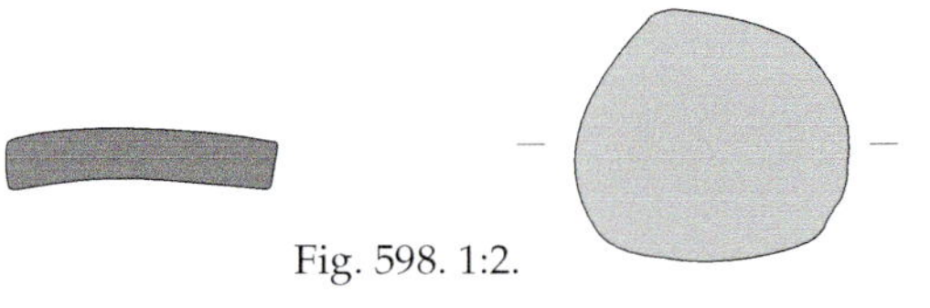
Fig. 598. 1:2.

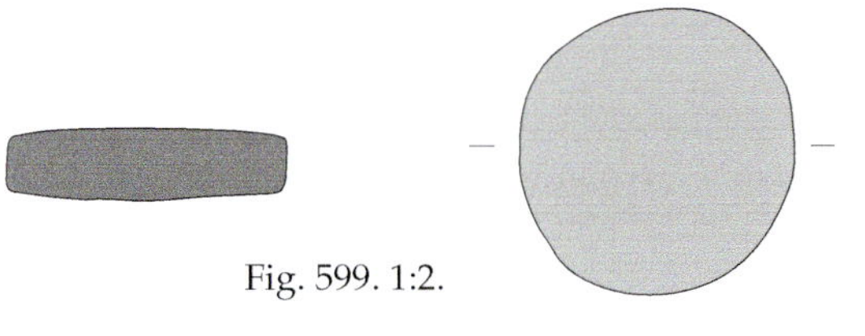
Fig. 599. 1:2.

Fig. 600. 1:1.

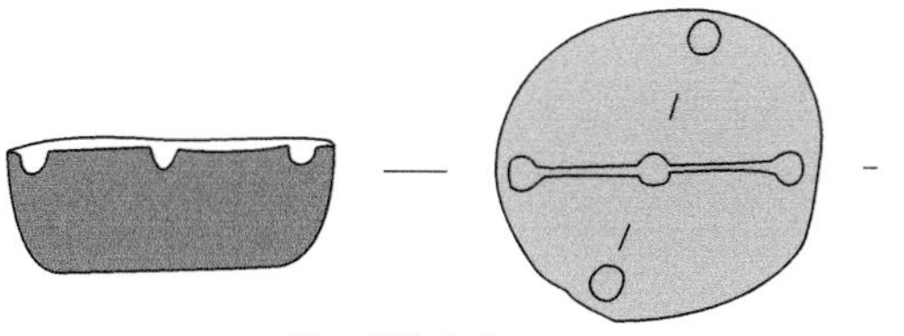
Fig. 601. 1:1.

Fig. 602. 1:1.

Fig. 603. 1:1.

Fig. 604. 1:1.

Fig. 605. 1:1.

Fig. 606. 1:2.

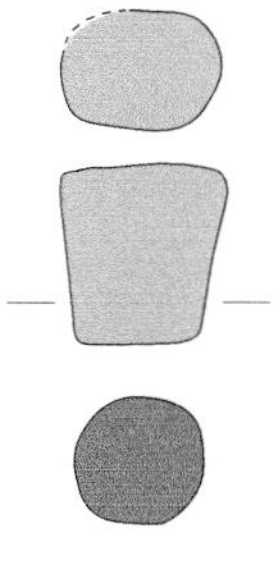
Fig. 607. 1:2.

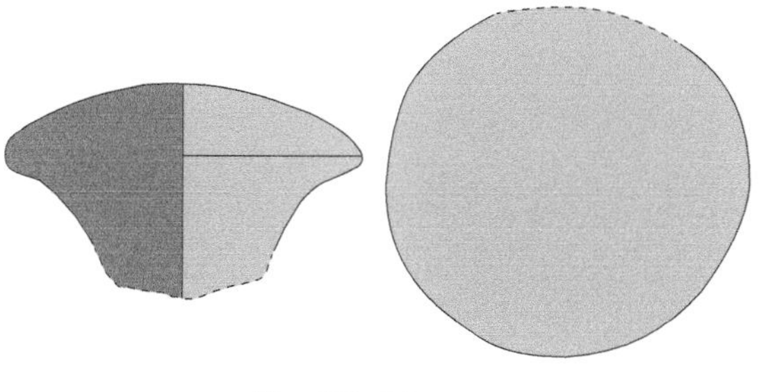
Fig. 608. 1:2.

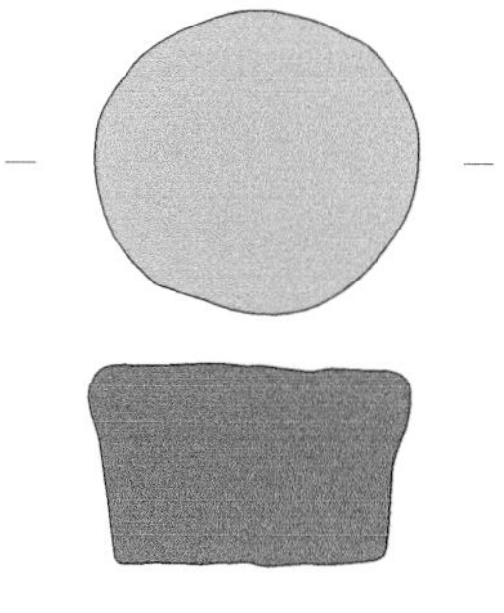
Fig. 609. 1:2.

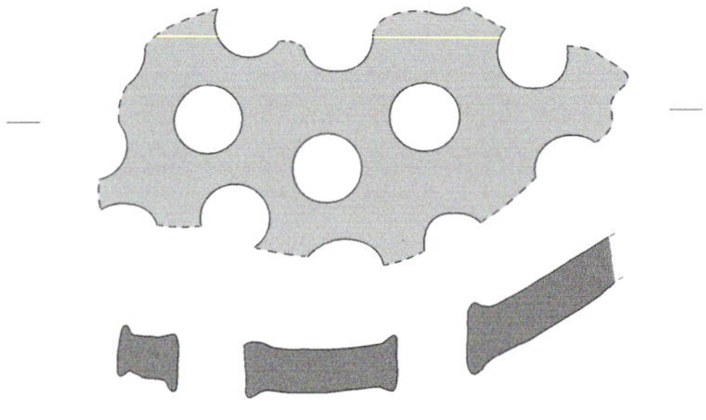

Fig. 610. 1:2.

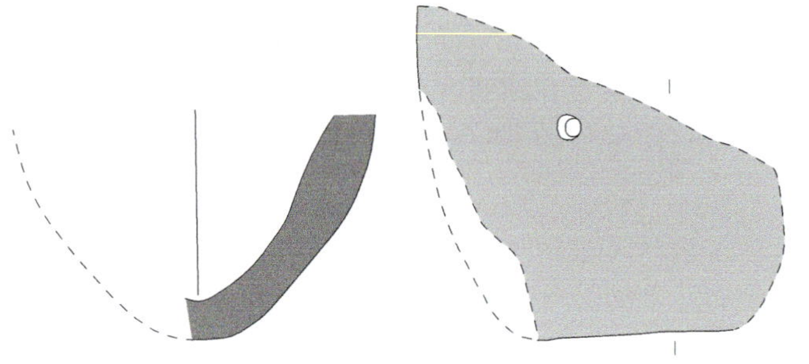

Fig. 611. 1:2.

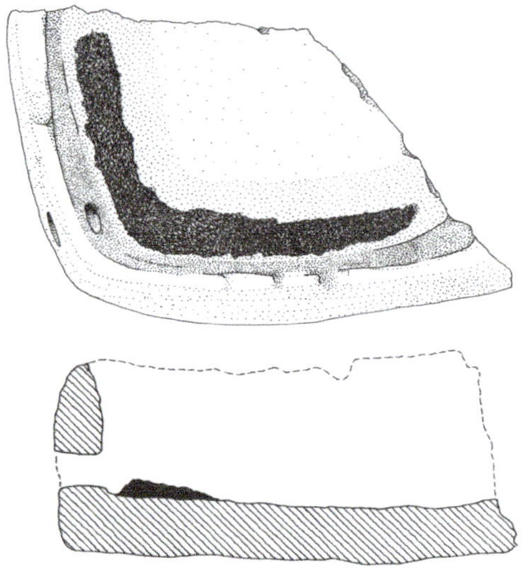

Fig. 612. 1:3.

Fig. 613. 1:1.

Fig. 614. 1:1.

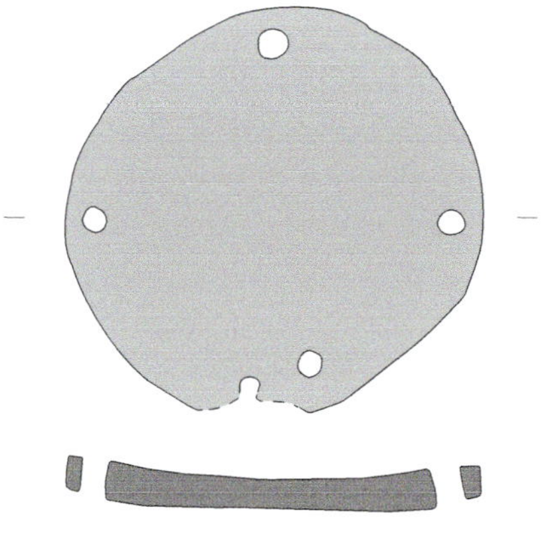

Fig. 615. 1:2.

10. Glass and glazed material

by Ann Andersson and Flemming Højlund

By far the majority of glass and glazed objects found during the 1958-1963 excavations consists of beads. A total of 81 glass and faience beads were included in the publication of beads from Tell F3 and Tell F6 (Andersson 2022). A further 109 glass beads and fragments of glass beads, which were not available until 2023, are treated by Andersson in an appendix below (p. 172). Besides, some fragments of vessels of glass or faience as well as amorphous lumps of glass will be described below.

Two fragments of a small glass bottle (possibly for makeup, perfume, or ointment), height 3.9 cm, diameter 1.5 cm (fig. 616) (F6.590). The variation in colours of the preserved glass (white, light brown and greyish black) indicates, that the vessel would originally have had several different colours. The vessel has a slender neck and body and a pointed base, and the rim is vertical and outwards thickened. Baulk between Trenches D2 and SN11-20, 14.5-16 N, 0-1 W, Room 3, level -1.28-1.56, i.e. from an area with a high frequency of glass beads (Andersson 2022 p. 38, fig. 71), probably stemming from a Period 4A hoard of beads disturbed by the Post 4A Period stone plundering of the "Palace" (see below, Andersson p. 172).

A sherd of glass or faience, 1.4 x 2 cm, 0.3-0.4 cm thick, with two, perhaps originally four, inlaid green circles and a green branch with yellow between the leaves on a whitish-grey background; in continuation of the branch are two green dots (fig. 617) (F3.adp). Trench D, level c. 7.07-6.77, sieve.

Glass sherd, green with degraded surface (F3.*41). Trench AK.

Two sherds, probably of faience, the surfaces are shiny, glassy, and veined, the veins being created by a mix of reddish-brown and cream material which can be seen both on the surfaces and in the breakages, 5-6 mm thick, curvature of both sherds suggests a small vessel (figs. 618-619) (cf. Starr 1937-1939 pl. 119: I-J, p. 461) (F3.xf). Trenches AE and AD, level 7.75-7.10. Associated pottery: Period 3A, 3B.

A sherd of veined faience, similar to previous two items (fig. 620) (F3.xg). Trench AB, sieve.

Four lumps of dark blue glass, 1 mm thick outer white layer (F3.mh). Trench J, north part, from surface to level 7.47. Associated pottery: Period 4B. Analysed by Pollard 1987 p. 190.

Small chip similar to above (F3.ån). Trench AF, sieve. Analysed by Pollard 1987 p. 190.

Lump of glass with a light yellowish-green surface, 1-3 mm from the surface it changes into a dark blue colour, 3.1 x 4.7 x 4.7 cm, broken into 14 fragments (fig. 621) (F3.bcf). Trench I, level 5.88-5.38. Associated pottery: Period 2.

Lump of dark blue glass, broken in two, 2 mm thick light brownish outer layer (F6.188). Trench C1, level +0.17. Analysed by Pollard 1987 p. 190.

Four irregular lumps of dark blue glass, light brownish-green surface, 2-8 mm thick, white, outer layer (F6.286). Trench SN 11.75-14 N, 0-1.5 E, level -0.89, outside the "Palace". Analysed by Pollard 1987 p. 190.

Lump of glass, light green in breakage, degraded, whitish-brown surface with black spots, 2 x 3.5 x 4.4 cm (fig. 622) (F6.482). Trench D2, level -1.60. Associated pottery: Period 1.

Lumps of light greenish-yellow glass with green spots and greyish, degraded surface, 1.3 x 2.5 x 4.3 cm (fig. 623) (F6.590.B). Trench SN 14.5-16 N, 0-1 W, level -1.28 to -1.56.

Lump of light green glazed material, 0.8 x 1.2 x 1.3 cm (F3.ib). Trench M, level 6.73-6.41. Associated pottery: Period 2.

Lump of glass? with herring-bone decoration on the surface, 6 x 7.5 cm (fig. 624) (no number).

The above-described lumps of glass may be raw materials for a production of glass items such as beads carried out in Tell F3 and/or Tell F6. Glass beads appear in small numbers in the Arabian Gulf as early as the late 3rd millennium. An Early Type burial in Wadi as-Sail in Bahrain, radiocarbon dated to c. 2200-2100 BC contained two beads of blue and golden glass (Højlund et al. 2008 figs. 17a-b), and two double-conic beads of blue glass were found from Period Ib layers (c. 2100 BC) at Qala'at al-Bahrain (Højlund & Andersen 1994 figs. 1941-1942, 1949). Furthermore, one turquoise-blue glass bead was found in Period IIc layer at Qala'at al-Bahrain (Højlund & Andersen 1994 fig. 1963).

Glass beads were rare in the 1958-1963 excavations in Tell F3 (N = 5), but more common in Tell F6 (N = 58) (Andersson 2022 p. 28). They occur in either a deep blue or turquoise colour. In the 2008-2012 excavations in Tell F6 nine glass beads were found, dating to Tell F6: Phases 7-8 (Period 4A-) (Andersson 2016 p. 183, figs. 906, 909-910 and 922). In the 2012-2017 excavations in Tell F3, three glass beads were found (Andersson 2021 figs. 421, 429-430). One blue bead dating to Tell F3: Phase 6 (Period 4A) and two light green beads dating to Tell F3: Phases 3 and 6 (Periods 3B and 4A).

Cylinder seals made of glass, often turquoise coloured, were also found in Tell F3 and F6 (Kjærum 1983 nos. 399-402, 404-406, 411-414 and 420-422).

A large amount of greenish, yellow, and golden glazed faience and pottery was found around House 30 in the latest occupation phase in Tell F3 dating to Period 4B (Højlund 1987 p. 95-98, figs. 395-430, 619. Pollard & Højlund 1983. Pollard 1987). Whether the glazing of this material could be related to the above-described glass lumps is uncertain.

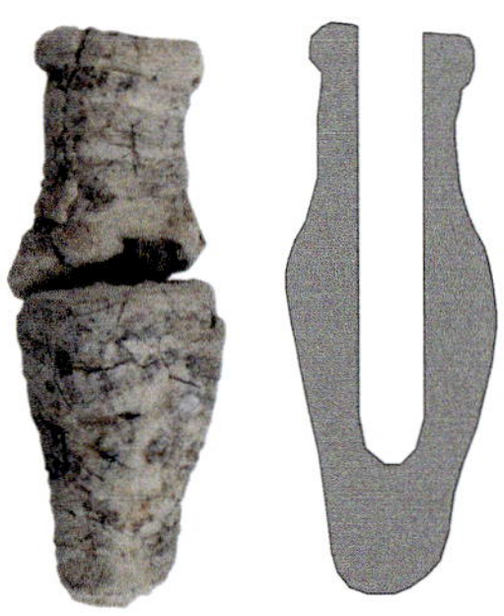

Fig. 616. 1:1.

Fig. 617. 2:1.

Fig. 618. 1:1.

Fig. 620. 1:1.

Fig. 621. 1:1.

Fig. 619. 1:1.

Fig. 622. 1:1.

Fig. 623. 1:1.

Fig. 624. 1:2.

11. Objects in bone, ivory, and shell

Handles

Handles for copper awls were made of the distal ends of the metapodia of sheep/goat (figs. 138-139, 145, 150, 152, 156, 158, 159-162, 164-166). The bone was sawn partly through and then broken, leaving behind the proximal end of the metapodia. The sawed-through end of the handle was always well smoothed, perhaps from use. Occasionally, the handle exhibits parallel striations from having been worked (cf. Killick & Moon 2005 fig. 5.6: c). Remains from the production of such handles were copious in the 2012-2017 excavations at Tell F3 (Højlund & Hilton 2021 p. 141, figs. 551-563).

A single handle made from the tarsometatarsus of a now extinct giant heron has been identified (see above p. 40, fig. 159).

Apart from the handles mounted with awls, loose handles were numerous in the excavation. No tool other than the awl has been seen hafted in this way. The tool was pushed into the spongious tissue of the bone, and this was enough to keep it fastened, no remains of bitumen or any other glue has been noted.

Broken bone handle, one end smooth, the other end broken, decorated with incised lines (fig. 625) (F3.oe). Trench I, level 5.85. Associated pottery: Period 2.

Handle, one end smoothed, the other end broken (fig. 626) (F3.ød). Trench AK, level 6.28.

Handle, broken at one end, smooth at the other end (fig. 627) (F3.aoø). Trench D.

Handle, fragment of tubular bone decorated with circular lines (fig. 628) (F3.bjl). Found in sieve.

Handle (F6.542). Trench D1, 7 N, 3 W, level -1.20.

Handle (F6.615). Trench SN11-20, 13.50 N, 0.50 E, -1.61. Associated pottery: Period 1.

Handle in bone or ivory, perforated with in situ copper rivet (fig. 629) (F6.949.R). Found in the sieve.

Bone awl (fig. 630) (F3.65). Trench RM, 11.25 N, 2.15 W, 1.73 m below surface.

Elephant tusks

by Helle Strehle and Flemming Højlund

Remains of several elephant tusks (F6.784) were found in 1961/62 in room 1 in the "Palace" in Tell F6. According to the diary they were found in Trench M2, at 13-14 N and 10.5 W, from level -0.15 to -0.41. This position corresponds to the middle of three buttresses built up against the northwestern wall of the building (Kjærum & Højlund 2014 fig. 138). The top of the buttress had a height of c. 30 cm above the latest ascertained floor (in level c. -0.70) in the room, and it was covered by a large stone flag. The find situation is documented in excavation photos (figs. 631-632) where several tusks can be seen lying both on top of the buttress and having slid partially off of it (fig. 633). Their position suggests a dating to the latest period of occupation in the "Palace", that is, Failaka Period 4A (fig. 7).

Judging from the photos, the longest fragments were c. 50-60 cm with a diameter of up to 10 cm. The material was extremely fragile and broke into numerous fragments during extraction. Two pieces were wrapped in gauze, and they now have, respectively, a length of c. 20 cm with a diameter of c. 8 cm and a length of c. 30 cm with a diameter of c. 9 cm.

Magnification (up to 60x) of cross sections of the material reveal Schreger lines (fig. 634) which have been examined by Dr Sonia O'Connor, University of Bradford, who reports: "From the appearance of the concentric cracking and the Schreger pattern this is clearly proboscidean ivory. The angle at which the Schreger lines cross in this pattern is quite narrow (less than ninety degrees). This can indicate mammoth ivory, but only if these acute angles are at the outer edge of the tusk. I think this fragment is from close to the centre of the tusk and so the features are consistent with those of elephant ivory."

Three samples of the ivory were analysed by Mass Spectrometry Analysis by Dr. Ashley Coutu of the University of York, and though it was not possible to make a confirmed and statistically significant species identification, two of the samples were a 'best match' to elephant (Coutu 2013).

Shell

Fragment of ostrich eggshell, 1.9 x 2.7 cm (F6.3). Trench SS, 27.8 S, 0.64 E.

Fragment of ostrich eggshell, 3 x 4.6 cm (F6.632). Trench F2, 19.5 N, 6 W, level +0.22.

Fragment of ostrich eggshell, 1.3 x 3.3 cm (F6.651). Trench F2, 17-20 N, 8 W, level -0.25.

Fragment of ostrich eggshell, 4.5 x 6.4 cm (F6.824). Trench M2, level +0.40.

Fig. 625. 1:2.

Fig. 626. 1:2.

Fig. 627. 1:2.

Fig. 628. 1:1.

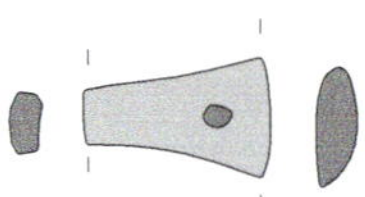

Fig. 629. 1:2.

Fig. 630. Ca. 1:2.

Fig. 631. Ivory lying on top of buttress in room 1 of the "Palace", looking NW.

Fig. 634. Unpolished breakage revealing Schreger lines indicative of elephant ivory.

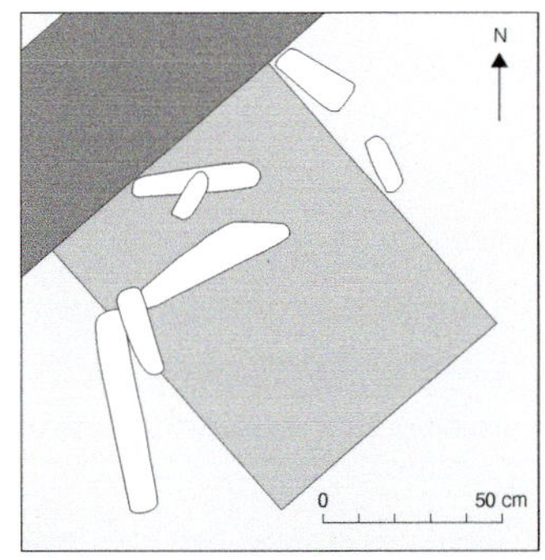

Fig. 633. Sketch of ivory lying on buttress in room 1 of the "Palace", based on figs. 631-632.

Fig. 632. Ivory lying on top of buttress in room 1 of the "Palace", looking N.

12. Gold objects

Three objects of gold found in the 1958-1963 excavations have already been published, namely a fitting for a round stamp seal in Style II (Kjærum 1983 no. 352), a cap for a lapis lazuli bead and a collared melon bead (Andersson 2022 figs. 554 and 578). Additionally, a gold ring found in Tell F3 must be mentioned, as well as a golden cylinder from Tell F6. A few fragments of gold sheet have appeared in later excavations in Tell F6 (Howard-Carter 1984 p. 20, FH1212. Højlund & Abu-Laban 2016 fig. 1135).

Fig. 635. 1:1.

Open ring tapering towards the ends, diameter 1.4 cm, maximum thickness 0.15 mm (fig. 635) (F3.272). Trench RM, 0-20 N, sieve.

Fig. 636. 1:1.

Cylinder of 0.5 mm thick sheet which overlaps 4 mm, strengthened with a narrow band at both ends (fig. 636) (F6.no number, KM1499).

13. Plaster objects

Architectural remains in plaster were frequently found during the 1958-1963 excavations, but only a few were kept. Some objects were also produced in plaster.

Jambs

Fragment of corner of two walls or a door jamb, 37 cm long, in white plaster (F3.bp). Trench A, 33.80 N, 2.50 E, level 7.33. Associated pottery: Period 3A. Cf. Højlund & Hilton 2021 figs. 511-512.

Wall plaster

Fragments of white wall plaster were quite common in the finds from both Tell F3 and Tell F6. Exceptional is a collection of c. 90 large fragments, up to 11 x 12 cm, of white wall plaster, rendered in two layers, 3-7 mm thick, both with remains of a plum red colour on the two faces (fig. 637) (F3.agi). Trench G, in the northwest corner of room 2 in House 6 dating to Period 3A (Kjærum & Højlund 2013 fig. 45).

During the recent excavations in Tell F6 a few fragments of what may have been wall plaster were also found to be coloured red (Højlund & Abu-Laban 2016 p. 221. Cf. Killick & Moon 2005 p. 155, fig. 5.23.f).

Roof

Remains of roof construction in plaster were copious in both Tell F3 and Tell F6, though few were kept, often showing impressions of palm trunks transversely covered with close-lying palm branch stems which must have been tied together to form "mats". Similar fragments of roof construction have been found in large numbers in recent excavations in Tell F6 (Højlund & Abu-Laban 2016 figs. 1100-1110) and Tell F3 (Højlund & Hilton 2021 p. 21 and 137-138, figs. 41-43, 506-509, 515 and 518), and occasionally at Saar Settlement (Killick & Moon 2005 p. 155). Only a few fragments were kept from the excavations at Qala'at al-Bahrain (Højlund & Andersen 1994 fig. 2040. Højlund & Andersen 1997 figs. 294-295), but many may have been left on the site.

Lump of white plaster with parallel impressions of palm branch stems, 5.8 x 6 cm (F3.vv). Trench Ø, level 7.04-6.79. Associated pottery: Period 2.

Fragment of plaster with one smooth, curved, convex side and the other side rough and concave, 13.6 x 17 cm (F3.aed). Trench C.

Corner of roof with impressions of parallel palm branch stems and possibly palm trunk (F3.aln). Trench K, level c. 7.20-7.00. Associated pottery: Period 3A.

Eight fragments of plaster with impressions of palm branch stems and transverse palm trunks (F3.ame). Trench K, level c. 7.20-7.00. Associated pottery: Period 3A.

Three fragments of plaster with parallel impressions of palm branch stems on one side and transverse palm trunks on the other (F3.asm). Trench K, level c. 7.00-6.50. Associated pottery: Period 3A.

Fragment of white plaster with impression of palm trunk on one side and transverse, parallel impressions of palm branch stems on the other side (fig. 638) (F3.bgv). From Trench AO, sieve from level 6.51-5.36. Associated pottery: Period 2, 3B/4A?

Fragment of white plaster with one smooth, even face and the other impressed with seven parallel stems of palm branch (fig. 639) (F6.478). Trench D2, level -1.32.

Two fragments of white plaster with one face impressed with palm branch stems (F6.622). Trench D2, 13-16 N, 1-3 W, level -2.03. Associated pottery: Period 1.

Two fragments of 2.6 cm thick, probably, roof plaster with impression of woven mat on one side. The strips are c. 1.2-2 cm wide and woven in a three-over-three-under, twill pattern displaced successively by one strip (fig. 640) (F3.no number). Found in SW section through temple platform in Tell F3.

Fragment of white plaster with impression of plaited mat, width of strips c. 2 cm (fig. 641) (881.SS). Trench RM, sieve.

Circular lids

Lid with oblique edge (fig. 642) (F3.afl). Trench D, level c. 6.77.

Lid, upper part splays near top (fig. 643) (F3.alo). Trench K, level c. 7.60. Associated pottery: Period 3A/4A.

Half a lid, one surface flat, the other slightly convex, 13 cm in diameter, 2.5 cm thick (F3.alt). Trench H, level c. 6.50-7.10.

Lid with flanged edge (fig. 644) (F3.ang). Trench K, level c. 7.00-6.50. Associated pottery: Period 3A.

Half a lid, discus-shaped, 9.1 cm in diameter, 2.8 cm thick (F3.arg). Trench K, level c. 7.40-7.90. Associated pottery: Period 3A/4A.

Lid, upper part splays near top to slightly convex face (fig. 645) (F3.asd). Trench C, level c. 7.00-6.50. Associated pottery: Period 3A.

Lid, diameter 10.5 cm, 3.6 cm thick, grey, ashy plaster (F3.tc). Trench AA, level 8.54-8.36. Associated pottery: Period 4.

Lid with fishhook-like figure applied to the upper surface (fig. 646) (F6.824) (cf. Killick & Moon 2005 fig. 5.21a). Trench M2, level +0.40.

Lid, circular (fig. 647) (KM364).

Fig. 637. 1:3.

Fig. 638. 1:2.

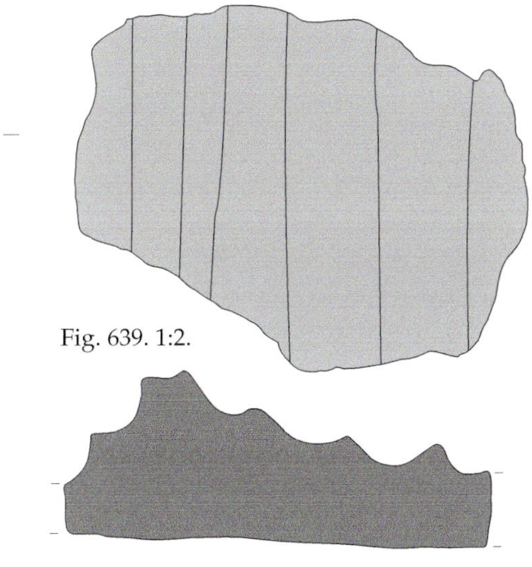

Fig. 639. 1:2.

Fig. 640. 1:2.

Fig. 641. 1:3.

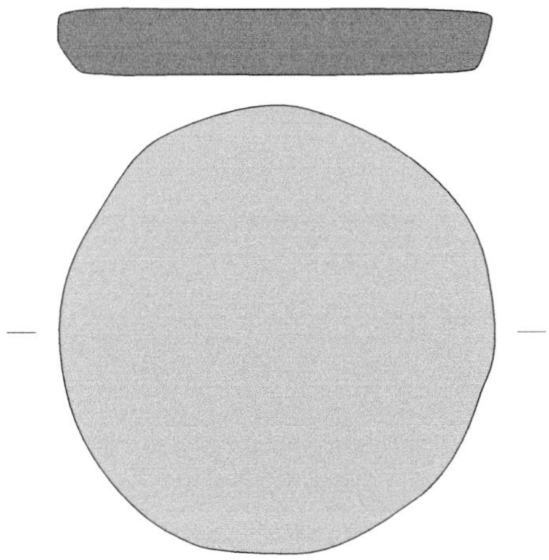

Fig. 642. 1:2.

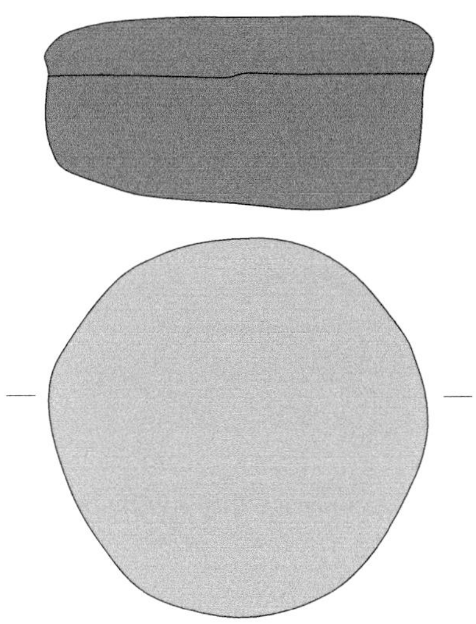

Fig. 643. 1:2.

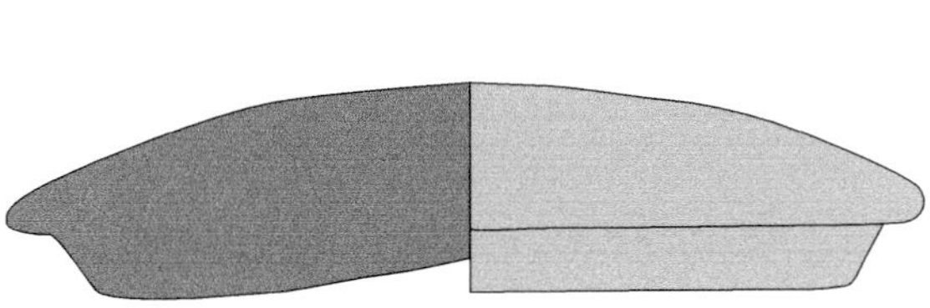

Fig. 644. 1:2.

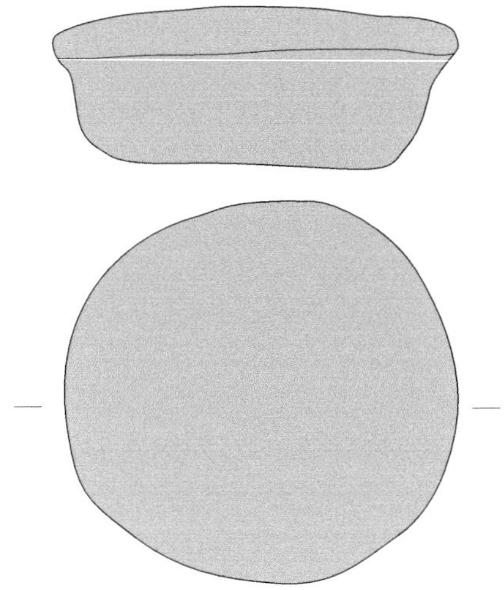

Fig. 645. 1:2.

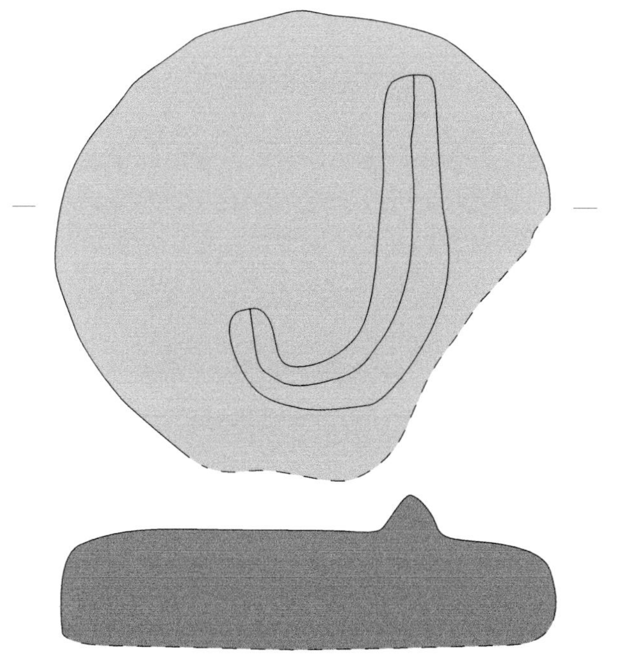

Fig. 646. 1:2.

Fig. 647. 1:3.

14. Miscellaneous objects

Pearls

A total of eleven pearls have been found in Tell F6 and none in Tell F3. During the 1958-1963 excavations four unpierced pearls, described below, were found in Tell F6, in addition to two pierced ones which have been published elsewhere (Andersson 2022 figs. 191-192). Two unpierced pearls derive from the 2008-2012 excavations in Tell F6, probably from the Ur III layer (Højlund & Abu-Laban 2016 p. 223, fig. 1127. Carter 2012 p. 8). Furthermore, three pearls, whether pierced or unpierced are uncertain, are said to have been found in "presumed Late Kassite contexts" in the northwest corner of the "Palace" (Howard-Carter 1986 p. 308, note 22. Quoted by Carter 2012 p. 8). The extreme northwest corner of the "Palace" was excavated by the Johns Hopkins Expedition (Kjærum & Højlund 2013 fig. 131), but there is no mention of any pearls in the report (Howard-Carter 1984).

Unpierced pearl, drop-shaped, length 7.5 mm, max diameter 5.5 mm, light yellowish shine (fig. 648) (F6.405). Trench D2, 15.8 N, 1.25 W, level -1.04.

Unpierced pearl, figure eight shaped, white, max diameter 3.5 mm (fig. 649) (F6.616.B). Trench D2, 11.4 N, 1.5 W, level -1.58. Associated pottery: Period 1.

Unpierced pearl, diameter 0.45 cm (fig. 650) (F6.no number, KM1666.A). Found in sieve.

Unpierced pearl, diameter 0.5 cm, flat side, brownish (fig. 651) (F6.no number, KM1666.B). Found in sieve.

Silver

Silver pin with elaborately decorated head (fig. 652) (F3.yu). Trench AB, sieve. Very similar metal to the next piece.

Awl of silver, both the pointed end and the butt end have a square section (fig. 653) (F3.ån). Trench AF, sieve.

Fragment of silver sheet with three rivets in situ and visible on both sides. On one side the rivet heads are flush with surrounding surface, on the other side they protrude up to 2 mm (fig. 654) (F3.ahi). Trench G, level c. 8.43-7.93. Associated pottery: Period 4A.

Iron

Iron fishhook. The shank is 2 mm thick and ends in a flat plate which is 1 x 5 mm (fig. 655) (F3.ky). Trench B, level 8.53, that is, c. 70 cm below surface.

Bitumen

Bitumen was commonly found in the excavation, but little was kept, mostly lumps with broken surfaces and a few "cakes" with smooth, unbroken surfaces.

One lump, 3.6 x 5.7 cm, showing the impression of some sort of textile (identified by conservator Helle Strehle). The weave is tabby and close, c. 11 threads per cm (fig. 656) (F3.amø). Trench D, level c. 8.10. Associated pottery: Period 4A.

One lump, 6 x 10 x 13 cm, shows the impression of 4 mm wide strips of plaited palm leaves over an area of 4.5 x 10 cm, probably deriving from a basket containing bitumen (fig. 657) (F6.309). Trench C1, 2 S, 1 E, level -1.11.

A triangular cake, all surfaces smooth and unbroken (fig. 658) (F6.486). Trench D1, level -0.30.

Fig. 648. 2:1.

Fig. 649. 2:1.

Fig. 650. 2:1.

Fig. 651. 2:1.

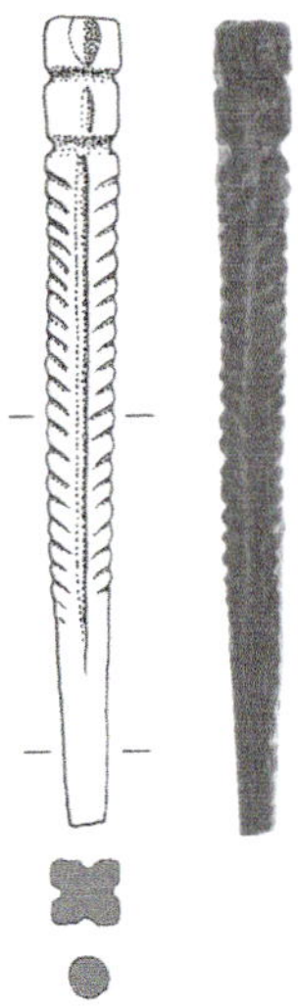

Fig. 652. 1:1.

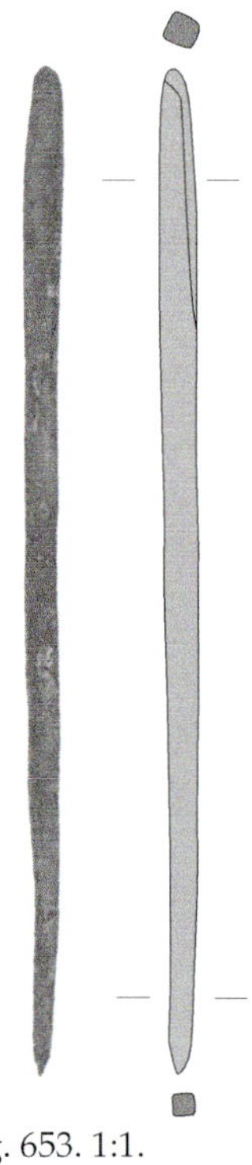

Fig. 653. 1:1.

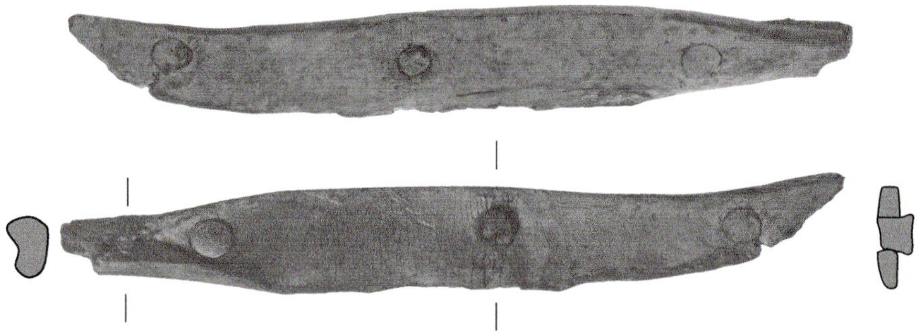

Fig. 654. 1:1.

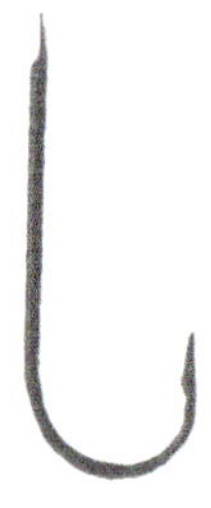

Fig. 655. 1:2.

Fig. 656.

Fig. 657. 1:2.

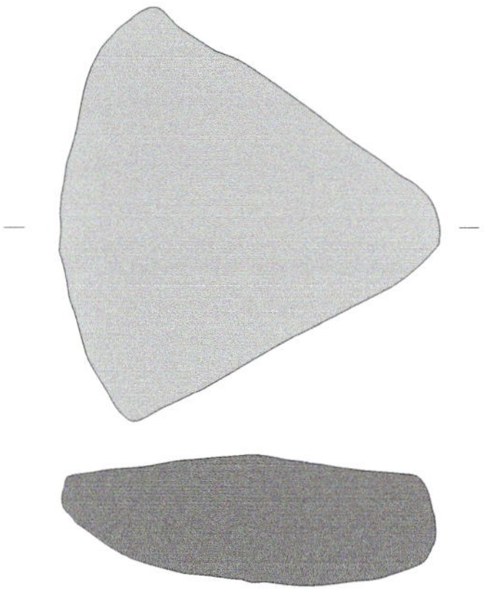

Fig. 658. 1:3.

15. Conclusions

The earliest human settlement on the island of Failaka dates from the end of the 3rd to the end of the 2nd millennium BC. During the major part of this millennium-long period the population of Failaka belonged to the Dilmun civilization that included both Bronze Age Bahrain and the Eastern Province of Saudi Arabia, as evidenced by a similar material culture in terms of pottery, stamp seals, burials, temples and domestic architecture. For brief periods, however, before and after the Dilmun occupation on Failaka, the island was settled by people from South Mesopotamia.

The Dilmun settlement

The major Dilmun occupation on Failaka was situated on the southwestern corner of the island with Tell F3 and Tell F6. The interpretation of these two tells is based on the differences in structure, dimensions, and functions of the architecture uncovered in combination with the pottery finds. The *"Palace" in Tell F6* was first interpreted as an administrative building for a ruler because of its size (c. 500 m^2) and main structure: an outer gate with a long corridor leading to an inner gate giving access to a large, pillared hall with a periphery of smaller rooms (Glob 1968 p. 132. Kjærum 1986a p. 79).

Based on an analysis of the internal installations of the building and the fact that the enormous pottery inventory consisted almost exclusively of storage vessels it is argued that it was instead intended for the production and storage of liquids, probably date juice (Højlund 1990a p. 79). Besides, there is evidence that the building was used for storage of trade goods, like beads (Andersson 2022 and below p. 172) and ivory (above p. 157).

A great temple, in front of the "Palace", was excavated in the 1980s (Calvet & Pic 2008). The proximity and relative layout of these two great buildings suggest that they belonged to the same organization (Kjærum & Højlund 2013 p. 105. Højlund & Abu-Laban 2016 p. 254). Judging from the cuneiform inscriptions found during the excavations, Inzak was the most important deity, being the most frequently attested god on Failaka, occurring in one text with the goddess Panipa, who appears to have been his divine consort (Marchesi above p. 102). It is presumed that the temple in Tell F6 is that of Inzak, probably named "The Great Palace" in cuneiform inscriptions found on Failaka (Calvet & Pic 1990 p. 115. Marchesi above p. 112).

The names of two Dilmun kings and a princess are recorded in the cuneiform inscriptions from Failaka (Marchesi above p. 110), in addition to the names of two Dilmun kings known from Bahrain (Marchesi 2017 p. 425-428). Since the title of the Dilmun kings was Servant of Inzak it is presumed that all of Tell F6 was under royal authority (Højlund & Abu-Laban 2016 p. 252).

The architecture of *Tell F3* is interpreted as a series of family-based houses, each consisting of a few small rooms adding up to a total floor area including a courtyard of between c. 12 and 50 m^2. The pottery excavated in the houses covers many different functional types, such as plates, bowls, cups, jugs, storage jars, and pithoi. This points to a variety of functions having taken place in each house and seems compatible with a family's habitation (Højlund 1987. Kjærum & Højlund 2013 p. 23).

The 400 m distance between Tell F3 and Tell F6 may reflect the social distance between its inhabitants in a society divided into two main castes, commoners and royalty.

Based on the finds dealt with in this volume a few observations may be added to the differences between the settlements of Tell F3 and Tell F6 described above.

The majority of the registered copper objects came from Tell F3, and less than a fourth derived from Tell F6. Part of this difference may be explained by the fact that the excavated surface of Tell F3 was larger than that of Tell F6 (1511 m2/617 m2) and that the trenches in Tell F3 were generally a little deeper than those in Tell F6. Nevertheless, it seems that some objects, like chisels/drills, awls, needles, and fishhooks, are far more common in Tell F3 than in Tell F6.

Twenty-one chisels/drills were found at Tell F3 and only three in Tell F6. The objects were likely used to drill holes in wooden planks for building or repairing boats and may suggest that such an activity was centred on Tell F3.

Thirty-two awls were found in Tell F3 and only four in Tell F6. Awls may have been a sort of all-round tool.

Twenty-seven needles derive from Tell F3 and only five from Tell F6. They may have been used for sewing textiles for boat sails, sewing palm leaf mats, or other production activities.

Thirty-three fishhooks were found in Tell F3 and only eight in Tell F6.

Conversely, of the six metal handles found - probably for basket-shaped containers - only one was found in Tell F3 and five in Tell F6. Perhaps baskets made of cheaper palm material were used more frequently in Tell F3.

With regards to materials other than copper, twenty-six spindle whorls made of pot sherds were found in Tell F3 and only two in Tell F6, suggesting that the act of spinning primarily took place at Tell F3.

Seventy objects produced from broken soft stone vessels, such as pendants, spindle whorls, and blanks, were found in Tell F3, only two came from Tell F6.

Conversely, beads were much more common in Tell F6 than in Tell F3 (Andersson below p. 172), and pearls, both pierced and unpierced, as well as ivory in the form of elephant tusks were exclusively found in Tell F6 and not in Tell F3 (above p. 157 and 163). Irregular lumps of copper, probably raw material for the production of copper artefacts, were found scattered over Tell F3 and Tell F6, but truly plano-convex copper ingots have only been found in the deepest layers of Tell F6.

Three small copper boxes of identical shape, one containing a black bituminous material, were found in Tell F6, and none are known from Tell F3.

Altogether, these observations add to the previous interpretation of Tell F3 as home to commoners working as craftsmen, fishers, and possibly farmers, whereas Tell F6 appears to have been the centre of royal authority that dealt with relations to the gods as well as large scale economics such as taxes and foreign trade.

Forty-eight cuneiform inscribed objects were found during the 1958-1963 excavations in Tell F3, Tell F5 and Tell F6. They have previously been examined by Glassner and others (Glassner 1984) but have in the context of this publication been re-studied by Marchesi, who has also included twenty-four inscriptions found on Failaka after 1963 in his study (Marchesi above p. 75, summarized on p. 110-112).

The animal bones from the 1958-1963 excavations of Tell F3 and Tell F6 were retrieved but have not been studied in the context of this publication. A cursory examination of the bones, however, indicates that the same animals found in the material from the 2008-2012 excavations of Tell F6 are present (Yeomans 2016 p. 228) and that the population inhabiting the settlement, therefore, was sustained by the herding of livestock (sheep/goat and cattle) as well as by fishing.

The presence of grinding stones (above p. 119) and baking plates (Højlund 1987 figs. 38, 43-44) suggests that seeds/grain and breadmaking may also have been of some importance. Similarly, the finds of numerous date pits and their frequent impressions in pottery and bitumen may point to a sizeable production of dates (Rowley-Conwy 1987 p. 181).

Whether farmers actually lived in Tell F3 is uncertain. Likely, there were agricultural villages on Failaka, supplying themselves and the settlements at Tell F3 and Tell F6 with foodstuff. They probably paid taxes to the authority at Tell F6, and quantities of dates paid as taxes may have been transformed into date juice in the "Palace" (Højlund 1990a).

Of other objects treated in this volume, five miniature altars must be mentioned. All five were found in Tell F3, suggesting, perhaps, that these objects were used in domestic rituals (above p. 125).

Furthermore, thirty-five rectangular, finely ground stones, including some with prongs, were found in Tell F3 and none in Tell F6, suggesting that they may also have been involved in some domestic activity, perhaps worship (above p. 125).

During all periods of occupation, copper working took place somewhere in the area around Tell F3 and Tell F6, as evidenced by the finds of crucible and mould fragments and waste from metal working. The exact location of such a workshop has, however, yet to be found. The produce of the workshop was a simple, utilitarian repertoire of weapons, tools and ornaments, based on the import of copper ingots from Southeast Arabia (Weeks et al. above p. 55).

During the first part of the occupation on Failaka (c. 2100-1740 BC, Tell F6 Phases 1-5) the trade in copper from Magan via Dilmun to Mesopotamia is well documented in the written sources found in South Mesopotamia. The study of the copper metals from Tell F3 and Tell F6 in a larger Gulf context suggests that this trade continues into the post-Old Babylonian period (Tell F6 Phases 6-8), when the cuneiform sources become silent on this theme (Weeks et al. above p. 73-74).

The dichotomy between the domestic Tell F3 and the public Tell F6 characterizes the *Dilmun* settlement in the early 2nd millennium BC, *Period 1-2*. In the north part of Tell F3 two houses with a floor area of each around 50 m^2 were excavated. They shared a long, north-south running wall and probably belonged to a row of houses that continued towards the east and west (Højlund & Hilton 2021 fig. 52). Each house consisted of approximately eight small rooms, measuring from 1 x 2 m to 2 x 3.5 m and presumably with an open courtyard in the middle. The houses had been extensively repaired and modified during their seemingly long occupation (Kjærum & Højlund 2013 p. 11, figs. 7 and 10, 104-109). South of these houses was an area with evidence of activities involving kilns and pithoi and generally littered with refuse (Kjærum & Højlund 2013 fig. 7. Højlund & Hilton 2021 fig. 52).

In contrast to the apparently long-term use of the two small Period 2 houses in Tell F3, the major structures in Tell F6 were repeatedly torn down and reconstructed during the same period, as observed during the 2008-2012 excavations (Højlund & Abu-Laban 2016 p. 252). The building activity began with two thick walls, one of them 75 cm thick, the other 1.4 x 1.85 m across, constructed on virgin soil (ibid. fig. 40) adjacent to several large fireplaces. Further to the west, below the "Palace" a few walls built on a smaller scale were excavated in 1960-1963 (Kjærum & Højlund 2013 fig. 132, p. 107).

The thick-walled buildings were subsequently torn down and replaced with a complex of smaller rooms bounded by thinner walls and fronted by a well-made pavement (Højlund & Abu-Laban 2016, fig. 46). The thin-walled house is contemporary with the first terrace around the nearby temple and therefore probably related to the construction of the great temple. Between the thin-walled house and the temple was an oven used to incinerate the sacrificial remains from the temple. The thin-walled house was thereafter razed to the ground and replaced by the "Palace" whereas the oven continued to be in use (ibid. fig. 53).

The large temple in Tell F6 was plundered to the foundation, but it is possible to separate at least two phases. The construction of the temple and its first surrounding terrace were contemporary with the thin-walled building. It was followed by the construction of a new terrace bordered by a channel, probably at the same time that the "Palace" was built (ibid. p. 259).

The length of Period 1-2 is debatable. If the relationship between Style II of the Dilmun stamp seals and the Mesopotamian cylinder seal drill-point-style appearing during the reign of King Samsuiluna is accepted (Kjærum 1980. Højlund & Hilton 2021 p. 85-86), then the dramatic building activity in Tell F6 described above (the construction of the thick-walled houses, the thin-walled house, the "Palace" and the temple), all took place within half a century. If, conversely, the Bayesian analysis of the radio-carbon dates from the 2008-2012 excavations is accepted, this period may have lasted several centuries (Heinemeier & Højlund 2016 p. 239. Højlund & Hilton 2021 fig. 50).

The continuation of the domestic occupation in Tell F3 in *Period 3A*, with a new row of small houses (Kjærum & Højlund 2013 fig. 7) combined with the sparse remains in Tell F6 dating to Period 3A, is taken as evidence of a collapse of public authority in Dilmun at this time (Højlund & Abu-Laban 2016 p. 256-257).

Half the pottery found in Period 3A consists of Mesopotamian imports, especially drinking and eating vessels. The partially abandonment of a unique Dilmun pottery style may be the consequence of economic recession and the fragmentation of the Dilmun kingdom in the shadow of an emerging Sealand Dynasty (Højlund & Abu-Laban 2016 p. 256. Calderbank 2018. 2021).

In *Period 3B*, the occupation not only of Tell F3 but also of Tell F6 resumed, an indication that public authority in Dilmun had been restored. In Tell F3 two phases of small-room architecture have been uncovered in addition to a third occupation phase suggested by layers of refuse from a hypothetical new building phase lying north of the excavated area (Højlund & Hilton 2021 p. 55). These three phases of occupation may correspond to three phases of a nearby open-air shrine that also date to Period 3B (Kjærum & Højlund 2013 fig. 8. Højlund & Hilton 2021 figs. 53-54, and 87).

We know that the large temple of Inzak in Tell F6 still existed in Period 3B because a thick "buttress" wall was built up against its outer walls in the subsequent Period 4A (Højlund & Abu-Laban 2016 p. 91). It is, therefore, remarkable that an additional shrine was constructed in Tell F3 in Period 3B. Three cuneiform inscriptions from Tell F3 contain dedications to Enki (Marchesi above p. 111-112) and since the earliest of these inscriptions seems to date to Period 3B it is possible that the open-air shrine in Tell F3 was related to the introduction of a new object of worship, namely of Enki. A small frog made in copper was found in the open-air shrine (fig. 434) and it may be relevant as there is a special relationship between Enki and a frog in the Sumerian poem "Inanna and Enki" (Black & Green 1992 p. 85).

A renaissance of Dilmun culture takes place in Period 3B with the reintroduction of the round stamp seal and a new royal burial mound in Bahrain (Højlund & Hilton 2021 p. 86-88. Laursen 2017). At the same time, a distinct cultural interaction with the Sealand of South Mesopotamia continues and expands, evidenced not just in the introduction of Enki worship, but also in a dominating morphological influence on the production of pottery in a local ware (Højlund 1989 p. 10-11) and the emergence of the Failaka Figurative Style of stone vessel decoration (Hilton 2014 p. 104).

The written sources found in Mesopotamia and at Qala'at al-Bahrain indicate that Dilmun was incorporated by the Sealand during the reign of Ea-gāmil (1460-1451 BC), the last king of the Sealand, or one of his predecessors (André-Salvini & Cavigneaux forth.; Marchesi above p. 111).

In *Period 4A*, domestic settlement continues in Tell F3 (Kjærum & Højlund 2013 fig. 8. Højlund & Hilton 2021 fig. 93), the "Palace" in Tell F6 is reconstructed (Kjærum & Højlund 2013 fig. 134), and the original structure of the great temple is surrounded by a heavy wall (Højlund & Abu-Laban 2016 p. 91). Pottery production continues to follow new Mesopotamian models but significantly, still in a local ware. Cylinder seals of Mesopotamian style were now extensively utilised in Failaka and Bahrain (Pittman 2016. 2021. Potts 2010), but stamp seals in a new style also occur (Højlund & Hilton 2021 p. 87-88).

Dilmun remains a province of Mesopotamia (Reade 1986) as it no doubt already was during the last phase of the Sealand Dynasty, but administrative correspondence from a Kassite governor referring to the gods of Dilmun (Cornwall & Goetze 1952 p. 141) indicates that Dilmun retained an important aspect of its identity despite of its evident emulation of Mesopotamian culture.

Five phases of occupational architecture have been uncovered in Tell F3, belonging to what in this chapter is called the Dilmun settlement, that is, Periods 1-4A: One belonging to Period 2, one to Period 3A, two to Period 3B and one to Period 4A. All of them show clear evidence of having been abandoned after a period of habitation and left to decay. Excavation has revealed how the clay washed down the walls, the roofs and the upper part of the walls collapsed, and the rubble was covered with layers of windblown sand (Højlund & Hilton 2021 p. 163. Kjærum & Højlund 2013 p. 11 and 17). The alternative explanation, that the inhabitants quietly moved from old houses into new ones does not fit the evidence as, in this case, the stones in the walls of the old houses would surely have been used to build the new ones, instead of being left to slowly collapse and be covered by drift sand.

The same picture of abandonment, collapse and rebuilding has been noted between Phase I and II of the "Palace" (cf. Kjærum & Højlund 2013 p. 103).

This characteristic abandonment-collapse-and-rebuilding pattern indicates how fragile a settlement on the small island of Failaka was, exposed to the constantly changing political relations between Dilmun and South Mesopotamia, alternating between stability and conflict. At the same time, it shows how indispensable such a station on Failaka was for trade through the Gulf.

Failaka before and after Dilmun

The dichotomy between the domestic Tell F3 and the public Tell F6 that characterises the Dilmun settlement is absent from those settlements of Failaka pre-dating and post-dating the Dilmun settlement.

The *Ur III settlement* uncovered in the bottom layers of Tell F6 during the 2008-2012 excavations, belongs to the end of the 3rd millennium BC and predates the Dilmun colonization of the island (Højlund & Abu-Laban 2016 fig. 9). It has no counterpart in Tell F3. The large pottery inventory makes it certain that this is a settlement belonging to Mesopotamian culture, and the several cylinder seals for officials in the Babylonian administrative hierarchy indicate that it was established by the Ur III state's bureau of foreign trade with a view to supporting and controlling trade towards the southeast, to the land of Magan, in order to procure copper and other products (Højlund & Abu-Laban 2016 p. 251. Laursen & Steinkeller 2017).

Likewise, the *Period 4B settlement* that crowns Tell F3 has no contemporary occupation in Tell F6 and, rather than a row of houses in the normal Dilmun way, it is structured as a compound of large rooms organized around a central courtyard in a typical Mesopotamian style (Kjærum & Højlund 2013 p. 21 and 88, figs. 8 and 110). The size of the uncovered rooms varies from 17 to 32 m^2 with a courtyard of perhaps 55 m^2. Thus, it far exceeds the size of the earlier Dilmun private houses.

In Bahrain there was an unbroken tradition of producing Mesopotamian pottery shapes in a local sand-tempered ware from c. 1600 BC to around 1000 BC (Qala'at al-Bahrain Periods IIIa, IIIb and IIIc) (Højlund 2019 p. 163). Conversely, the Failaka Period 4B pottery reflects a genuine Mesopotamian tradition with mostly straw-tempered ware, as well as a sizeable component of glazed pottery and faience, evidence of a new technology developed in Mesopotamia. It may well be argued that the Period 4B assemblage on Failaka is the remains of a direct colonization from Mesopotamia rather than the continuation of a Dilmun settlement acculturated into a Mesopotamian lifestyle. A cuneiform inscription found in Tell F3 mentioning the Kassite ruler Adad-šuma-uṣur attests to Babylonian control of Failaka in the late 13th and early 12th centuries BC (Marchesi above p. 111) which may well be contemporary with Failaka Period 4B.

Appendix 1. Addendum: Stamp seals

The following three seals can be added to the stamp seals from the 1958-1963 excavations at Failaka previously published (Kjærum 1983).

Bifacial stamp seal, oval (fig. 659) (F3.61). Trench RM, 15.70 N, 1.25 W, 1.07 m below surface. The seal is known only through the photo, so material and thickness are unknown. Face 1: Two dotted circles and between them a Z-shaped figure. Along the edge a denticulated line. Face 2: Two dotted circles. Along the edge a denticulated line. The oval shape of the seal and the ornamentation have a close parallel in a scaraboid stamp seal from Tell F6 (Højlund & Abu-Laban 2016 fig. 750. Sperveslage 2016. Karim et al. 2017).

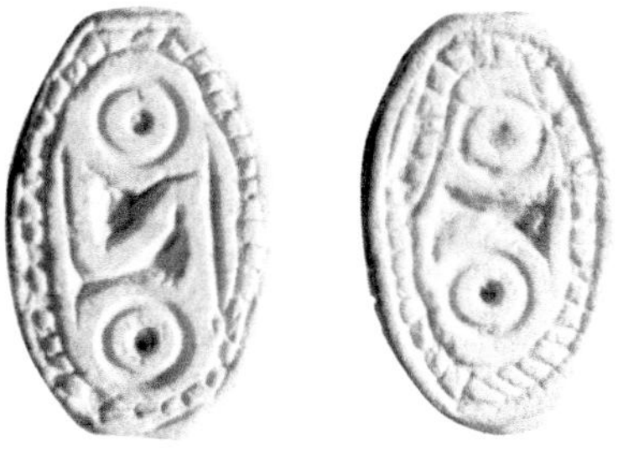

Fig. 659. 2:1.

Fragmented stamp seal in bright green-blue stone (Amazonite?) with cuneiform inscription on one side (Marchesi above p. 76: CFa 1, fig. 388) and the other side broken, c. 2.2 cm diameter, 0.3 cm thick (F3.109). Trench RM, 1-15 N, 1-2.45 m below surface, sieve.

Stamp seal fragment with cuneiform inscription on one side (Marchesi above p. 77, CFa 3, fig. 390) (F5. nw; KM1502). D 1.7, Th 0.8 cm. Green jasper. Unifacial (Style III). The boss is partially preserved and has part of a circle.

Appendix 2. Addendum: Stone vessels

by Anna Hilton

To the stone vessels from the 1958-1963 excavations at Failaka previously published (Hilton 2014), the following ten fragments of vessels in harder stones, not originally available to the author, should be added.

Fragment of open plain conical bowl, everted straight sloping rim with pointed lip and flat base with rounded base edge in calcite (Type 14) (fig. 660) (F3.bs). Trench A, 31.20 N, 1.30 E, level 6.86. Associated pottery: Period 2 (Casanova 1991 fig. 12: 151, Série XVIb and Pl. 11. Hilton 2016 p. 165, fig. 771. Hakemi 1997 p. 606, fig. Fb.7. Ciarla 1979 tab. 1.a, tab. 2.a. Potts 1989 p. 153-154, figs. 1 and 4).

Fragment of vessel with thick base in white calcite (fig. 661) (F3.bw). Trench B, 37.40 N, 3.20 E, level 7.47. Associated pottery: Period 3A/3B.

Fragment of the lower body of a vessel in calcite, wall thickness ranging from 1.5 to 2.5 cm, approximate diameter 18 cm (F3.kn). Trench Q, level 7.70-6.30.

Fragment of base of a vase in cream coloured, layered, calcite with traces of secondary external crushing (fig. 662) (F3.lj). Trench B, level 7.85-6.85. Associated pottery: Period 2, 3A/3B (Casanova 2003 figs. 761, 763-764. 1991 fig. 3: 41 and 46, Série IVa and fig. 4: 48-49, Série IVc).

Body sherd, 2.5 x 3.5 cm, of calcite vessel with c. 6 cm diameter, traces of secondary cutting (F3.ån). Trench AF, sieve.

Simple rim of calcite vessel (fig. 663) (F3.abj). Trench D, 40.25 N, 7.26 W, level 8.55. Associated pottery: Period 4A.

Fragment of bowl in brownish hard stone with uneven, eroded surface (fig. 664) (F3.aea). Trench G, level 9.43-8.93. Associated pottery: Period 4A.

Fragment of closed plain vase, vertical rim externally thickened lip in calcite (fig. 665) (F3.amo). From the area west of Trench RM (Casanova 1991 fig. 2: Série IIa and figs. 3-4: Série IVa-c. Hilton 2014 p. 30, 66, fig. 85 (type 39B). Hilton 2016 p. 165, figs. 772 and 773 (type 39B). Casanova 2003 p. 283. Potts, T.F. 1994 p. 228-232, tab. 6.2, fig. 1).

Jar with plain flat base with rounded edge of cream coloured, layered, calcite (fig. 666) (F3.aqh). Trench O, level c. 7.20-6.60. Associated pottery: Period 3A/4A (Hilton 2014 p. 35 and 67, fig. 87, type 58A).

Fragment of lower body of vessel in brownish, layered hard stone, wall thickness from 0.9 to 1.6 cm (fig. 667) (F3.aqø). Trench K, level c. 7.90-7.40. Associated pottery: Period 3A/4A.

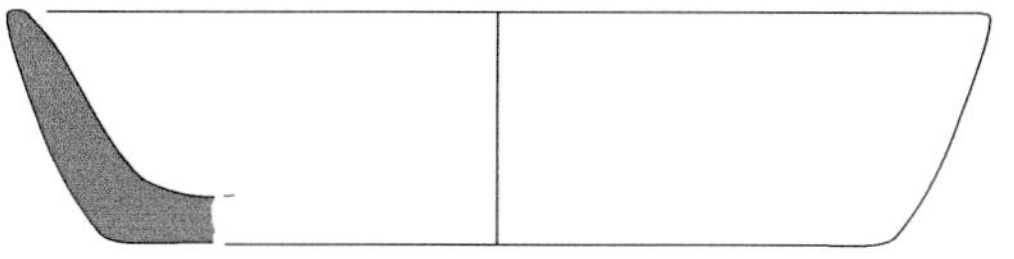

Fig. 660. 1:2.

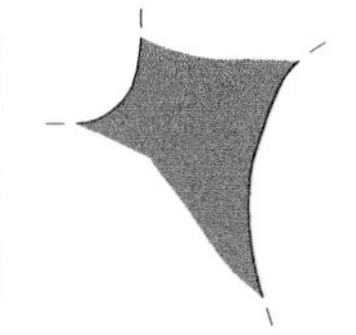

Fig. 661. 1:2.

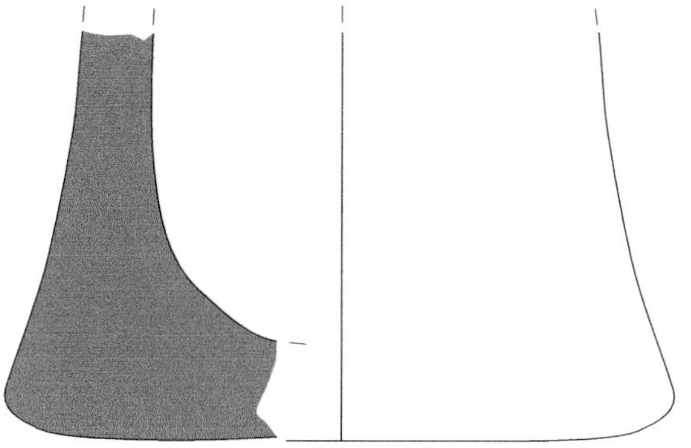

Fig. 662. 1:2.

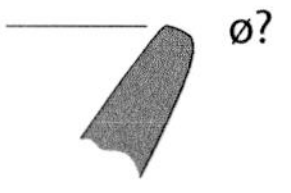

Fig. 663. 1:2.

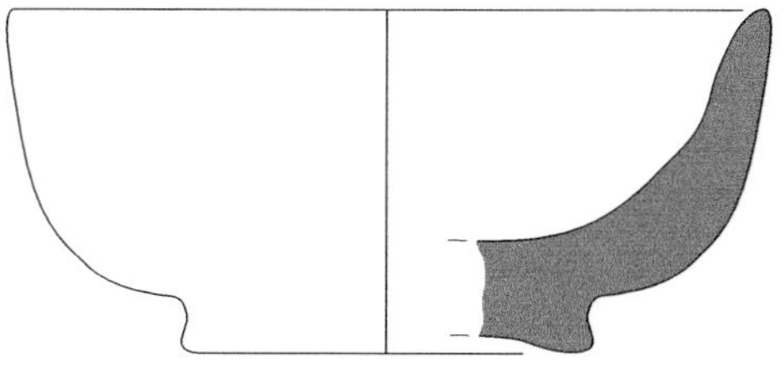

Fig. 664. 1:2.

Fig. 665. 1:2.

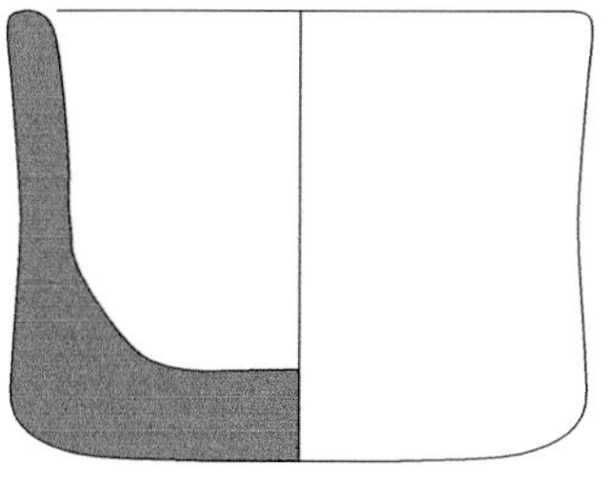

Fig. 666. 1:2.

Fig. 667. 1:2.

Appendix 3. Addendum: Beads

by Ann Andersson

To the 515 beads from the 1958-1963 excavations at Failaka previously published (Andersson 2022), the following 114 beads and bead fragments of semi-precious stones, shell and especially glass, which were not available until 2023, should be added. The beads have been classified using Beck's system from *Classification and Nomenclature of Beads and Pendants* (Beck 1928), which has also been applied in previous publications of beads from the Danish excavations on Failaka from 1958-1963, 2008-2012, and 2012-2017 (Andersson 2016, 2021 and 2022).

Three of the beads treated in this addendum come from Tell F3. Two were found in the sieve from Trenches AE and RM (F3.øp and F3.144) and have no dating information, while one (F3.afp) was found in Trench G and is tentatively dated to period 4A.

The vast majority of the beads, however, come from Tell F6 (n=111). Some belong to find numbers which have already been partially published (i.e. find numbers F6.362, F6.393, F6.406, F6.417, F6.482, F6.590, and F6.666 in Andersson 2022). Most of the glass beads come from Trenches D2, SN11-20, E2, and F2 located in the northern part of the "Palace", primarily rooms 2 and 3, and from vertical levels spanning from level -0.46 to -1.60. This corresponds well with the previously published material, where a large number of beads were found to be concentrated in this area and from the same levels (Andersson 2022 fig. 71). The most likely interpretation of this distribution pattern is that these beads were originally part of a hoard belonging to the last occupation of the building dating to Period 4A, and that this hoard was disturbed and scattered by the post-4A Period stone plundering of the building (Højlund & Abu-Laban 2016 p. 59). Due to the nature of the "Palace" building, as a storage and production facility, this could indicate a controlled storage of beads, presumably as trade goods, by a central authority (Andersson 2022 p. 38-40).

The glass beads are generally badly preserved and very fragmented, and in some glass beads only the inner clay core is still present. Part of the glass beads examined here has remains of a dark grey to black surface color on top of the white or light brown glass core (figs. 684, 691-692, 694, 696, 699-700).

Despite their poor state of preservation, most of the forms (spheres and barrels with circular cross sections) have good parallels in the previously published bead assemblage. A few beads stand out, being almost completely preserved. Especially notable are some of the relatively long glass barrel beads (figs. 680, 684 and 691). A new glass bead form seen in the assemblage is a long, slim barrel bead with slightly bulbous ends. A complete example of such a bead has been preserved (fig. 683) along with fragments, which may belong to the same type (see for instance fig. 678). No parallels for this bead form have been found in contemporary sites in the Gulf, Mesopotamia, or the Indus region.

A very fragmentary glass object (fig. 692) was originally a long bicone with a plano-convex cross section. This form may also be called a diamond shape. It may have been a glass bead or a kind of decorative glass inlay, but since no perforation is preserved, it is not possible to determine the function of the object. If it is a bead, the form is unknown in the previously published assemblage, but diamond shaped beads in different materials, forms and sizes are known to occur in other bead assemblages (cf. Limper 1988 p. 11-12).

Another form of glass beads previously recognized in the Failaka assemblage are eye-beads (Andersson 2022 p. 83, figs. 380 and 382). Fig. 687 is the same kind of eye-bead, although it is very badly preserved. It has lost most of its "pupil and iris" decoration through the disintegration of the glass and loss of original glass color.

A few of the glass beads have different types of decoration preserved that have not been observed in the previously published assemblage. A fragmented barrel bead (fig. 690) shows a design with a raised line of white glass wound in a spiral around the surface of the bead. Another type of decoration occurs on a cylinder bead (fig. 686) with a square cross section and a vertical design, demonstrated by two different colors. The design was created by applying a spiral glass design on the bead while the glass was still malleable, drawing the glass vertically down the middle of the surface, in one direction at one side of the bead and in the other direction at the other side, creating a pattern of chevrons in alternating colors.

All the beads made from semiprecious stone find good parallels in the previously published material, both in terms of form and materials. One agate eye-bead (fig. 668) is oval in profile and somewhat smaller than other eye-beads in the assemblage. It shows evidence of being broken during use and re-drilled, as it has both a horizontal and vertical drilling. The horizontal drilling is the secondary drilling. Another bead (fig. 673) is partially drilled from both ends, with the perforation almost meeting at the middle of the bead, but the last bit of drilling was never finished. A small number of blanks and semi-drilled beads was included in the previously published assemblage and may be either a result of accidental imports of unfinished products or evidence of a minor local production at Failaka (cf. Andersson 2022 p. 41 and 52).

The single shell "plate" pendant from Tell F3 (fig. 700) finds a good parallel in the already published bead assemblage (Andersson 2022 p. 33 and fig. 583). Both pendants are identified as made from spiny oyster shell (*spondylus exilis*).

Beads of semi-precious stone

Eye-bead (fig. 668) (F3.144). *Context:* Trench RM, sieve. *Type:* Varia; Eye-bead; XLVI.A.1.a. *Dimensions:* L 9.85, W 11.40, H 4.40 mm. *Material:* Agate. *Condition:* Fragmented. *Perforation:* Type II; Drilled horizontally and vertically (re-drilled after breakage); PD 2.00 and PD 1.60-1.70 mm.

Bead (fig. 669) (F3.øp). *Context:* Trench AE, sieve. *Type:* Long barrel/Circular; I.D.1.b. *Dimensions:* L 24.00, D 9.80 mm. *Material:* Agate. *Condition:* Complete. *Perforation:* Type II; PD 2.30-2.50 mm.

Bead (fig. 670) (F6.97). *Context:* Trench A1, 3.7 S, 2.85 W, level -0.26. *Type:* Long barrel/Circular; I.D.1.b. *Dimensions:* L 20.90, D 6.60 mm. *Material:* Jasper. *Condition:* Complete. *Perforation:* Type II; PD 2.50-2.70 mm.

Bead (fig. 671) (F6.217). *Context:* Trench SN11-20, 14 N, 0.50 W, level -0.53. *Type:* Long barrel/Semicircular; VI.D.1.b. *Dimensions:* L 23.80, W 14.15, H 8.45 mm. *Material:* Jasper. *Condition:* Complete. *Perforation:* Type II; PD 2.50 mm.

Bead (fig. 672) (F6.590.9). *Context:* Trench D2, 14.5-16 N, 0-1 W, level -1.28/1.58. *Type:* Long barrel/Circle and flat; VII.D.1.b. *Dimensions:* L 21.00, W 11.40, H 10.60 mm. *Material:* Agate. *Condition:* Complete. *Perforation:* Type II; PD 2.20-2.30 mm.

Bead (fig. 673) (F6.827). *Context:* Trench M2, sieve. *Type:* Long barrel/Circular; I.D.1.b. *Dimensions:* L 17.80, D. 7.20 mm. *Material:* Jasper. *Condition:* Complete. *Perforation:* Type II (semi-drilled from both ends); PD 2.00-2.20 mm.

Bead (fig. 674) (F6.without no. 56). *Context:* No provenience; Unknown; No information. *Type:* Long barrel/Circular; I.D.1.b. *Dimensions:* L 23.35, D 8.25 mm. *Material:* Agate. *Condition:* Complete. *Perforation:* Type II; PD 2.30-2.40 mm.

Bead (fig. 675) (F6.without no. 57). *Context:* No provenience; Unknown; No information. *Type:* Long barrel/Circular; I.D.1.b. *Dimensions:* L 18.85, D 8.70 mm. *Material:* Agate. *Condition:* Complete. *Perforation:* Type II; PD 2.50-2.95 mm.

Glass beads

Glass bead (fig. 676) (F6.361.1). *Context:* Trench D2, 15.5 N, 2.6 W, level -0.46. *Type:* Long barrel/Circular; I.D.1.b. *Dimensions:* L 23.00, D 8.75 mm. *Condition:* Fragmented. *Perforation:* Type IV; PD 2.15 mm.

Glass bead (fig. 677) (F6.361.2). *Context:* Trench D2, 15.5 N, 2.6 W, level -0.46. *Type:* Long barrel/Circular; I.D.1.b. *Dimensions:* L 21.60, D 7.30 mm. *Condition:* Fragmented. *Perforation:* Type IV; PD 3.20 mm.

Glass bead (fig. 678) (F6.361.3). *Context:* Trench D2, 15.5 N, 2.6 W, level -0.46. *Type:* Varia; Long Barrel/Circular with bulbous ends; I.D.1.b. *Dimensions:* L 13.20, D 4.50 mm. *Condition:* Fragmented. *Perforation:* Type IV; PD 1.60 mm.

Glass bead (fig. 679) (F6.362.15). *Context:* Trench D2, 14-15 N, 3.5-4 W, level -0.59. *Type:* Long barrel/Circular; I.D.1.b. *Dimensions:* L 25.10, D 8.45 mm. *Condition:* Fragmented. *Perforation:* Type IV; PD 2.80 mm.

Glass bead (fig. 680) (F6.362.16). *Context:* Trench D2, 14-15 N, 3.5-4 W, level -0.59. *Type:* Long Barrel/Circular, I.D.1.b. *Dimensions:* L 29.25, D 8.40 mm. *Condition:* Fragmented. *Perforation:* Type IV; PD 2.80 mm.

Glass bead (fig. 681) (F6.362.17). *Context:* Trench D2, 14-15 N, 3.5-4 W, level -0.59. *Type:* Oblate/Circular; I.B.1.a. *Dimensions:* L 5.95, D 8.20 mm. *Condition:* Fragmented. *Perforation:* Type IV; PD 2.10-2.30 mm.

Glass bead (F6.362.18). *Context:* Trench D2, 14-15 N, 3.5-4 W, level -0.59. *Type:* Oblate/Circular; I.B.1.a. *Dimensions:* L 10.60, D 12.00 mm. *Condition:* Fragmented. *Perforation:* Type IV; PD 2.50 mm.

Glass bead (F6.362.19). *Context:* Trench D2, 14-15 N, 3.5-4 W, level -0.59. *Type:* Long barrel/Circular; I.D.1.b. *Dimensions:* L 11.60, D 6.85 mm. *Condition:* Fragmented. *Perforation:* Type IV; PD 2.60 mm.

Glass bead (F6.362.20). *Context:* Trench D2, 14-15 N, 3.5-4 W, level -0.59. *Type:* Long barrel/Circular; I.D.1.b. *Dimensions:* L 10.10, D 9.40 mm. *Condition:* Fragmented. *Perforation:* Type IV; PD 2.20 mm.

Glass bead (F6.362.21). *Context:* Trench D2, 14-15 N, 3.5-4 W, level -0.59. *Type:* Long barrel/Circular; I.D.1.b. *Dimensions:* L 8.05, D 7.30 mm. *Condition:* Fragmented. *Perforation:* Type IV; PD 2.50 mm.

Glass bead (F6.362.22). *Context:* Trench D2, 14-15 N, 3.5-4 W, level -0.59. *Type:* Long barrel/Circular; I.D.1.b. *Dimensions:* L 10.90, D 6.10 mm. *Condition:* Fragmented. *Perforation:* Type IV; PD 2.55 mm.

Glass bead (F6.362.23). *Context:* Trench D2, 14-15 N, 3.5-4 W, level -0.59. *Type:* Unidentified. *Dimensions:* L 8.00, D 8.60 mm. *Condition:* Fragmented. *Perforation:* Type IV; PD 2.80 mm.

Glass bead (F6.362.24). *Context:* Trench D2, 14-15 N, 3.5-4 W, level -0.59. *Type:* Long barrel/Circular; I.D.1.b. *Dimensions:* L 5.80, D 5.40 mm. *Condition:* Fragmented. *Perforation:* Type IV; PD 1.50 mm.

Glass bead (F6.362.25). *Context:* Trench D2, 14-15 N, 3.5-4 W, level -0.59. *Type:* Long barrel/Circular; I.D.1.b. *Dimensions:* L 10.75, W 6.55 mm. *Condition:* Fragmented. *Perforation:* Type IV; PD 2.30 mm.

Glass bead (F6.362.26). *Context:* Trench D2, 14-15 N, 3.5-4 W, level -0.59. *Type:* Oblate /Circular; I.B.1.a. *Dimensions:* L 8.70, D 10.50 mm. *Condition:* Fragmented. *Perforation:* Not preserved.

Glass bead (F6.362.27). *Context:* Trench D2, 14-15 N, 3.5-4 W, level -0.59. *Type:* Long barrel/Circular; I.D.1.b. *Dimensions:* L 9.60, D 5.50 mm. *Condition:* Fragmented. *Perforation:* Type IV; PD 2.20 mm.

Glass bead (fig. 682) (F6.362.28). *Context:* Trench D2, 14-15 N, 3.5-4 W, level -0.59. *Type:* Oblate/Circular; I.B.1.a. *Dimensions:* L 6.60, D 9.30 mm. *Condition:* Fragmented. *Perforation:* Type IV; PD 3.25 mm.

Glass bead (F6.362.29). *Context:* Trench D2, 14-15 N, 3.5-4 W, level -0.59. *Type:* Unidentified. *Dimensions:* L 9.00, W 13.30 mm. *Condition:* Fragmented. *Perforation:* Not preserved.

Glass bead (F6.362.30). *Context:* Trench D2, 14-15 N, 3.5-4 W, level -0.59. *Type:* Unidentified. *Dimensions:* L 11.30, W 8.00 mm. *Condition:* Fragmented. *Perforation:* Not preserved.

Glass bead (F6.362.31). *Context:* Trench D2, 14-15 N, 3.5-4 W, level -0.59. *Type:* Long barrel/Circular; I.D.1.b. *Dimensions:* L 14.90, D 8.50 mm. *Condition:* Fragmented. *Perforation:* Type IV; PD 2.60 mm.

Glass bead (F6.362.32). *Context:* Trench D2, 14-15 N, 3.5-4 W, level -0.59. *Type:* Oblate /Circular; I.B.1.a. *Dimensions:* L 6.00, D 10.50 mm. *Condition:* Fragmented. *Perforation:* Type IV; PD 1.90 mm.

Glass bead (F6.362.33). *Context:* Trench D2, 14-15 N, 3.5-4 W, level -0.59. *Type:* Long barrel/Circular; I.D.1.b. *Dimensions:* L 9.10, D 6.60 mm. *Condition:* Fragmented. *Perforation:* Type IV; PD 2.40 mm.

Glass bead (F6.362.34). *Context:* Trench D2, 14-15 N, 3.5-4 W, level -0.59. *Type:* Long barrel/Circular; I.D.1.b. *Dimensions:* L 11.35, D 7.00 mm. *Condition:* Fragmented. *Perforation:* Type IV; PD 2.35 mm.

Glass bead (F6.362.35). *Context:* Trench D2, 14-15 N, 3.5-4 W, level -0.59. *Type:* Long barrel/Circular; I.D.1.b. *Dimensions:* L 11.35, D 6.60 mm. *Condition:* Fragmented. *Perforation:* Type IV; PD 2.35 mm.

Glass bead (F6.362.36). *Context:* Trench D2, 14-15 N, 3.5-4 W, level -0.59. *Type:* Long barrel/Circular; I.D.1.b. *Dimensions:* L 10.10, D 6.20 mm. *Condition:* Fragmented. *Perforation:* Type IV; PD 2.60-2.65 mm.

Glass bead (F6.362.37). *Context:* Trench D2, 14-15 N, 3.5-4 W, level -0.59. *Type:* Long barrel/Circular; I.D.1.b. *Dimensions:* L 14.30, D 8.90 mm. *Condition:* Fragmented. *Perforation:* Type IV; PD 2.65 mm.

Glass bead (F6.362.38). *Context:* Trench D2, 14-15 N, 3.5-4 W, level -0.59. *Type:* Long barrel/Circular; I.D.1.b. *Dimensions:* L 9.60, D 9.10 mm. *Condition:* Fragmented. *Perforation:* Type IV; PD 2.80 mm.

Glass bead (F6.362.39). *Context:* Trench D2, 14-15 N, 3.5-4 W, level -0.59. *Type:* Oblate/Circular; I.B.1.a. *Dimensions:* L 4.70, D 8.80 mm. *Condition:* Fragmented. *Perforation:* Type IV; PD 2.45 mm.

Glass bead (F6.362.40). *Context:* Trench D2, 14-15 N, 3.5-4 W, level -0.59. *Type:* Unidentified. *Dimensions:* L 8.35, W 8.00, H 6.15 mm. *Condition:* Fragmented. *Perforation:* Not preserved.

Glass bead (F6.362.41). *Context:* Trench D2, 14-15 N, 3.5-4 W, level -0.59. *Type:* Oblate/Circular; I.B.1.a. *Dimensions:* L 4.15, D 7.75 mm. *Condition:* Fragmented. *Perforation:* Type IV; PD 2.10 mm.

Glass bead (F6.362.42). *Context:* Trench D2, 14-15 N, 3.5-4 W, level -0.59. *Type:* Oblate/Circular; I.B.1.a. *Dimensions:* L 6.40, D 8.25 mm. *Condition:* Fragmented. *Perforation:* Type IV; PD 2.60 mm.

Glass bead (fig. 683) (F6.393.4). *Context:* Trench D2, 14-15 N, 3.5-4 W, level -0.96. *Type:* Varia; Long Barrel/Circular with bulbous ends; I.D.1.b. *Dimensions:* L 35.10, D 6.00 mm. *Condition:* Fragmented. *Perforation:* Type IV; PD 1.70 mm.

Glass bead (fig. 684) (F6.393.5). *Context:* Trench D2, 14-15 N, 3.5-4 W, level -0.96. *Type:* Long barrel/Circular; I.D.1.b. *Dimensions:* L 26.00, D 10.80 mm. *Condition:* Fragmented. *Perforation:* Type IV; PD 3.60 mm.

Glass bead (fig. 685) (F6.393.6). *Context:* Trench D2, 14-15 N, 3.5-4 W, level -0.96. *Type:* Long barrel/Circular; I.D.1.b. *Dimensions:* L 24.00, D 8.00 mm. *Condition:* Fragmented. *Perforation:* Type IV; PD 2.50 mm.

Glass bead (F6.393.7). *Context:* Trench D2, 14-15 N, 3.5-4 W, level -0.96. *Type:* Long barrel/Circular; I.D.1.b. *Dimensions:* L 19.00, D 8.20 mm. *Condition:* Fragmented. *Perforation:* Type IV; PD 2.25 mm.

Glass bead (F6.393.8). *Context:* Trench D2, 14-15 N, 3.5-4 W, level -0.96. *Type:* Long barrel/Circular. *Dimensions:* L 13.10, D 7.80 mm. *Condition:* Fragmented. *Perforation:* Type IV; PD 2.80 mm.

Glass bead (F6.393.9). *Context:* Trench D2, 14-15 N, 3.5-4 W, level -0.96. *Type:* Long barrel/Circular; I.D.1.b. *Dimensions:* L 14.50, D 7.20 mm. *Condition:* Fragmented. *Perforation:* Type IV; PD 1.00 mm.

Glass bead (fig. 686) (F6.393.10). *Context:* Trench D2, 14-15 N, 3.5-4 W, level -0.96. *Type:* Cylinder/Square; IX.C.2.b. *Dimensions:* L 15.50, W 7.50, H 7.25 mm. *Condition:* Fragmented. *Perforation:* Type IV; PD 2.40 mm.

Glass bead (F6.393.11). *Context:* Trench D2, 14-15 N, 3.5-4 W, level -0.96. *Type:* Long barrel/Circular; I.D.1.b. *Dimensions:* L 14.60, D 8.00 mm. *Condition:* Fragmented. *Perforation:* Type IV; PD 3.15 mm.

Glass bead (F6.393.12). *Context:* Trench D2, 14-15 N, 3.5-4 W, level -0.96. *Type:* Long barrel/Circular; I.D.1.b. *Dimensions:* L 8.20, D 14.00 mm. *Condition:* Fragmented. *Perforation:* Type IV; PD 3.50 mm.

Glass bead (F6.393.13). *Context:* Trench D2, 14-15 N, 3.5-4 W, level -0.96. *Type:* Long barrel/Cylinder; I.D.1.b. *Dimensions:* L 15.65, D 7.30 mm. *Condition:* Fragmented. *Perforation:* Type IV; PD 1.50 mm.

Glass bead (F6.393.14). *Context:* Trench D2, 14-15 N, 3.5-4 W, level -0.96. *Type:* Long barrel/Circular; I.D.1.b. *Dimensions:* L 8.35, D 6.00 mm. *Condition:* Fragmented. *Perforation:* Type IV; PD 1.50 mm.

Glass bead (F6.393.15). *Context:* Trench D2, 14-15 N, 3.5-4 W, level -0.96. *Type:* Long barrel/Circular; I.D.1.b. *Dimensions:* L 18.55, D 5.70 mm. *Condition:* Fragmented. *Perforation:* Type IV; PD 1.00 mm.

Glass bead (F6.393.16). *Context:* Trench D2, 14-15 N, 3.5-4 W, level -0.96. *Type:* Long barrel/Circular; I.D.1.b. *Dimensions:* L 6.70, D 6.80 mm. *Condition:* Fragmented. *Perforation:* Type IV; PD 2.50 mm.

Glass bead (F6.393.17). *Context:* Trench D2, 14-15 N, 3.5-4 W, level -0.96. *Type:* Long barrel/Circular; I.D.1.b. *Dimensions:* L 8.20, D 6.00 mm. *Condition:* Fragmented. *Perforation:* Type IV; PD 2.00 mm.

Glass bead (F6.393.18). *Context:* Trench D2, 14-15 N, 3.5-4 W, level -0.96. *Type:* Long barrel/Circular; I.D.1.b. *Dimensions:* L 8.80, D 4.70 mm. *Condition:* Fragmented. *Perforation:* Type IV; PD 1.50 mm.

Glass bead (F6.393.19). *Context:* Trench D2, 14-15 N, 3.5-4 W, level -0.96. *Type:* Long barrel/Circular; I.D.1.b. *Dimensions:* L 8.40, D 7.85 mm. *Condition:* Fragmented. *Perforation:* Type IV; PD 2.40 mm.

Glass bead (F6.393.20). *Context:* Trench D2, 14-15 N, 3.5-4 W, level -0.96. *Type:* Long barrel/Circular; I.D.1.b. *Dimensions:* L 6.00, D 6.00 mm. *Condition:* Fragmented. *Perforation:* Type IV; PD 2.15 mm.

Glass bead (F6.393.21). *Context:* Trench D2, 14-15 N, 3.5-4 W, level -0.96. *Type:* Unidentified. *Dimensions:* L 9.50, W 7.30, H 4.20 mm. *Condition:* Fragmented. *Perforation:* Not preserved.

Glass bead (F6.393.22). *Context:* Trench D2, 14-15 N, 3.5-4 W, level -0.96. *Type:* Long cylinder/Circular; I.D.2.b. *Dimensions:* L 8.00, D 4.85 mm. *Condition:* Fragmented. *Perforation:* Type IV; PD 1.80 mm.

Glass bead (F6.393.23). *Context:* Trench D2, 14-15 N, 3.5-4 W, level -0.96. *Type:* Long cylinder/Circular; I.D.2.b. *Dimensions:* L 11.75, D 6.00 mm. *Condition:* Fragmented. *Perforation:* Type IV; PD 1.30-1.90 mm.

Glass bead (F6.393.24). *Context:* Trench D2, 14-15 N, 3.5-4 W, level -0.96. *Type:* Long barrel/Circular; I.D.1.b. *Dimensions:* L 9.65, D 10.50 mm. *Condition:* Fragmented. *Perforation:* Type IV; PD 2.40 mm.

Glass bead (F6.393.25). *Context:* Trench D2, 14-15 N, 3.5-4 W, level -0.96. *Type:* Oblate /Circular; I.B.1.a. *Dimensions:* L 4.15, D 6.40 mm. *Condition:* Fragmented. *Perforation:* Type IV; PD 2.70 mm.

Glass bead (F6.393.26). *Context:* Trench D2, 14-15 N, 3.5-4 W, level -0.96. *Type:* Unidentified. *Dimensions:* L 7.75, W 8.75 mm. *Condition:* Fragmented. *Perforation:* Not preserved.

Glass bead (F6.393.27). *Context:* Trench D2, 14-15 N, 3.5-4 W, level -0.96. *Type:* Long cylinder/Circular; I.D.2.b. *Dimensions:* L 15.50, D 3.50 mm. *Material:* Glass/Clay. *Condition:* Fragmented. *Perforation:* Type IV; PD 1.85 mm.

Glass bead (F6.393.28). *Context:* Trench D2, 14-15 N, 3.5-4 W, level -0.96. *Type:* Long cylinder/Circular; I.D.2.b. *Dimensions:* L 9.50, D 3.50 mm. *Material:* Glass/Clay. *Condition:* Fragmented. *Perforation:* Type IV; PD 1.80 mm.

Glass bead (F6.393.29). *Context:* Trench D2, 14-15 N, 3.5-4 W, level -0.96. *Type:* Long cylinder/Circular; I.D.2.b. *Dimensions:* L 11.35, D 3.50 mm. *Material:* Glass/Clay. *Condition:* Fragmented. *Perforation:* Type IV; PD 1.90 mm.

Glass bead (F6.393.30). *Context:* Trench D2, 14-15 N, 3.5-4 W, level -0.96. *Type:* Long cylinder/Circular; I.D.2.b. *Dimensions:* L 4.70, D 3.20 mm. *Material:* Glass/Clay. *Condition:* Fragmented. *Perforation:* Type IV; PD 1.95 mm.

Glass bead (F6.393.31). *Context:* Trench D2, 14-15 N, 3.5-4 W, level -0.96. *Type:* Long cylinder/Circular; I.D.2.b. *Dimensions:* L 6.70, D 5.50 mm. *Condition:* Fragmented. *Perforation:* Not preserved.

Glass bead (F6.393.32). *Context:* Trench D2, 14-15 N, 3.5-4 W, level -0.96. *Type:* Unidentified. *Dimensions:* L 8.85, W 6.85 mm. *Condition:* Fragmented. *Perforation:* Not preserved.

Glass eye-bead (fig. 687) (F6.406.7). *Context:* Trench D2, 13-15 N, 2.5-4 W, level -1.08. *Type:* Short Barrel/Plano-convex; V.B.1.b. *Dimensions:* L 19.70, W 25.60, H 9.30 mm. *Condition:* Fragmented. *Perforation:* Type IV; PD 3.30 mm.

Glass bead (F6.406.8). *Context:* Trench D2, 13-15 N, 2.5-4 W, level -1.08. *Type:* Long barrel/Circular; I.D.1.b. *Dimensions:* L 15.10, D 7.90 mm. *Condition:* Fragmented. *Perforation:* Type IV; PD 1.90 mm.

Glass bead (fig. 688) (F6.406.9). *Context:* Trench D2, 13-15 N, 2.5-4 W, level -1.08. *Type:* Long barrel/Circular; I.D.1.b. *Dimensions:* L 14.80, D 10.35 mm. *Condition:* Fragmented. *Perforation:* Type IV; PD 2.00 mm.

Glass bead (fig. 689) (F6.406.10). *Context:* Trench D2, 13-15 N, 2.5-4 W, level -1.08. *Type:* Long barrel/Circular; I.D.1.b. *Dimensions:* L 19.50 D 6.50 mm. *Condition:* Fragmented. *Perforation:* Type IV; PD 2.40 mm.

Glass bead (F6.406.11). *Context:* Trench D2, 13-15 N, 2.5-4 W, level -1.08. *Type:* Long barrel/Circular; I.D.1.b. *Dimensions:* L 13.20, D 7.25 mm. *Condition:* Fragmented. *Perforation:* Type IV; PD 3.20 mm.

Glass bead (F6.406.12). *Context:* Trench D2, 13-15 N, 2.5-4 W, level -1.08. *Type:* Long barrel/Circular; I.D.1.b. *Dimensions:* L 27.90, D 10.90 mm. *Condition:* Fragmented. *Perforation:* Type IV; PD 2.90 mm.

Glass bead (F6.406.13). *Context:* Trench D2, 13-15 N, 2.5-4 W, level -1.08. *Type:* Long barrel/Circular. *Dimensions:* L 17.55, D 9.75 mm. *Condition:* Fragmented. *Perforation:* Type IV; PD 4.50 mm.

Glass bead (F6.406.14). *Context:* Trench D2, 13-15 N, 2.5-4 W, level -1.08. *Type:* Long barrel/Circular. *Dimensions:* L 18.60, D 5.75 mm. *Condition:* Fragmented. *Perforation:* Type IV; PD 2.00 mm.

Glass bead (F6.417.12). *Context:* Trench D2, 13-15 N, 2.5-4 W, level -1.08. *Type:* Long barrel/Circular; I.D.1.b. *Dimensions:* L 24.60, D 10.35 mm. *Condition:* Fragmented. *Perforation:* Type IV; PD 2.70 mm.

Glass bead (F6.417.13). *Context:* Trench D2, 13-15 N, 2.5-4 W, level -1.08. *Type:* Long barrel/Circular; I.D.1.b. *Dimensions:* L 27.60, D 11.50 mm. *Condition:* Fragmented. *Perforation:* Type IV; PD 3.50 mm.

Glass bead (F6.417.14). *Context:* Trench D2, 13-15 N, 2.5-4 W, level -1.08. *Type:* Long barrel/Circular; I.D.1.b. *Dimensions:* L 22.00, D 9.10 mm. *Condition:* Fragmented. *Perforation:* Type IV; PD 2.85 mm.

Glass bead (F6.417.15). *Context:* Trench D2, 13-15 N, 2.5-4 W, level -1.08. *Type:* Long barrel/Circular; I.D.1.b. *Dimensions:* L 20.50, D 9.20 mm. *Condition:* Fragmented. *Perforation:* Type IV; PD 2.20 mm.

Glass bead (fig. 690) (F6.417.16). *Context:* Trench D2, 13-15 N, 2.5-4 W, level -1.08. *Type:* Long barrel/Circular; I.D.1.b. *Dimensions:* L 19.40, D 6.40 mm. *Condition:* Fragmented. *Perforation:* Type IV; PD 2.75 mm.

Glass bead (fig. 691) (F6.417.17). *Context:* Trench D2, 13-15 N, 2.5-4 W, level -1.08. *Type:* Long barrel/Circular; I.D.1.b. *Dimensions:* L 41.20, D 10.30 mm. *Condition:* Fragmented. *Perforation:* Type IV; PD 2.20 mm.

Glass bead (F6.417.18). *Context:* Trench D2, 13-15 N, 2.5-4 W, level -1.08. *Type:* Oblate/Circular; I.B.1.a. *Dimensions:* L 6.20, D 8.30 mm. *Condition:* Fragmented. *Perforation:* Type IV; PD 1.70 mm.

Glass bead (F6.417.19). *Context:* Trench D2, 13-15 N, 2.5-4 W, level -1.08. *Type:* Long barrel/Circular; I.D.1.b. *Dimensions:* L 9.50, D 9.00 mm. *Condition:* Fragmented. *Perforation:* Type IV; PD 2.50 mm.

Glass bead (F6.417.20). *Context:* Trench D2, 13-15 N, 2.5-4 W, level -1.08. *Type:* Long barrel/Circular; I.D.1.b. *Dimensions:* L 9.60, D 5.60 mm. *Condition:* Fragmented. *Perforation:* Type IV; PD 2.50 mm.

Glass bead (F6.417.21). *Context:* Trench D2, 13-15 N, 2.5-4 W, level -1.08. *Type:* Oblate /Circular; I.B.1.a. *Dimensions:* L 7.50, W 7.30. *Condition:* Fragmented. *Perforation:* Not preserved.

Glass bead (F6.417.22). *Context:* Trench D2, 13-15 N, 2.5-4 W, level -1.08. *Type:* Unidentified. *Dimensions:* L 8.30, W 7.00 mm. *Condition:* Fragmented. *Perforation:* Not preserved.

Glass bead (F6.417.23). *Context:* Trench D2, 13-15 N, 2.5-4 W, level -1.08. *Type:* Oblate/Circular; I.B.1.a. *Dimensions:* L 8.30, W 6.65 mm. *Condition:* Fragmented. *Perforation:* Type IV; PD 2.20 mm.

Glass bead (F6.417.24). *Context:* Trench D2, 13-15 N, 2.5-4 W, level -1.08. *Type:* Long barrel/Circular; I.D.1.b. *Dimensions:* L 18.40, D 10.30 mm. *Condition:* Fragmented. *Perforation:* Type IV; PD 2.20 mm.

Glass bead (F6.417.25). *Context:* Trench D2, 13-15 N, 2.5-4 W, level -1.08. *Type:* Long barrel/Circular; I.D.1.b. *Dimensions:* L 6.30, D 9.00 mm. *Condition:* Fragmented. *Perforation:* Type IV; PD 2.10 mm.

Glass bead (F6.417.26). *Context:* Trench D2, 13-15 N, 2.5-4 W, level -1.08. *Type:* Long cylinder/Circular; I.D.2.b. *Dimensions:* L 13.40, D 4.20 mm. *Condition:* Fragmented. *Perforation:* Type IV; PD 1.50 mm.

Glass bead (F6.417.27). *Context:* Trench D2, 13-15 N, 2.5-4 W, level -1.08. *Type:* Long barrel/Circular; I.D.1.b. *Dimensions:* L 7.00, D 7.80 mm. *Condition:* Fragmented. *Perforation:* Type IV; PD 3.90 mm.

Glass bead (F6.417.28). *Context:* Trench D2, 13-15 N, 2.5-4 W, level -1.08. *Type:* Long barrel/Circular; I.D.1.b. *Dimensions:* L 10.50, D 6.25 mm. *Condition:* Fragmented. *Perforation:* Type IV; PD 2.00 mm.

Glass bead (F6.417.29). *Context:* Trench D2, 13-15 N, 2.5-4 W, level -1.08. *Type:* Long barrel/Circular; I.D.1.b. *Dimensions:* L 10.30, D 7.85 mm. *Condition:* Fragmented. *Perforation:* Type IV; PD 1.40 mm.

Glass bead (F6.417.30). *Context:* Trench D2, 13-15 N, 2.5-4 W, level -1.08. *Type:* Long cylinder/Circular; I.D.2.b. *Dimensions:* L 11.10, D 4.15 mm. *Condition:* Fragmented. *Perforation:* Type IV; PD 1.30 mm.

Glass bead (F6.417.31). *Context:* Trench D2, 13-15 N, 2.5-4 W, level -1.08. *Type:* Long barrel/Circular; I.D.1.b. *Dimensions:* L 11.20, D 6.60 mm. *Condition:* Fragmented. *Perforation:* Type IV; PD 2.10 mm.

Glass bead (F6.417.32). *Context:* Trench D2, 13-15 N, 2.5-4 W, level -1.08. *Type:* Long barrel/Circular; I.D.1.b. *Dimensions:* L 11.80, D 6.50 mm. *Condition:* Fragmented. *Perforation:* Type IV; PD 2.70 mm.

Glass bead (F6.417.33). *Context:* Trench D2, 13-15 N, 2.5-4 W, level -1.08. *Type:* Long barrel/Circular; I.D.1.b. *Dimensions:* L 8.15, D 5.70 mm. *Condition:* Fragmented. *Perforation:* Type IV; PD 2.00 mm.

Glass inlay or bead (fig. 692) (F6.417.34). *Context:* Trench D2, 13-15 N, 2.5-4 W, level -1.08. *Type:* Varia; Long bicone/Plano-convex; V.D.2.e. *Dimensions:* L 26.80, W 16.30, H 6.60 mm. *Condition:* Fragmented. *Perforation:* Not preserved.

Glass bead (fig. 693) (F6.482.2). *Context:* Trench D2, 16 N, 3-4 W, level -1.60. *Type:* Oblate/Circular; I.B.1.a. *Dimensions:* L 14.25, D 18.60 mm. *Condition:* Fragmented. *Perforation:* Type IV; PD 4.00-4.50 mm.

Glass bead (F6.482.3). *Context:* Trench D2, 16 N, 3-4 W, level -1.60. *Type:* Oblate/Circular; I.B.1.a. *Dimensions:* L 8.00, D 10.80 mm. *Condition:* Fragmented. *Perforation:* Type IV; PD 2.00.2.50 mm.

Glass bead (fig. 694) (F6.482.4). *Context:* Trench D2, 16 N, 3-4 W, level -1.60. *Type:* Standard Cone/Circular; I.C.2.c. *Dimensions:* L 14.35, D 13.95 mm. *Condition:* Fragmented. *Perforation:* Type IV; PD 3.50 mm.

Glass bead (fig. 695) (F6.482.5). *Context:* Trench D2, 16 N, 3-4 W, level -1.60. *Type:* Long barrel/Circular; I.D.1.b. *Dimensions:* L 18.70, D 6.60 mm. *Condition:* Fragmented. *Perforation:* Type IV; PD 2.00 mm.

Glass bead (F6.482.6). *Context:* Trench D2, 16 N, 3-4 W, level -1.60. *Type:* Long Barrel/Circular; I.D.1.b. *Dimensions:* L 24.15, D 7.50 mm. *Condition:* Fragmented. *Perforation:* Type IV; PD 1.90 mm.

Glass bead (fig. 696) (F6.590.10). *Context:* Baulk between Trenches D2 and SN11-20, 14.5 -16 N, 0-1 W, level -1.28-1.56. *Type:* Oblate/Circular; I.B.1.a. *Dimensions:* L 8.30, D 9.60 mm. *Condition:* Complete. *Perforation:* Type IV; PD 2.20-2.70 mm.

Glass bead (fig. 697) (F6.590.11). *Context:* Baulk between Trenches D2 and SN11-20, 14.5-16 N, 0-1 W, level -1.28-1.56. *Type:* Oblate/Circular; I.B.1.a. *Dimensions:* L 10.15, D 13.10 mm. *Condition:* Complete. *Perforation:* Type IV; PD 3.35 mm.

Glass bead (fig. 698) (F6.590.12). *Context:* Baulk between Trenches D2 and SN11-20, 14.5-16 N, 0-1 W, level -1.28-1.56. *Type:* Long barrel/Circular; I.D.1.b. *Dimensions:* L 15.60, D 6.60 mm. *Condition:* Complete. *Perforation:* Type IV; PD 1.60 mm.

Glass bead (F6.666.4). *Context:* Trench F2, 13 N, 5 W, level -0.78. *Type:* Long barrel/Circular; I.D.1.b. *Dimensions:* L 17.20, D 8.65 mm. *Condition:* Fragmented. *Perforation:* Type IV; PD 3.10 mm.

Glass bead (F6.666.5). *Context:* Trench F2, 13 N, 5 W, level -0.78. *Type:* Long barrel/Circular; I.D.1.b. *Dimensions:* L 15.20, D 5.50 mm. *Material:* Glass/Clay. *Condition:* Fragmented. *Perforation:* Type IV; PD 0.50 mm.

Glass bead (F6.666.6). *Context:* Trench F2, 13 N, 5 W, level -0.78. *Type:* Oblate/Circular; I.B.1.a. *Dimensions:* L 7.75, W 9.90, H 4.25 mm. *Condition:* Fragmented. *Perforation:* Type IV; Not preserved.

Glass bead (F6.666.7). *Context:* Trench F2, 13 N, 5 W, level -0.78. *Type:* Long barrel/Circular; I.D.1.b. *Dimensions:* L 10.50, D 7.30 mm. *Condition:* Fragmented. *Perforation:* Type IV; PD 2.20 mm.

Glass bead (F6.666.8). *Context:* Trench F2, 13 N, 5 W, level -0.78. *Type:* Long barrel/Circular; I.D.1.b. *Dimensions:* L 7.15, D 2.55 mm. *Condition:* Fragmented. *Perforation:* Type IV; PD 1.50 mm.

Glass bead (fig. 699) (F6.895). *Context:* Trench F2, 14 N, 6-7 W, level -1.82. *Type:* Long barrel/Circular; I.D.1.b. *Dimensions:* L 19.00, D 7.80 mm. *Condition:* Complete. *Perforation:* Type IV; PD 2.20 mm.

Shell beads

Shell bead (fig. 700) (F3.afp). *Context:* Trench G, between c. level 8.93-8.43. *Type:* Varia (shell "plate" pendant). *Dimensions:* L 26.00, W 16.00, H 2.00 mm. *Material:* Shell (spiny oyster; *Spondylus Exilis*). *Condition:* Complete. *Perforation:* Type III; PD 2.30-2.60 mm.

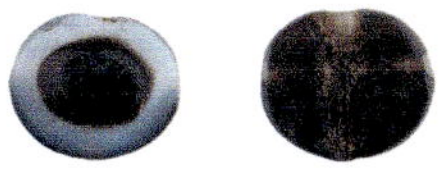
Fig. 668. 1:1.

Fig. 669. 1:1.

Fig. 670. 1:1.

Fig. 671. 1:1.

Fig. 672. 1:1.

Fig. 673. 1:1.

Fig. 674. 1:1.

Fig. 675. 1:1.

Fig. 676. 1:1.

Fig. 677. 1:1.

Fig. 678. 1:1.

Fig. 679. 1:1.

Fig. 680. 1:1.

Fig. 681. 1:1.

Fig. 682. 1:1.

Fig. 683. 1:1.

Fig. 684. 1:1.

Fig. 685. 1:1.

Fig. 686. 1:1.

Fig. 687. 1:1.

Fig. 688. 1:1.

Fig. 689. 1:1.

Fig. 690. 1:1.

Fig. 691. 1:1.

Fig. 692. 1:1.

Fig. 693. 1:1.

Fig. 694. 1:1.

Fig. 695. 1:1.

Fig. 696. 1:1.

Fig. 697. 1:1.

Fig. 698. 1:1.

Fig. 699. 1:1.

Fig. 700. 1:1.

Appendix 4. Bronze Age finds from Tell F5

A number of Bronze Age finds derive from the Danish excavations of the Hellenistic Tell F5 in 1958-1963. They include pottery (Hannestad 1983 p. 123, note 1), twenty-eight stamp seals (Kjærum 1983 p. 8-13), a further stamp seal (see above Marchesi fig. 390, CFa3), twenty-nine stone vessel fragments (Hilton 2014 p. 167, 177-191, fig. 449), and a few other finds described below.

According to Kjærum these finds occurred partly in the Hellenistic layer and partly in a thin occupation layer from the second millennium at the base of the tell (Kjærum 1983 p. 8).

Similarly, the American and French excavations in Tell F5 have produced Bronze Age finds (Howard-Carter 1984). The early French excavators described these finds as random intrusions into the Hellenistic layers (Gachet & Salles 1986 p. 304). During the recent French excavations led by M. Gelin, a level containing mid 2nd millennium BC pottery was uncovered below the Hellenistic fortress architecture (pers.comm. Gelin 2017).

Fragment of object in soft stone of Hilton's type 4 (Hilton 2014 p. 13), decorated with fine engravings, perhaps head/neck of ram (fig. 701) (F5.AET).

Head of a bearded man

by David Mulder & Holly Pittman

Greyish-brown soft stone with black inclusions (bitumen compound?), height 4 cm (fig. 702) (F5. No. 5585/1960, KM58).

This head would have been part of a composite sculpture, attached to the torso by a dowel inserted into the 5.6 mm hole in the neck. An encircling band, perhaps of precious metal, would likely have covered what is now a flat recessed strip across the upper forehead and hair. The eyes, now round and empty and giving the work a vaguely skeletal appearance, would certainly have been inlaid, probably with shell.

The work initially calls to mind Mesopotamian statuary of the Early Dynastic period with its exaggeratedly large eyes, geometric stylization of the facial features, and rendering of the hair through frond-like diagonal and vertical hatching. The gridded square cross-hatching of the beard, however, is unlike the usual parallel zigzags and/or broad horizontal ridges typical of Early Dynastic sculptures. Square grids are used as abbreviated renderings of the curls of the beard in artworks of the Ur III and Old Babylonian periods, particularly in terracottas,[1] a practice that extends through the first millennium BCE in Assyria and Babylonia.[2] The hair worn relatively long and falling to the neck is more reminiscent of Kassite, Middle/Neo-Assyrian, and Neo-Babylonian styles in Mesopotamia than of the shorter cut and brimmed cap typical of the Neo-Sumerian and Old Babylonian periods, or of the late Early Dynastic and Akkadian chignon. A terminus post quem for the Failaka head in the latter half of the second millennium might therefore be suggested.

The closest parallel to the rendering of the face in the Failaka work is to be found in a bitumen mastic statuette fragment from Susa,[3] where we can observe a strikingly similar rendering of the eyes through broad, crater-like depressions surrounded by sharply protruding ridges. One of the eyes on the Susa piece retains its inlay, allowing us to envision the original appearance of the now-hollow sockets on the Failaka head. The ears of both works are also similar, consisting of simple flat ovals within which are smooth and shallowly cut concavities. The flattened faces and tubular necks of both works also speak to a close kinship. Some of the Susa fragment's other attributes differ from those of the Failaka work, as the former's face is not bearded, and the hair is clearly pulled into a flat bun at the back of the head. The Susa sculpture most likely represents a woman. The date of the Susa head is also uncertain, and proposals have ranged from the middle of the third to the end of the second millennium BCE. Deschesne provisionally dates it to ca. 2300 BCE but notes its resemblance to certain Middle Elamite heads in terracotta, which would suggest instead a date in the latter half of the second millennium.[4] The stylistic links to the Middle Elamite heads (including the emphatic ridges encircling the eyes, flat, nearly triangular face, concave oval for the ear, and hairstyle with a flat top encircled by a braid) are more compelling than the association of the hairstyle with the late Early Dynastic/Akkadian royal chignon, to which it bears only a faint resemblance.[5]

While there remains a certain degree of uncertainty regarding the date and origins of the head from Failaka, its shared stylistic and material properties with the head from Susa indicate that it may have been imported to Failaka from southwestern Iran. The hairstyle is consistent with a date in the late second millennium BCE, a period to which its companion at Susa can also be attributed based on comparison with sculpture in terracotta of the Middle Elamite era.

1. E.g., Woolley & Mallowan 1976, pls. 63 (U.16993) and 74.95. Cf. the hair on a bronze statuette from the Ishtar Temple, Assur (dated by context to the Ur III period): Spycket 1981, p. 213, fig. 63; and the beard of the "Adorant de Larsa" figure (ibid., pl. 169; Louvre, AO 15704).

2. Cf. VA 3135/Bab 44400, a figurine from Babylon. Numerous Neo-Assyrian reliefs, particularly from the Southwest Palace at Nineveh, can also be cited; see for example Barnett, Bleibtreu & Turner 1998 pls. 27.14c, 29.16a, 177.244b, etc.

3. Louvre Sb 14238; Connan & Deschesne 1996, p. 190-191, no. 120.

4. Connan & Deschesne 1996 p. 191. Examples of such heads can be found in Amiet 1966, p. 440-441, no. 336a-b; and Spycket 1992, pl. 136, no. 1204, and pls. 138-139.

5. A better case might be made for an Early Dynastic date by comparing the hairstyle with those of some votive statues from the Diyala region: cf. Frankfort 1939, pl. 90. The overall stylistic resemblance to Middle Elamite sculptures nevertheless remains the more convincing chronological datum.

Fig. 701. 2:1.

Fig. 702. 1:1 and 2:1.

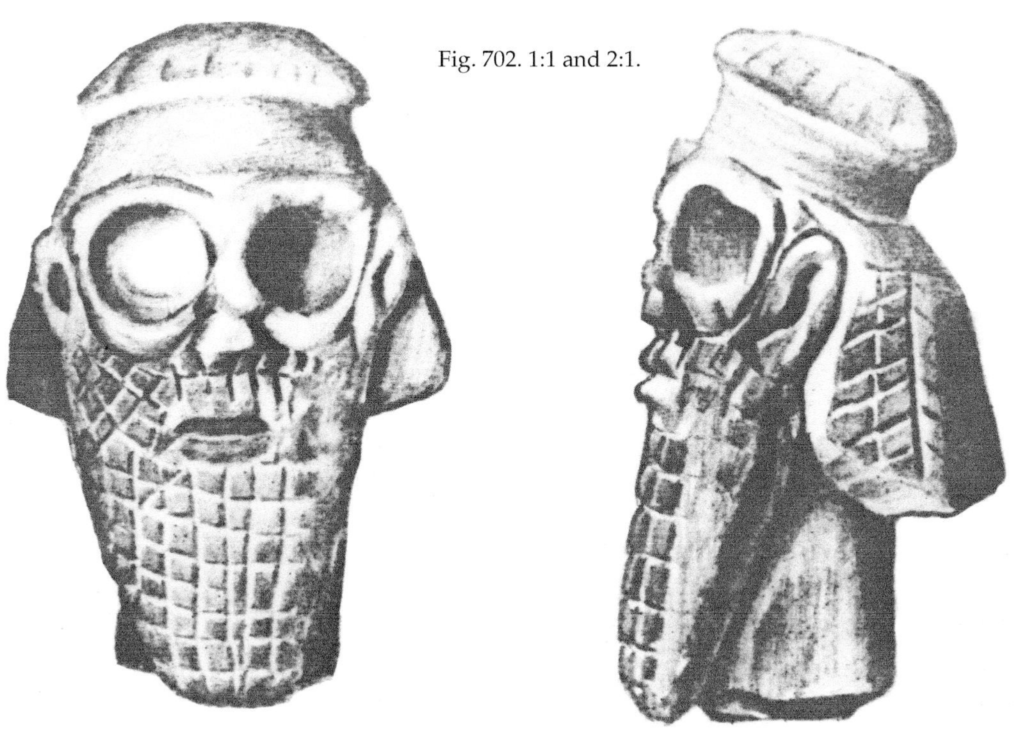

Appendix 5. Conservation of bituminous finds

by Helle Strehle

One of the big attractions about bituminous-based finds is that they in some cases bear, by coincidence or by human action, impressions of organic matter which, due to their perishable nature, normally leave very meagre or incidental traces. Bitumen-based compounds may therefore offer a small glimpse into otherwise vanished *materials* that were part of everyday life such as wood, textile, reeds or leaves. Finds of bitumen may also reveal interesting insight in *techniques* such as the waterproofing of roofs, boats and containers as well as the closing, sealing and gluing of pottery, adhesion for ornamental purposes and mortaring in architecture (Højlund & Andersen 1994 p. 408-412. Wilcox 1994 p. 460. Højlund 1995 p. 100-102. Killick & Moon 2005 p. 193-198).

In order to study and document these traces of organic matter, the bituminous finds often need consolidation, and a challenging aspect is how to conserve a material, which consists of a combination of organic and mineral matter. Further, the organic component is to some extent still water-repellent and soluble in some non-polar solvents, which rules out a series of materials normally used in conservation.

Composition of bitumen

Technically bitumen is a pure organic hydrocarbon without any filler or temper. Bitumen can be produced from crude oil in modern distilleries, but its natural origin is seepages from tar-sands and sticky outcrops or sometimes caught by water in areas with reservoirs of oil. In the Near East bitumen surfaces naturally and several studies inspired by organo-geochemical methods known to the oil industry have been made to try to couple the archaeological bitumen to specific geological sources (Marschner & Wright 1978 p. 150. Connan et al. 1998. Connan & Carter 2007). Bitumen samples from the Danish excavations at Tell F6, 2008-2012, were found to originate from sources in Iran. Other Bronze Age finds of bitumen from Failaka derive from Iraq and Kuwait (Van de Velde 2016 p. 214-220).

Archaeological bitumen is never found pure but will always be an artificial mixture of pure bitumen and a temper of combined inorganic and organic origin. The *inorganic* part is typically minerals from the sandy or clayey environment such as calcite, dolomite, quartz and plagioclase as well as shell debris (Marschner & Wright 1978 p. 150-171. Connan et al. 2005 p. 25, 38. Connan & Carter 2007 p. 139-181).

Further, archaeological bitumen is intentionally tempered with a *vegetal* filler (Lahanier 1977 p. 47. Connan & Van de Velde 2010 p. 2). Studies of the vegetal additive have identified chopped straw, chaff, stems and leaves from reed, palm and crop (Connan et al. 2005 p. 25. Wilcox 1994 p. 460).

The proportions between pure bitumen, organic temper and mineral temper may vary considerably according to date, site and use, but an average content seems to be: pure bitumen: 10-35% (normally more than 20%), vegetal temper: 10-35% and mineral temper ca. 50% of the total weight (Connan et al. 2005 p. 55).

The additives in the bituminous finds from the Danish excavations 2008-2017 have not been studied in detail by archaeo-botanists or geologists but rather macroscopically checked (Van de Velde 2016 p. 215). Examining the bituminous finds from the Danish excavations at Failaka 2008-2017 the present writer was able to ascertain that the majority had visible remnants of both mineral and vegetal temper (Strehle 2022).

Despite the composite nature of bituminous compounds, i.e. mixtures of bitumen with organic and mineral temper, the shorter term 'bitumen' is widely used in the archaeological literature. Mixtures with minerals alone are in the chemical and technical literature denoted as 'asphalt'. Archaeological 'asphalt' is considered a product of human intention whereas geological asphalt develops naturally by contact between bitumen and the surrounding soil (Marschner & Wright 1978 p. 150). In this text, the terms 'bitumen' and 'archaeological bitumen' are used in accordance with archaeological terminology for mixtures containing bitumen, 'bituminous compounds'. Bitumen is sometimes confused with 'tar' or 'pitch', which are man-made distillations from wood (or coal).

Physical and chemical characterization

The tempering, whether mineral or vegetal, has a profound effect on the physical and chemical properties: its viscosity and workability, the temperatures by which it softens, melts and burns, its solubility and the long-term degradation. Natural, pure bitumen has a melting interval between 120-150 °C and might float when subjected to direct sunlight. In nature, bitumen will always be mixed up with sand (becoming an asphalt) and thereby reaches a sticky, viscous state and a melting interval between 136-165 °C (Darbandizadeh 2023). With mineral temper the mixture may solidify in ambient temperatures and if heated it becomes pourable (Connan & Van de Velde 2010 p. 2-4). The tempering with vegetal ingredients adds strength, cohesion and flexibility and prevents the mixture from sweating and flowing under high ambient temperatures (Connan et al. 2005 p. 55-58).

Degradation of bituminous compounds

Natural, pure bitumen consists of three fractions: hydrocarbons, resins and asphaltenes. Studies of archaeological and weathered bitumen indicate that the fractions degrade progressively and differently loosing matter over time and leaving the asphalthenes behind as the end product (Connan et al. 2005 p. 21). It is suggested, "that the terminal product of exposure to the elements is much the same whether it occurs over geological ages deep underground or over archaeological millennia near the surface" (Marschner & Wright 1978 p. 159 and 166). The asphaltenes are soluble in aromatic solvents like xylene, benzene and toluene and not susceptible to biodegradation.

The vegetal temper tends to wither away and completely dissolve by oxidation and biodegradation exhibiting voids left by the organic material (Connan et al. 2005 p. 23 and 59).

The environmental conditions at Failaka being at times extremely hot, temporarily humid and exposed to haline precipitation have altered the original composition of the bituminous compound. The bituminous finds from Failaka showed mineral temper, voids and impressions after the degraded organic temper and the bituminous matrix was changed from sticky and viscous to desiccated, fragile, crumbly and porous. The surfaces were fragile to the touch and the objects were often encrusted with sand and earth, obscuring the surface details. The condition of the fragments varied, some of them were extremely desiccated and crumbly while others could be handled with some care. None of them could withstand impressions being taken without smearing out the details or causing further fragmentation.

The bituminous objects

Bitumen occurred in all phases and all layers of the excavations at Tell F6 in 2008-2012 and Tell F3 in 2012-2017. Most of the finds were small amorphous lumps, but some had shapes and textures suggesting an original use as either raw material, repair of pottery or waterproofing of mats, roofs and boats. Several fragments had impressions of reeds, weeds or leaf in a plaited system or intricate impressions of horizontal and vertical string or wood. The presence of barnacles (one fragment) further indicates the use of bitumen on sea-faring boats. Bitumen was also used for fixing a bronze blade into an ivory handle. Waterproofing with bitumen also appear together with lime mortar also suitable as a water repellent (Højlund & Abu Laban 2016 p. 210-213. Højlund & Hilton 2021 p. 139-140).

Conservation

Consolidation was necessary to allow cleaning, examination, and photography of the bituminous finds. For a closer study of the impressions, the consolidation should ideally allow moulding the impressions.

Working on very degraded Ubaid and Dilmunite bitumen Norman (2005) has reported excellent results using a water-based emulsion (Vinamul 6825®, a polyvinyl acetate) and a water-based dispersion (Vinamul 3252®, a 50:50 copolymer of polyvinyl acetate/polyethylene). The Vinamul was used in a 5-10 % concentration sometimes in combination with Klucel G (an inert cellulose filler). The consolidant was applied by pipette and brush at intervals (Norman 2005).

None of these consolidants were accessible at Failaka, but another water based acrylic dispersion, Primal WS 24® (a copolymer of methyl methacrylate/ethylacrylate), was available. WS24 seemed promising because of its very small particle size, 0,03 microns, and because it is widely used to conserve composite organic and mineral objects. Also, Mowilith® (a polyvinyl buthyral, PVB) soluble in organic solvents was available.

A series of experiments were carried out on small indiscriminative bitumen lumps to decide for a feasible conservation procedure: The water based consolidant, WS 24, proved unable to penetrate the bitumen regardless of applying method (brush, pipette, immersion), treatment time or concentration of the consolidant. The WS 24 left the bitumen surface a little shiny and the core still fragile. The PVB consolidant, when diluted in the polar solvent, ethanol, had a better wetting ability and was able to penetrate and stabilize the core of the bitumen lumps without dissolving the bituminous matter.

After several different applying methods were tested, the following standard procedure was chosen: The bitumen was placed on a stainless-steel net and immersed in a 5% w/v PVB in ethanol. The object was monitored and removed from the consolidant, when air bubbles ceased to escape (fig. 703). The treatment time being between 30 and 180 seconds.

The surface was generally left non-glossy, if the impregnated object was twisted and turned until the consolidant started to cure. Some objects with smooth surfaces needed a special measure to prevent glossiness: the bitumen was left to cure while sitting on a net in a chamber saturated with fumes from ethanol. Protruding areas, which dried up faster than the rest, were able to suck an extra helping of 5% PVB applied by a fine brush.

Prior to consolidation, the objects were carefully cleaned using sable hair brush, customized wooden sticks and a 'puffer' (a small photography air brush). The cleaning procedure was performed under a stereo microscope to prevent harming the surface details. Following cleaning and consolidating it was possible to mould the - now much clearer - impression present in the bitumen. Among several available moulding materials a plasticine, Farcolina®, was chosen because it is soft, flexible and well suited for photography (fig. 704). The Farcolina left no visible traces at the surfaces but is not meant to survive in hot weather conditions. Therefore, photo documentation was carried out at site.

The treatment appeared to be successful, and the objects could be handled much more safely after consolidation. This allowed moulding and detailed study of the impressions left by otherwise totally degraded organic constructions.

Fig. 703. Immersion of bitumen fragment in consolidant, 1:2.

Fig. 704. Left: Fragment of bitumen with impression of lashing in plant material (Højlund & Abu-Laban 2016 fig. 1074). Right: Mould of same in plasticine, 1:1.

Bibliographic abbreviations

AAE *Arabian Archaeology and Epigraphy*. Wiley.

CAD *Chicago Assyrian Dictionary* = Oppenheim, A.L., Reiner, E., Biggs, R.D., Roth, M.T. (eds.), *The Assyrian Dictionary of the Oriental Institute of the University of Chicago*. The Oriental Institute, Chicago (1956-2010).

CDLI *Cuneiform Digital Library Initiative*: https://cdli.mpiwg-berlin.mpg.de/

DRS Cohen, D., Bron, F., Lonnet, A., *Dictionnaire des racines sémitiques ou attestées dans les langues sémitiques*. Mouton, Paris/La Haye / Peeters, Leuven (1970-...)

HALOT Koehler, L., Baumgartner, W., Stamm, J.J., *The Hebrew and Aramaic Lexicon of the Old Testament*. Translated and edited under the supervision of M.E.J. Richardson. E.J. Brill, Leiden/New York/Köln (1994).

JASP *Jutland Archaeological Society Publications*. Moesgaard. Højbjerg/Aarhus.

PNA Radner, K. & Baker, H.D. (eds.), *The Prosopography of the Neo-Assyrian Empire*. The Neo-Assyrian Text Corpus Project, Helsinki (1998-2011).

PSAS *Proceedings of the Seminar for Arabian Studies*. Archaeopress.

Bibliography

Alster, B. 1983: Dilmun, Bahrain, and the Alleged Paradise in Sumerian Myth and Literature. In: Potts, D.T. (ed.), *Dilmun. New Studies in the Archaeology and Early History of Bahrain*. Berliner Beiträge zum Vorderen Orient Bd. 2, Dietrich Reimer Verlag, Berlin, p. 39-124.

Amiet, P. 1966: *Élam*. Archée Editeur, Auvers-sur-Oise.

Andersen, H.H. & Højlund, F. 2003: *The Barbar Temples*, vols. 1-2. *JASP* vol. 48. Jutland Archaeological Society & Moesgaard Museum, Højbjerg / Ministry of Information, Bahrain.

Andersen, S.F. & Kennet, D. 2003: Sasanian and Islamic Pottery. In: Andersen, H.H. & Højlund, F. (eds) 2003: *The Barbar Temples*, Vol. 1. *JASP* vol. 48, Højbjerg, p. 307-310.

Andersson, A. 2016: The Beads. In: Højlund, F. & Abu-Laban, A. 2016: *Tell F6 on Failaka Island. Kuwaiti-Danish Excavations 2008-2012*. *JASP* vol. 92, Jutland Archaeological Society & Moesgaard Museum, Højbjerg / National Council for Culture, Arts and Letters, Kuwait City, Højbjerg, p. 176-198.

Andersson, A. 2021: Beads. In: Højlund, F. & Hilton, A. 2021: *Tell F3 on Failaka Island. Kuwaiti-Danish Excavations 2012-2017*. *JASP* vol. 116, Jutland Archaeological Society & Moesgaard Museum, Højbjerg / National Council for Culture, Arts and Letters, Kuwait City, Højbjerg, p. 117-122.

Andersson, A. 2022: *Failaka/Dilmun. The Second Millennium Settlements* vol. 5: *The Beads*. *JASP* vol. 17:5, Jutland Archaeological Society & Moesgaard Museum, Højbjerg / National Council for Culture, Arts and Letters, Kuwait City.

André-Salvini, B. & Cavigneaux, A. forth.: Cuneiform Tablets from Qal'a. Dilmun and the Sealand at the dawn of the Kassite era. In: Lombard, P. & Al Sindi, Kh.M. (eds.), *Twenty Years of Bahrain Archaeology, 1986-2006. Actes du colloque international de Manama, 9-12 décembre 2007*. Ministry of Culture, Bahrain.

Anonymous 1964: *Archaeological Investigations in the Island of Failaka 1958-1964* [in Arabic]. Ministry of Guidance & Information—Department of Antiquity & Museums, Kuwait.

Archi, A. 1993: Bronze Alloys in Ebla. In: Frangipane, M., Hauptmann, H., Liverani, M., Matthiae, P. & Mellink, M. (eds) 1993: *Between the Rivers and Over the Mountains. Archaeologica Anatolica et Mesopotamica alba Palmieri Dedicata*, Dipartimento di Scienze Storiche Archeologiche e Anthropologiche dell'Antichità Università di Roma "La Sapienza", Rome, p. 615-625.

Arnaud, D. 1998: Cinq dédicaces d'époque cassite provenant de Babylonie et de Syrie. *Studi Micenei ed Egeo-Anatolici* 40 p. 197-204.

Arnaud, D. 2004: *Nabuchodonosor II: Roi de Babylone*. Fayard, Paris.

Aruz, J. & Wallenfels, R. (eds.) 2003: *Art of the First Cities: The Third Millennium B.C. from the Mediterranean to the Indus*. New York, NY: The Metropolitan Museum of Art.

Ashkanani, H. 2021: *Antiquities Treasures From Kuwait National Museum*. Kuwait.

Attinger, P. 1984: Enki et Ninḫursaĝa. *Zeitschrift für Assyriologie und Vorderasitische Archäologie* 74 p. 1-52.

Attinger, P. 2021: *Glossaire sumérien-français principalement des textes littéraires paléobabyloniens*. Harrassowitz, Wiesbaden.

Balke, Th.E. 2017: *Das altsumerische Onomastikon. Namengebung und Prosopografie nach den Quellen aus Lagas*. Dubsar 1, Zaphon, Münster.

Barjamovic, G. 2018: Interlocking commercial networks and the infrastructure of trade in western Asia during the Bronze Age. In: Kristiansen, K. et al. (eds), 2018: *Trade and Civilisation: Economic Networks and Cultural Ties, from*

Prehistory to the Early Modern Era. Cambridge University Press, p. 133-167.

Barnett, R.D., Bleibtreu, E. & Turner, G. 1998: *Sculptures from the Southwest Palace of Sennacherib at Nineveh*. London: British Museum Press.

Barrelet, M.-Th. 1968: *Figurines et reliefs en terre cuite de la Mésopotamie antique I: potiers, termes de métier, proceeds de fabrication et production*. Paris: Librairie orientaliste Paul Geuthner.

Barta, P., Benediková, L., Hajnalová, M., Miklíková, Z., Belanová, T., Shehab, S.A.H. 2008: Al-Khidr on Failaka Island: Preliminary Results of the Fieldworks at a Dilmun Culture Settlement in Kuwait. *TÜBA-AR* (*Türkiye Bilimler Akademisi Arkeoloji Dergisi*) 11 p. 121-134.

Bartelmus, A. 2016: *Fragmente einer großen Sprache. Sumerisch im Kontext der Schreiberausbildung des kassitenzeitlichen Babylonien*. Untersuchungen zur Assyriologie und Vorderasiatischen Archäologie Bd. 12, De Gruyter, Boston/Berlin.

Beaulieu, P.-A. 2017: Palaces of Babylon and Palaces of Babylonian Kings. *The Canadian Society for Mesopotamian Studies—Journal* 11-12, p. 5-14.

Beaulieu, P.-A. 2019: What's in a Name? Babylon and its Designations throughout History. *The Canadian Society for Mesopotamian Studies—Journal* 14, p. 29-37.

Beck, H.C. 1928: The Classification and Nomenclature of Beads and Pendants. *In: Archaeologia. The Society of Antiquaries of London*, vol. 77 p. 1-76.

Becker, A. 1993: *Uruk. Kleinfunde I: Stein*. Ausgrabungen in Uruk-Warka—Endberichte Bd. 6, Philipp von Zabern, Mainz am Rhein.

Begemann, F. & Schmitt-Strecker, S. 2009: Über das frühe Kupfer Mesopotamiens. *Iranica Antiqua* 44, p. 1–45.

Begemann, F., Hauptmann, A., Schmitt-Strecker, S. and Weisgerber, G. 2010: Lead Isotope and Chemical Signature of Copper from Oman and its Occurrence in Mesopotamia and Sites on the Arabian Gulf Coast. *AAE* 21, p. 135-169.

Benediková, L. (ed.) 2010: *Al-Khidr 2004-2009. Primary Scientific Report on the Activities of the Kuwait-Slovak Archaeological Mission*. National Council for Culture, Arts & Letters, Kuwait City / Archeologicky ústav Slovenska akadémie vied, Nitra.

Benz, F.L. 1972: *Personal Names in the Phoenician and Punic Inscriptions*. Studia Pohl 8, Biblical Institute Press, Rome.

Berger, D., Soles, J.S., Giumlia-Mair, A.R., Brügmann, G., Galili, E., Lockhoff, N. & Pernicka, E. 2019: Isotope systematics and chemical composition of tin ingots from Mochlos (Crete) and other Late Bronze Age sites in the eastern Mediterranean Sea: An ultimate key to tin provenance? *PLoS ONE* 14, p. 1–46.

Berger, D., Brügmann, G., Friedrich, R., Lutz, J., Meyer, H.-P., & Pernicka, E. 2022. Shiny bronze in glassy matter: an inconspicuous piece of slag from the Bronze Age mining site of Mušiston (Tajikistan) and its significance for the development of tin metallurgy in Central Asia. *Archaeological and Anthropological Sciences* 14:150. https://doi.org/10.1007/s12520-022-01606-2

Bibby, T.G. 1965: Arabian Gulf archeology. *Kuml* 1964 p. 86-111.

Bibby, G. 1969: *Looking for Dilmun*. Alfred A. Knopf, New York.

Bisht, R.S. 2015: *Excavations at Dholavira (1989-1990 to 2004-2005)*. Archaeological Survey of India, New Dheli.

Black, J. & Green, A. 1992: *Gods, Demons and Symbols of Ancient Mesopotamia. An Illustrated Dictionary*. British Museum Press, London.

Boehmer, R.M. 1965: *Die Entwicklung der Glyptik während der Akkad-Zeit*. Berlin: Walter De Gruyter.

Boivin, O., 2018: *The First Dynasty of the Sealand in Mesopotamia*. Studies in Ancient Near Eastern Records vol. 20, De Gruyter: Boston/Berlin.

Borger, R. 2003: *Mesopotamisches Zeichenlexikon*. Alter Orient und Altes Testament Bd. 305, Ugarit Verlag, Münster.

Braun-Holzinger, E.A. 1991: *Mesopotamische Weihgaben der frühdynastichen bis altbabylonischen Zeit*. Heidelberger Studien zum Alten Orient Bd. 3, Heidelberger Orientverlag, Heidelberg.

Braun-Holzinger, E.A. 2007: *Das Herrscherbild in Mesopotamien und Elam. Spätes 4. Bis frühes 2. Jt. v. Chr.* Münster: Ugarit-Verlag.

Bray, P., Cuénod, A., Gosden, C. et al. 2015: Form and flow: the 'karmic cycle' of copper. *Journal of Archaeological Science* 56, p. 202–209.

Brinkman, J.A. 1993: A Kassite Seal Mentioning a Babylonian Governor of Dilmun. *NABU* 1993/106.

Buchanan, B. 1981: *Early Near Eastern Seals in the Yale Babylonian Collection*. Yale University Press, New Haven/ London.

Calderbank, D. 2018: *Moulding clay to model Sealand society. Pottery production and function at Tell Khaiber, Southern Iraq*. PhD dissertation, University of Manchester.

Calderbank, D. 2021: *Pottery from Tell Khaiber. A Craft Tradition of the First Sealand Dynasty*. Archaeology of Ancient Iraq vol. 1. Moonrise Press, Ludlow.

Calvet, Y. 1984: La Fouille de l'Age du Bronze (G3). In: Salles, J.-F. (ed.), *Failaka. Fouilles françaises 1983*. Travaux de la Maison de l'Orient n° 9, Lyon, p. 51-72.

Calvet, Y. 2005: Agarum, une île de la civilisation de Dilmoun. In: Callot, O. et al. 2005: *L'île de Failaka. Archéologie du Koweït*. Musée des Beaux-Arts de Lyon, Lyon, p. 41-61.

Calvet, Y. & Glassner, J.-J. 1986: Un fragment de vase inscrit. In: Calvet, Y. & Salles, J.-F. (eds.), *Failaka. Fouilles françaises 1984-1985*. Travaux de la Maison de l'Orient n° 12, Lyon, p. 105-106.

Calvet, Y. & Pic, M. 1986: Un nouveau bâtiment de l'Age du Bronze sur le Tell F6. In: Calvet, Y. & Salles, J.-F. (eds.), *Failaka. Fouilles françaises 1984-1985*. Travaux de la Maison de l'Orient n° 12, Lyon, p. 13-87.

Calvet, Y. & Pic, M. 1990: Un temple-tour de l'âge du Bronze à Failaka. In: Calvet, Y. & Gachet, J. (eds.), *Failaka. Fouilles françaises 1986-1988*. Travaux de la Maison de l'Orient n° 18, Lyon, p. 103-122.

Calvet, Y. & Pic, M. (eds.) 2008: *Failaka. Fouilles françaises 1984-1988. Matériel céramique du temple-tour et épigraphie*. Travaux de la Maison de L'Orient et de la Méditerranée n° 48, Lyon.

Carter, R.A. 2012: *Sea of Pearls. Seven Thousand Years of the Industry that Shaped the Gulf*. Arabian Publishing, London.

Casanova, M. 1991: *La vaisselle d'albatre de Mésopotamie, d'Iran et d'Asie centrale aux IIIe et IIe millénaires av. J.-C.* Èditions Recherche sur les Civilisations, Paris.

Casanova, M. 2003: Alabaster and Calcite Vessels. *In:* Andersen, H.H. & Højlund, F. 2003: *The Barbar Temples*, vols. 1. *JASP* vol. 48. Jutland Archaeological Society & Moesgaard Museum, Højbjerg / Ministry of Information, Bahrain, p. 283-288.

Caubet, A. & Salles, J.-F. 1984: Le Sanctuaire Hellénistique

(B6). In: Salles, J.-F. (ed.), *Failaka. Fouilles françaises 1983.* Travaux de la Maison de l'Orient n° 9, Lyon, p. 73-156.
Charpin, D. 1980: *Archives familiales et proprieté privée en Babylonie ancienne: Étude des documents de "Tell Sifr".* Hautes études orientales n° 12, Librairie Droz, Genève.
Charpin, D. 1984: Inscriptions votives d'époque assyrienne. *MARI* 3 p. 41-81.
Ciarla, R. 1979: The Manufacture of Alabaster Vessels at Shahr-I Sokhta and Mundigak in the 3rd Mill. BC. A Problem of Cultural Identity. In: Gnoli, G. & Rossi, A.V. (eds.), *Iranica.* Seminario di Studi Asiatici—Series minor vol. 10, Istituto Universitario Orientale, Napoli, p. 319-335.
Ciarla, R. 1985: Bronze-Age Crafts at Failaka: Some Preliminary Observations on Stone Vase Fragments. *East and West* 35 p. 396-406.
Ciarla, R. 1990: Fragments of Stone Vessels as a Base Material. Two Case Studies: Failaka and Shahr-I Sohkta. In: Taddei, M. (ed.): *South Asian Archaeology 1987, part 1.* Istituto Italiano per il Medio ed Estremo Oriente, Rome, p. 475-491.
Cifola, B. 1988: A Kudurru Fragment from the Reign of Enlil-nādin-aḫi. *Vicino Oriente* 7 p. 249-252.
Civil, M. 1971: *Izi* = išātu, *Ká-gal* = abullu *and Níg-ga* = makkūru. Materials for the Sumerian Lexicon vol. 13, Pontificium Institutum Biblicum, Roma.
Civil, M. 2010: *The Lexical Texts in the Schøyen Collection.* Cornell University Studies in Assyriology and Sumerology vol. 12, CDL Press, Bethesda, Maryland.
Clay, A.T. 1912: *Personal Names from Cuneiform Inscriptions of the Cassite Period.* Yale Oriental Series vol. 1, Yale University Press, New Haven.
Clayden, T. 2020: Ur in the Kassite Period. In: Paulus, S. & Clayden, T. (eds.), *Babylonia under the Sealand and Kassite Dynasties.* Studies in Ancient Near Eastern Records vol. 24, De Gruyter, Boston/Berlin, p. 88-124.
Cleuziou, S. & Tosi, M. 2020: *In the Shadow of the Ancestors. The Prehistoric Foundations of the Early Arabian Civilization in Oman.* 2nd edition. Archaeopress, Oxford.
Collon, D. 1986: *Catalogue of the Western Asiatic Seals in the British Museum. Cylinder Seals III: Isin-Larsa and Old Babylonian Periods.* The Trustees of the British Museum, London.
Collon, D. 1987: *First Impressions. Cylinder Seals in the Ancient Near East.* British Museum Publications, London.
Connan, J. 2012: *Le bitumen dans l'Antiquité.* Editions errance.
Connan, J. & Deschesne, O. 1996: *Le Bitume à Suse. Collection du Musée du Louvre.* Réunion des Musées Nationaux, Paris.
Connan, J., Lombard, P., Killick, R., Højlund, F., Salles, J-F. & Khalaf, A. 1998: The archaeological bitumens of Bahrain from the Early Dilmun period (c. 2200 BC) to the sixteenth century AD: A problem of sources and trade. *AAE* 9, p. 141–181.
Connan, J., Carter, R., Crawford, H., Tobey, M., Charrié-Duhaut, A., Jarvie, D., Albrecht, P. & Norman, K. 2005: A comparative geochemical study of bituminous boat remains from H3, As-Sabiyah (Kuwait), and RJ-2, Ra's al-Jinz (Oman). *AAE* 16, p. 21–66.
Connan, J. & Carter, R. 2007: A geochemical study of bituminous mixtures from Failaka and Umm an-Namel (Kuwait), from the Early Dilmun to the Early Islamic period. *AAE* p. 139-181.
Connan, J. & Van de Velde, T. 2010: An overview of bitumen trade in the Near East from the Neolithic (c. 8000 BC) to the early Islamic period. *AAE*, p. 1-19.
Cornwall, P.B. & Goetze, A. 1952: Two letters from Dilmun. *Journal of Cuneiform Studies* 6 p. 137-145.
Coutu, A. 2013: ZooMS analysis of Failaka ivory fragments. Report from the BioArCh laboratories at the University of York.
Craddock, P.T. & Meeks, N.D. 1987: Iron in ancient copper. *Archaeometry* 29, p. 187-204.
Cuenod, A. 2012: Rethinking the Bronze-Iron Transition in Iran: Copper and Iron Metallurgy Before the Achaemenid Period. Unpublished PhD dissertation, Oxford University.
Cuenod, A., Bray, P. & Pollard, A.M. 2015: The "Tin Problem" in the Prehistoric Near East: Further Insights from a Study of Chemical Datasets on Copper Alloys from Iran and Mesopotamia. *Iran* 53, p. 29-48. DOI: 10.1080/05786967.2015.11834749
Dalley, S. 2013: Gods from north-eastern and north-western Arabia in cuneiform texts from the First Sealand Dynasty, and a cuneiform inscription from Tell en-Nasbeh, c. 1500 BC. *AAE* 25 p. 177-185.
Darbandizadeh, M. 2023: https://www.linkedin.com/pulse/what-differences-between-bitumen-tar-asphalt-mozh-deh-darbandizadeh. Accessed 12.1.2024.
David-Cuny, H. and Azpeitia, J. 2012: *Failaka Seals Catalogue* vol. 1: *Al-Khidr.* Ed. S.A.H. Shehab. National Council for Culture, Arts and Letters, State of Kuwait, Kuwait City.
David-Cuny, H. & Neyme, D. 2016: *Failaka Seals Catalogue* vol. 2: *Tell F6 "The Palace".* National Council for Culture, Arts and Letters, Kuwait City.
Denton, B.E. 1997: "Style III" seals from Bahrain. *AAE* 8 p. 174-189.
Dijk, J. van 1962: *Note préliminaire sur les documents inscripts provenant de Failaka et de Bahrein.* Unpublished report from the Assyriological Institute, University of Copenhagen.
Dossin, G. 1962: Bronzes inscrits du Luristan de la collection Foroughi. *Iranica Antiqua* 2 p. 149-164.
Durand, J.-M. 2023: *Les primières années du roy Zimrî-Lîm de Mari. Deuxième Partie.* Archives royales de Mari 34, Peeters, Leuven.
Eidem, J. 1987: The inscribed pottery. In: Højlund, F., *Failaka/Dilmun. The Second Millennium Settlements* vol. 2: *The Bronze Age Pottery. JASP* vol. 17:2, Jysk Arkæologisk Selskab, Højbjerg / Kuwait National Museum, Kuwait City, p. 179-180.
Eidem, J. 1994: Cuneiform inscriptions. In: Højlund, F. & Andersen, H.H., *Qala'at al-Bahrain* vol. 1: *The Northern City Wall and the Islamic Fortress. JASP* vol. 30:1, p. 301-303.
Eidem, J. 1997: Cuneiform inscriptions. In: Højlund, F. & Andersen, H.H., *Qala'at al-Bahrain* vol. 2. *The Central Monumental Buildings. JASP* vol. 30:2, p. 76-80.
Eidem, J. 2016: Cuneiform inscriptions. In: Højlund, F. & Abu-Laban, A., *Tell F6 on Failaka Island. Kuwaiti-Danish Excavations 2008-2012. JASP* vol. 92, Jutland Archaeological Society & Moesgaard Museum, Højbjerg / National Council for Culture, Arts and Letters, Kuwait City, p. 162-163.
Eidem, J. 2021: Cuneiform inscribed tablet. In: Højlund, F. & Hilton, A., *Tell F3 on Failaka Island. Kuwaiti-Danish Excavations 2012-2017. JASP* vol. 116, Jutland Archaeological Society & Moesgaard Museum, Højbjerg / National Council for Culture, Arts and Letters, Kuwait City, p. 100.
Eidem, J. & Højlund, F. 1993: Trade or Diplomacy? Assyria and Dilmun in the Eighteenth Century BC. *World Archaeology* 24 p. 441-448.
Eidem, J. & Højlund, F. 1997: Assyria and Dilmun revisited.

In: Waetzoldt, H. & Hauptmann, H. (eds.), *Assyrien im Wandel der Zeiten. XXXIXe Rencontre assyriologique internationale, Heidelberg, 6.-10. Juli 1992.* Heidelberger Studien zum Alten Orient Bd. 6, Heidelberger Orientalverlag, Heidelberg, p. 25-31.

Elayi, J. 2023: Les dattes de Dilmun et Nabuchodonosor II. *NABU* 2023/50.

Eppihimer, M. 2019: *Exemplars of Kingship: Art, Tradition, and the Legacy of the Akkadians.* Oxford University Press.

Ferdinand, K. 1993: *Bedouins of Qatar.* Rhodos International, Copenhagen / Thames and Hudson, London.

Ferrara, A.J. 1975: An Inscribed Stone Slab of Nebuchadnezzar II. *Journal of Cuneiform Studies* 27, p. 231-232.

Ferrara, A.J. 1977: A Kassite Cylinder Seal from the Arabian Gulf. *Bulletin of the American Schools of Oriental Research* 225, p. 69.

Figulla, H.H. & Martin, W.J. 1953: *Letters and Documents of the Old-Babylonian Period.* Ur Excavations—Texts vol. 5, The Trustees of the two Museums, London.

Fossey, Ch. 1926: *Manuel d'assyriologie. Tome deuxième: Évolution des cunéiformes.* Louis Conard, Paris.

Frankfort, H. 1939: *Sculpture of the Third Millennium B.C. from Tell Asmar and Khafājah.* Chicago, IL: the University of Chicago Press.

Frayne, D.R. 1990: *Old Babylonian Period (2003-1595 BC).* The Royal Inscriptions of Mesopotamia—Early Periods vol. 4, University of Toronto Press, Toronto.

Frayne, D.R. & Stuckey, J.H. 2021: *A Handbook of Gods and Goddesses of the Ancient Near East. Three Thousand Deities of Anatolia, Syria, Israel, Sumer, Babylonia, Assyria, and Elam.* The Pennsylvania State University, University Park, Pennsylvania.

Frenez, D. 2021: A non-Egyptian «Egyptian» stone vessel from Ras Al-Jinz RJ-2, Sultanate of Oman: Critical review of an entrenched hypothesis. *Academia Letters*, Article 445. https://doi.org/10.20935/AL445.

Frifelt, K. 1995: *The Island of Umm an-Nar* vol. 2: *Third Millennium Settlement. JASP* vol. 26:2, Højbjerg.

Gabbay, Y. & Boivin, O. 2018: A Hymn of Ayadaragalama, King of the First Sealand Dynasty, to the Gods of Nippur: The Fate of Nippur and Its Cult during the First Sealand Dynasty. *Zeitschrift für Assyriologie und Vorderasiatische Archäologie* 108 p. 22-42.

Gachet, J. & Salles, J.-F. 1986: Preliminary report: 1985 excavations on F5. In: Calvet, Y. & Salles, J.-F. (eds.), *Failaka. Fouilles françaises 1984-1985.* Travaux de la Maison de l'Orient n° 12, Lyon, p. 297-330.

Galter, H.D. 1983: *Der Gott Ea/Enki in der akkadischen Überlieferung. Eine Bestandsaufnahme des vorhandenen Materials.* Dissertationen der Karl-Franzens-Universität Graz, dbv-Verlag, Graz.

Garner, J. 2015: Bronze Age tin mines in Central Asia. In: Hauptmann, A. & Modaressi-Tehrani, D. (eds) 2015: *Archaeometallurgy in Europe III: Proceedings of the 3rd International Conference, 29 June to 1 July 2011.* Der Anschnitt, Beiheft 26. Deutsches Bergbau-Museum, Bochum, p. 135–142.

Gasche, H. & Pons, N. 2014: *Floraison de l'art Populaire. Les terres cuites de Tell ed-Der (Sippar Amnanum).* Mesopotamian History and Environment II—Memoirs n° 7, Recherches et Publications, Neuchatel, Ghent.

Gelb, I.J. 1977: Typology of Mesopotamian Seal Inscriptions. In: Gibson, McG. & Biggs, R.D. (eds.), *Seals and Sealing in the Ancient Near East.* Bibliotheca Mesopotamica vol. 6, Undena Publications, Malibu, p. 107-126.

Gelb, I.J. 1980: *Computer-Aided Analysis of Amorite.* Assyriological Studies no. 21, The Oriental Institute of the University of Chicago, Chicago.

Genouillac, H. de 1922: *Textes économiques d'Oumma de l'époque d'Our.* Textes cunéiformes Musée du Louvre—textes cunéiformes tome 5, Paul Geuthner, Paris.

George, A.R. 1993: *House Most High. The Temples of Ancient Mesopotamia.* Mesopotamian Civilizations vol. 5, Eisenbrauns, Winona Lake, Indiana.

Al-Ghabban et al. 2010: *Roads of Arabia. Archaeology and History of the Kingdom of Saudi Arabia.* Somogy Art Publishers.

Gharbia, E., Al Najjar, J., Al Baghly, I.T. 1990: *Cuneiform Inscriptions at Kuwait National Museum.* The Kuwait Government Printing Press, Kuwait.

Glassner, J.J. 1984: Inscriptions cunéiformes de Failaka. In: Salles, J.F. (ed.), *Failaka. Fouilles françaises 1983.* Travaux de la Maison de l'Orient n° 9, Lyon, p. 31-50.

Glassner, J.-J. 1990: Inscriptions cunéiformes de Failaka. Complément. In: Calvet, Y. & Gachet, J. (eds.) 1990, *Failaka. Fouilles françaises 1986-1988.* Travaux de la Maison de l'Orient n° 18, Lyon, p. 123-124.

Glassner, J.-J. 1996: Dilmun, Magan and Meluhha: some Observations on Language, Toponymy, Anthroponymy and Theonimy. In: Reade, J. (ed.), *The Indian Ocean in Antiquity.* KPI, London, p. 235-248.

Glassner, J.-J. 2002: Dilmun et Magan: le peuplement, l'organisation politique, la question des Amorrites et la place de l'écriture. Point de vue de l'assyriologue. In: Cleuziou, S., Tosi, M., Zarins, J. (eds.), *Essays on the Late Prehistory of the Arabian Peninsula*, Serie Orientale Roma vol. 93, Istituto Italiano per l'Africa e l'Oriente, Roma, p. 337-381.

Glassner, J.J. 2008: Textes Cunéiformes. In: Calvet, Y. & Pic, M. (eds.), *Failaka. Fouilles françaises 1984-1988. Matériel céramique du temple-tour et épigraphie.* Travaux de la Maison de L'Orient et de la Méditerranée n° 48, Lyon, p. 171-205.

Glob, P.V. 1959a: Investigations in Kuwait. *Kuml* 1958 p. 166-171.

Glob, P.V. 1959b: Archeological Investigations in Four Arab States. *Kuml* 1959 p. 233-239.

Glob, P.V. 1960: Danish Archeologists in the Persian Gulf. *Kuml* 1960 p. 208-213.

Glob, P.V. 1968: *Al-Bahrain. De danske ekspeditioner til oldtidens Dilmun.* Gyldendal.

Golinets, V. 2018: *Das amurritische Onomastikon der altbabylonischen Zeit* Bd. 2: *Verbalmorphologie des Amurritischen und Glossar der Verbalwurzeln.* Alter Orient und Altes Testament Bd. 271/2, Ugarit Verlag, Münster.

Gregoricka, L.A. 2013a: Residential mobility and social identity in the periphery: strontium isotope analysis of archaeological tooth enamel from southeastern Arabia. *Journal of Archaeological Science* 40 p. 452-464.

Gregoricka, L.A. 2013b: Geographic Origins and Dietary Transitions During the Bronze Age in the Oman Peninsula. *American Journal of Physical Anthropology* 152 p. 353-369.

Groneberg, B. 1992: Le golfe arabo-persique, vu depuis Mari. In: Durand, J.-M. (ed.), *Florilegium marianum. Recueil d'études en l'honneur de Michel Fleury.* Mémoires de NABU 1, SEPOA, Paris, p. 69-80.

Hakemi, A. 1997: *Shahdad. Archaeological Excavations of a Bronze Age Center in Iran.* Reports and Memoirs vol. 27. IsMEO.

Hannestad, L. 1983: *The Hellenistic Pottery from Failaka.* Ikaros. The Hellenistic Settlements 2:1-2. *JASP* vol. 16:2, Højbjerg.
Hallo, W.W. 1965: A Mercantile Agreement from the Reign of Gungunum of Larsa. In: Güterbock, H.G. & Jacobsen, Th. (eds.), *Studies in Honor of Benno Landsberger on His Seventy-Fifth Birthday April 21, 1965.* Assyriological Studies no. 16, The University of Chicago Press, Chicago, p. 199-203.
Hansen, D.P. 1988: A Sculpture of Gudea, Governor of Lagash. *Bulletin of the Detroit Institute of Arts* 64.1.
Hauptmann, A. 1985: *5000 Jahre Kupfer in Oman. Band 1: Die Entwicklung der Kupfermetallurgie vom 3. Jahrtausend bis zur Neuzeit.* Der Anschnitt Beiheft 4. Deutsches Bergbau Museum, Bochum.
Hauptmann, A. 2014: The Investigation of Archaeometallurgical Slag. In: Roberts, B. & Thornton, C. (eds.) 2014: *Archaeometallurgy in Global Perspective: Methods and Syntheses.* Springer, New York, p. 91-106.
Heinemeier, J. & Højlund, F. 2016: Radiocarbon chronology. In: Højlund, F. & Abu-Laban, A., *Tell F6 on Failaka Island. Kuwaiti-Danish Excavations 2008-2012.* Jutland Archaeological Society Publications vol. 92, Højbjerg, p. 239-250.
Helwing, B. 2021: Patterns of early metallurgy on the Iranian Plateau, from the beginnings to the end of the Bronze Age. In: Marro, C. & Stöllner, T. (eds) 2021: *On Salt, Copper and Gold: The Origins of Early Mining and Metallurgy in the Caucasus.* Mom Éditions, Lyon, p. 201–230.
Heskel, D. 2003: Metal Analyses. In: Andersen, H.H. & Højlund, F. (eds) 2003: *The Barbar Temples,* Vol. 2. *JASP* vol. 48, Højbjerg, p. 21-34.
Hill, H.D., Jacobsen, Th. & Delougaz, P. 1990: *Old Babylonian Public Buildings in the Diyala Region,* Oriental Institute Publications 98. Chicago, IL: The Oriental Institute of the University of Chicago.
Hilton, A., Højlund, F., David-Cuny, H., Eidem, J. 2012: Altar Plates from Second Millennium BC Failaka, Kuwait. *Bibliotheca Orientalis* 69, col. 411-420.
Hilton, A. 2014: *The Stone Vessels.* Failaka/Dilmun. The Second Millennium Settlements, vol. 4. Jutland Archaeological Society Publications vol. 17:4, Højbjerg.
Hilton, A. 2016: Stone vessels. In: Højlund, F. & Abu-Laban, A., *Tell F6 on Failaka Island. Kuwaiti-Danish Excavations 2008-2012. JASP* vol. 92, Højbjerg, p. 164-175.
Hoch, E. 1979: Reflections on prehistoric life at Umm an-Nar (Trucial Oman) based on faunal remains from the third millennium BC. In: Taddei, M. 1979: *South Asian Archaeology 1977.* Seminario di Studi Asiatici Series Minor 6. Napoli, p. 589-638.
Hoftijzer, J., & Jongeling, K. 1995: *Dictionary of the North-West Semitic Inscriptions.* Handbuch der Orientalistik—Erste Abteilung: Der Nahe und Mittlere Osten Bd. 21, E.J. Brill, Leiden/New York/Köln.
Holes, C. 2005: *Dialect, Culture, and Society in Eastern Arabia,* vol. 2. Handbook Oriental Studies: Near and Middle East vol. 51, Brill.
Howard-Carter, Th. 1980-1983: Kuwait. In: Edzard, D.O. (ed.), *Reallexikon der Assyriologie und Vorderasiatischen Archäologie* Bd. 7: *Klagegesang—Libanon.* De Gruyter, Berlin/New York, p. 389-397.
Howard-Carter, T. 1984: *The Johns Hopkins University Expedition to Failaka Island 1973-1974.* Unpublished report on file in the Kuwait National Museum.
Howard-Carter, T. 1986: Eyestones and Pearls. In: Al Khalifa, H. & Rice, M. (eds.), *Bahrain through the ages, the Archaeology,* London, p. 305-310.
Howard-Carter, Th. 1987: Dilmun: At Sea or not at Sea? *Journal of Cuneiform Studies* 39 p. 54-117.
Howarth, P. 2018: *Tracing Traditions: Patterns of technological innovation and the circulation of copper in Southwest Asia from the 8th to 1st millennia BCE.* Unpublished PhD dissertation, University of Oxford.
Huber Vulliet, F. 2010: Un festival nippurite à l'époque paléobabylonienne. In: Baker, H.D., Robson, E., & Zólyomi, G. (eds.), *Your Praise Is Sweet. A Memorial Volume for Jeremy Black from Students, Colleagues and Friends.* British Institute for the Study of Iraq, London, p. 125-150.
Huot, J.-L. (ed.) 2003: *Larsa. Travaux de 1987 et 1989.* Bibliothèque Archéologique et Historique 165. Beirut, Institut Français d'Archéologie du Proche-Orient.
Hurtel, L., & Tallon, F. 1990: Le Métal en provenance du Tell F6, description des objets et Analyses. In : Calvet, Y. & Gachet, J. (eds.), *Failaka Fouilles Francaises 1986–1988* (Travaux de la Maison de l'Orient 8, Paris), p. 49–54.
Højlund, F. 1987: *The Bronze Age Pottery.* Failaka/Dilmun. The Second Millennium Settlements 2. *JASP* vol. 17:2, Højbjerg.
Højlund, F. 1989: Dilmun and the Sealand. *Northern Akkad Project Reports* 2, p. 9-14.
Højlund, F. 1990a: Date Honey Production of Dilmun in the Mid 2nd Millennium B.C.: Steps in the Technological Evolution of the Madbasa. *Paléorient* 16:1 p. 77-86.
Højlund, F. 1990b: Perlekøbmandens vægt. *Sfinx* 1990: 4 p. 151-155.
Højlund, F. 1995: Bitumen-coated basketry in Bahraini burials. *AAE 6:2,* p. 100-102.
Højlund, F. 2007: *The Burial Mounds of Bahrain. Social complexity in Early Dilmun. JASP* vol. 58, Højbjerg.
Højlund, F. 2008a: *The Danish Archaeological Expedition to Kuwait 1958-1963. A glimpse into the archives of Moesgård Museum.* Moesgård Museum (also in Arabic).
Højlund, F. 2008b: The *true* story about Failaka's ancient artefacts (in Arabic). *Al Houyah.*
Højlund, F. 2016a: Copper. In: Højlund, F. & Abu-Laban, A. 2016: *Tell F6 on Failaka Island. Kuwaiti-Danish Excavations 2008-2012. JASP* vol. 92, Højbjerg, p. 207-210.
Højlund, F. 2016b: Moesgård Museum's Investigations of the History and Culture of Kuwait 1958-2012. *Hadeeth ad-Dar* 40 p. 7-11.
Højlund, F. 2019: *Qala'at al-Bahrain* vol. 3. *The Western and Southern City Walls and Other Excavations. JASP* vol. 30:2, Højbjerg.
Højlund, F. 2021: Copper. In: Højlund, F. & Hilton, A. 2021: *Tell F3 on Failaka Island. Kuwaiti-Danish Excavations 2012-2017. JASP* vol. 116, Højbjerg, p. 130-136.
Højlund, F. & Andersen, H.H. 1994: *Qala'at al-Bahrain* vol. 1. *The Northern City Wall and the Islamic Fortress. JAS* vol. 30:1, Højbjerg.
Højlund, F. & Andersen, H.H. 1997: *Qala'at al-Bahrain* vol. 2. *The Central Monumental Buildings. JASP* vol. 30:2, Højbjerg.
Højlund, F., Bangsgaard, P., Hansen, J., Haue, N., Kjærum, P. & Lund, D.D. 2005: New excavations at the Barbar Temple, Bahrain. *AAE* 16 p. 1-24.
Højlund, F., Hilton, A.S., Juel, C., Kirkeby, N., Laursen, S.T. & Nielsen, L.E. 2008: Late third millennium elite burials in Bahrain. *AAE* 19 p. 143-154.
Højlund, F. & Abu-Laban, A. 2016: *Tell F6 on Failaka Island. Kuwaiti-Danish Excavations 2008-2012. JASP* vol. 92, Højbjerg.

Højlund, F. & Hagelquist, C.P. 2019: A new temple platform at Tell F6 on Failaka Island, Kuwait. *AAE* 30 p. 173–178.

Højlund, F. & Hilton, A. 2021: *Tell F3 on Failaka Island. Kuwaiti-Danish Excavations 2012-2017. JASP* vol. 116. Jutland Archaeological Society & Moesgaard Museum, Højbjerg / National Council for Culture, Arts and Letters, Kuwait City.

Hölscher, M. 1996: *Die Personennamen der kassitenzeitlichen Texte aus Nippur.* Imgula Bd. 1, Rhema-Verlag, Münster.

Ibrahim, M. 1982: *Excavations of the Arab Expedition at Sar el-Jisr, Bahrain.* Ministry of Information. Bahrain.

Insoll, T., Almahari, S., MacLean, R., Priestman, S., Al-Maeraj, M. & Overton, N. 2016: Bilad al Qadim revisited: recent archaeological research at the Al-Khamis mosque, Ain Abu Zaydan and Abu Anbra, Bahrain. *AAE* 27 p. 215-242.

Joannès, F. 1991: L'Etain, de l'Elam a Mari. In: Meyer, L.D. & Gasche, H. (eds) 1991: *Mésopotamie et Elam.* Mesopotamian History and Environment Occasional Publications 1, Ghent, p. 67-76.

Joshi, J.P. & Parpola, A. (eds.) 1987: *Corpus of Indus seals and inscriptions 1. Collections in India.* Annales Academiae Scientiarum Fennicae B239 & Memoirs of the Archaeological Survey of India 86. Suomalainen Tiedeakatemia. Helsinki.

Karim, M.B.R., David-Cuny, H., Mahmoud, A. & Al-Ali, Y.Y. 2017: *Iron Age Seals at Saruq al-Hadid (Dubai, UAE).* Poster from the Seminar for Arabian Studies 2017, British Museum.

Kawami, T.S. & Olbrantz, J. 2013: *Breath of Heaven, Breath of Earth: Ancient Near Eastern Art from American Collections.* Hallie Ford Museum of Art, Willamette University.

Killick, R. & Moon, J. 2005: *The Early Dilmun Settlement at Saar.* London-Bahrain Archaeological Expedition. Saar Excavation Report 3. Archaeology International Ltd, Ludlow, UK.

Kjærum, P. 1980: Seals of "Dilmun-Type" from Failaka, Kuwait. *PSAS* 10 p. 45-53.

Kjærum, P. 1983: *The Stamp and Cylinder Seals. Plates and Catalogue Descriptions.* Failaka/Dilmun. The Second Millennium Settlements vol. 1. *JASP* vol. 17:1, Højbjerg.

Kjærum, P. 1986a: Architecture and Settlement Patterns in 2nd Mill. Failaka. *PSAS* 16 p. 77-88.

Kjærum, P. 1986b: The Dilmun seals as evidence of long distance relations in the early second millennium B.C. In: Al Khalifa, H. & Rice, M. (eds.), *Bahrain through the Ages: the Archaeology*, London, p. 269-277.

Kjærum, P. & Højlund, F. 2013: *The Bronze Age Architecture.* Failaka/Dilmun. The Second Millennium Settlements vol. 3. *JASP* vol. 17:3, Højbjerg.

Knudsen, E.E. 1982: An Analysis of Amorite. A Review Article. *Journal of Cuneiform Studies* 34 p. 1-18.

Koldewey, R. 1913: *Das wieder erstehende Babylon. Die bisherigen Ergebnisse der deutschen Ausgrabungen.* 6. Sendschrift der Deutschen Orient-Gesellschaft, J.C. Hinrichs'sche Buchhandlung, Leipzig.

Koppen, F. van 1997: L'expédition à Tilmun et la révolte des bédouins. *MARI* 8 p. 417-429.

Koppen, F. van 2017: The Early Kassite Period. In: Bartelmus, A. & Sternitzke, K. (eds.), *Karduniaš. Babylonia under the Kassites. The Proceedings of the Symposium Held in Munich 30 June to 2 July 2011.* Untersuchungen zur Assyriologie und Vorderasiatischen Archäologie Bd. 11, De Gruyter, Boston/Berlin, p. 45-92.

Krebernik, M. 1993-1997: Meskilak, Mesikila, Ninsikila. In: Edzard, D.O. (ed.), *Reallexikon der Assyriologie und Vorderasiatischen Archäologie* Bd. 8: *Meek—Mythologie.* Walter de Gruyter, Berlin/New York, p. 93-94.

Krebernik, M. 2003-2005a: ^{d}PA, $^{mul/múl}$PA. In: Edzard, D.O. & Streck, M.P. (eds.), *Reallexikon der Assyriologie und Vorderasiatischen Archäologie* Bd. 10: *Oannes—Priesterverkleidung.* Walter de Gruyter, Berlin/New York, p. 160.

Krebernik, M. 2003-2005b: ^{d}PA.NI.PA. In: Edzard, D.O. & Streck, M.P. (eds.), *Reallexikon der Assyriologie und Vorderasiatischen Archäologie* Bd. 10: *Oannes—Priesterverkleidung.* Walter de Gruyter, Berlin/New York, p. 294.

Lahanier, C. 1977: Analyse d´objects en bitume de Suse, p. 47-68. In: Laboratoire de Reherche des Musées de France, Annales.

Laursen, S.T. 2016: Symbols of Dilmun's royal house – a primitive system of communication adopted from the late Indus world? *AAE* 27, p. 2-18.

Laursen, S.T. 2017: *The Royal Mounds of A'ali in Bahrain. The Emergence of Kingship in Early Dilmun. JASP* vol. 100, Højbjerg.

Laursen, S.T. 2018: Seals and Sealing Technology in the Dilmun Culture: The Post-Harappan Life of the Indus Valley Sealing Tradition. In: Ameri, M., Costello, S.K., Jamison, G. & Scott, S.J. (eds.) 2018: *Seals and Sealing in the Ancient World: Case Studies from the Near East, Egypt, the Aegean, and South Asia.* Cambridge University Press, Cambridge, p. 204–226.

Laursen, S.T. & Steinkeller, P. 2017: *Babylonia, the Gulf Region and the Indus. Archaeological and Textual Evidence for Contact in the Third and Early Second Millennium B.C.* Winona Lake, Eisenbrauns.

Laursen, S.T. & Al-Otaibi, F. 2022: From Dilmun to Wādī al-Fāw: A forgotten desert corridor, c. 2000 BC. *AAE 2022* p. 1-24.

Laursen, S.T., Al Shaikh, N., Reeler, C., Lombard, P. & Marchesi, G. forth.: Stamped Tokens with Cuneiform Inscriptions from Bahrain: New Light on Kingship and the Gods in Early Second Millennium BC Dilmun.

Leese, M.N., Craddock, P.T., Freestone, I.P. & Rothenberg, B. 1986: The composition of ores and metal objects from Timna, Israel. *Wiener Berichte über Naturwissenschaft in der Kunst* 2/3, p. 90-120.

Lieberman, S.J. 1977: *The Sumerian Loanwords in Old-Babylonian Akkadian* vol. 1: *Prolegomena and Evidence.* Harvard Semitic Studies no. 22, Scholars Press, Missoula, Montana.

Limet, H. 1968: *L'anthroponymie sumérienne dans les documents de la 3ᵉ dynastie d'Ur.* Bibliothèque de la Faculté de Philosophie et Lettres de l'Université de Liège fasc. 180, Société d'édition "Les Belles Lettres", Paris.

Limet, H. 1985: La technique du Bronze dans les archives de Mari. In: Durand, J.M. & Kupper, J.R. (éds): *Miscellanea Babylonica. Mélanges Offerts* à *Maurice Birot.* Editions Recherche sur les Civilisations, Paris, p. 201-210.

Limet, H. 1993: Metalle und metallurgie. A. I. In Mesopotamien. *Reallexikon der Assyriologie* 8, p. 96-112.

Limper, K. 1988: *Uruk. Perlen, Ketten, Anhänger.* Grabungen 1912-1985. Ausgrabungen in Uruk-Warka Endberichte. Band 2. Verlag Philipp Von Zabern. Mainz am Rhein.

Lombard, P. (ed.) 1999: *Bahrain. The Civilisation of the Two Seas, from Dilmun to Tylos.* Institut du Monde Arabe, Paris.

Lombard, P. & Kervran, M. (eds.) 1989: *Bahrain National Museum Archaeological Collections. Vol. I.* Ministry of Information. Bahrain.

Mackay, E.J.H. 1937-1938: *Further Excavations at Mohenjo-Daro.* Government of India Press. New Delhi.

Mackay, E.J.H. 1943: *Chanhu-Daro Excavations 1935-36*. American Oriental Series 20. New Haven, Connecticut.

Malfoy, J.-M. & Menu, M. 1987: La Métallurgie du cuivre à Suse aux IVe et IIIe millénaires: analyses en laboratoire. In: Tallon, F. 1987: *Métallurgie susienne I. De la fondation de Suse au XVIIIe avant J.-C.* (2 vols). Editions de la Réunion des musées nationaux, Paris, p. 355–373.

Marchesi, G. 2004: Who Was Buried in the Royal Tombs of Ur? The Epigraphic and Textual Data. *Orientalia* 73 p. 153-197.

Marchesi, G. 2011: Goods from the Queen of Tilmun. In: Barjamovic, G. et al. (eds.), *Akkade Is King. A Collection of Papers by Friends and Colleagues Presented to Aage Westenholz on the Occasion of His 70th Birthday 15th of May 2009*. Publications de l'Institut historique-archéologique néerlandais de Stamboul n° 118, Nederlands Instituut voor het Nabije Oosten, Leiden, p. 189-199.

Marchesi, G. 2014-2016: Tilmun (Dilmun). A. Philologisch. In: Streck, M.P. (ed.), *Reallexikon der Assyriologie und Vorderasiatischen Archäologie* Bd. 14: *Tiergefäß—Waša/ezzil(i)*. De Gruyter, Berlin/Boston, p. 50-52.

Marchesi, G. 2017: Inscriptions from the Royal Mounds of A'ali (Bahrain) and related texts. Appendix 5. In: Laursen, S.T., *The Royal Mounds of A'ali in Bahrain. The Emergence of Kingship in Early Dilmun. JASP* vol. 100, Højbjerg, p. 425-437.

Marchesi, G. forth.: On the Name of the Last Kassite King (to appear in *NABU*).

Marchesi, G. & Marchetti, N. 2011: *Royal Statuary of Early Dynastic Mesopotamia*. Mesopotamian Civilizations vol. 14, Eisenbrauns, Winona Lake, Indiana.

Marschner, R.F. & Wright, H. 1978: *Asphalts from Middle Eastern Archaeological Sites*. In: Carter, G. (ed.), *Archaeological Chemistry II, American Chemical Society, Advances in Chemistry Series 171*, Washington, p. 150-171.

Martinon-Torres, M. 2023: Making and Using Metals: Contributions from Archaeological Science. In: Pollard, A.M., Armitage, R.A. & Makarewicz, C.A. 2023: *Handbook of Archaeological Sciences*, Second Edition (2 Vols.). Wiley, New York, p. 935-952.

Mathiesen, H.E. 1982: *The Terracotta Figurines*. Ikaros. The Hellenistic Settlements 1. *JASP* vol. 16:1, Højbjerg.

Merkel, J.F. 1990: Experimental reconstruction of Bronze Age copper smelting based on the archaeological evidence from Timna. In: Rothenberg, B. (ed.) 1990: *The Ancient Metallurgy of Copper: Archaeology-Experiment-Theory*. Institute for Archaeo-Metallurgical Studies, London, p. 78-122.

Meyer-Laurin, V. 2011: Die "Zeichenpaare" im sargonischen Akkadisch aus sumerologischer Sicht. *Die Welt des Orients* 41 p. 27-68.

Montero Fenollos, J.-L. 2019: Mari and the use of tin within the context of the Near East during the 3rd and 2nd millennia BC. *Oriens Antiquus. Serie Nova* 2019, p. 121-126.

Moon, J. (ed.) 2023: *Tell Khaiber: A Fortified Centre of the First Sealand Dynasty*. Archaeology of Ancient Iraq 2, Moonrise Press: Ludlow.

Mughal, M.R. 1983: *The Dilmun Burial Complex at Sar. The 1980-82 Excavations in Bahrain*. Ministry of Information. Bahrain.

Nashef, Kh. 1982: *Die Orts- und Gewässernamen der mittelbabylonischen und mittelassyrischen Zeit*. Répertoire Géographique des Textes Cunéiformes Bd. 5, Ludwig Reichert Verlag, Wiesbaden.

Nashef, Kh. 1984: The Deities of Dilmun. *Akkadica* 38 p. 1-33 (Republished in: Al Khalifa, H. & Rice, M. (eds.), *Bahrain through the Ages: the Archaeology*. KPI, London: 1986, p. 340-366).

Neumann, G. 2013: Elams Kulturkontakte mit seiner Nachbarn im Spiegel der Glyptik des 2. Jahrtausends v. Chr. In: De Graef, K. & Tavernier, J. (eds) 2013: *Susa and Elam. Archaeological, Philological, Historical and Geographical Perspectives. Proceedings of the International Congress Held at Ghent University. December 14–17, 2009*. Brill, Leiden, p. 83–128.

Norman, K. 2005: *Conservation of the bitumen finds from H3*. Unpublished report.

Oppenheim, L. 1954: The Seafaring Merchants of Ur. *Journal of the American Oriental Society* 74 p. 6-17.

Oshima, T.M. 2020: The Bilingual Syncretistic Hymn to Nanāya "One-God(dess)"-theism in Mesopotamia. In: Gabbay, U. & Pérennès, J.-J. (eds.), *Des polytheismes aux monotheismes. Melanges d'assyriologie offerts à Marcel Sigrist*. Peeters, Leuven, p. 335-398.

Oudbashi, O. 2018: A methodological approach to estimate soil corrosivity for archaeological copper alloy artefacts. *Heritage Science* 6, p. 1-15. https://doi.org/10.1186/s40494-018-0167-4

Oudbashi, O., Emamie, S.M. & Davami, P. 2012: Bronze in Archaeology: A Review of the Archaeometallurgy of Bronze in Ancient Iran. In: Collini, L. (ed.) 2014. *Copper Alloys – Early Applications and Current Performance-Enhancing Processes*. InTech, Croatia, p. 153-178.

Oudbashi, O. & Davami, P. 2014: Investigation on manufacturing process in some Elamite copper alloy artefacts from Haft Tappeh, Southwest Iran. *Microscopy and Microanalysis* 20, p. 2034–2035.

Oudbashi, O., Agha-Aligol. D., Mishmastnehi, M. & Barnoos, V. 2019: The Elamite metalworkers: multianalytical study on copper objects and ingots from second millennium BC of southwestern Iran. *Archaeological and Anthropological Sciences* 11, p. 2059–2072.

Pagan, J.M. 1998: *A Morphological and Lexical Study of Personal Names in the Ebla texts*. Archivi Reali di Ebla—Studi vol. 3, Missione Archeologica Italiana in Siria, Roma.

Paulus, S. 2014: *Die babylonischen Kudurru-Inschriften von der kassitischen bis zu frühneubabylonischen Zeit. Untersucht unter besonderer Berücksichtigung gesellschafts- und rechtshistorischer Fragestellungen*. Alter Orient und Altes Testament Bd. 51, Ugarit-Verlag, Münster.

Peyronel, L. 1997: La glittica a stampo dilmunita in età paleobabilonese classica e cassita. *Contributi e materiali di archeologia orientale* 7 p. 407-435.

Peyronel, L. 2008: Some Thoughts on Iconographic Relations between the Arabian Gulf and Syria-Mesopotamia during the Middle Bronze Age. In: *Olijdam, E. & Spoor, R.H. (eds.), Intercultural Relations Between South and Southwest Asia. Studies in Commemoration of E.C.L. During Caspers (1934-1996). BAR International Series* 1826 p. 236-252.

Pic, M. 1990: Quelques éléments de glyptique. In: Calvet, Y. & Gachet, J. (eds.), *Failaka. Fouilles françaises 1986-1988*. Travaux de la Maison de l'Orient n° 18, Lyon, p. 125-140.

Picchioni, S.A. 1987-1988: L'amuleto cassita RB 20. *Studi Orientali e Linguistici* 4 p. 15-20.

Pigott, V.C. 2021: The acquisition of tin in Bronze Age Southwest Asia. In: Lyonnet, B. & Dubova, N.A., (eds.) 2021: *The World of the Oxus Civilization*. Routledge, London, p. 827–862.

Pigott, V.C., Rogers, H.C. & Nash, S.K. 2003: Archaeometallurgical Investigations at Tal-e Malyan: The Evidence for Tin-Bronze in the Kaftari Phase. In: Miller, N.F. & Abdi, K. (eds.) 2003: *Yeki Bud, Yeki Nabud: Essays on the Archaeology of Iran in Honor of William M. Sumner.* University of Pennsylvania Museum, Philadelphia, p. 161–175.

Pittman, H. 2016: Mesopotamian cylinder seals. In: Højlund, F. & Abu-Laban, A., *Tell F6 on Failaka Island. Kuwaiti-Danish Excavations 2008-2012.* Jutland Archaeological Society Publications vol. 92, Højbjerg, p. 157-161.

Pittman, H. 2021: Mesopotamian cylinder seals. In: Højlund, F. & Hilton, A., *Tell F3 on Failaka Island. Kuwaiti-Danish Excavations 2012-2017. JASP* vol. 116, Jutland Archaeological Society & Moesgaard Museum, Højbjerg / National Council for Culture, Arts and Letters, Kuwait City, p. 97-99.

Pollard, A.M. 1987: Report on the analysis of Failaka glass, glazed pottery and faience. In: Højlund, F. 1987: *The Bronze Age Pottery.* Failaka/Dilmun. The Second Millennium Settlements 2. *JASP* vol. 17:2, Højbjerg, p. 184-195.

Pollard, A.M. 2018: *Beyond Provenance: The Interpretation of Chemical and Isotopic Data in Archaeological Bronzes.* Studies in Archaeological Science. University of Leuven Press.

Pollard, A.M. & Højlund, F. 1983: High-magnesium glazed sherds from Bronze Age tells on Failaka, Kuwait. *Archaeometry* 25, p. 196-200.

Potts, D.T. 1990: *The Arabian Gulf in Antiquity* vol. 1: *From Prehistory to the Fall of the Achaemenid Empire.* Clarendon Press, Oxford.

Potts, D.T. 1994: Contributions to the agrarian history of Eastern Arabia I. Implements and cultivation techniques. *AAE* 5 p. 158-168.

Potts, D.T. 1999: *The Archaeology of Elam: Formation and Transformation of an Ancient Iranian State.* Cambridge World Archaeology.

Potts, D.T. 2010: Cylinder seals and their use in the Arabian Peninsula. *AAE* 21 p. 20-40.

Potts, T.F. 1989: Foreign Stone Vessels of the Late Third Millennium B.C. from Southern Mesopotamia: Their Origins and Mechanisms of Exchange. *Iraq* 51, p. 123-164.

Potts, T.F. 1994: *Mesopotamia and the East – An Archaeological and Historical Study of Foreign Relations ca. 3400-2000 BC.* Oxford: Oxford University Committee for Archaeology.

Powell, W., Johnson, M., Pulak, C., Yener, K.A, Mathur, R., Bankoff, H.A., Godfrey, L., Price, M. &. Galili, E. 2021: From peaks to ports: Insights into tin provenance, production, and distribution from adapted applications of lead isotopic analysis of the Uluburun tin ingots. *Journal of Archaeological Science* 134, 105455.

Powell, W., Frachetti, M., Pulak, C., Bankoff, H.A., Barjamovic, G., Johnson, M., Mathur, R., Pigott, V.C. Price, M. & Yener, K.A. 2022: Tin from Uluburun shipwreck shows small-scale commodity exchange fuelled continental tin supply across Late Bronze Age Eurasia. *Science Advances* 8 (48), eabq3766. DOI: 10.1126/sciadv.abq3766

Prange, M.K. 2001: 5000 Jahre Kupfer in Oman. Band II. Vergleichende Untersuchungen zur Charakterisierung des omanischen Kupfers mittels chemischer und isotopischer Analysenmethoden. *Metalla* 8, p. 1–126.

Rafiei Alavi, B. 2015: *Archäologische Untersuchungen der Metallartefakte aus Haft Tappeh* (2 vols.). Unpublished PhD dissertation, Johann Wolfgang Goethe-Universität.

Reade, J. 1986: Commerce or Conquest: Variations in the Mesopotamian – Dilmun relationship. In: Al Khalifa, H. & Rice, M. (eds.), *Bahrain through the Ages: the Archaeology,* London, p. 325-334.

Rehren, Th. & Northover, P. 1991: Selenium and Tellurium in Ancient Copper Ingots. In: *Archaeometry '90.* Birkhauser Verlag, Basel, p. 221-228.

Rostoker, W., Pigott, V.C. & Dvorak, J. 1989: Direct reduction of copper metal by oxide-sulphide mineral interaction. *Archaeomaterials* 3, p. 69–87.

Rouault, O. & Masetti-Rouault, M.G. (eds.) 1993: *L'Eufrate e il tempo: Le civiltà del medio Eufrate e della Gezira siriana.* Exhibition catalogue, Sala dell'Arengo and Palazzo del Podesta, Rimini. Milan: Electa.

Rovsing Olsen, P. 2002: *Music in Bahrain. Traditional Music of the Arabian Gulf. JASP* vol. 42.

Rowley-Conwy, P. 1987: Remains of date (Phoenix dactilifera) from Failaka, Kuwait. In: Højlund, F. 1987: *The Bronze Age Pottery.* Failaka/Dilmun. The Second Millennium Settlements 2. *JASP* vol. 17:2, Højbjerg, p. 181-183.

Salles, J.-F. 1986: Terracotta figurines at Tell Khazneh. In: Calvet, Y. & Salles, J.-F. (eds.), *Failaka. Fouilles françaises 1984-1985.* Travaux de la Maison de l'Orient n° 12, Lyon, p. 143-200.

Salles, J.-F. 2005: IKAROS, de la conquête d'Alexandre au 1er siècle après J.-C. In: Callot, O. et al. 2005: *L'île de Failaka. Archéologie du Koweït.* Musée des Beaux-Arts de Lyon, Lyon, p. 63-93.

Sangmeister, E. 2003: Metal Analyses. In: Andersen, H.H. & Højlund, F. (eds): *The Barbar Temples,* vol. 2. *JASP* vol. 48, Højbjerg, p. 19-20.

Sassmannshausen, L. 2008: Dilmun, Baḫrain und Babylonien im 15.-14. Jahrhundert v.Chr. aus assyriologischer Sicht. In: Olijdam, E. & Spoor, R.H. (eds.), *Intercultural Relations between South and Western Asia. Studies in commemoration of E.C.L. During Caspers (1934-1996).* Society for Arabian Studies Monographs no. 7, BAR International Series no. 1826, Archaeopress, Oxford, p. 316-328.

Schaudig, H.-P. 2001: *Die Inschriften Nabonids von Babylon und Kyros' des Grossen samt den in ihrem Umfeld entstandenen Tendenzschriften. Textausgabe und Grammatik.* Alter Orient und Altes Testament Bd. 256, Ugarit-Verlag, Münster.

Scheil, V. 1917: Notules. *Revue d'Assyriologie et d'Archéologie Orientale* 14 p. 177-185.

Scheil, V. 1939: *Mélanges épigraphiques.* Mémoires de la mission archéologique de Perse tome 28, Libraire Ernest Leroux, Paris.

Schorsch, D. 2014: A Conservator's Perspective on Ancient Metallurgy. In: Roberts, B. & Thornton, C.P. (eds.) 2014: *Archaeometallurgy in Global Perspective: Methods and Syntheses.* Springer, New York, p. 269-302.

Schroeder, O. 1920: *Keilschrifttexte aus Assur verschiedenen Inhalts.* Ausgrabungen der Deutschen Orient-Gesellschaft E: Inschriften Bd. 3, J.C. Hinrichs'sche Buchhandlung, Leipzig.

Seidl, U. 1989: *Die babylonischen Kudurru-Reliefs: Symbole mesopotamischer Gottheiten.* Orbis Biblicus et Orientalis 87, Universitätsverlag, Freiburg (Schweiz) / Vandenhoeck & Ruprecht, Göttingen.

Seux, M.-J. 1967: *Épithètes royales akkadiennes et sumériennes.* Letouzey et Ané, Paris.

Soden, W. von & Röllig, W. 1991: *Das akkadische Syllabar.* 4., durchgesehene und erweiterte Auflage. Analecta Orientalia 42, Pontificio Istituto Biblico, Roma.

Soldi, S. 2017: "Assyrian Clay Hands" in the Architecture of the Ancient Near East. *Metropolitan Museum Journal* 52 p. 9-24.

Soldt, W.H. van 2021: Middle Babylonian. In: Vita, J.P. (ed.), *History of the Akkadian Language* vol. 2: *The Second and First*

Millennia BCE; Afterlife. Handbook of Oriental Studies sect. 1: The Ancient Near East vol. 152/2, Brill, Leiden/ Boston, p. 1039-1102.

Sperveslage, G. 2016: A scarab. In: Højlund, F. & Abu-Laban, A.: Tell F6 on Failaka Island. Kuwait-Danish Excavations 2008-2012. *JASP* vol. 92, Jutland Archaeological Society & Moesgaard Museum, Højbjerg / National Council for Culture, Arts and Letters, Kuwait City, p. 155-156, n. 6.

Spycket, A. 1981: *La statuaire du Proche-Orient ancient.* Leiden: E. J. Brill.

Spycket, A. 1992: *Les figurines de Suse: Volume I – Les figurines humaines, IVe-IIe millénaires av. J. C.* Paris: Gabalda.

Srivastava, K.M. 1991: *Madinat Hamad. Burial Mounds 1984-85.* Ministry of Information and Bahrain National Museum, Manama.

Stamm, J.J. 1968: *Die akkadische Namengebung.* Wissenschaftliche Buchgesellschaft, Darmstadt.

Starr, R.F.S. 1937-1939: *Nuzi. Report on the Excavations at Yorgan Tepa near Kirkuk, Iraq, Conducted by Harvard University in Conjunction with the American Schools of Oriental Research and the University Museum of Philadelphia 1927-1931*, vol. 1-2. Harvard University Press, Cambridge, Massachusetts.

Steele, F.R. 1951: Writing and History: The New Tablets from Nippur. *The University Museum Bulletin* 16/2 (July 1951) p. 21-27.

Stein, P. 2000: *Die mittel- und neubabylonischen Königsinschriften bis zum Ende der Assyrerherrschaft. Grammatische Untersuchungen.* Jenaer Beiträge zum Vorderen Orient Bd. 3, Harrassowitz Verlag, Wiesbaden.

Steinkeller, P. 2016: The Role of Iran in the Inter-Regional Exchange of Metals: Tin, Copper, Silver and Gold in the Second Half of the Third Millennium BC. In: Maekawa, K., (ed.) 2016: *Ancient Iran: New Perspectives from Archaeology and Cuneiform Studies. Proceedings of the International Colloquium held at the Center for Eurasian Cultural Studies, Kyoto University, December 6–7, 2014.* Iran-Japan Project of Ancient Texts, Tehran and Kyoto, p. 127–150.

Steinkeller, P. 2017: An Estimate of the Population of the City of Umma in Ur III Times. In: Heffron, Y., Stone, A., Worthington, M. (eds.), *Ancient Near Eastern Studies in Honour of J. N. Postgate.* Eisenbrauns, Winona Lake, Indiana, p. 535-566.

Stiehler-Alegria, G. 1996: *Die kassitische Glyptik.* Münchener vorderasiatische Studien Bd. 18, Profil Verlag, München/ Wien.

Stiehler-Alegria, G. 2011-2012: Bemerkungen zur Datierung und Interpretation kassitischer Siegelthemen unter Berücksichtigung interaktiver Begegnungen mit der Dilmun Glyptik. *Isimu* 14-15 p. 13-27.

Streck, M.P. 2000: *Das amurritische Onomastikon der altbabylonischen Zeit* Bd. 1: *Die Amurriter; Die onomastische Forschung; Orthographie und Phonologie; Nominalmorphologie.* Alter Orient und Altes Testament Bd. 271/1, Ugarit Verlag, Münster.

Streck, M.P. 2004: Die Amurriter der altbabylonischen Zeit im Spiegel des Onomastikons. Eine ethno-linguistische Evaluierung. In: Meyer, J.-W. & Sommerfeld, W. (eds.), *2000 v. Chr.: Politische, Wirtschaftliche und Kulturelle Entwicklung im Zeichen einer Jahrtausendwende. 3. Internationales Colloquium der Deutschen Orient-Gesellschaf, 4.-7. April 2000 in Frankfurt/Mainz und Marburg/Lahn*. Saarbrücker Druckerei und Verlag, Saarbrücken, p. 313-355.

Strehle, H. 2021: Hook and line. In: Højlund, F. & Hilton, A. 2021: *Tell F3 on Failaka Island. Kuwaiti-Danish Excavations 2012-2017. JASP* vol. 116, Jutland Archaeological Society & Moesgaard Museum, Højbjerg / National Council for Culture, Arts and Letters, Kuwait City, p. 165-166.

Strehle, H. 2022: *Conservation Journals*, The Kuwaiti-Danish Archaeological Mission to Failaka, 2010-2022. Unpublished report on file at Moesgaard Museum.

Strommenger, E. 1971: Mesopotamische Gewandtypen von der Frühsumerischen bis zur Larsa Zeit. *Acta praehistorica et archaeologica* 2, p. 37-55.

Suter, C.E. 1991-1993: A Shulgi Statuette from Tello. *Journal of Cuneiform Studies* 43-45, p. 63-70.

Thornton, C.P. 2007: Of brass and bronze in prehistoric Southwest Asia. In: La Niece, S., Hook, D. & Craddock, P.T. (eds.) 2007: *Metals and Mines: Studies in Archaeometallurgy.* Archetype and the British Museum, London, p. 123-135.

Thornton, C.P., Lamberg-Karlovsky, C.C., Liezers, M. & Young, S.M.M. 2002: On pins and needles: tracing the evolution of copper-base alloying at Tepe Yahya, Iran, via ICP-MS analysis of common-place items. *Journal of Archaeological Science* 29, p. 1451–1460.

Trier, J. & Højlund, F. 1986: *Register of Metal Finds in the Bahrain National Museum 1986.* Report on file at Moesgaard Museum.

Tylecote, R.F., Ghaznavi, H.A. & Boydell, P.J. 1977: Partitioning of Trace Elements Between the Ores, Fluxes, Slags and Metal During the Smelting of Copper. *Journal of Archaeological Science* 4, p. 305-333.

Van de Velde, T. 2016: Bitumen provenience. In: Højlund, F. & Abu-Laban, A.: *Tell F6 on Failaka Island. Kuwaiti-Danish Excavations 2008-2012. JASP*, 92, Højbjerg p. 214-220

Velde, C. 2003: Wadi Suq and Late Bronze Age in the Oman Peninsula. In: Potts, D., Naboodah, H.A., Hellyer, P. (eds.), *Proceedings of the First International Conference on the Archaeology of the U.A.E.* Trident Press, London, p. 102-113.

Vine, P. 1993. *Bahrain National Museum.* Immel Publishing, London.

Vosmer, T. 1996: Watercraft and Navigation in the Indian Ocean: An Evolutionary Perspective. In: Afanas'ev, G., Cleuziou, S., Lukacs, J.R. & Tosi, M. (eds.), *The Prehistory of Asia and Oceania*, vol. 16 of the *XIII International Congress of Prehistoric and Protohistoric Sciences. Forlì (Italia), 8-14 September 1996.* ABACO, Forlì, p. 223-242.

Waetzoldt, H. 1981: Zur Terminologie der Metall in den Texten aus Ebla. In: Cagni, L., (ed.) 1981: *La Lingua di Ebla.* Istituto Universitario Orientale, Seminario di Studi Asiatici, Naples, p. 363-378.

Waetzoldt, H. & Bachmann, H.G. 1984: Zinn- und Arsenbronzen in den Texten aus Ebla und aus dem Mesopotamien des 3. Jahrtausends. *Oriens Antiquus* 23, p. 1-18.

Weeks, L.R. 2003: *Early Metallurgy of the Persian Gulf. Technology, Trade, and the Bronze Age World.* American School of Prehistoric Research Monograph Series vol. 2, Brill, Boston/Leiden.

Weeks, L. & Collerson, K. 2005: Archaeometallurgical studies. In: Killick, R. & Moon, J. 2005: *The Early Dilmun Settlement at Saar.* London-Bahrain Archaeological Expedition—Saar Excavation Report 3, Archaeology International Ltd, Ludlow p. 309-324.

Weeks, L., Faber, E., Goodburn Brown, D., Zhao, J., Nguyen, A.D. & Feng, Y. In press: Qarn al-Harf Metal Artefacts and Archaeometallurgical Analyses. In: Kennet, D., In press: *Excavations at Qarn al-Harf.* Oxbow, Oxford.

Weisgerber, G. 1988: Oman: a bronze-producing centre during the 1st Half of the 1st millennium BC. In: Curtis, J. (ed.) 1988: *Bronzeworking Centres of Western Asia c. 1000-539 B.C.* Keegan Paul International, London, p. 285-295.

Weisgerber, G. 1991: Archäologisches Fundgut des 2. Jahrtausends v. Chr. in Oman. Möglichkeiten zur chronologischen Gliederung. In: Schippmann, K., Herling, A. & Salles, J.-F., (eds.) 1991: *Golf-Archäologie: Mesopotamien, Iran, Kuwait, Bahrain, Vereinigte Arabische Emirate und Oman.* Internationale Archäologie 6, p. 321-330.

Weisgerber, G. 2007: Sites of multi-period copper production in the Sultanate of Oman. In: *Proceedings of the International Symposium: Archaeology of the Arabian Peninsula through the Ages (7th–9th May 2006).* Muscat: Ministry of Heritage and Culture.

Weisgerber, G. 2020: Copper in the Wadi Suq Period (Second millennium BC). In: Cleuziou, S. & Tosi, M. 2020: *In the Shadow of the Ancestors: The Prehistoric Foundations of the Early Arabian Civilization in Oman* (second expanded edition, ed. Frenez, D. & Garba, R.). Ministry of Heritage and Tourism, Sultanate of Oman, Muscat, p. 434-435.

Wilcox, G. 1994: Archaeobotanical finds. In: Højlund, F. & Andersen, H.H. 1994: *Qala'at al-Bahrain vol 1. The Northern City Wall and the Islamic Fortress. JASP* 30:1, p. 459-462

Winter, I.J. 2009: The Body of the Able Ruler: Toward an Understanding of the Statues of Gudea. In: *On Art in the Ancient Near East.* Leiden: Brill, vol. 2, p. 151-165.

Woolley, L. & Mallowan, M. 1976: *Ur Excavations, Volume VII: The Old Babylonian Period.* London: British Museum Publications.

Wäfler, M. 1993: Tell al-Hamidiya. In: Rouault, O. & Masetti-Rouault, M.G. (eds.), *L'Eufrate e il tempo: Le civiltà del medio Eufrate e della Gezira siriana.* Electa, Milano, p. 193-198 [plus catalogue entries on p. 464].

Yeomans, L. 2016: Animal bones. In: Højlund, F. & Abu-Laban, A., *Tell F6 on Failaka Island. Kuwaiti-Danish Excavations 2008-2012. JASP* vol. 92, Jutland Archaeological Society & Moesgaard Museum, Højbjerg / National Council for Culture, Arts and Letters, Kuwait City, p. 228-238.

Yıldız, F. & Gomi, T. 1993: *Die Umma-Texte aus den Archäologischen Museen zu Istanbul.* Bd III *(Nr. 1601-2300).* CDL Press, Bethesda, Maryland.

Yule, P. & Weisgerber, G. 2015: Al-Wasit tomb W1 and other sites: Redefining the second millennium BCE chronology in south-eastern Arabia. In: Yule, P. (ed.) 2015: *Archaeological Research in the Sultanate of Oman: Bronze and Iron Age Graveyards. The Expedition of the Deutsches Bergbau-Museum Bochum in Oman 1.* Der Anschnitt Beiheft 28. Deutsches Bergbau-Museum, Bochum, p. 9-108.

Zadok, R. 1984: *The Elamite Onomasticon.* Supplemento n. 40 agli Annali, Istituto Universitario Orientale, Napoli.

Ziegler, N. 2008: Tilmuniter im Königreich Samsî-Addus. In: Olijdam, E. & Spoor, R.H. (eds.), *Intercultural Relations between South and Western Asia. Studies in commemoration of E.C.L. During Caspers (1934-1996).* Society for Arabian Studies Monographs no. 7, BAR International Series no. 1826, Archaeopress, Oxford, p. 253-259.

Contributors

Ann Andersson, National Museum, Denmark, anan@natmus.dk

Eddy Faber, School of Archaeological and Forensic Sciences, University of Bradford, UK

Anna Hilton, Moesgaard Museum, Denmark, annaohilton@hotmail.com

Flemming Højlund, flemminghojlund24@gmail.com

Gianni Marchesi, University of Bologna, Italy, gianni.marchesi@unibo.it

Sarah Morriss, Independent scholar, UK

David Mulder, University of Pennsylvania, USA, mulder@sas.upenn.edu

Holly Pittman, University of Pennsylvania, USA, hpittman@sas.upenn.edu

Helle Strehle, Moesgaard Museum, Denmark, hs@moesgaardmuseum.dk

Emma Watt, University of New England, Australia

Lloyd Weeks, University of New England, Australia, lweeks2@une.edu.au